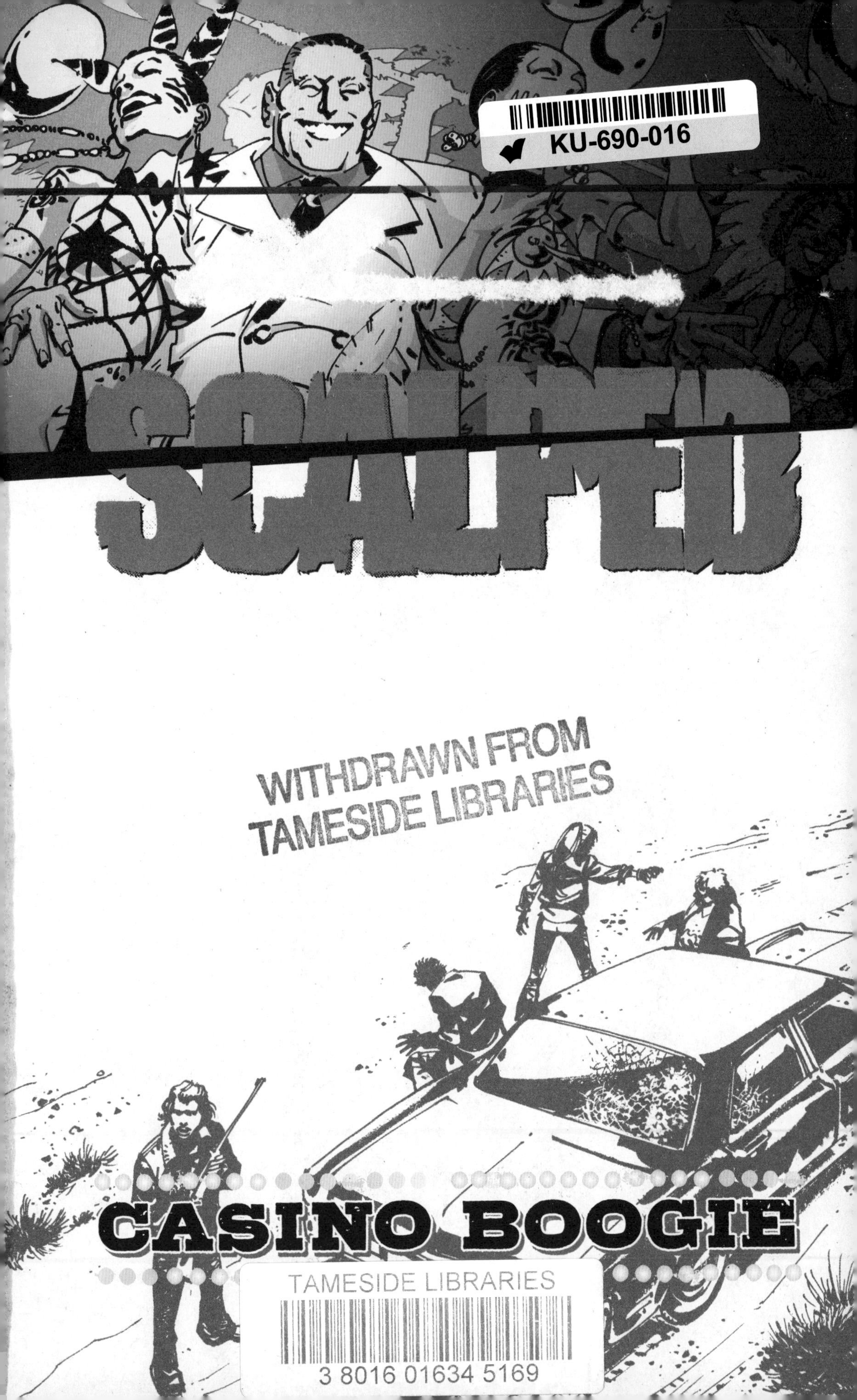
SCALPED
CASINO BOOGIE

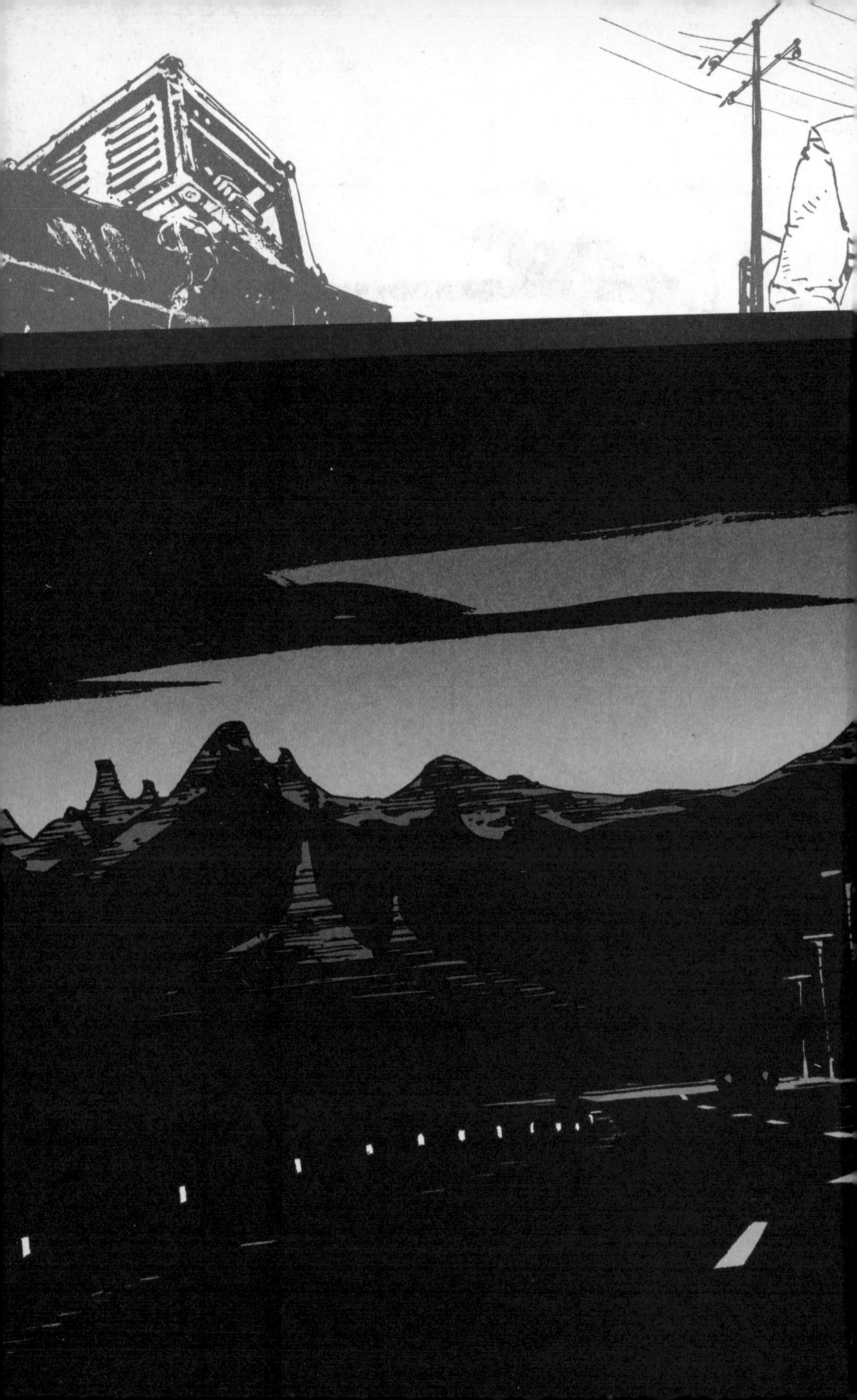

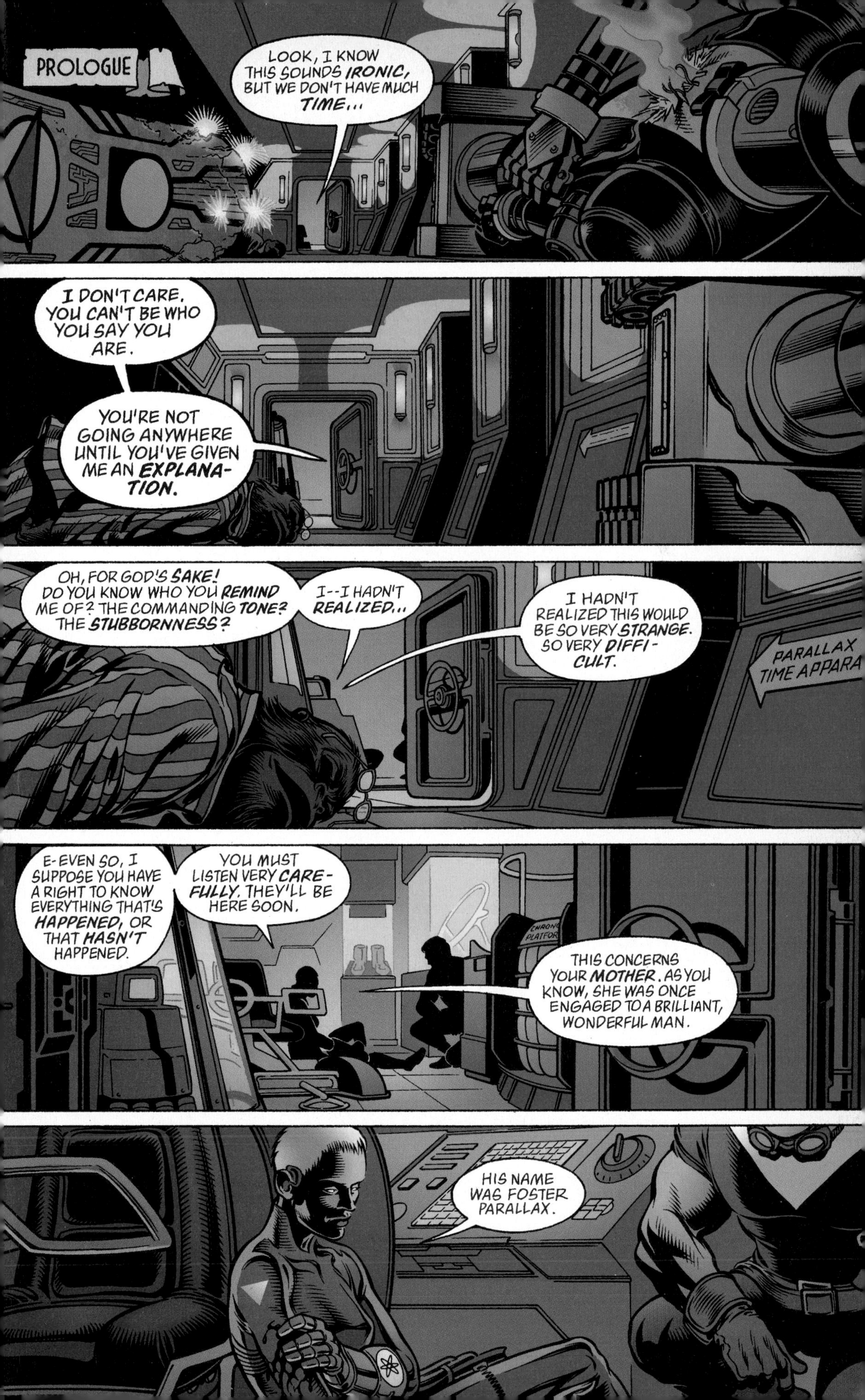

PROLOGUE
LOOK, I KNOW THIS SOUNDS IRONIC, BUT WE DON'T HAVE MUCH TIME...
I DON'T CARE. YOU CAN'T BE WHO YOU SAY YOU ARE.
YOU'RE NOT GOING ANYWHERE UNTIL YOU'VE GIVEN ME AN EXPLANATION.
OH, FOR GOD'S SAKE! DO YOU KNOW WHO YOU REMIND ME OF? THE COMMANDING TONE? THE STUBBORNNESS?
I--I HADN'T REALIZED...
I HADN'T REALIZED THIS WOULD BE SO VERY STRANGE. SO VERY DIFFICULT.
PARALLAX TIME APPARA
E-EVEN SO, I SUPPOSE YOU HAVE A RIGHT TO KNOW EVERYTHING THAT'S HAPPENED, OR THAT HASN'T HAPPENED.
YOU MUST LISTEN VERY CAREFULLY. THEY'LL BE HERE SOON.
THIS CONCERNS YOUR MOTHER. AS YOU KNOW, SHE WAS ONCE ENGAGED TO A BRILLIANT, WONDERFUL MAN.
HIS NAME WAS FOSTER PARALLAX.

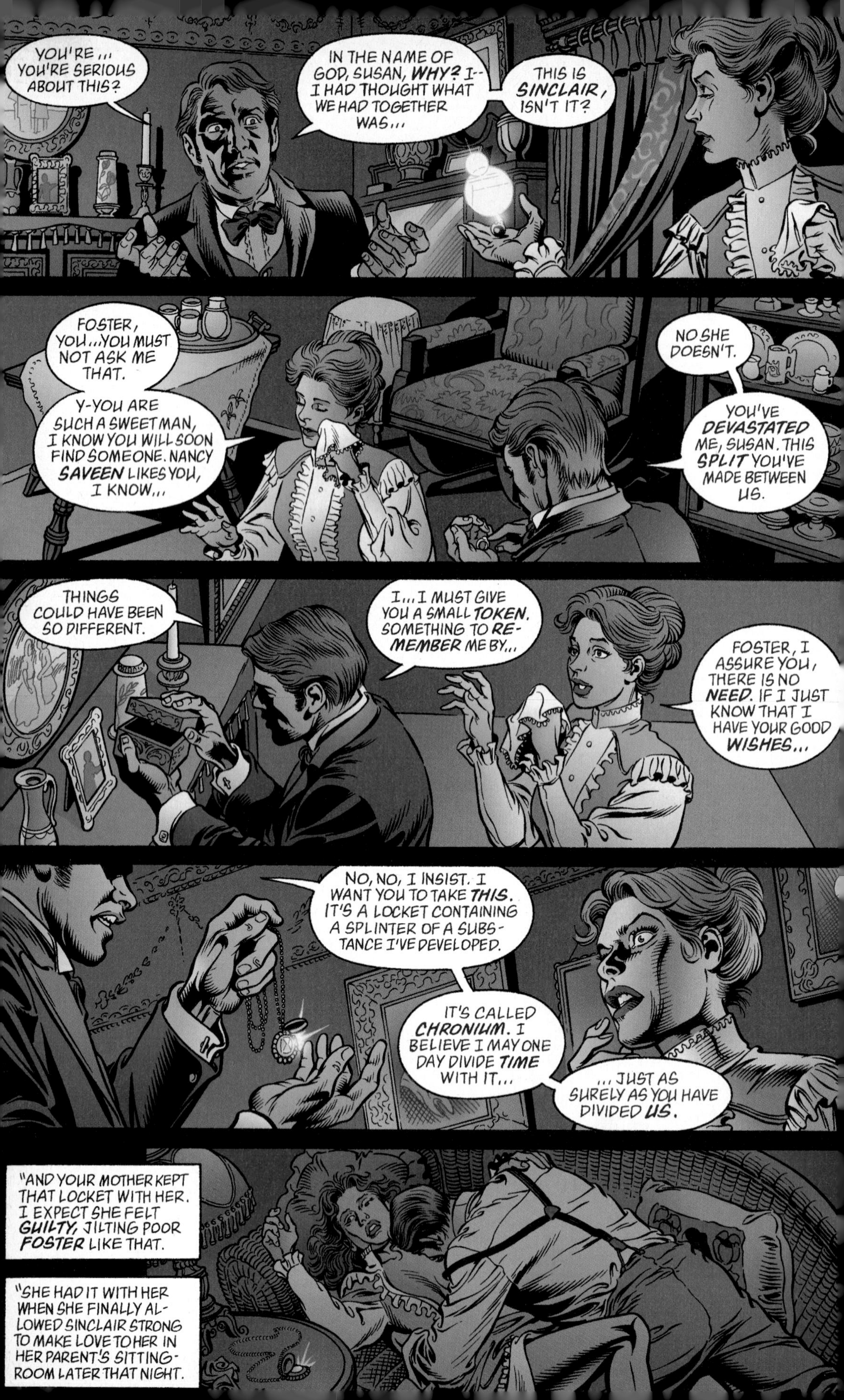

YOU'RE... YOU'RE SERIOUS ABOUT THIS?
IN THE NAME OF GOD, SUSAN, WHY? I-- I HAD THOUGHT WHAT WE HAD TOGETHER WAS...
THIS IS SINCLAIR, ISN'T IT?
FOSTER, YOU...YOU MUST NOT ASK ME THAT.
Y-YOU ARE SUCH A SWEET MAN, I KNOW YOU WILL SOON FIND SOMEONE. NANCY SAVEEN LIKES YOU, I KNOW...
NO SHE DOESN'T.
YOU'VE DEVASTATED ME, SUSAN. THIS SPLIT YOU'VE MADE BETWEEN US.
THINGS COULD HAVE BEEN SO DIFFERENT.
I... I MUST GIVE YOU A SMALL TOKEN. SOMETHING TO REMEMBER ME BY...
FOSTER, I ASSURE YOU, THERE IS NO NEED. IF I JUST KNOW THAT I HAVE YOUR GOOD WISHES...
NO, NO, I INSIST. I WANT YOU TO TAKE THIS. IT'S A LOCKET CONTAINING A SPLINTER OF A SUBSTANCE I'VE DEVELOPED.
IT'S CALLED CHRONIUM. I BELIEVE I MAY ONE DAY DIVIDE TIME WITH IT...
...JUST AS SURELY AS YOU HAVE DIVIDED US.
"AND YOUR MOTHER KEPT THAT LOCKET WITH HER. I EXPECT SHE FELT GUILTY, JILTING POOR FOSTER LIKE THAT.
"SHE HAD IT WITH HER WHEN SHE FINALLY ALLOWED SINCLAIR STRONG TO MAKE LOVE TO HER IN HER PARENT'S SITTING-ROOM LATER THAT NIGHT.

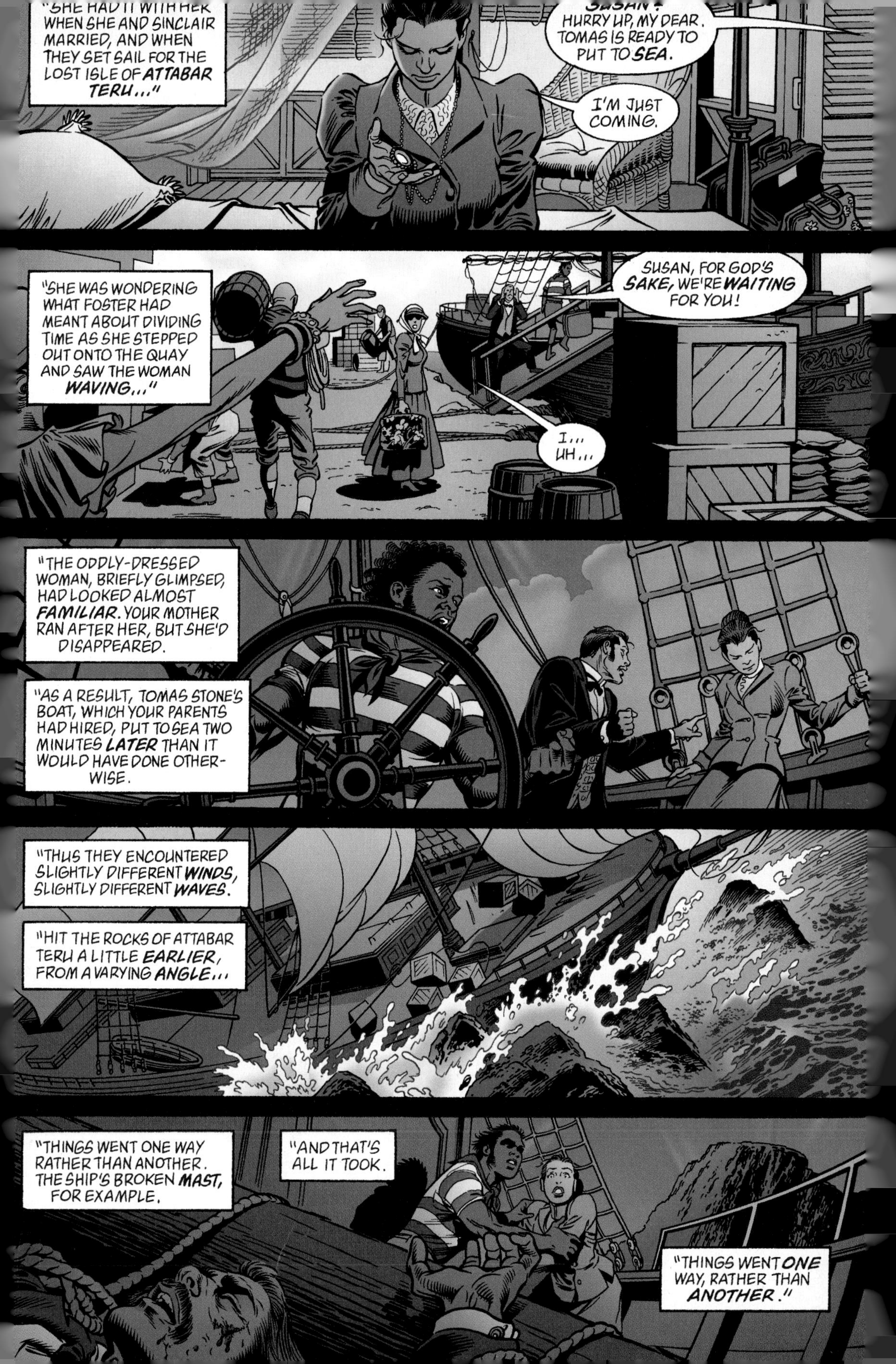
"SHE HAD IT WITH HER WHEN SHE AND SINCLAIR MARRIED, AND WHEN THEY SET SAIL FOR THE LOST ISLE OF ATTABAR TERU..."
SUSAN! HURRY UP, MY DEAR. TOMAS IS READY TO PUT TO SEA.
I'M JUST COMING.
"SHE WAS WONDERING WHAT FOSTER HAD MEANT ABOUT DIVIDING TIME AS SHE STEPPED OUT ONTO THE QUAY AND SAW THE WOMAN WAVING..."
SUSAN, FOR GOD'S SAKE, WE'RE WAITING FOR YOU!
I... UH...
"THE ODDLY-DRESSED WOMAN, BRIEFLY GLIMPSED, HAD LOOKED ALMOST FAMILIAR. YOUR MOTHER RAN AFTER HER, BUT SHE'D DISAPPEARED.
"AS A RESULT, TOMAS STONE'S BOAT, WHICH YOUR PARENTS HAD HIRED, PUT TO SEA TWO MINUTES LATER THAN IT WOULD HAVE DONE OTHER-WISE.
"THUS THEY ENCOUNTERED SLIGHTLY DIFFERENT WINDS, SLIGHTLY DIFFERENT WAVES.
"HIT THE ROCKS OF ATTABAR TERU A LITTLE EARLIER, FROM A VARYING ANGLE...
"THINGS WENT ONE WAY RATHER THAN ANOTHER. THE SHIP'S BROKEN MAST, FOR EXAMPLE.
"AND THAT'S ALL IT TOOK.
"THINGS WENT ONE WAY, RATHER THAN ANOTHER."

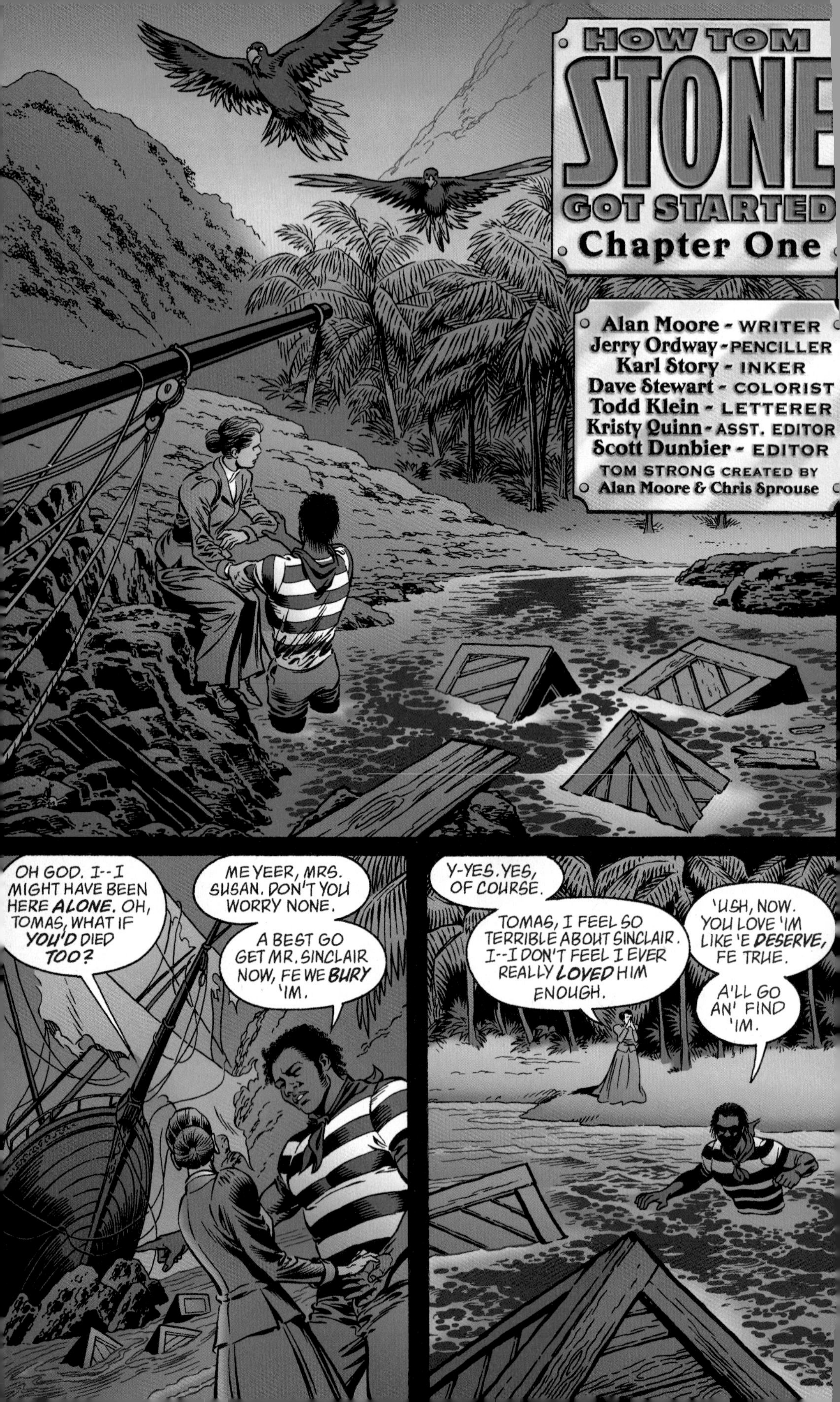
HOW TOM STONE GOT STARTED
Chapter One
Alan Moore - WRITER
Jerry Ordway - PENCILLER
Karl Story - INKER
Dave Stewart - COLORIST
Todd Klein - LETTERER
Kristy Quinn - ASST. EDITOR
Scott Dunbier - EDITOR
TOM STRONG CREATED BY
Alan Moore & Chris Sprouse
OH GOD. I--I MIGHT HAVE BEEN HERE ALONE. OH, TOMAS, WHAT IF YOU'D DIED TOO?
ME YEER, MRS. SUSAN. DON'T YOU WORRY NONE.
A BEST GO GET MR. SINCLAIR NOW, FE WE BURY 'IM.
Y-YES. YES, OF COURSE.
TOMAS, I FEEL SO TERRIBLE ABOUT SINCLAIR. I--I DON'T FEEL I EVER REALLY LOVED HIM ENOUGH.
'USH, NOW. YOU LOVE 'IM LIKE 'E DESERVE, FE TRUE.
A'LL GO AN' FIND 'IM.

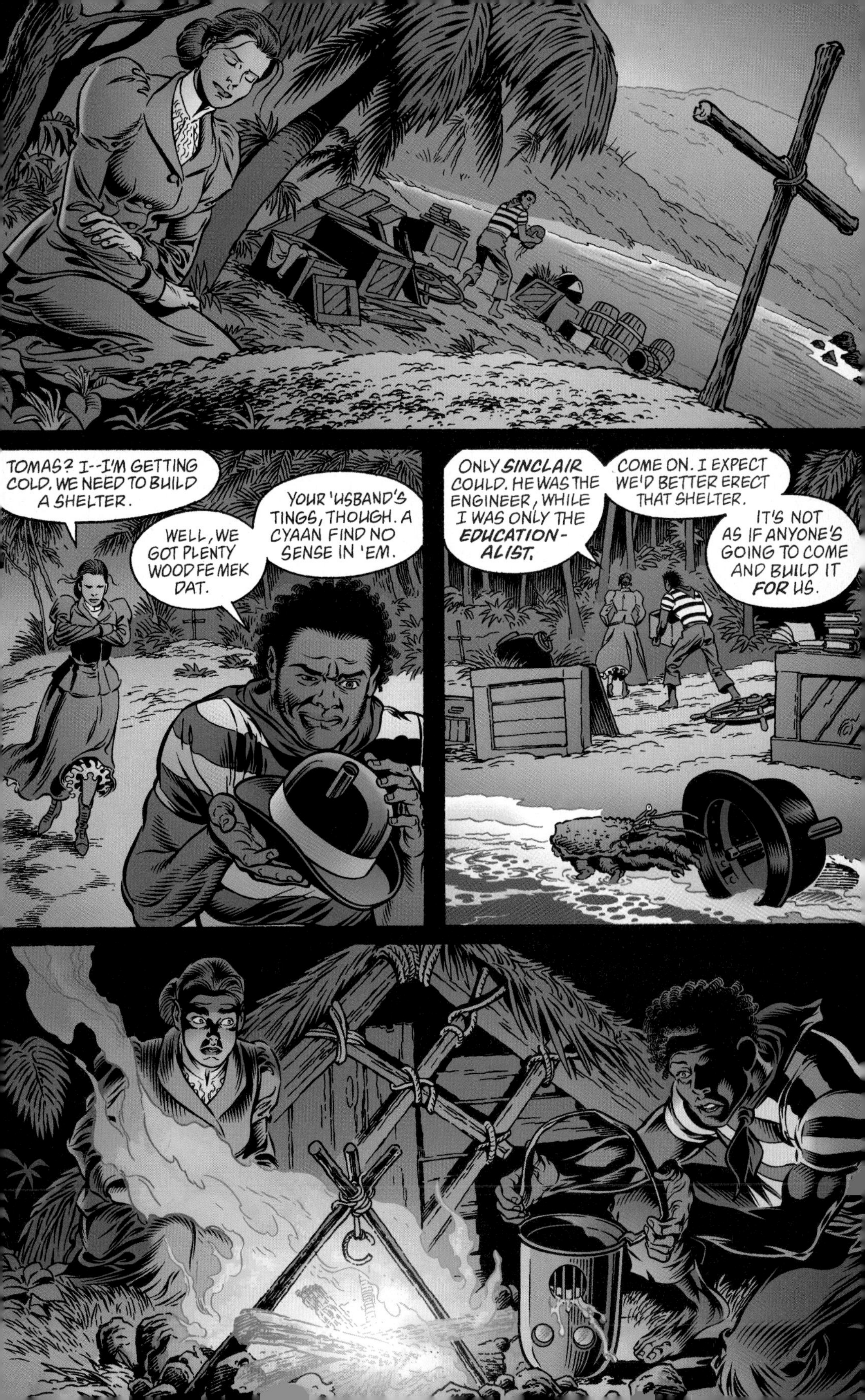
TOMAS? I--I'M GETTING COLD. WE NEED TO BUILD A SHELTER.
WELL, WE GOT PLENTY WOOD FE MEK DAT.
YOUR 'USBAND'S TINGS, THOUGH. A CYAAN FIND NO SENSE IN 'EM.
ONLY SINCLAIR COULD. HE WAS THE ENGINEER, WHILE I WAS ONLY THE EDUCATION-ALIST.
COME ON. I EXPECT WE'D BETTER ERECT THAT SHELTER.
IT'S NOT AS IF ANYONE'S GOING TO COME AND BUILD IT FOR US.

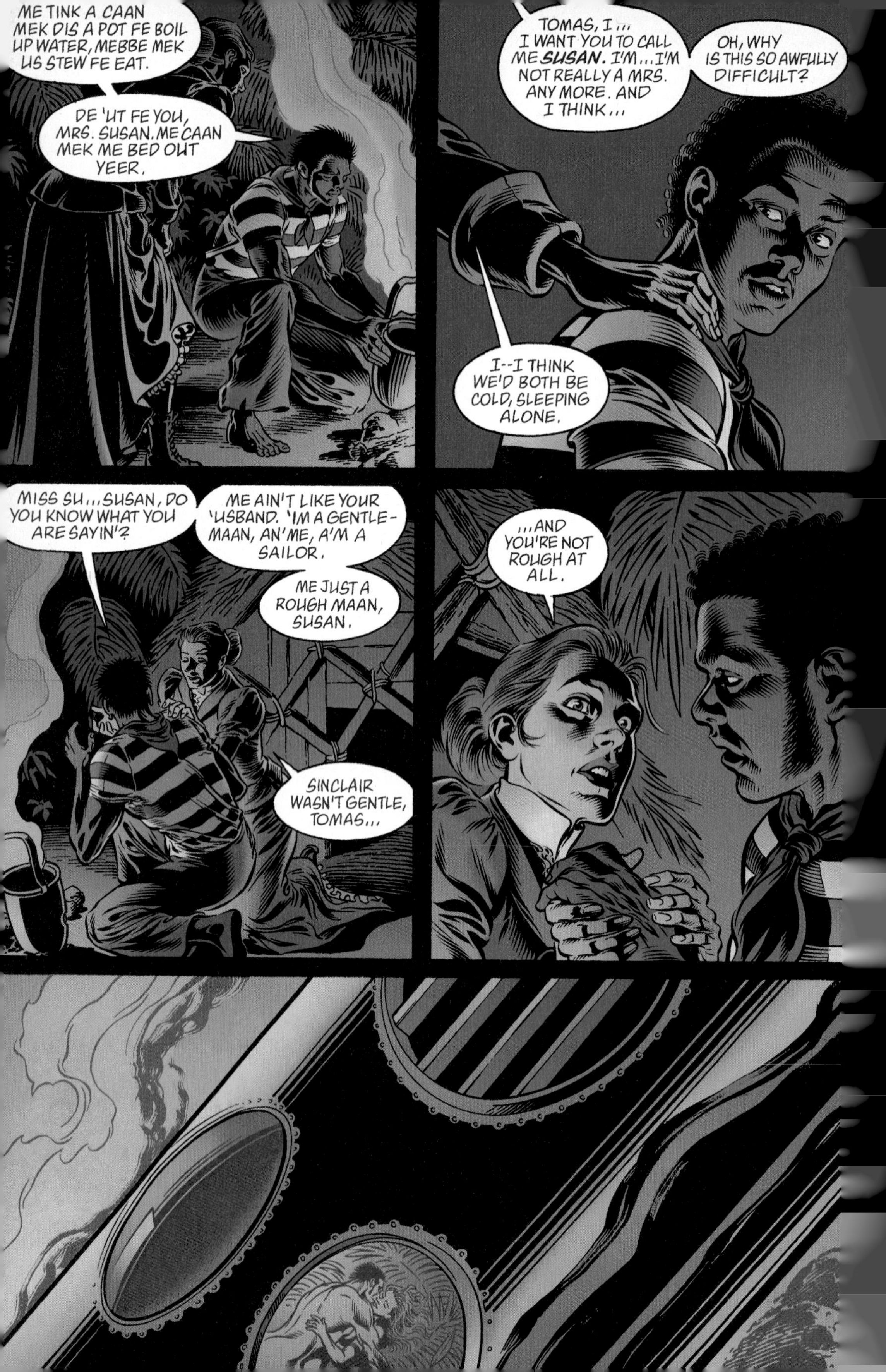
ME TINK A CAAN MEK DIS A POT FE BOIL UP WATER, MEBBE MEK US STEW FE EAT.
DE 'UT FE YOU, MRS. SUSAN. ME CAAN MEK ME BED OUT YEER.
TOMAS, I... I WANT YOU TO CALL ME SUSAN. I'M... I'M NOT REALLY A MRS. ANY MORE. AND I THINK...
OH, WHY IS THIS SO AWFULLY DIFFICULT?
I--I THINK WE'D BOTH BE COLD, SLEEPING ALONE.
MISS SU... SUSAN, DO YOU KNOW WHAT YOU ARE SAYIN'?
ME AIN'T LIKE YOUR 'USBAND. 'IM A GENTLE-MAAN, AN' ME, A'M A SAILOR.
ME JUST A ROUGH MAAN, SUSAN.
SINCLAIR WASN'T GENTLE, TOMAS...
...AND YOU'RE NOT ROUGH AT ALL.

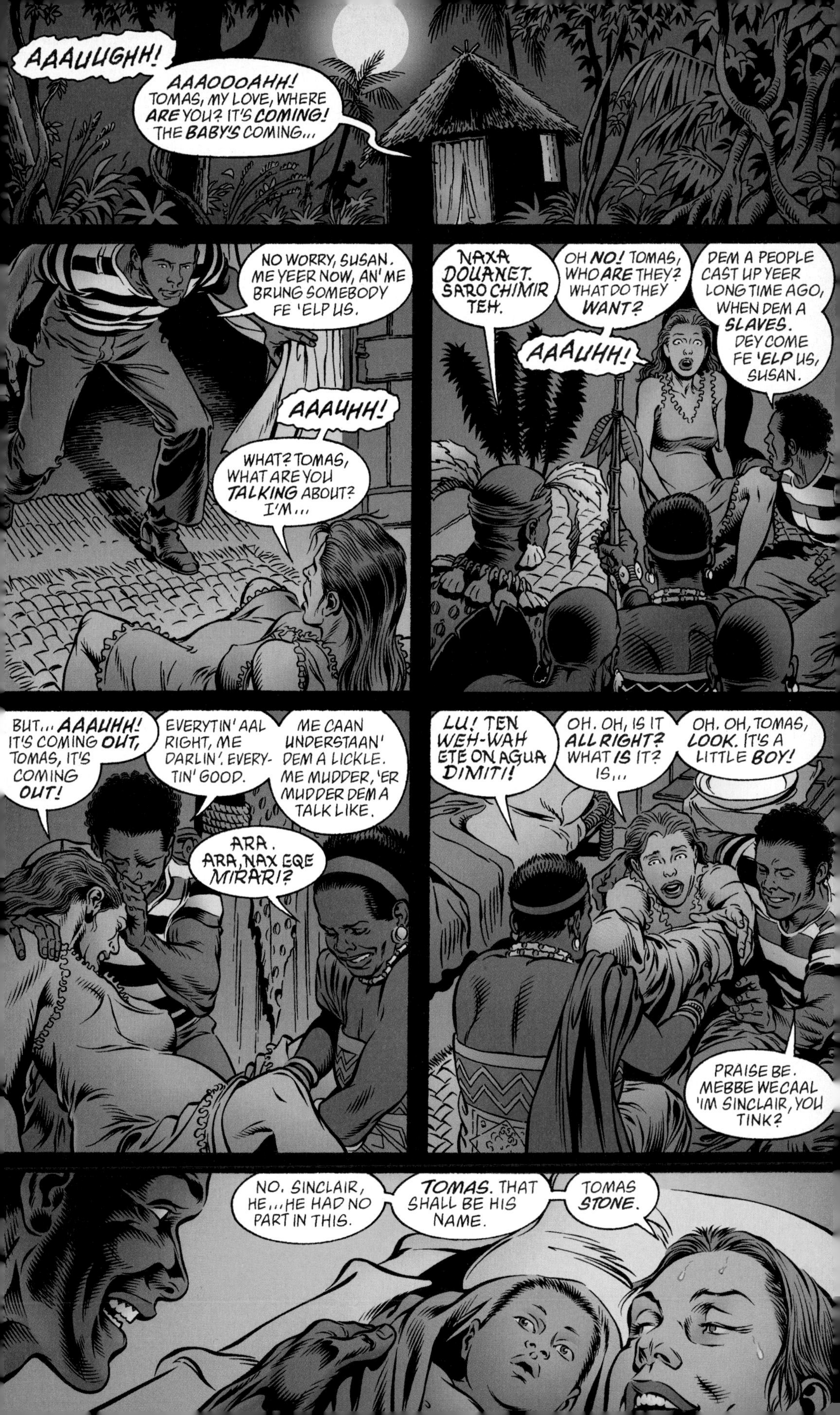
AAAUUGHH!
AAAOOOAHH! TOMAS, MY LOVE, WHERE ARE YOU? IT'S COMING! THE BABY'S COMING...
NO WORRY, SUSAN. ME YEER NOW, AN' ME BRUNG SOMEBODY FE 'ELP US.
AAAUHH!
WHAT? TOMAS, WHAT ARE YOU TALKING ABOUT? I'M...
NAXA DOUANET. SARO CHIMIR TEH.
OH NO! TOMAS, WHO ARE THEY? WHAT DO THEY WANT?
AAAUHH!
DEM A PEOPLE CAST UP YEER LONG TIME AGO, WHEN DEM A SLAVES. DEY COME FE 'ELP US, SUSAN.
BUT... AAAUHH! IT'S COMING OUT, TOMAS, IT'S COMING OUT!
EVERYTIN' AAL RIGHT, ME DARLIN'. EVERY-TIN' GOOD.
ME CAAN UNDERSTAAN' DEM A LICKLE. ME MUDDER, 'ER MUDDER DEM A TALK LIKE.
ARA. ARA, NAX EQE MIRARI?
LU! TEN WEH-WAH ETE ON AGUA DIMITI!
OH. OH, IS IT ALL RIGHT? WHAT IS IT? IS...
OH. OH, TOMAS, LOOK. IT'S A LITTLE BOY!
PRAISE BE. MEBBE WE CAAL 'IM SINCLAIR, YOU TINK?
NO. SINCLAIR, HE... HE HAD NO PART IN THIS.
TOMAS. THAT SHALL BE HIS NAME.
TOMAS STONE.

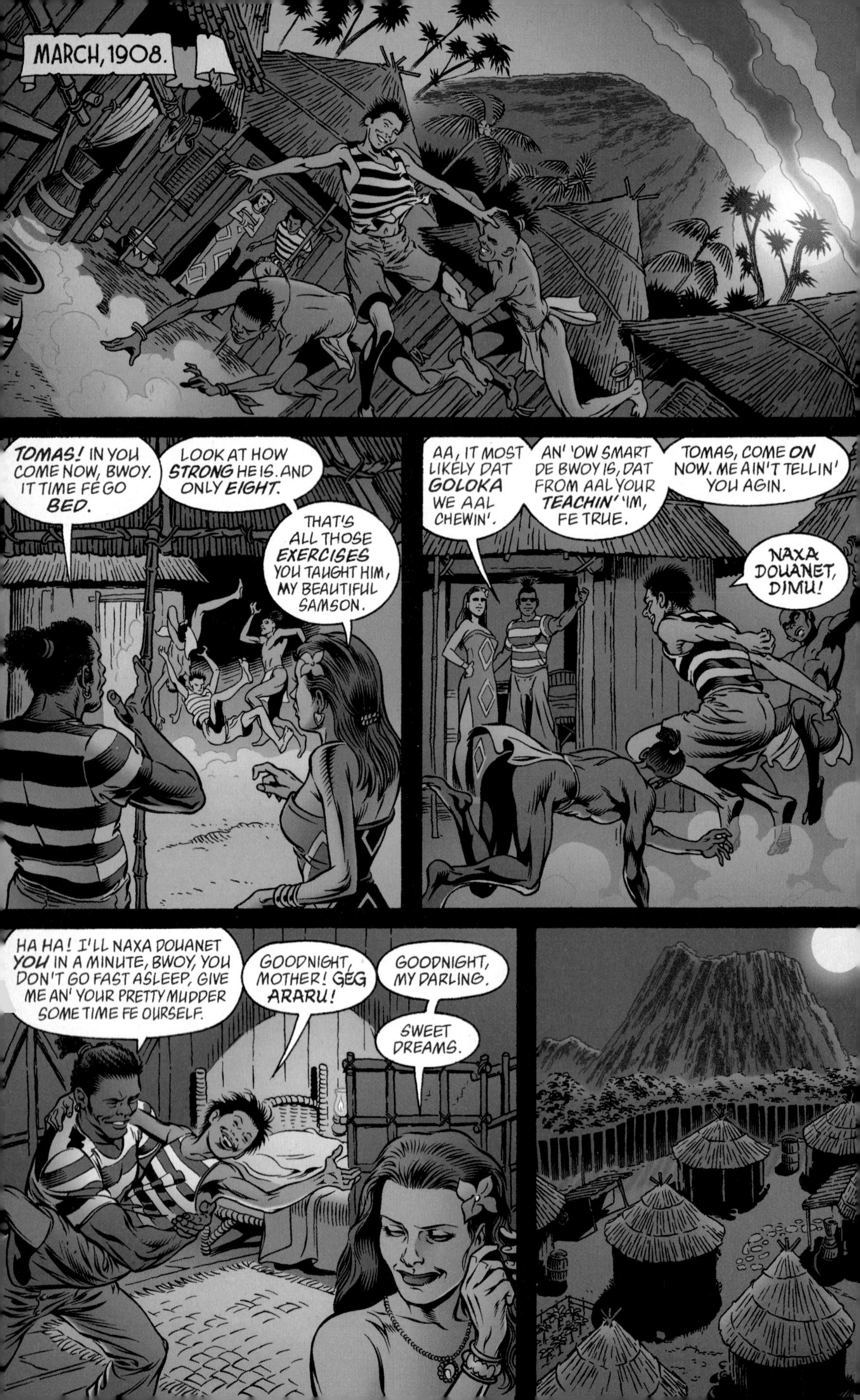
MARCH, 1908.
TOMAS! IN YOU COME NOW, BWOY. IT TIME FE GO BED.
LOOK AT HOW STRONG HE IS. AND ONLY EIGHT.
THAT'S ALL THOSE EXERCISES YOU TAUGHT HIM, MY BEAUTIFUL SAMSON.
AA, IT MOST LIKELY DAT GOLOKA WE AAL CHEWIN'.
AN' 'OW SMART DE BWOY IS, DAT FROM AAL YOUR TEACHIN' 'IM, FE TRUE.
TOMAS, COME ON NOW. ME AIN'T TELLIN' YOU AGIN.
NAXA DOUANET, DIMU!
HA HA! I'LL NAXA DOUANET YOU IN A MINUTE, BWOY, YOU DON'T GO FAST ASLEEP, GIVE ME AN' YOUR PRETTY MUDDER SOME TIME FE OURSELF.
GOODNIGHT, MOTHER! GEG ARARU!
GOODNIGHT, MY DARLING.
SWEET DREAMS.

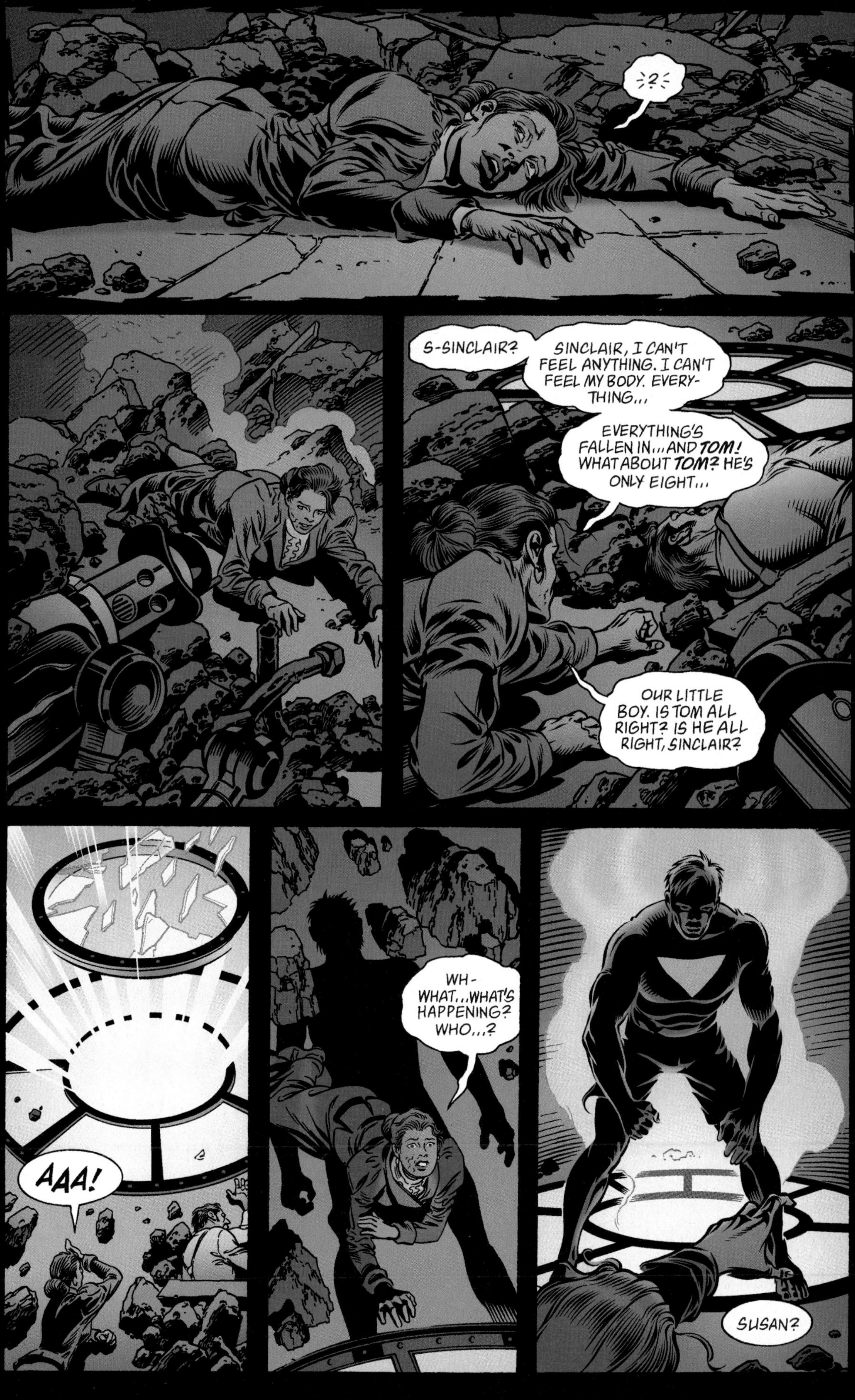
?
S-SINCLAIR?
SINCLAIR, I CAN'T FEEL ANYTHING. I CAN'T FEEL MY BODY. EVERY-THING...
EVERYTHING'S FALLEN IN... AND TOM! WHAT ABOUT TOM? HE'S ONLY EIGHT...
OUR LITTLE BOY. IS TOM ALL RIGHT? IS HE ALL RIGHT, SINCLAIR?
AAA!
WH- WHAT... WHAT'S HAPPENING? WHO...?
SUSAN?

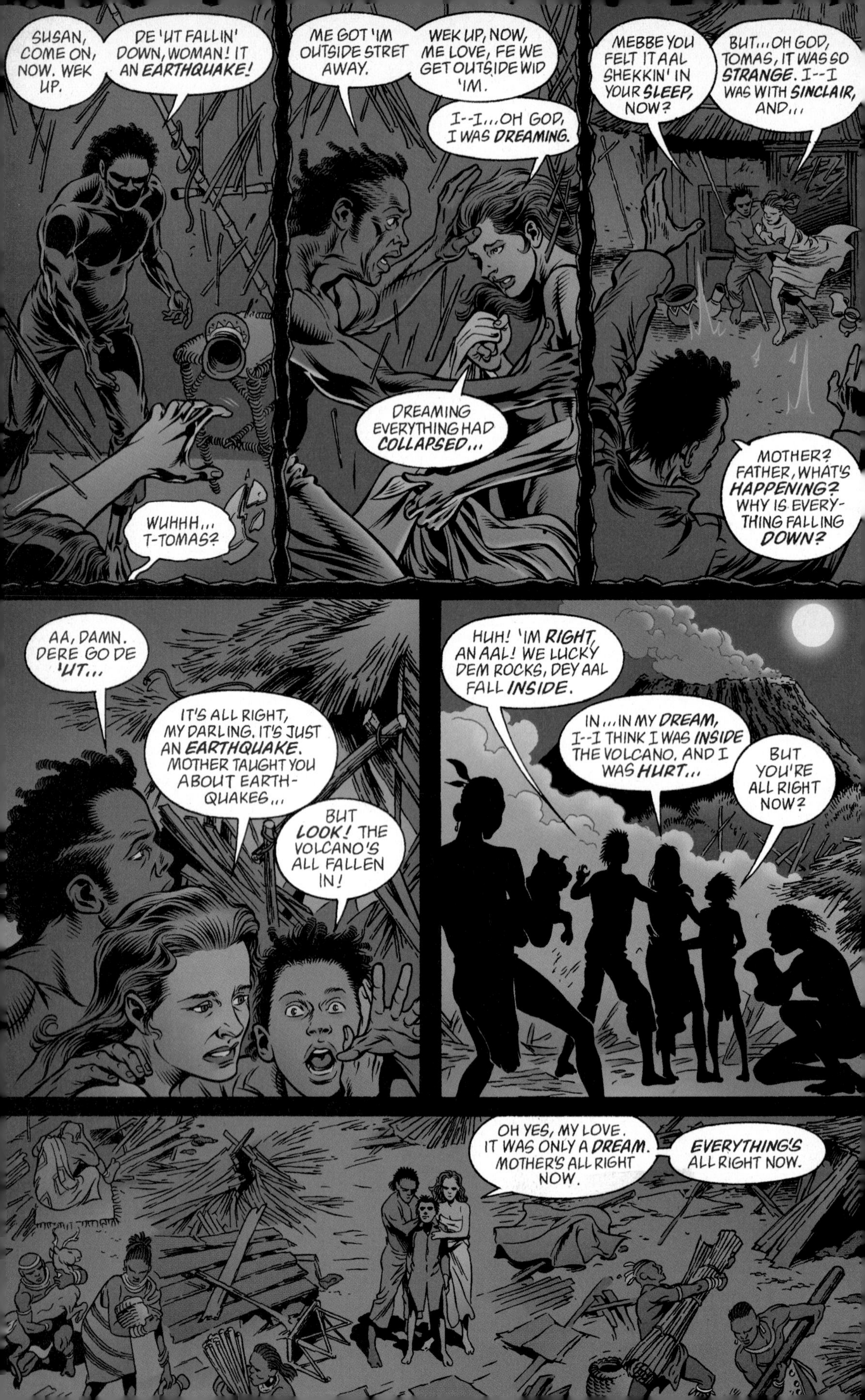
SUSAN, COME ON, NOW. WEK UP.
DE 'UT FALLIN' DOWN, WOMAN! IT AN EARTHQUAKE!
WUHHH... T-TOMAS?
ME GOT 'IM OUTSIDE STRET AWAY.
WEK UP, NOW, ME LOVE, FE WE GET OUTSIDE WID 'IM.
I--I...OH GOD, I WAS DREAMING.
DREAMING EVERYTHING HAD COLLAPSED...
MEBBE YOU FELT IT AAL SHEKKIN' IN YOUR SLEEP, NOW?
BUT...OH GOD, TOMAS, IT WAS SO STRANGE. I--I WAS WITH SINCLAIR, AND...
MOTHER? FATHER, WHAT'S HAPPENING? WHY IS EVERY-THING FALLING DOWN?
AA, DAMN. DERE GO DE 'UT...
IT'S ALL RIGHT, MY DARLING. IT'S JUST AN EARTHQUAKE. MOTHER TAUGHT YOU ABOUT EARTH-QUAKES...
BUT LOOK! THE VOLCANO'S ALL FALLEN IN!
HUH! 'IM RIGHT, AN AAL! WE LUCKY DEM ROCKS, DEY AAL FALL INSIDE.
IN...IN MY DREAM, I--I THINK I WAS INSIDE THE VOLCANO. AND I WAS HURT...
BUT YOU'RE ALL RIGHT NOW?
OH YES, MY LOVE. IT WAS ONLY A DREAM. MOTHER'S ALL RIGHT NOW.
EVERYTHING'S ALL RIGHT NOW.

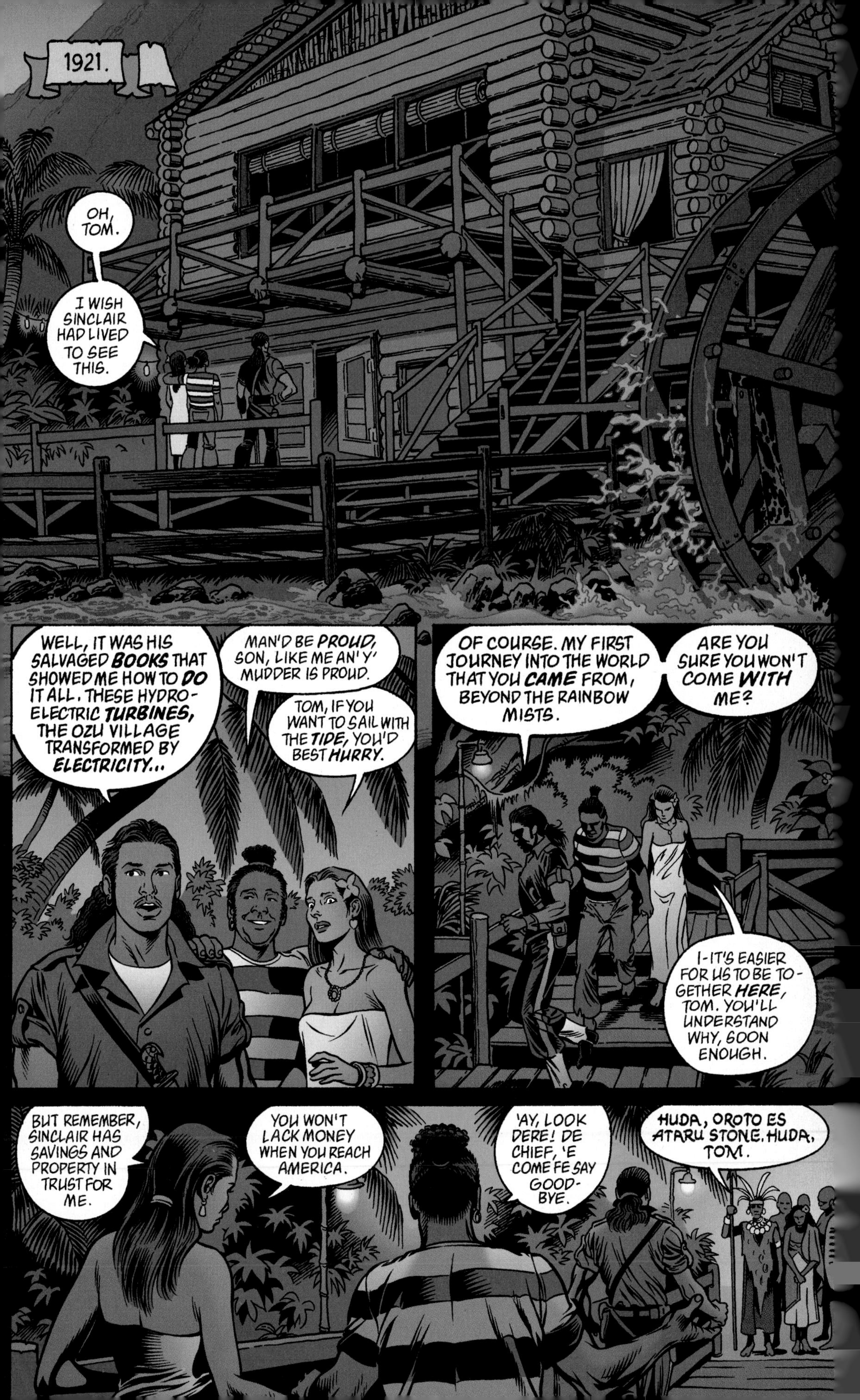
1921.
OH, TOM.
I WISH SINCLAIR HAD LIVED TO SEE THIS.
WELL, IT WAS HIS SALVAGED BOOKS THAT SHOWED ME HOW TO DO IT ALL. THESE HYDRO-ELECTRIC TURBINES, THE OZU VILLAGE TRANSFORMED BY ELECTRICITY...
MAN'D BE PROUD, SON, LIKE ME AN' Y' MUDDER IS PROUD.
TOM, IF YOU WANT TO SAIL WITH THE TIDE, YOU'D BEST HURRY.
OF COURSE. MY FIRST JOURNEY INTO THE WORLD THAT YOU CAME FROM, BEYOND THE RAINBOW MISTS.
ARE YOU SURE YOU WON'T COME WITH ME?
I-IT'S EASIER FOR US TO BE TO-GETHER HERE, TOM. YOU'LL UNDERSTAND WHY, SOON ENOUGH.
BUT REMEMBER, SINCLAIR HAS SAVINGS AND PROPERTY IN TRUST FOR ME.
YOU WON'T LACK MONEY WHEN YOU REACH AMERICA.
'AY, LOOK DERE! DE CHIEF, 'E COME FE SAY GOOD-BYE.
HUDA, OROTO ES ATARU STONE. HUDA, TOM.

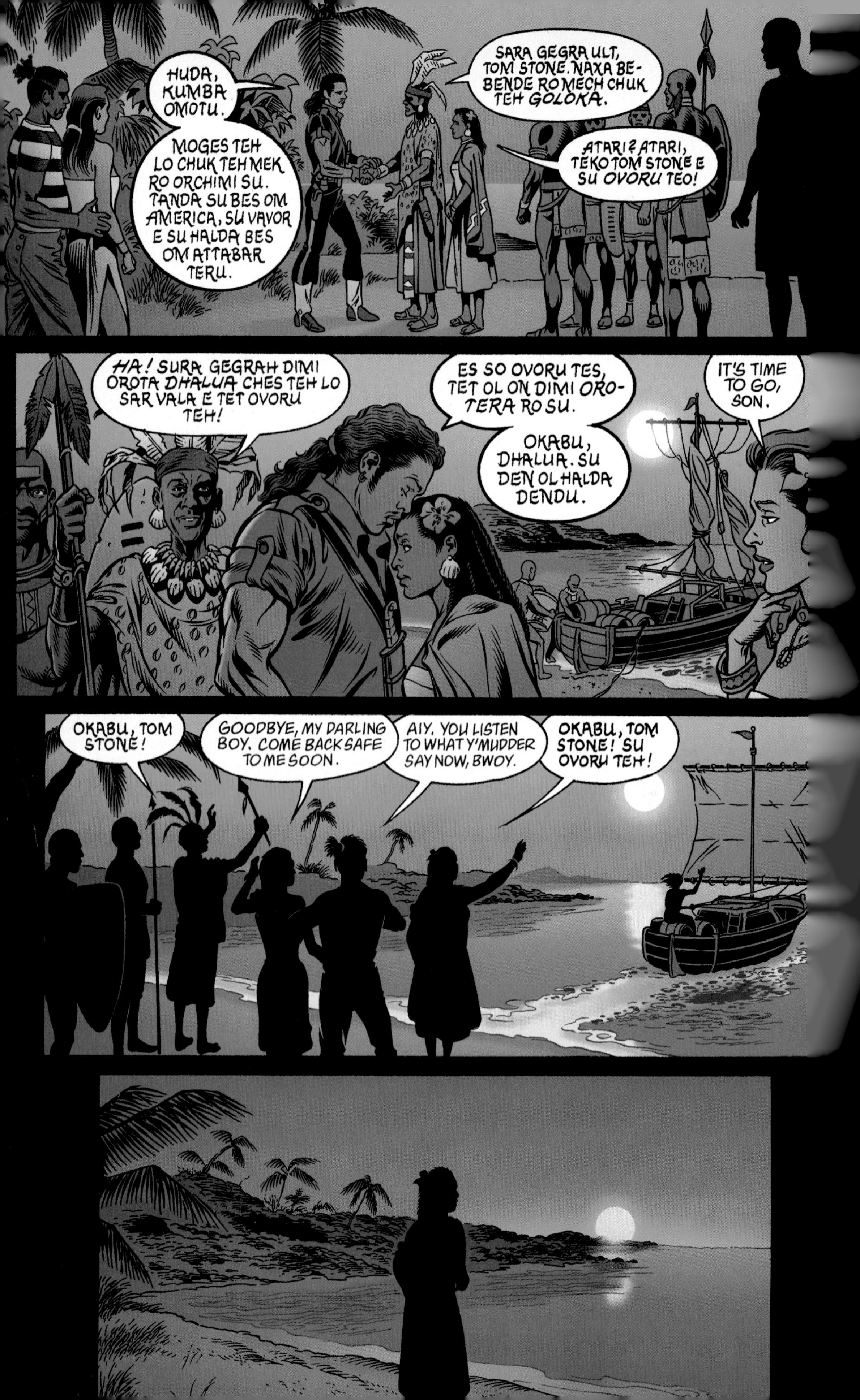
HUDA, KUMBA OMOTU.
MOGES TEH LO CHUK TEH MEK RO ORCHIMI SU. TANDA SU BES OM AMERICA, SU VAVOR E SU HALDA BES OM ATTABAR TERU.
SARA GEGRA ULT, TOM STONE. NAXA BEBENDE RO MECH CHUK TEH GOLOKA.
ATARI? ATARI, TEKO TOM STONE E SU OVORU TEO!
HA! SURA GEGRAH DIMI OROTA DHALUA CHES TEH LO SAR VALA E TET OVORU TEH!
ES SO OVORU TES, TET OL ON DIMI OROTERA RO SU.
OKABU, DHALUA. SU DEN OL HALDA DENDU.
IT'S TIME TO GO, SON.
OKABU, TOM STONE!
GOODBYE, MY DARLING BOY. COME BACK SAFE TO ME SOON.
AIY. YOU LISTEN TO WHAT Y'MUDDER SAY NOW, BWOY.
OKABU, TOM STONE! SU OVORU TEH!

# THE MILLENNIUM CITIZEN

METRO-POLITAN EDITION, BRINGING YOU ALL THE NEWS

TWO CENTS

MORNING EDITION · MILLENNIUM CITY, SEPTEMBER 21st, 1921 · VOLUME XIV, NO. 345

Today: Sunny. Temperatures in the mid 60s. Tonight: colder, clouds moving into area.

TWO CENTS

## NEGRO FOILS ROBBERY
### Charlie "Bones" Costanza Believed Dead

*Exclusive by Chick Johnson*

In a spectacular and daring escapade high over the streets of Millennium City, a muscular daredevil put on a show for an amazed crowd last night as he rescued a damsel in distress while spoiling the evil plan of well-known criminal mastermind Charlie "Bones" Costanza. The young lady, one Grace seemed shaken but unhurt as she told this re...

≥HAHHHHHHH≤

OH, *MY.* SOMEBODY CERTAINLY SOUNDS FED UP.

YOU MUST BE THE WONDER FROM THE *JUNGLE* I'VE HEARD SO MUCH ABOUT.

DO YOU MIND IF I *JOIN* YOU?

HMM. WELL, I'M TOLD IT'S A FREE COUNTRY. BE MY GUEST, MR...?

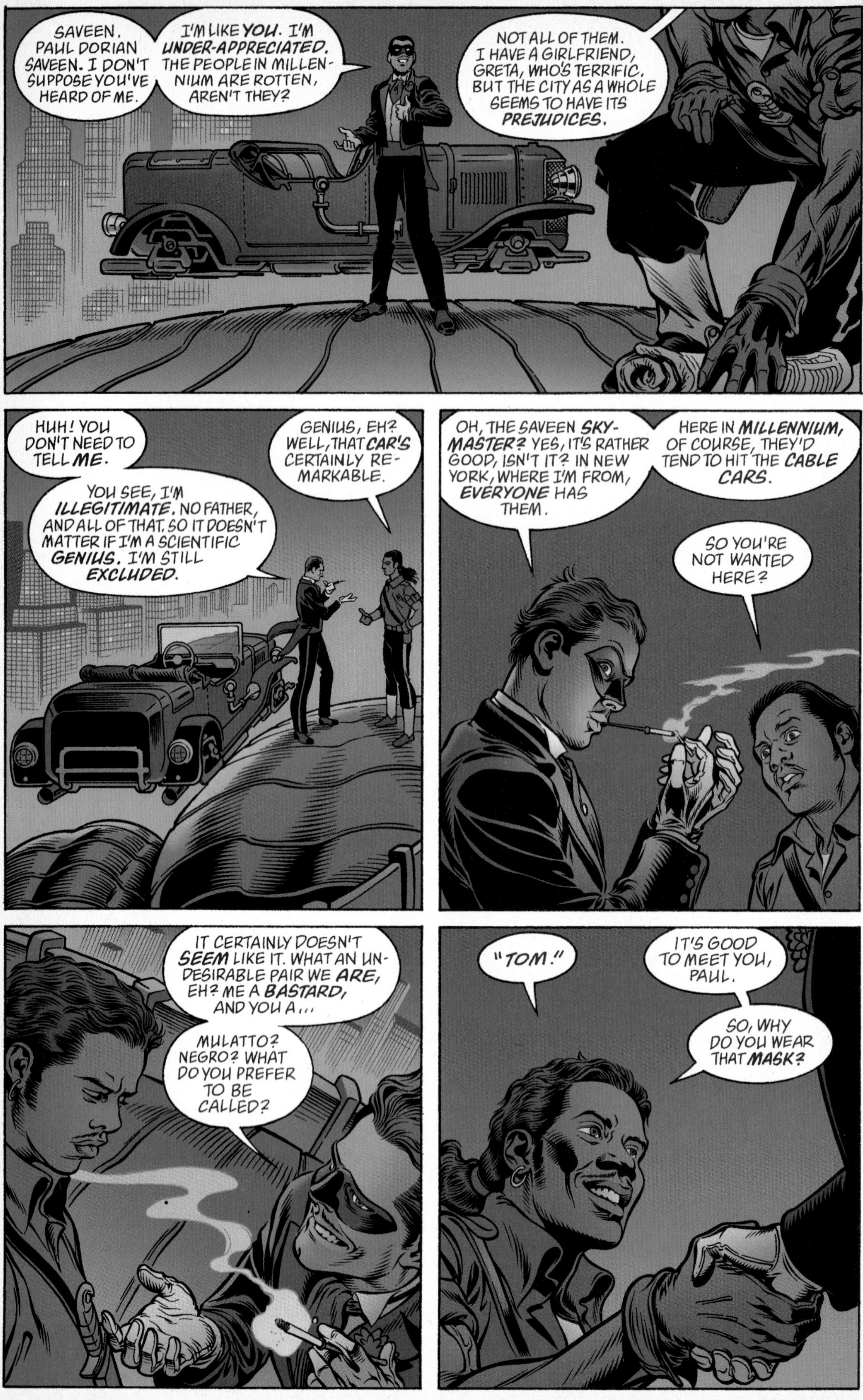
SAVEEN. PAUL DORIAN SAVEEN. I DON'T SUPPOSE YOU'VE HEARD OF ME.
I'M LIKE YOU. I'M UNDER-APPRECIATED. THE PEOPLE IN MILLENNIUM ARE ROTTEN, AREN'T THEY?
NOT ALL OF THEM. I HAVE A GIRLFRIEND, GRETA, WHO'S TERRIFIC, BUT THE CITY AS A WHOLE SEEMS TO HAVE ITS PREJUDICES.
HUH! YOU DON'T NEED TO TELL ME.
YOU SEE, I'M ILLEGITIMATE. NO FATHER, AND ALL OF THAT. SO IT DOESN'T MATTER IF I'M A SCIENTIFIC GENIUS. I'M STILL EXCLUDED.
GENIUS, EH? WELL, THAT CAR'S CERTAINLY REMARKABLE.
OH, THE SAVEEN SKY-MASTER? YES, IT'S RATHER GOOD, ISN'T IT? IN NEW YORK, WHERE I'M FROM, EVERYONE HAS THEM.
HERE IN MILLENNIUM, OF COURSE, THEY'D TEND TO HIT THE CABLE CARS.
SO YOU'RE NOT WANTED HERE?
IT CERTAINLY DOESN'T SEEM LIKE IT. WHAT AN UNDESIRABLE PAIR WE ARE, EH? ME A BASTARD, AND YOU A...
MULATTO? NEGRO? WHAT DO YOU PREFER TO BE CALLED?
"TOM."
IT'S GOOD TO MEET YOU, PAUL.
SO, WHY DO YOU WEAR THAT MASK?

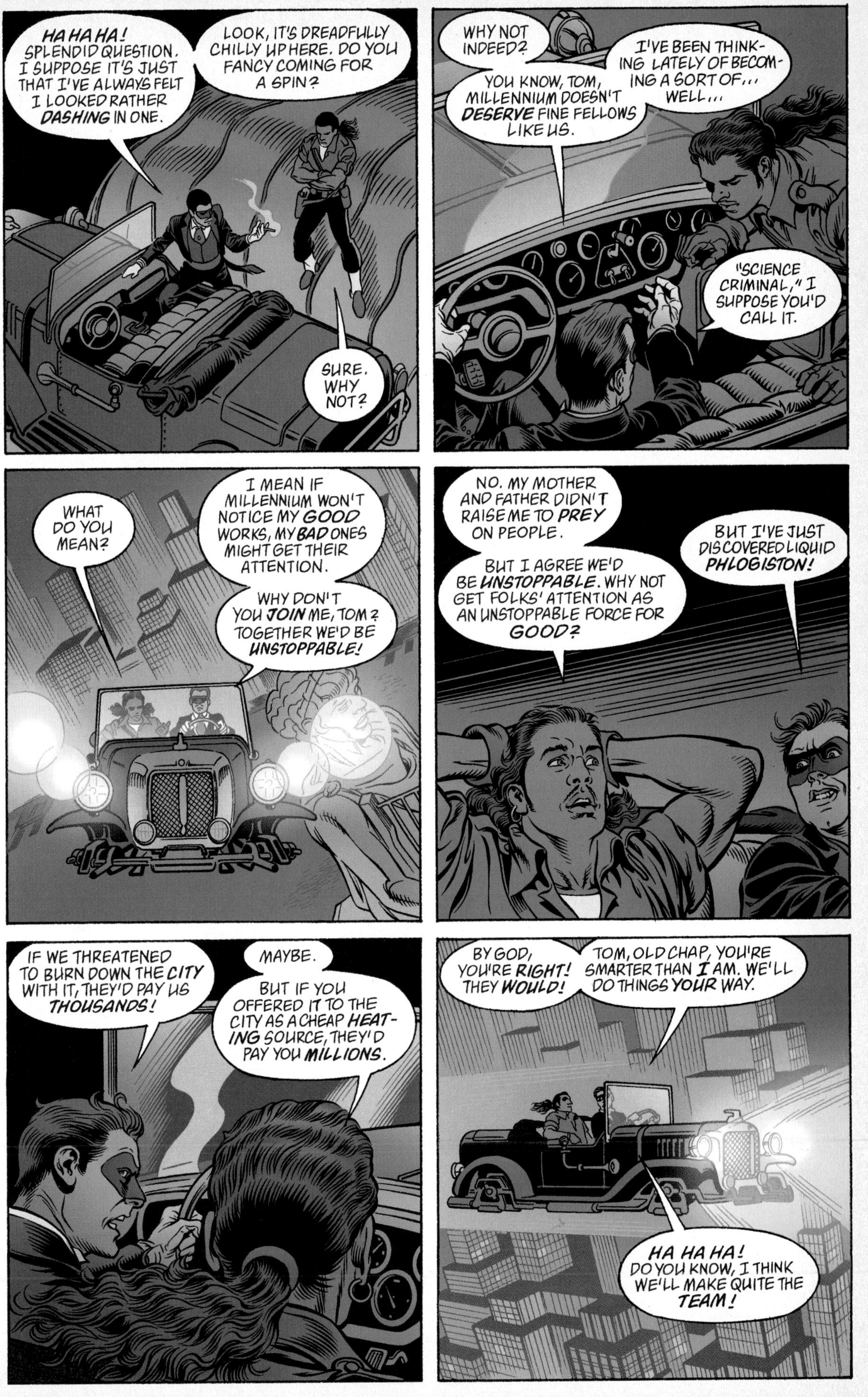
HA HA HA! SPLENDID QUESTION. I SUPPOSE IT'S JUST THAT I'VE ALWAYS FELT I LOOKED RATHER DASHING IN ONE.
LOOK, IT'S DREADFULLY CHILLY UP HERE. DO YOU FANCY COMING FOR A SPIN?
SURE. WHY NOT?
WHY NOT INDEED?
YOU KNOW, TOM, MILLENNIUM DOESN'T DESERVE FINE FELLOWS LIKE US.
I'VE BEEN THINKING LATELY OF BECOMING A SORT OF... WELL...
"SCIENCE CRIMINAL," I SUPPOSE YOU'D CALL IT.
WHAT DO YOU MEAN?
I MEAN IF MILLENNIUM WON'T NOTICE MY GOOD WORKS, MY BAD ONES MIGHT GET THEIR ATTENTION.
WHY DON'T YOU JOIN ME, TOM? TOGETHER WE'D BE UNSTOPPABLE!
NO. MY MOTHER AND FATHER DIDN'T RAISE ME TO PREY ON PEOPLE.
BUT I AGREE WE'D BE UNSTOPPABLE. WHY NOT GET FOLKS' ATTENTION AS AN UNSTOPPABLE FORCE FOR GOOD?
BUT I'VE JUST DISCOVERED LIQUID PHLOGISTON!
IF WE THREATENED TO BURN DOWN THE CITY WITH IT, THEY'D PAY US THOUSANDS!
MAYBE.
BUT IF YOU OFFERED IT TO THE CITY AS A CHEAP HEATING SOURCE, THEY'D PAY YOU MILLIONS.
BY GOD, YOU'RE RIGHT! THEY WOULD!
TOM, OLD CHAP, YOU'RE SMARTER THAN I AM. WE'LL DO THINGS YOUR WAY.
HA HA HA! DO YOU KNOW, I THINK WE'LL MAKE QUITE THE TEAM!

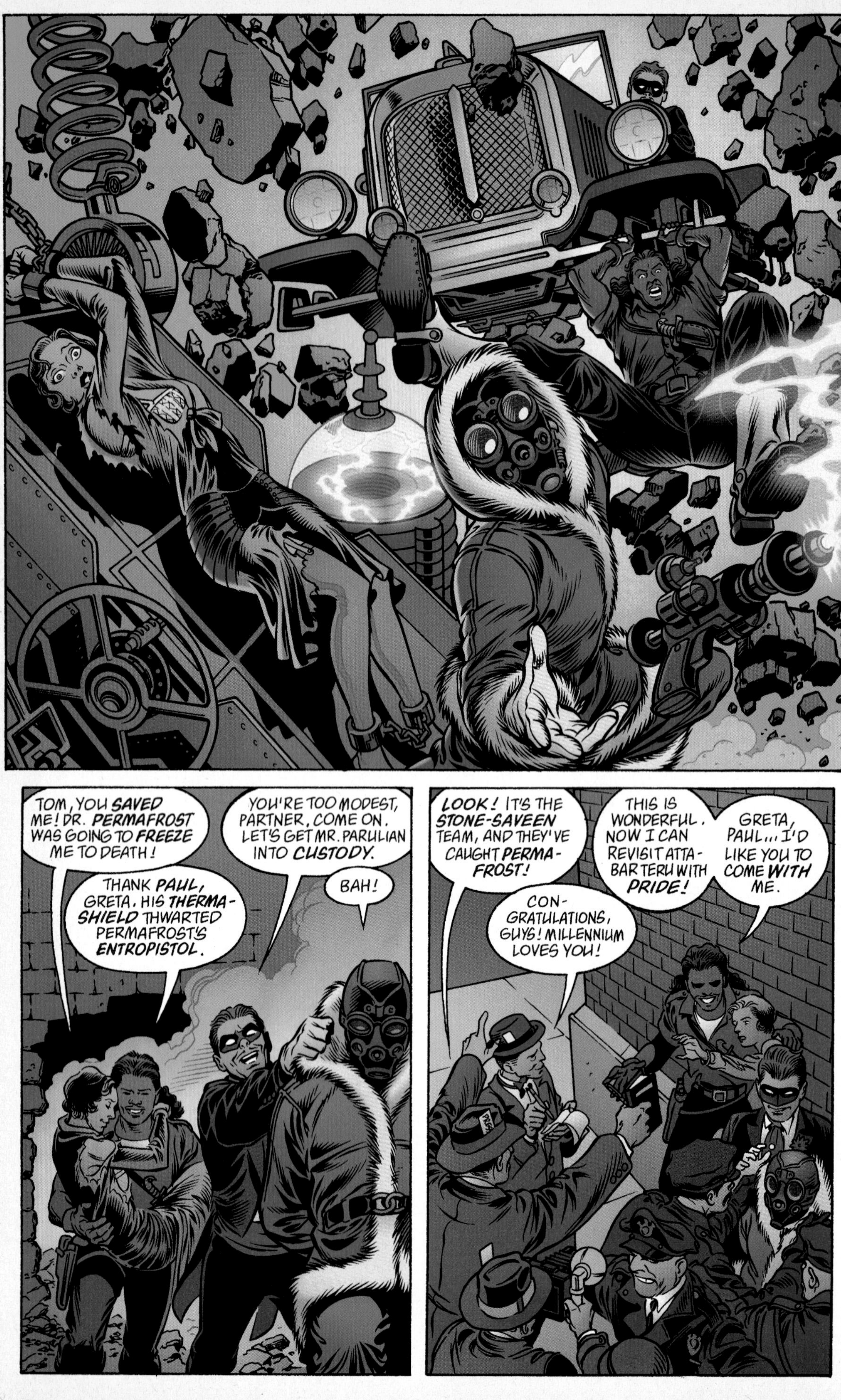

TOM, YOU SAVED ME! DR. PERMAFROST WAS GOING TO FREEZE ME TO DEATH!
THANK PAUL, GRETA. HIS THERMA-SHIELD THWARTED PERMAFROST'S ENTROPISTOL.
YOU'RE TOO MODEST, PARTNER, COME ON. LET'S GET MR. PARULIAN INTO CUSTODY.
BAH!
LOOK! IT'S THE STONE-SAVEEN TEAM, AND THEY'VE CAUGHT PERMA-FROST!
CON-GRATULATIONS, GUYS! MILLENNIUM LOVES YOU!
THIS IS WONDERFUL. NOW I CAN REVISIT ATTA-BAR TERU WITH PRIDE!
GRETA, PAUL... I'D LIKE YOU TO COME WITH ME.

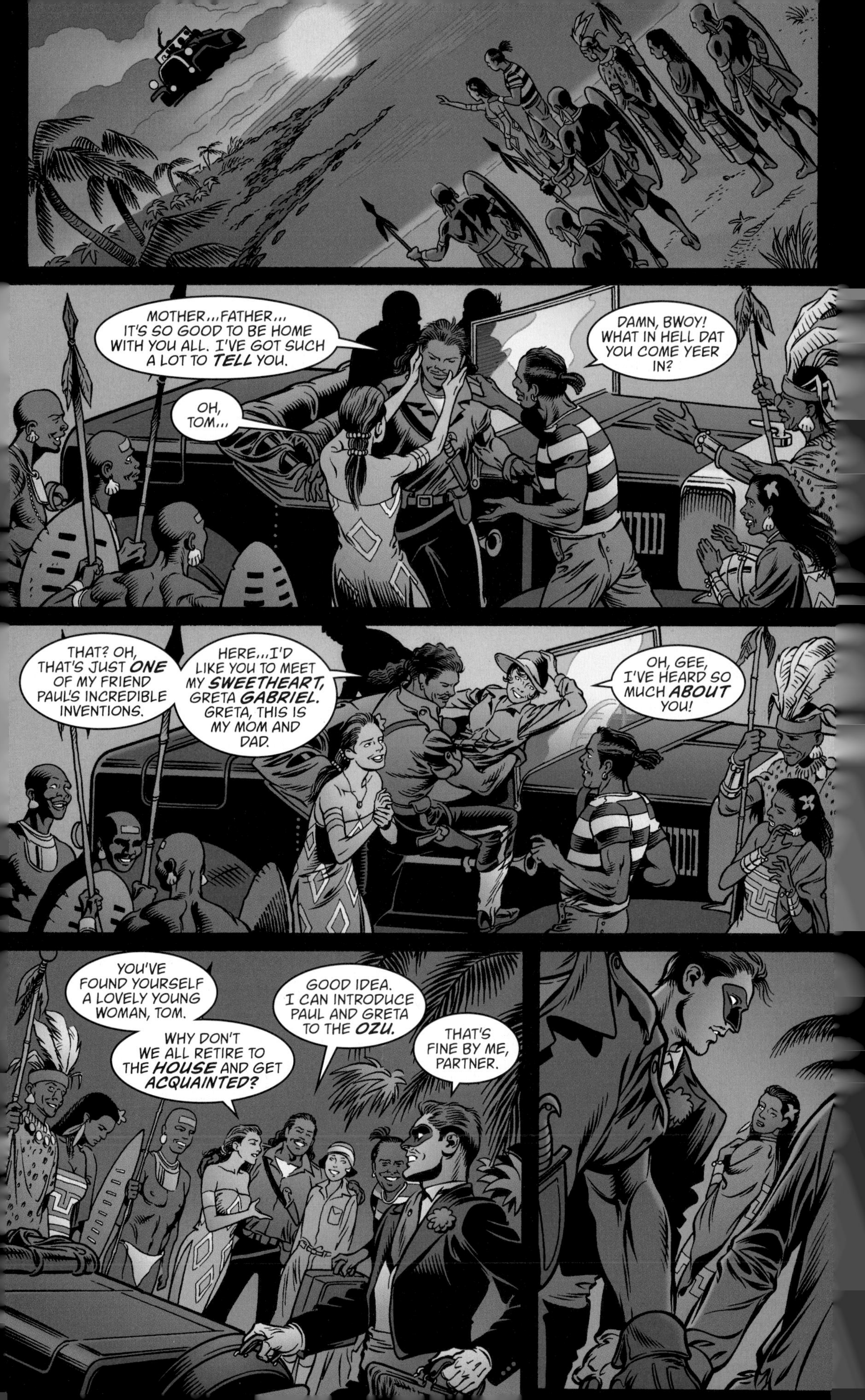
MOTHER...FATHER... IT'S SO GOOD TO BE HOME WITH YOU ALL. I'VE GOT SUCH A LOT TO TELL YOU.
OH, TOM...
DAMN, BWOY! WHAT IN HELL DAT YOU COME YEER IN?
THAT? OH, THAT'S JUST ONE OF MY FRIEND PAUL'S INCREDIBLE INVENTIONS.
HERE...I'D LIKE YOU TO MEET MY SWEETHEART, GRETA GABRIEL. GRETA, THIS IS MY MOM AND DAD.
OH, GEE, I'VE HEARD SO MUCH ABOUT YOU!
YOU'VE FOUND YOURSELF A LOVELY YOUNG WOMAN, TOM.
WHY DON'T WE ALL RETIRE TO THE HOUSE AND GET ACQUAINTED?
GOOD IDEA. I CAN INTRODUCE PAUL AND GRETA TO THE OZU.
THAT'S FINE BY ME, PARTNER.

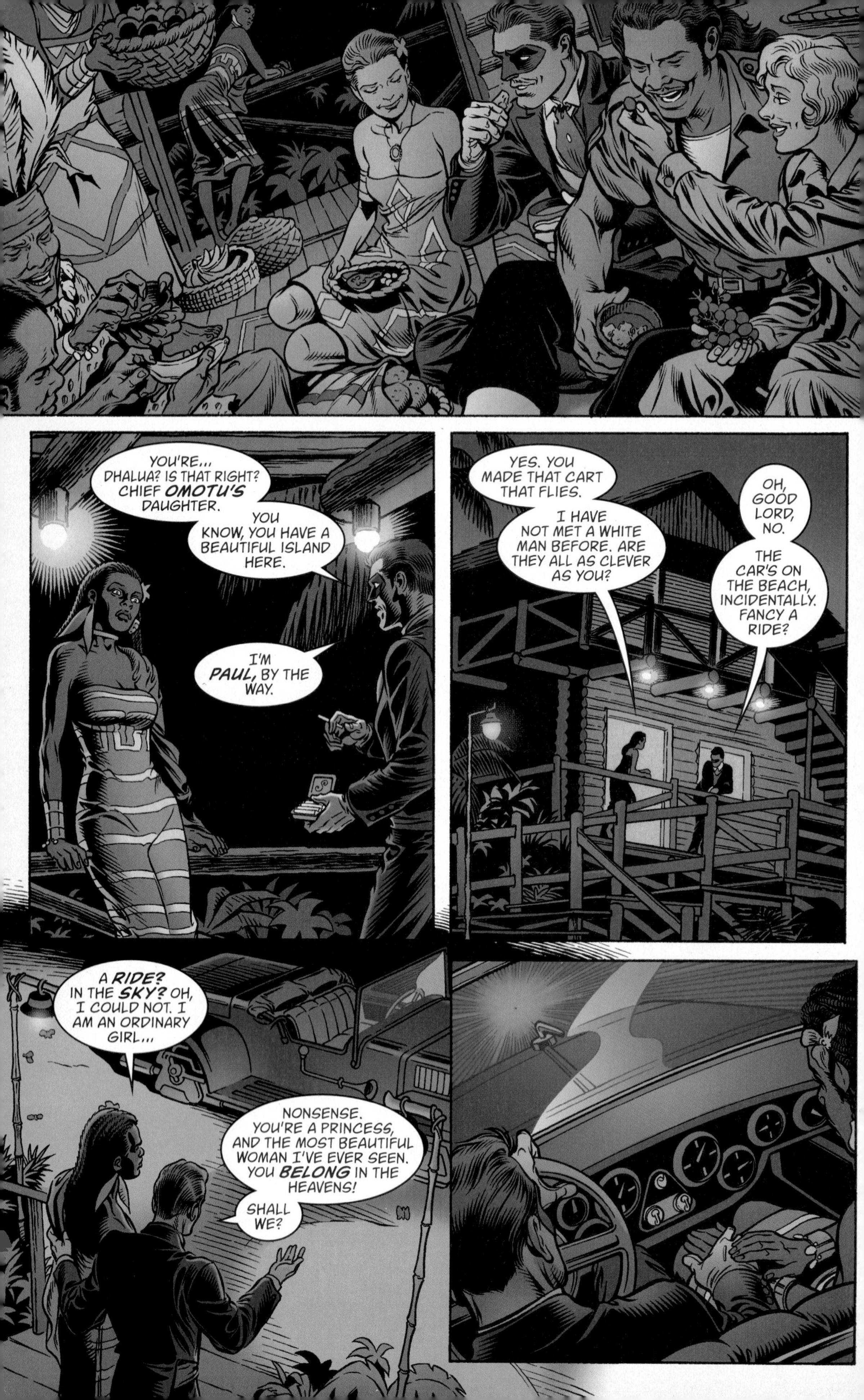
YOU'RE... DHALUA? IS THAT RIGHT? CHIEF OMOTU'S DAUGHTER.
YOU KNOW, YOU HAVE A BEAUTIFUL ISLAND HERE.
I'M PAUL, BY THE WAY.
YES. YOU MADE THAT CART THAT FLIES.
I HAVE NOT MET A WHITE MAN BEFORE. ARE THEY ALL AS CLEVER AS YOU?
OH, GOOD LORD, NO.
THE CAR'S ON THE BEACH, INCIDENTALLY. FANCY A RIDE?
A RIDE? IN THE SKY? OH, I COULD NOT. I AM AN ORDINARY GIRL...
NONSENSE. YOU'RE A PRINCESS, AND THE MOST BEAUTIFUL WOMAN I'VE EVER SEEN. YOU BELONG IN THE HEAVENS!
SHALL WE?

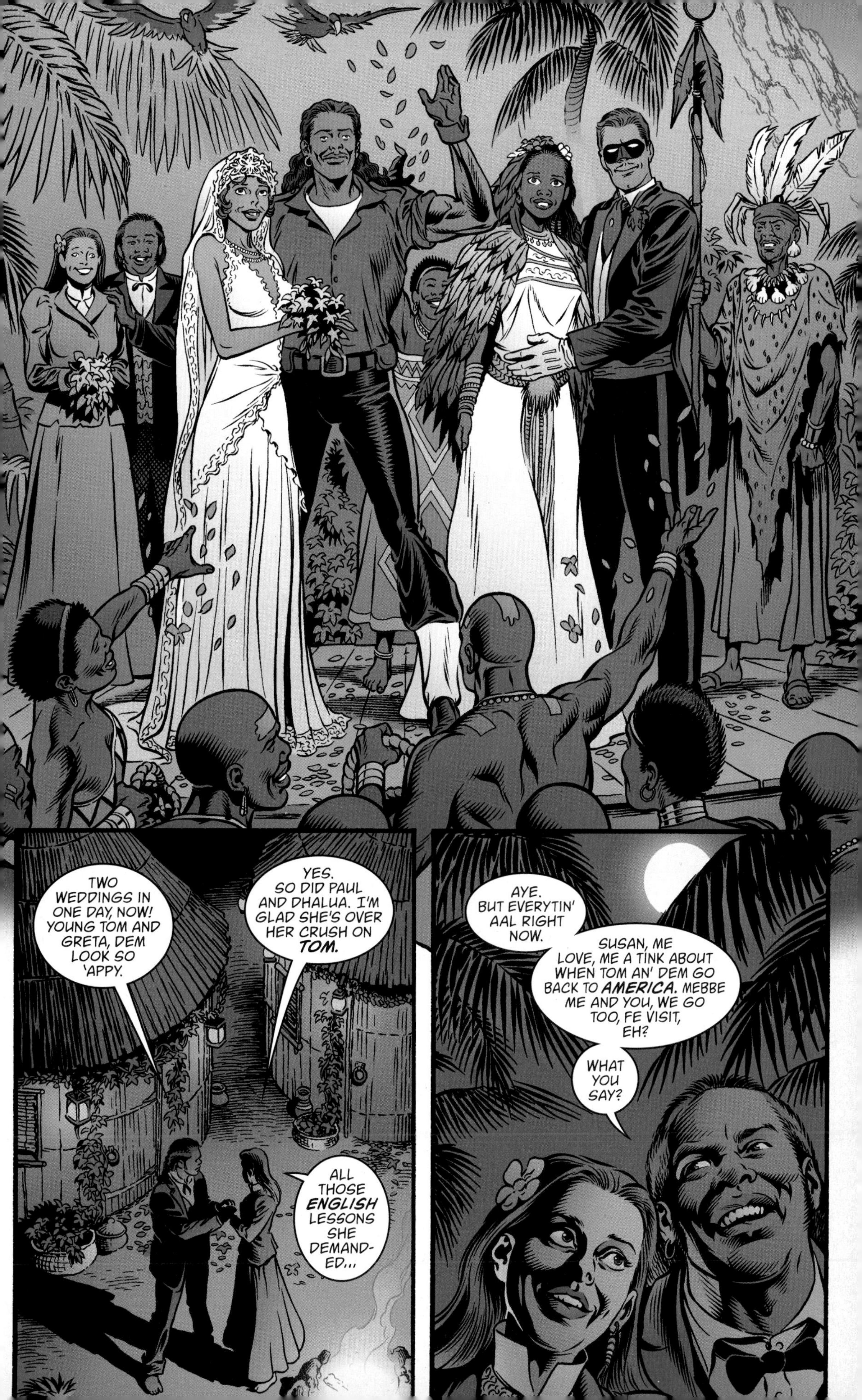

TWO WEDDINGS IN ONE DAY, NOW! YOUNG TOM AND GRETA, DEM LOOK SO 'APPY.
YES. SO DID PAUL AND DHALUA. I'M GLAD SHE'S OVER HER CRUSH ON TOM.
ALL THOSE ENGLISH LESSONS SHE DEMAND-ED...
AYE. BUT EVERYTIN' AAL RIGHT NOW.
SUSAN, ME LOVE, ME A TINK ABOUT WHEN TOM AN' DEM GO BACK TO AMERICA. MEBBE ME AND YOU, WE GO TOO, FE VISIT, EH?
WHAT YOU SAY?

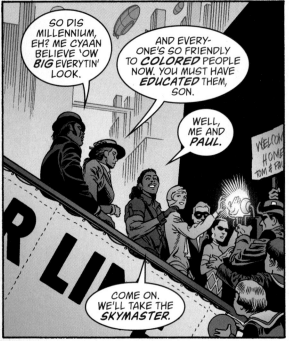

SO DIS *MILLENNIUM*, EH? ME CYAAN BELIEVE 'OW *BIG* EVERYTIN' LOOK.

AND EVERYONE'S SO FRIENDLY TO *COLORED* PEOPLE NOW. YOU MUST HAVE *EDUCATED* THEM, SON.

WELL, ME AND *PAUL*.

COME ON. WE'LL TAKE THE *SKYMASTER*.

WHERE ARE WE GOING?

TO THE PLACE WE CAN CALL *HOME* WHILE WE'RE NOT ON *ATTABAR TERU*.

ABSOLUTELY. IT'S THE BUILDING YOUR LATE HUSBAND OWNED HERE IN MILLENNIUM, MRS. STONE.

IT'S BECOME OUR *HEADQUARTERS*.

NATURALLY, WE'VE REFURBISHED THE PLACE WITH MY SCIENTIFIC DISCOVERIES, BUT IT'S A WONDERFUL BASE FOR THE *STONE-SAVEEN* TEAM.

YES. AND WE NAMED IT TO COMMEMORATE ITS ORIGINAL OWNER, SINCLAIR *STRONG*.

REALLY? WHAT'S IT CALLED?

THE STRONGHOLD.

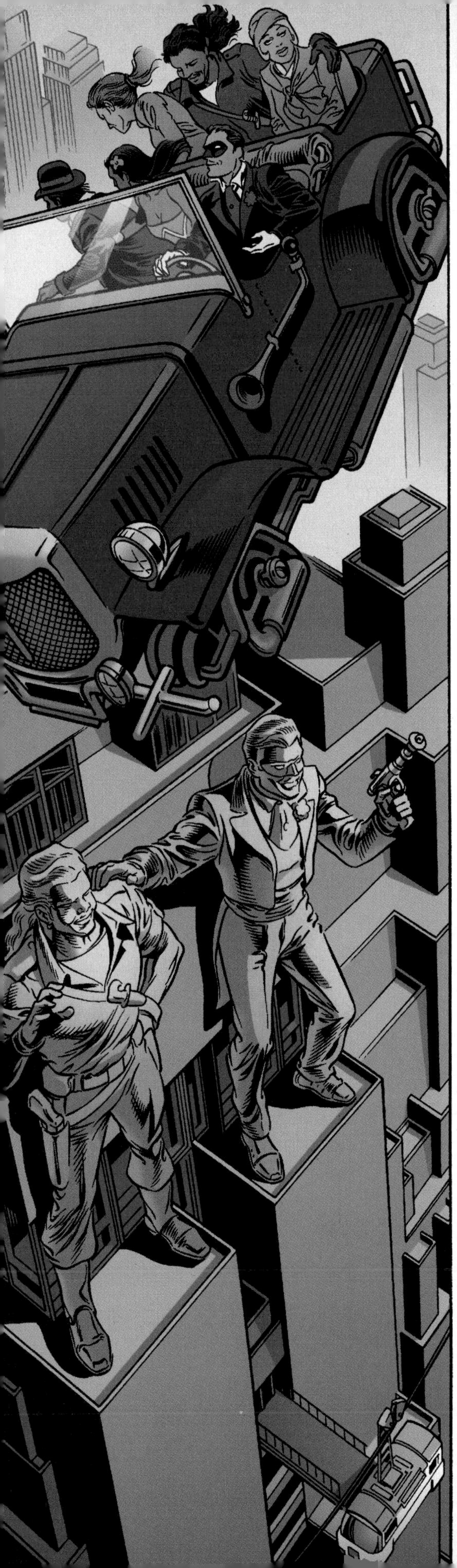

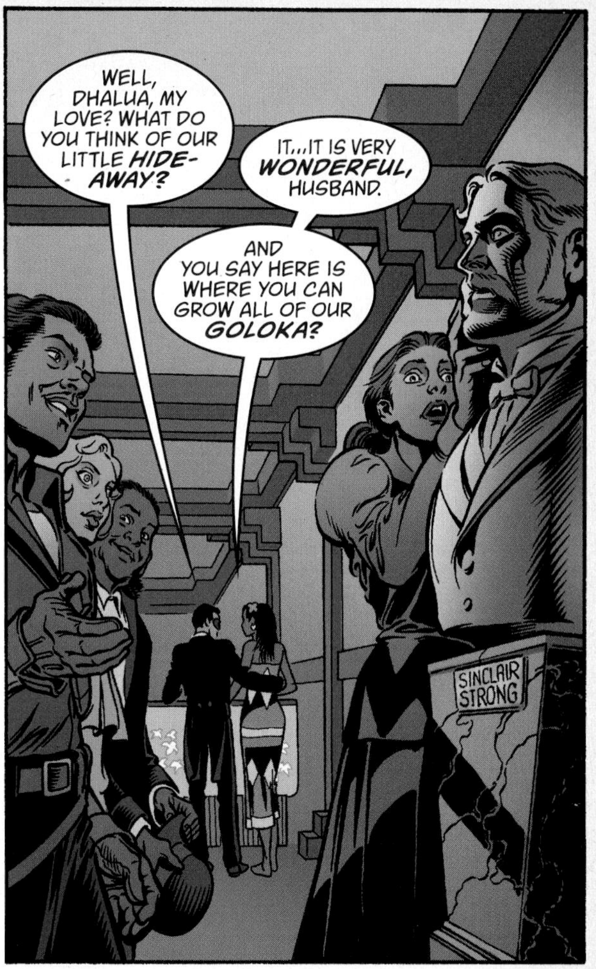
WELL, DHALUA, MY LOVE? WHAT DO YOU THINK OF OUR LITTLE HIDE-AWAY?
IT...IT IS VERY WONDERFUL, HUSBAND.
AND YOU SAY HERE IS WHERE YOU CAN GROW ALL OF OUR GOLOKA?
SINCLAIR STRONG

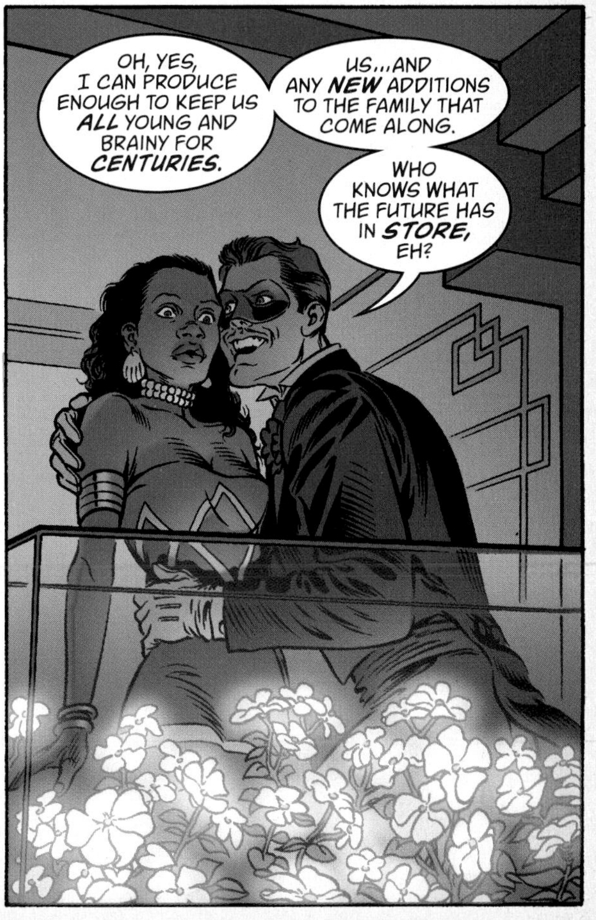
OH, YES, I CAN PRODUCE ENOUGH TO KEEP US ALL YOUNG AND BRAINY FOR CENTURIES.
US...AND ANY NEW ADDITIONS TO THE FAMILY THAT COME ALONG.
WHO KNOWS WHAT THE FUTURE HAS IN STORE, EH?

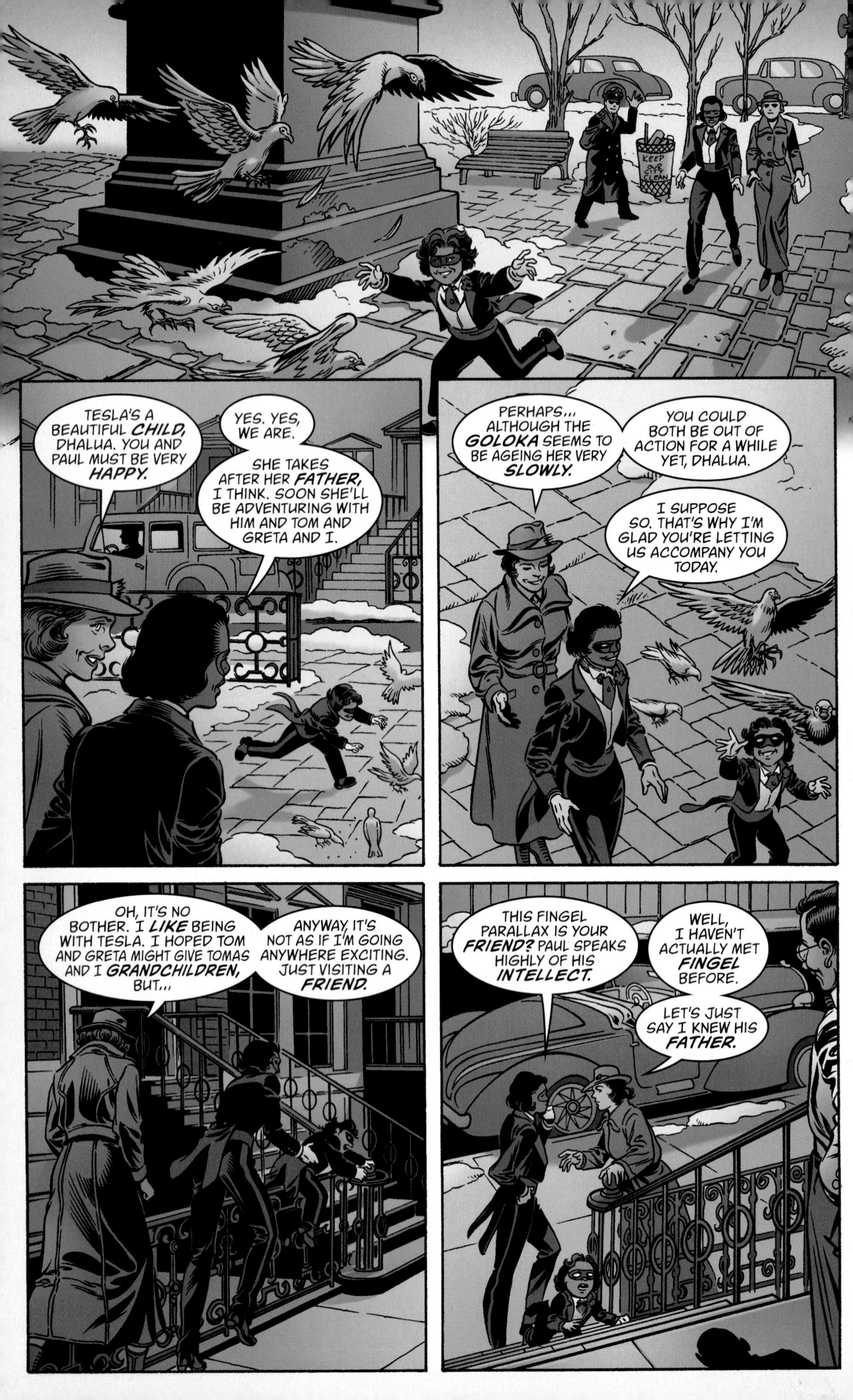
KEEP OUR CITY CLEAN
TESLA'S A BEAUTIFUL CHILD, DHALUA. YOU AND PAUL MUST BE VERY HAPPY.
YES. YES, WE ARE.
SHE TAKES AFTER HER FATHER, I THINK. SOON SHE'LL BE ADVENTURING WITH HIM AND TOM AND GRETA AND I.
PERHAPS... ALTHOUGH THE GOLOKA SEEMS TO BE AGEING HER VERY SLOWLY.
YOU COULD BOTH BE OUT OF ACTION FOR A WHILE YET, DHALUA.
I SUPPOSE SO. THAT'S WHY I'M GLAD YOU'RE LETTING US ACCOMPANY YOU TODAY.
OH, IT'S NO BOTHER. I LIKE BEING WITH TESLA. I HOPED TOM AND GRETA MIGHT GIVE TOMAS AND I GRANDCHILDREN, BUT...
ANYWAY, IT'S NOT AS IF I'M GOING ANYWHERE EXCITING. JUST VISITING A FRIEND.
THIS FINGEL PARALLAX IS YOUR FRIEND? PAUL SPEAKS HIGHLY OF HIS INTELLECT.
WELL, I HAVEN'T ACTUALLY MET FINGEL BEFORE.
LET'S JUST SAY I KNEW HIS FATHER.

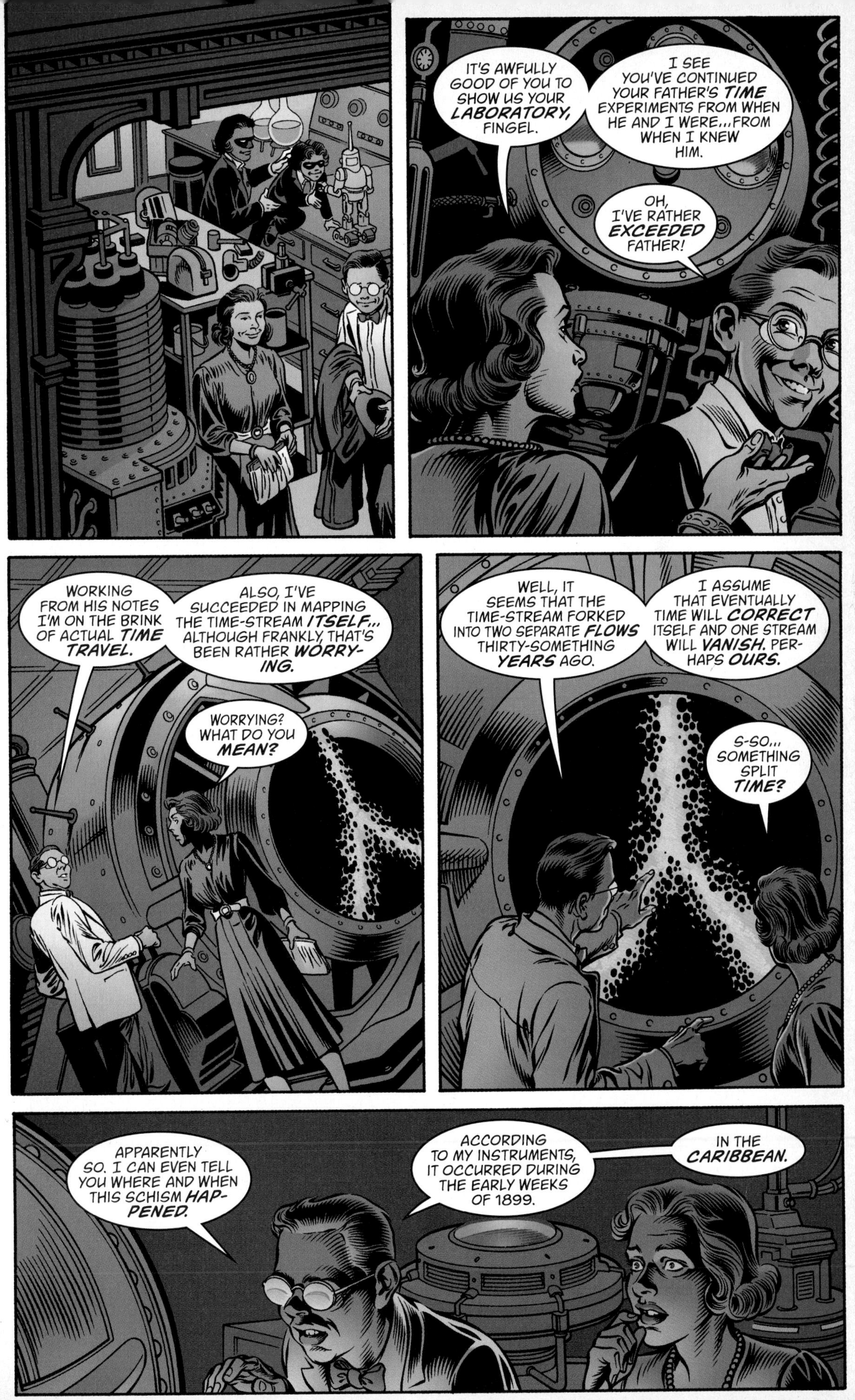
IT'S AWFULLY GOOD OF YOU TO SHOW US YOUR LABORATORY, FINGEL.
I SEE YOU'VE CONTINUED YOUR FATHER'S TIME EXPERIMENTS FROM WHEN HE AND I WERE... FROM WHEN I KNEW HIM.
OH, I'VE RATHER EXCEEDED FATHER!
WORKING FROM HIS NOTES I'M ON THE BRINK OF ACTUAL TIME TRAVEL.
ALSO, I'VE SUCCEEDED IN MAPPING THE TIME-STREAM ITSELF... ALTHOUGH FRANKLY, THAT'S BEEN RATHER WORRYING.
WORRYING? WHAT DO YOU MEAN?
WELL, IT SEEMS THAT THE TIME-STREAM FORKED INTO TWO SEPARATE FLOWS THIRTY-SOMETHING YEARS AGO.
I ASSUME THAT EVENTUALLY TIME WILL CORRECT ITSELF AND ONE STREAM WILL VANISH. PERHAPS OURS.
S-SO... SOMETHING SPLIT TIME?
APPARENTLY SO. I CAN EVEN TELL YOU WHERE AND WHEN THIS SCHISM HAPPENED.
ACCORDING TO MY INSTRUMENTS, IT OCCURRED DURING THE EARLY WEEKS OF 1899.
IN THE CARIBBEAN.

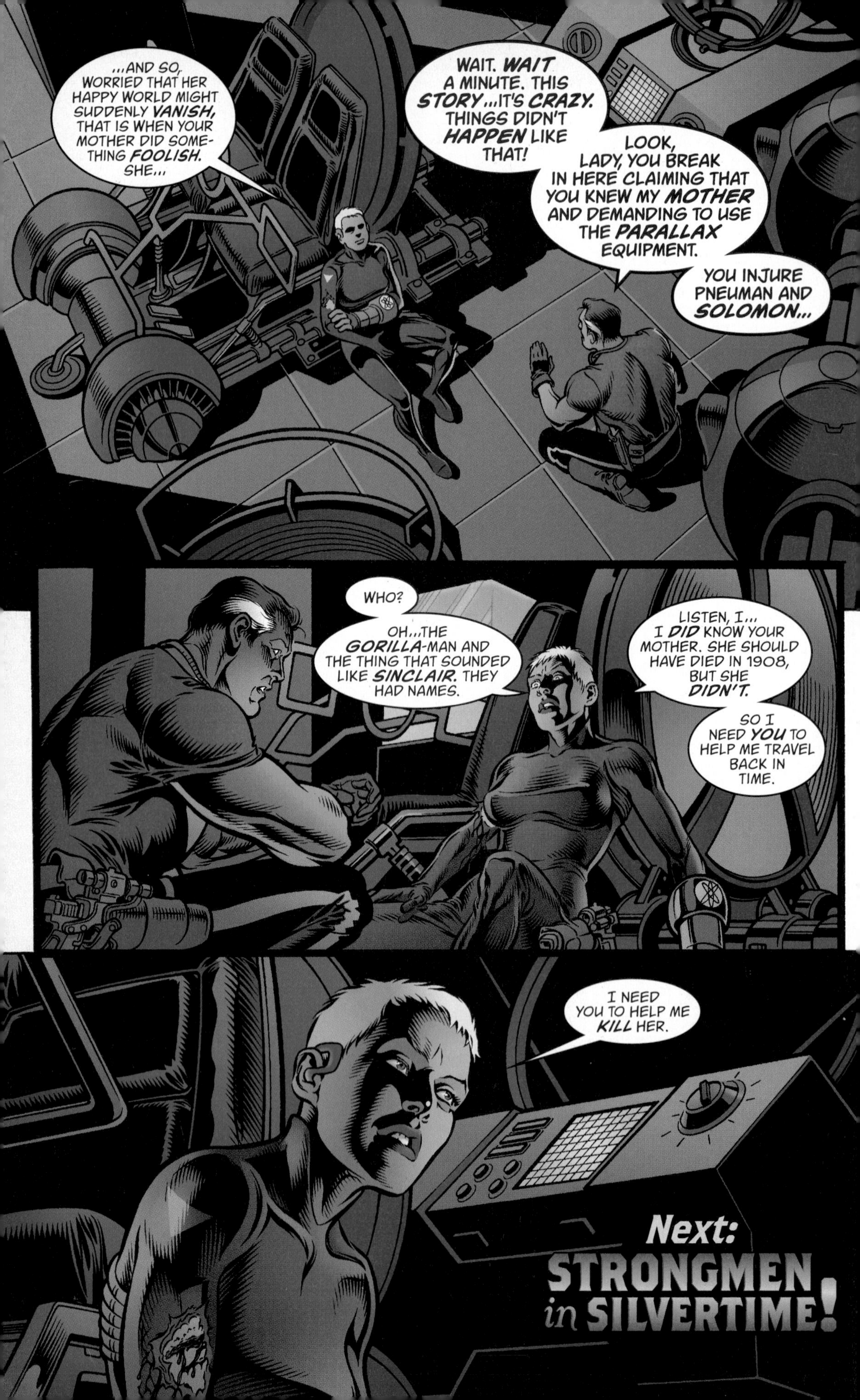
...AND SO, WORRIED THAT HER HAPPY WORLD MIGHT SUDDENLY VANISH, THAT IS WHEN YOUR MOTHER DID SOMETHING FOOLISH. SHE...
WAIT. WAIT A MINUTE. THIS STORY...IT'S CRAZY. THINGS DIDN'T HAPPEN LIKE THAT!
LOOK, LADY, YOU BREAK IN HERE CLAIMING THAT YOU KNEW MY MOTHER AND DEMANDING TO USE THE PARALLAX EQUIPMENT.
YOU INJURE PNEUMAN AND SOLOMON...
WHO?
OH...THE GORILLA-MAN AND THE THING THAT SOUNDED LIKE SINCLAIR. THEY HAD NAMES.
LISTEN, I... I DID KNOW YOUR MOTHER. SHE SHOULD HAVE DIED IN 1908, BUT SHE DIDN'T.
SO I NEED YOU TO HELP ME TRAVEL BACK IN TIME.
I NEED YOU TO HELP ME KILL HER.
Next: STRONGMEN in SILVERTIME!

# CHAPTER TWO

**In which Stone and Saveen gather allies, a new age of heroes sweeps the world, and Dhalua meets the storyteller.**

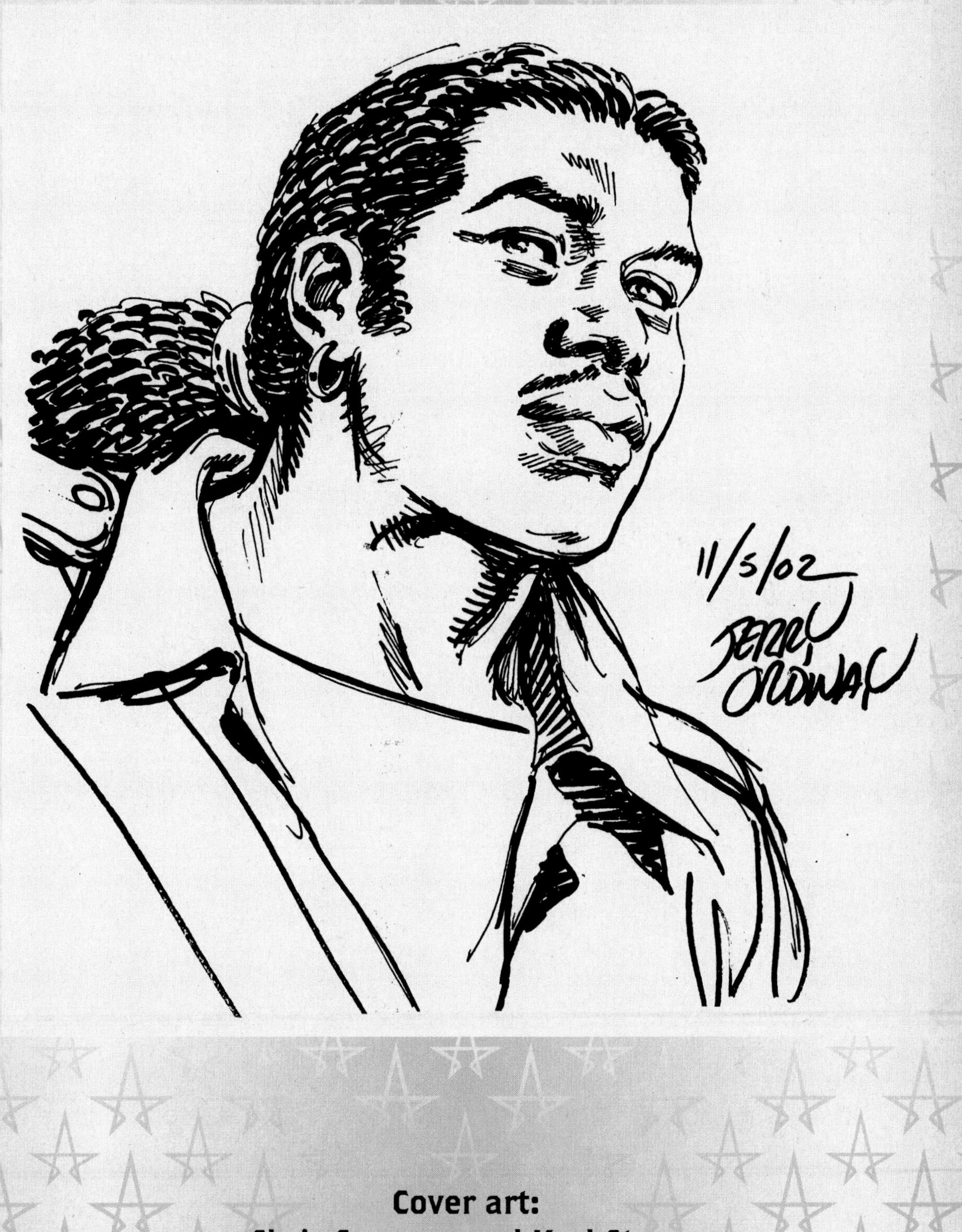
11/5/02

**Cover art:**
**Chris Sprouse and Karl Story**

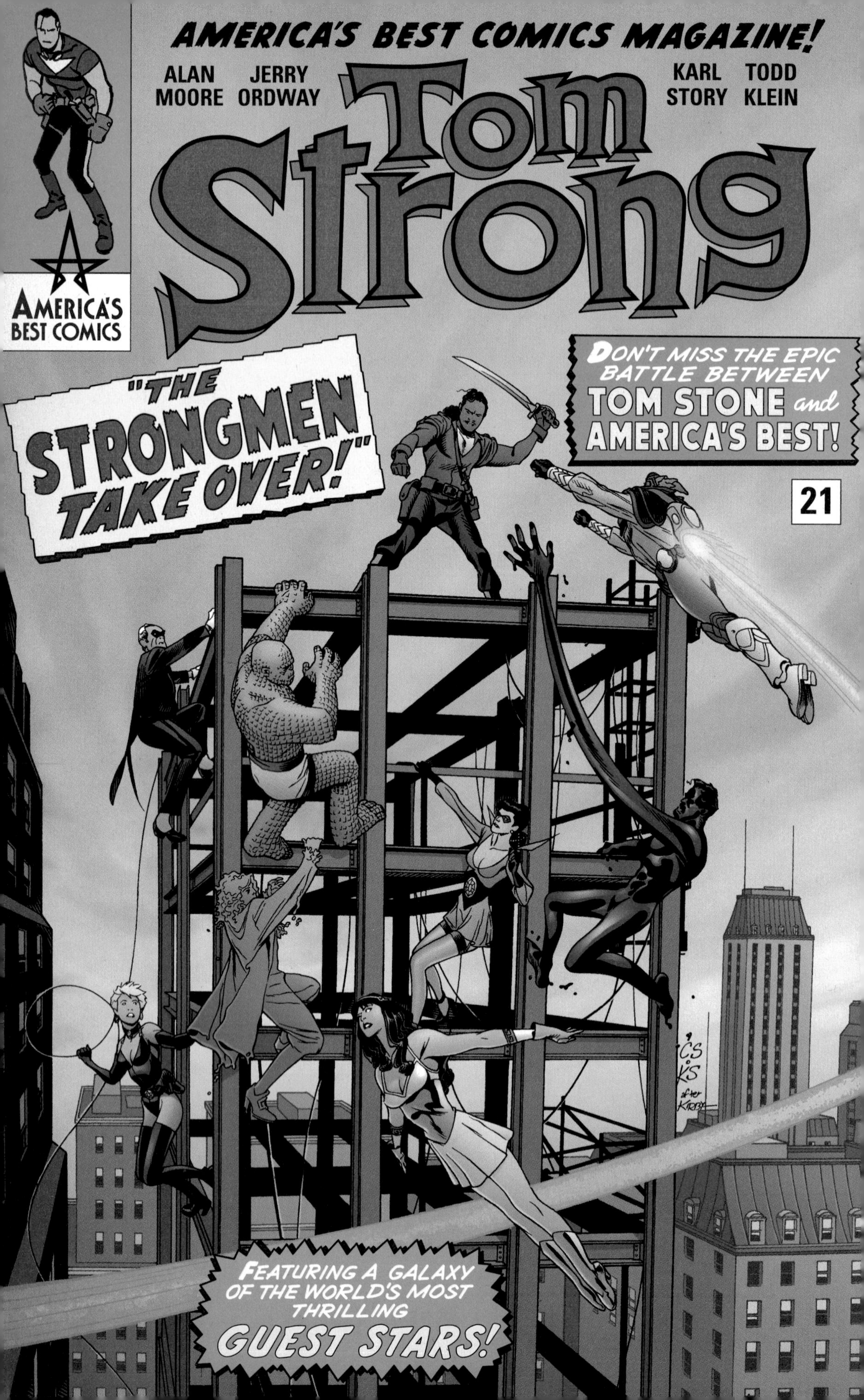
AMERICA'S BEST COMICS MAGAZINE!
ALAN MOORE
JERRY ORDWAY
KARL STORY
TODD KLEIN
Tom Strong
AMERICA'S BEST COMICS
"THE STRONGMEN TAKE OVER!"
DON'T MISS THE EPIC BATTLE BETWEEN TOM STONE and AMERICA'S BEST!
21
FEATURING A GALAXY OF THE WORLD'S MOST THRILLING GUEST STARS!

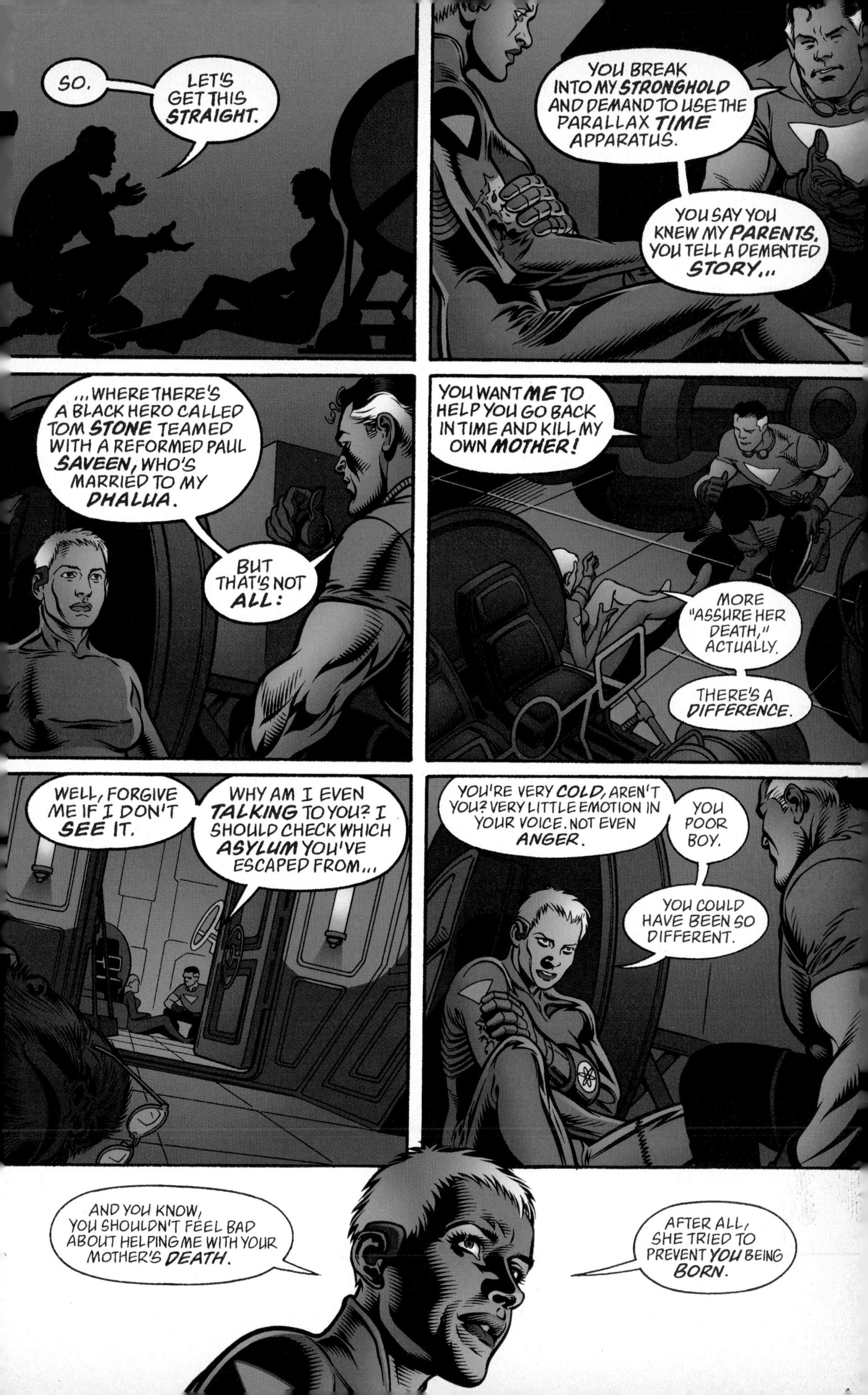
SO.
LET'S GET THIS STRAIGHT.
YOU BREAK INTO MY STRONGHOLD AND DEMAND TO USE THE PARALLAX TIME APPARATUS.
YOU SAY YOU KNEW MY PARENTS. YOU TELL A DEMENTED STORY...
...WHERE THERE'S A BLACK HERO CALLED TOM STONE TEAMED WITH A REFORMED PAUL SAVEEN, WHO'S MARRIED TO MY DHALUA.
BUT THAT'S NOT ALL:
YOU WANT ME TO HELP YOU GO BACK IN TIME AND KILL MY OWN MOTHER!
MORE "ASSURE HER DEATH," ACTUALLY.
THERE'S A DIFFERENCE.
WELL, FORGIVE ME IF I DON'T SEE IT.
WHY AM I EVEN TALKING TO YOU? I SHOULD CHECK WHICH ASYLUM YOU'VE ESCAPED FROM...
YOU'RE VERY COLD, AREN'T YOU? VERY LITTLE EMOTION IN YOUR VOICE. NOT EVEN ANGER.
YOU POOR BOY.
YOU COULD HAVE BEEN SO DIFFERENT.
AND YOU KNOW, YOU SHOULDN'T FEEL BAD ABOUT HELPING ME WITH YOUR MOTHER'S DEATH.
AFTER ALL, SHE TRIED TO PREVENT YOU BEING BORN.

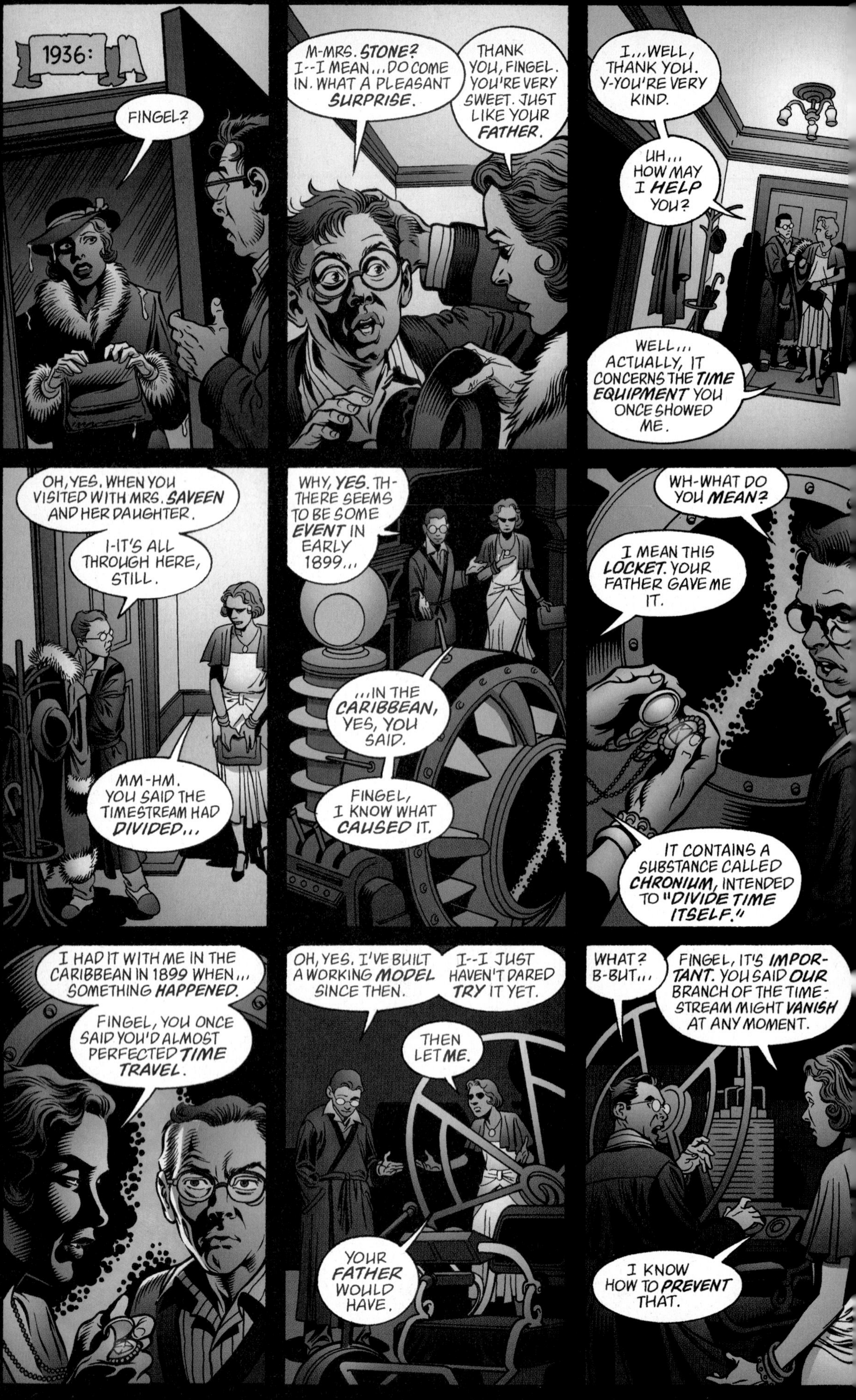
1936:
FINGEL?
M-MRS. STONE? I--I MEAN... DO COME IN. WHAT A PLEASANT SURPRISE.
THANK YOU, FINGEL. YOU'RE VERY SWEET. JUST LIKE YOUR FATHER.
I... WELL, THANK YOU. Y-YOU'RE VERY KIND.
UH... HOW MAY I HELP YOU?
WELL... ACTUALLY, IT CONCERNS THE TIME EQUIPMENT YOU ONCE SHOWED ME.
OH, YES. WHEN YOU VISITED WITH MRS. SAVEEN AND HER DAUGHTER.
I-IT'S ALL THROUGH HERE, STILL.
MM-HM. YOU SAID THE TIMESTREAM HAD DIVIDED...
WHY, YES. TH-THERE SEEMS TO BE SOME EVENT IN EARLY 1899...
...IN THE CARIBBEAN, YES, YOU SAID.
FINGEL, I KNOW WHAT CAUSED IT.
WH-WHAT DO YOU MEAN?
I MEAN THIS LOCKET. YOUR FATHER GAVE ME IT.
IT CONTAINS A SUBSTANCE CALLED CHRONIUM, INTENDED TO "DIVIDE TIME ITSELF."
I HAD IT WITH ME IN THE CARIBBEAN IN 1899 WHEN... SOMETHING HAPPENED.
FINGEL, YOU ONCE SAID YOU'D ALMOST PERFECTED TIME TRAVEL.
OH, YES. I'VE BUILT A WORKING MODEL SINCE THEN.
I--I JUST HAVEN'T DARED TRY IT YET.
THEN LET ME.
YOUR FATHER WOULD HAVE.
WHAT? B-BUT...
FINGEL, IT'S IMPORTANT. YOU SAID OUR BRANCH OF THE TIME-STREAM MIGHT VANISH AT ANY MOMENT.
I KNOW HOW TO PREVENT THAT.

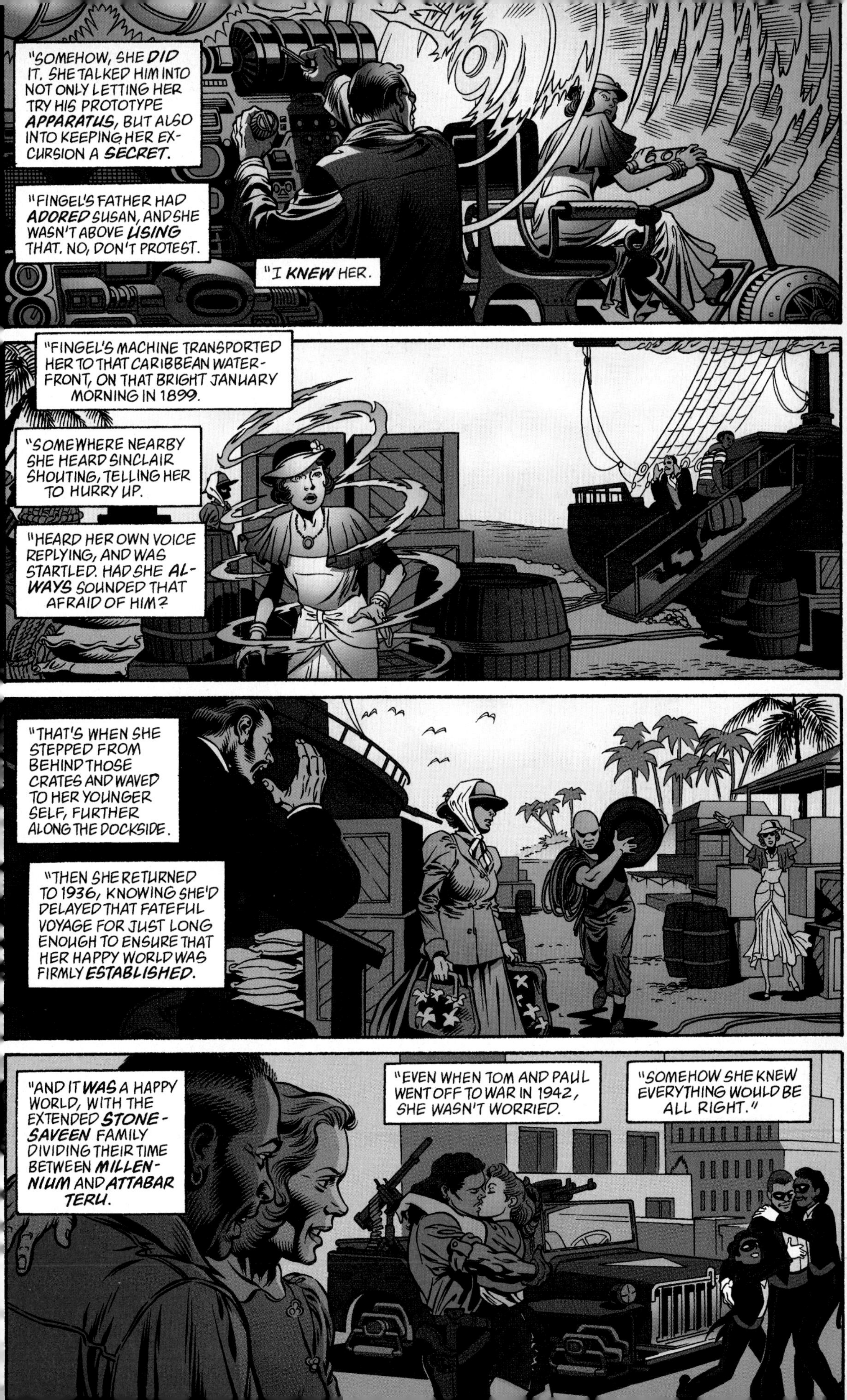
"SOMEHOW, SHE DID IT. SHE TALKED HIM INTO NOT ONLY LETTING HER TRY HIS PROTOTYPE APPARATUS, BUT ALSO INTO KEEPING HER EXCURSION A SECRET.
"FINGEL'S FATHER HAD ADORED SUSAN, AND SHE WASN'T ABOVE USING THAT. NO, DON'T PROTEST.
"I KNEW HER.
"FINGEL'S MACHINE TRANSPORTED HER TO THAT CARIBBEAN WATERFRONT, ON THAT BRIGHT JANUARY MORNING IN 1899.
"SOMEWHERE NEARBY SHE HEARD SINCLAIR SHOUTING, TELLING HER TO HURRY UP.
"HEARD HER OWN VOICE REPLYING, AND WAS STARTLED. HAD SHE ALWAYS SOUNDED THAT AFRAID OF HIM?
"THAT'S WHEN SHE STEPPED FROM BEHIND THOSE CRATES AND WAVED TO HER YOUNGER SELF, FURTHER ALONG THE DOCKSIDE.
"THEN SHE RETURNED TO 1936, KNOWING SHE'D DELAYED THAT FATEFUL VOYAGE FOR JUST LONG ENOUGH TO ENSURE THAT HER HAPPY WORLD WAS FIRMLY ESTABLISHED.
"AND IT WAS A HAPPY WORLD, WITH THE EXTENDED STONE-SAVEEN FAMILY DIVIDING THEIR TIME BETWEEN MILLENNIUM AND ATTABAR TERU.
"EVEN WHEN TOM AND PAUL WENT OFF TO WAR IN 1942, SHE WASN'T WORRIED.
"SOMEHOW SHE KNEW EVERYTHING WOULD BE ALL RIGHT."

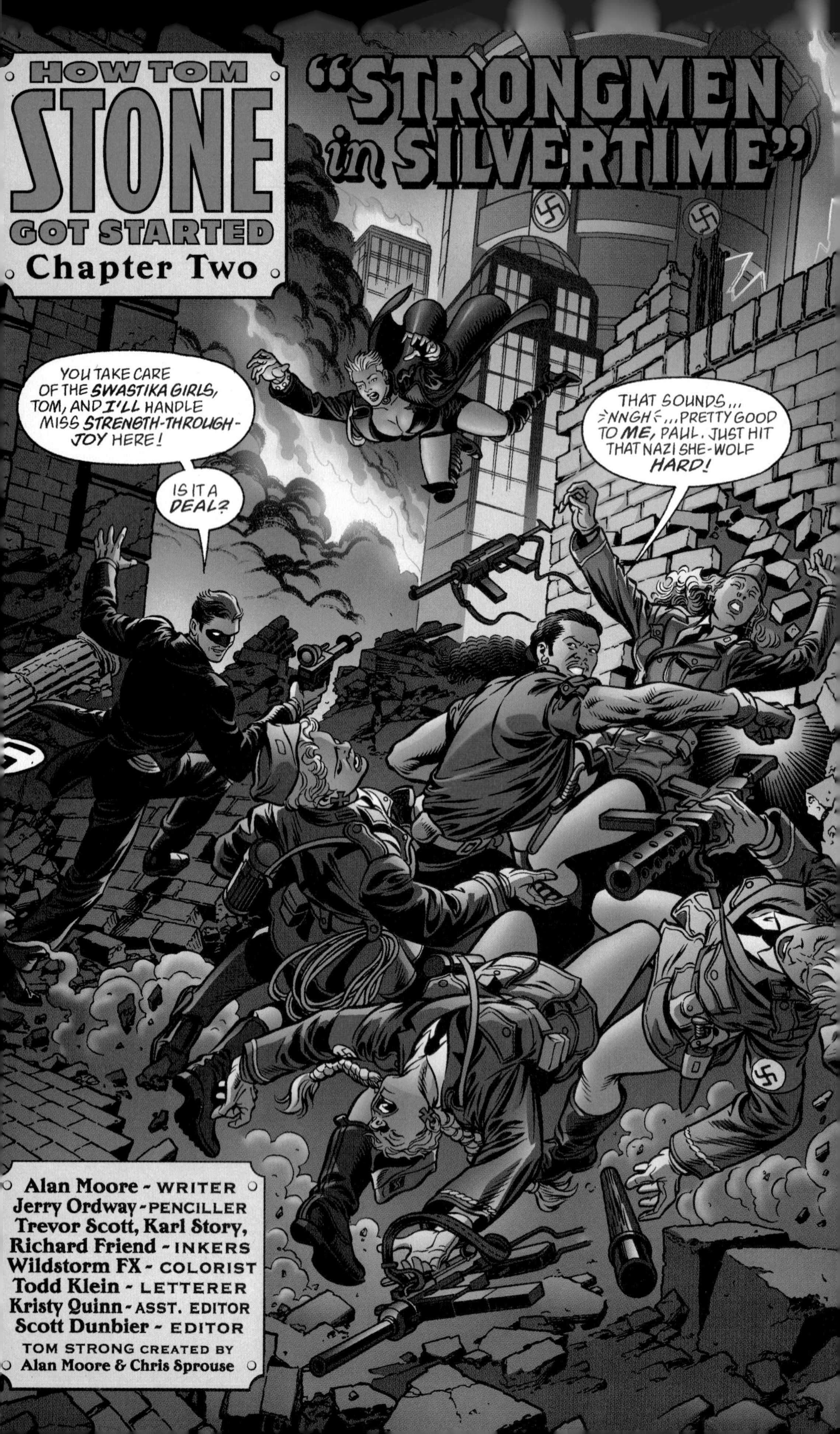
HOW TOM STONE GOT STARTED
Chapter Two
"STRONGMEN in SILVERTIME"
YOU TAKE CARE OF THE SWASTIKA GIRLS, TOM, AND I'LL HANDLE MISS STRENGTH-THROUGH-JOY HERE!
IS IT A DEAL?
THAT SOUNDS... =NNGH=... PRETTY GOOD TO ME, PAUL. JUST HIT THAT NAZI SHE-WOLF HARD!
Alan Moore - WRITER
Jerry Ordway - PENCILLER
Trevor Scott, Karl Story, Richard Friend - INKERS
Wildstorm FX - COLORIST
Todd Klein - LETTERER
Kristy Quinn - ASST. EDITOR
Scott Dunbier - EDITOR
TOM STRONG CREATED BY
Alan Moore & Chris Sprouse

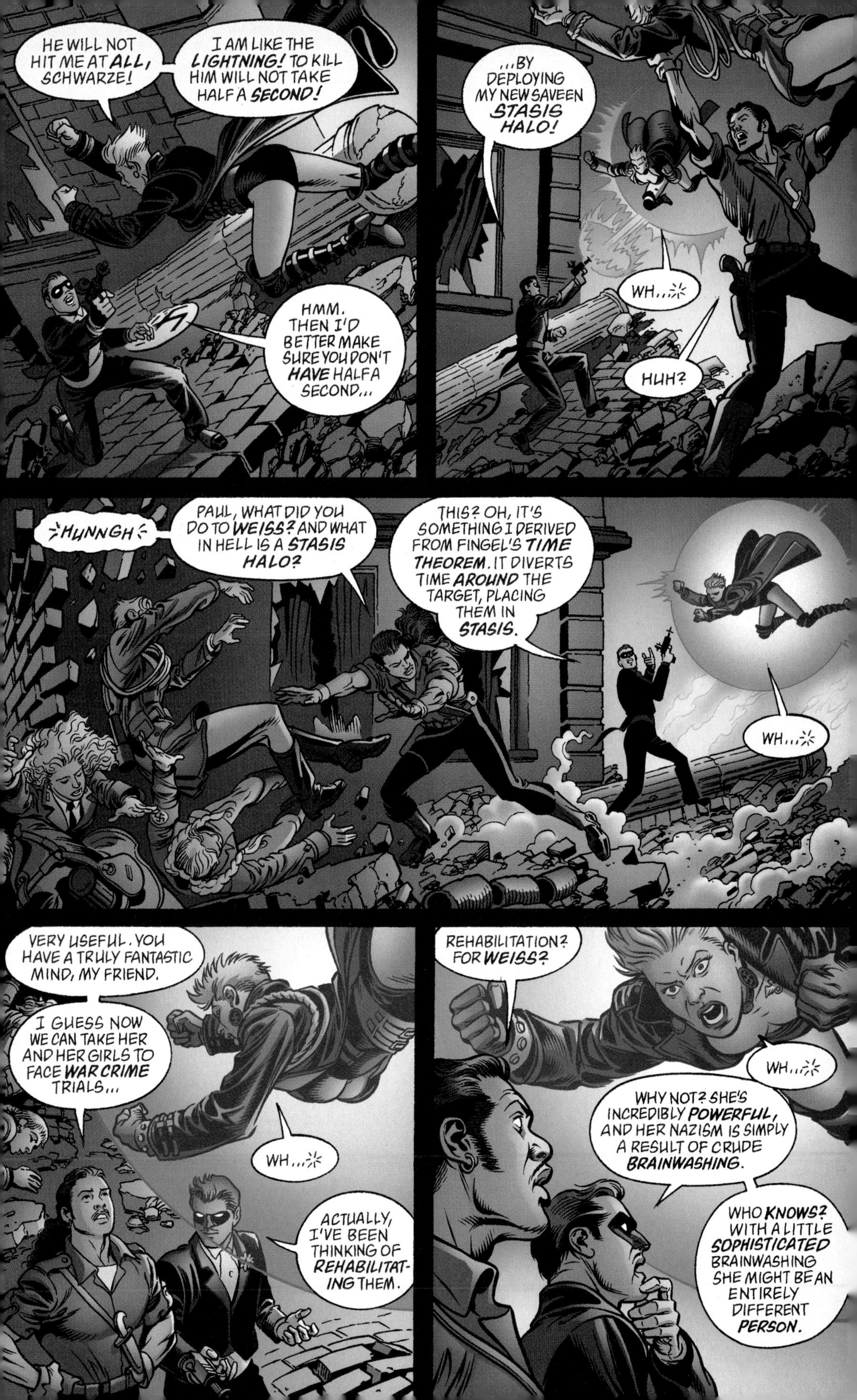
HE WILL NOT HIT ME AT ALL, SCHWARZE!
I AM LIKE THE LIGHTNING! TO KILL HIM WILL NOT TAKE HALF A SECOND!
HMM. THEN I'D BETTER MAKE SURE YOU DON'T HAVE HALFA SECOND...
...BY DEPLOYING MY NEW SAVEEN STASIS HALO!
WH...
HUH?
HUNNGH
PAUL, WHAT DID YOU DO TO WEISS? AND WHAT IN HELL IS A STASIS HALO?
THIS? OH, IT'S SOMETHING I DERIVED FROM FINGEL'S TIME THEOREM. IT DIVERTS TIME AROUND THE TARGET, PLACING THEM IN STASIS.
WH...
VERY USEFUL. YOU HAVE A TRULY FANTASTIC MIND, MY FRIEND.
I GUESS NOW WE CAN TAKE HER AND HER GIRLS TO FACE WAR CRIME TRIALS...
WH...
ACTUALLY, I'VE BEEN THINKING OF REHABILITATING THEM.
REHABILITATION? FOR WEISS?
WH...
WHY NOT? SHE'S INCREDIBLY POWERFUL, AND HER NAZISM IS SIMPLY A RESULT OF CRUDE BRAINWASHING.
WHO KNOWS? WITH A LITTLE SOPHISTICATED BRAINWASHING SHE MIGHT BE AN ENTIRELY DIFFERENT PERSON.

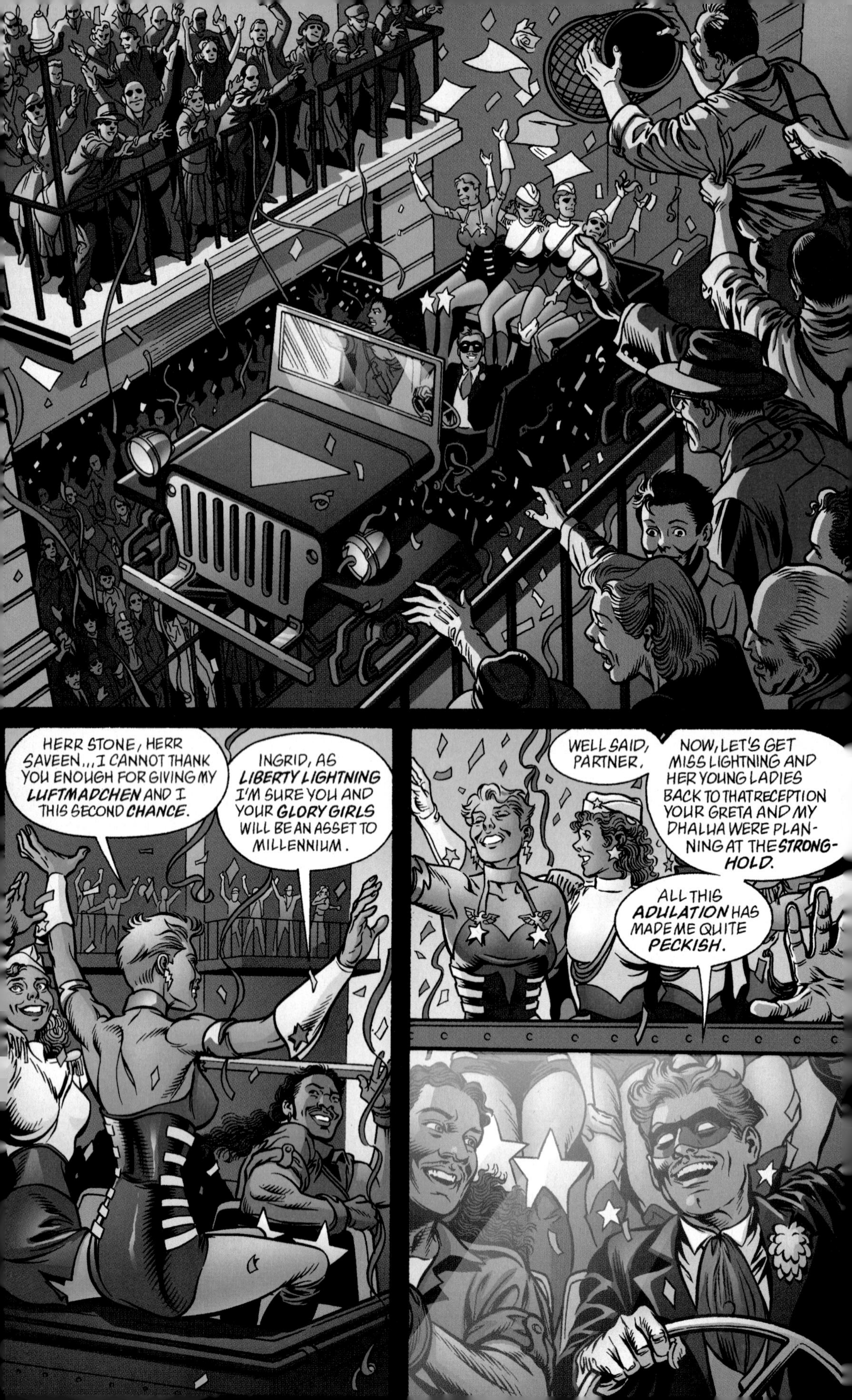
HERR STONE, HERR SAVEEN... I CANNOT THANK YOU ENOUGH FOR GIVING MY LUFTMADCHEN AND I THIS SECOND CHANCE.
INGRID, AS LIBERTY LIGHTNING I'M SURE YOU AND YOUR GLORY GIRLS WILL BE AN ASSET TO MILLENNIUM.
WELL SAID, PARTNER.
NOW, LET'S GET MISS LIGHTNING AND HER YOUNG LADIES BACK TO THATRECEPTION YOUR GRETA AND MY DHALUA WERE PLANNING AT THE STRONGHOLD.
ALL THIS ADULATION HAS MADE ME QUITE PECKISH.

TOM, BWOY, DEM A FINE LOT O' FRIENDS YOU GOT DERE, FE TRUE.

YOUR FATHER'S RIGHT, SON. REFORMING *INGRID* AND COMPANY IS LITTLE SHORT OF *MIRACU-LOUS...*

...ALTHOUGH "*LIBERTY LIGHTNING*" WILL TAKE SOME GETTING USED TO.

INGRID CHOSE THE NAME HERSELF. NOW SHE'S DEVOTED TO *AMERICA*, SHE WANTED TO SOUND *PATRIOTIC*.

BUT YOU'RE RIGHT, DAD. THEY *ARE* A FINE CROWD.

NOW THE WAR'S OVER, MAYBE WE CAN REALLY *HELP* THIS COUNTRY.

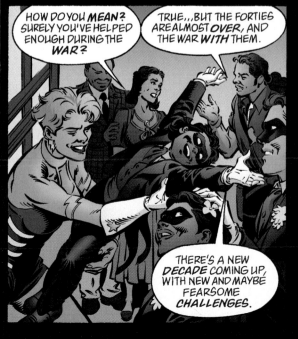

HOW DO YOU *MEAN?* SURELY YOU'VE HELPED ENOUGH DURING THE *WAR?*

TRUE,,,BUT THE FORTIES ARE ALMOST *OVER*, AND THE WAR *WITH* THEM.

THERE'S A NEW *DECADE* COMING UP, WITH NEW AND MAYBE FEARSOME *CHALLENGES.*

I WANT US ALL TO BE *READY.* US, AMERICA, THE WHOLE *WORLD.*

I WANT US TO BE READY FOR THE *1950S.*

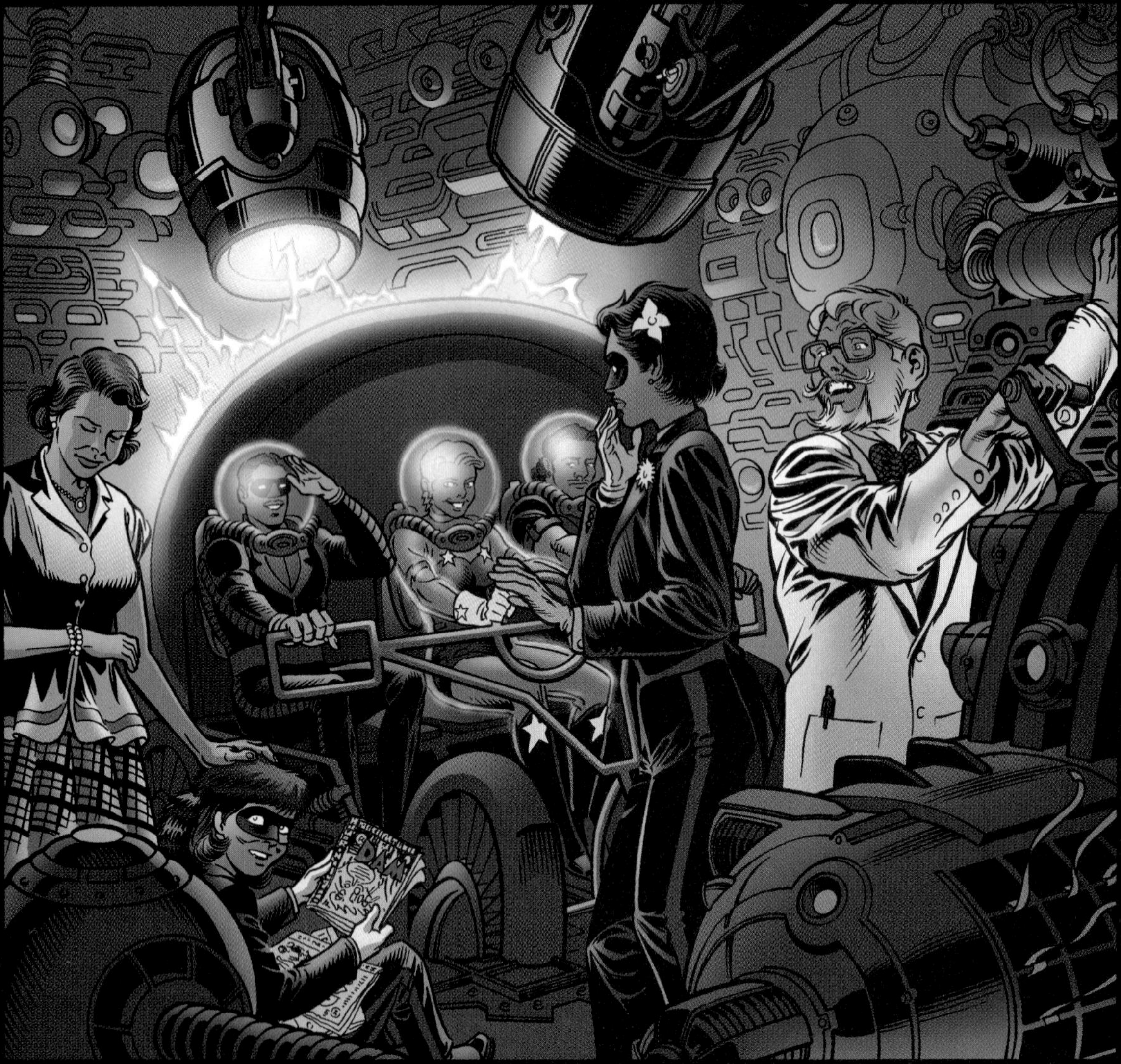

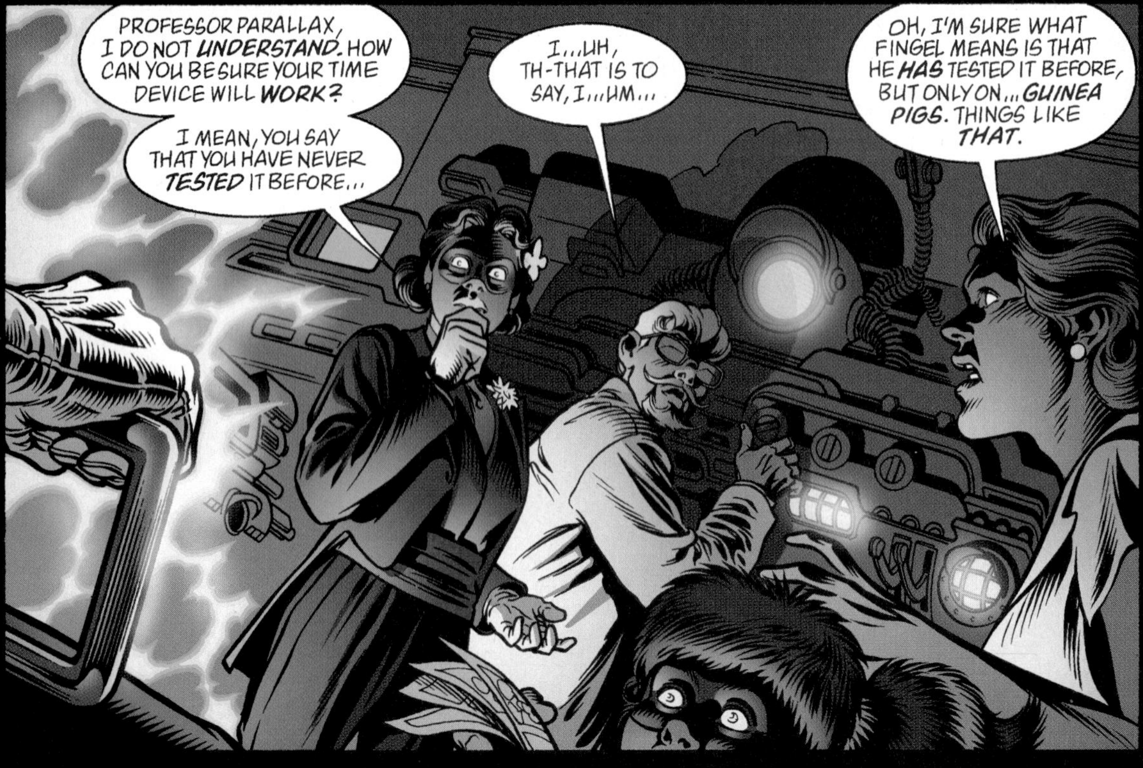

PROFESSOR PARALLAX, I DO NOT UNDERSTAND. HOW CAN YOU BE SURE YOUR TIME DEVICE WILL WORK?
I MEAN, YOU SAY THAT YOU HAVE NEVER TESTED IT BEFORE...
I...UH, TH-THAT IS TO SAY, I...UM...
OH, I'M SURE WHAT FINGEL MEANS IS THAT HE HAS TESTED IT BEFORE, BUT ONLY ON...GUINEA PIGS. THINGS LIKE THAT.

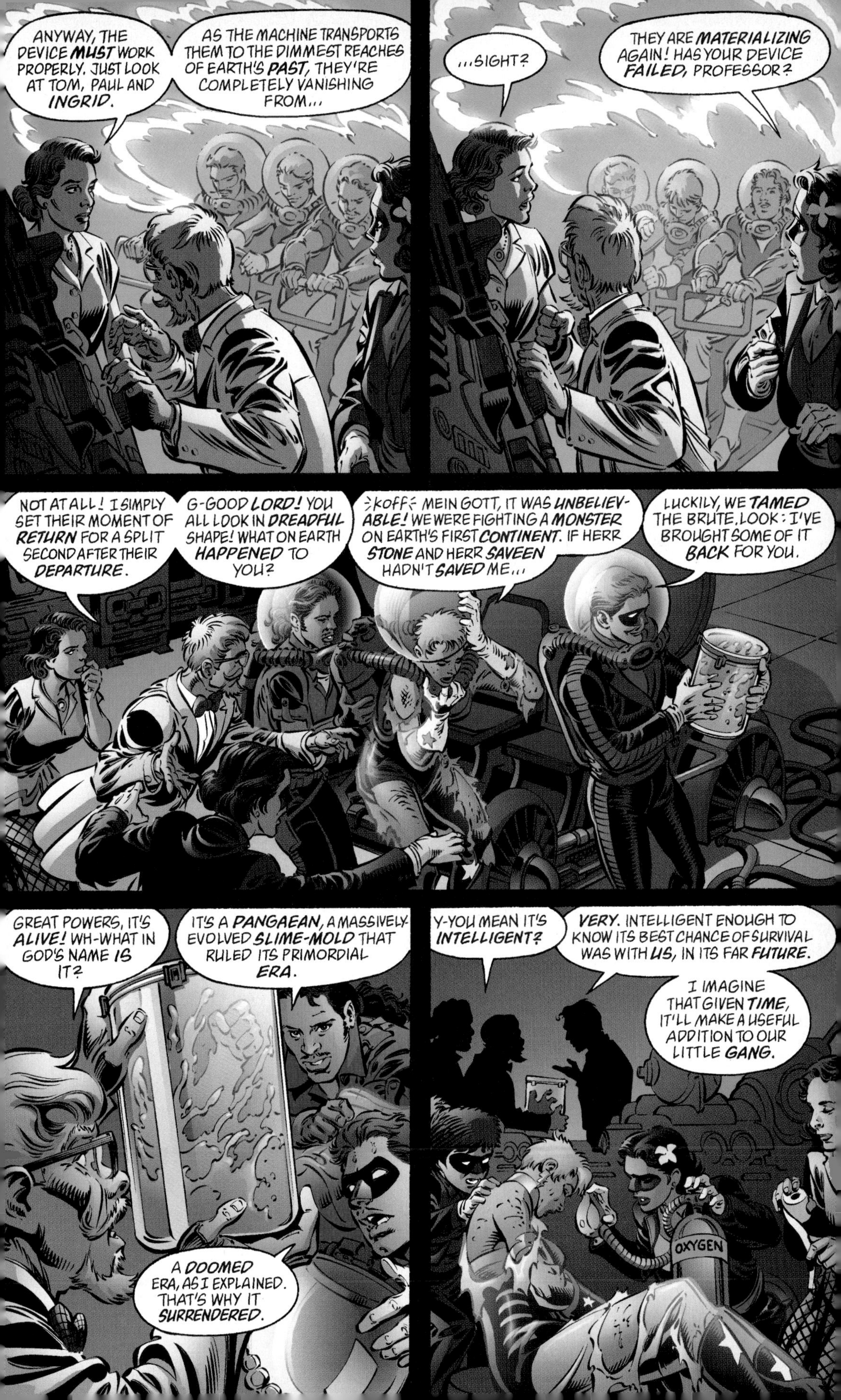
ANYWAY, THE DEVICE MUST WORK PROPERLY. JUST LOOK AT TOM, PAUL AND INGRID.
AS THE MACHINE TRANSPORTS THEM TO THE DIMMEST REACHES OF EARTH'S PAST, THEY'RE COMPLETELY VANISHING FROM...
...SIGHT?
THEY ARE MATERIALIZING AGAIN! HAS YOUR DEVICE FAILED, PROFESSOR?
NOT AT ALL! I SIMPLY SET THEIR MOMENT OF RETURN FOR A SPLIT SECOND AFTER THEIR DEPARTURE.
G-GOOD LORD! YOU ALL LOOK IN DREADFUL SHAPE! WHAT ON EARTH HAPPENED TO YOU?
*KOFF* MEIN GOTT, IT WAS UNBELIEVABLE! WE WERE FIGHTING A MONSTER ON EARTH'S FIRST CONTINENT. IF HERR STONE AND HERR SAVEEN HADN'T SAVED ME...
LUCKILY, WE TAMED THE BRUTE. LOOK: I'VE BROUGHT SOME OF IT BACK FOR YOU.
GREAT POWERS, IT'S ALIVE! WH-WHAT IN GOD'S NAME IS IT?
IT'S A PANGAEAN, A MASSIVELY-EVOLVED SLIME-MOLD THAT RULED ITS PRIMORDIAL ERA.
A DOOMED ERA, AS I EXPLAINED. THAT'S WHY IT SURRENDERED.
Y-YOU MEAN IT'S INTELLIGENT?
VERY. INTELLIGENT ENOUGH TO KNOW ITS BEST CHANCE OF SURVIVAL WAS WITH US, IN ITS FAR FUTURE.
I IMAGINE THAT GIVEN TIME, IT'LL MAKE A USEFUL ADDITION TO OUR LITTLE GANG.
OXYGEN

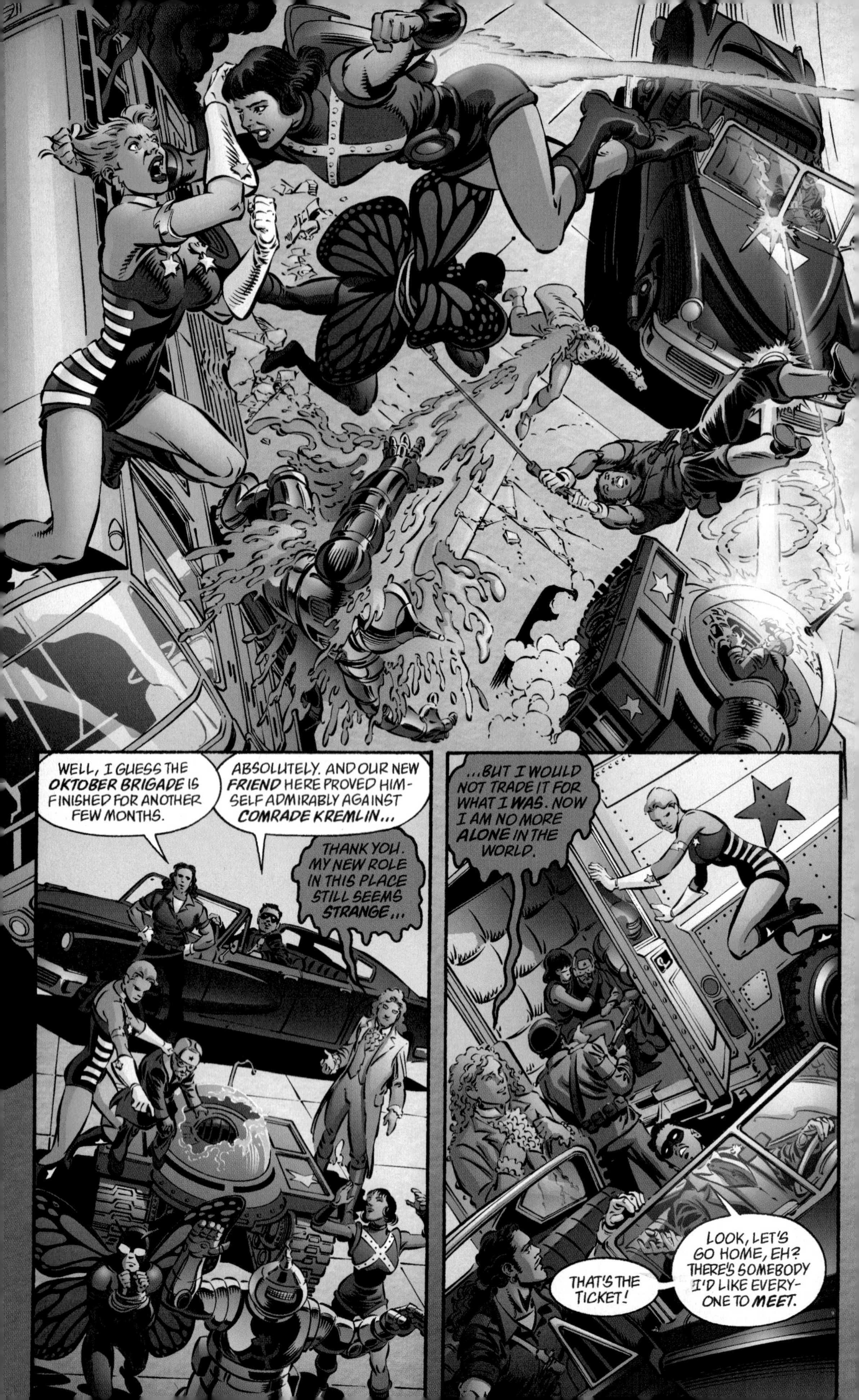

WELL, I GUESS THE OKTOBER BRIGADE IS FINISHED FOR ANOTHER FEW MONTHS.
ABSOLUTELY. AND OUR NEW FRIEND HERE PROVED HIM-SELF ADMIRABLY AGAINST COMRADE KREMLIN...
THANK YOU. MY NEW ROLE IN THIS PLACE STILL SEEMS STRANGE...
...BUT I WOULD NOT TRADE IT FOR WHAT I WAS. NOW I AM NO MORE ALONE IN THE WORLD.
LOOK, LET'S GO HOME, EH? THERE'S SOMEBODY I'D LIKE EVERY-ONE TO MEET.
THAT'S THE TICKET!

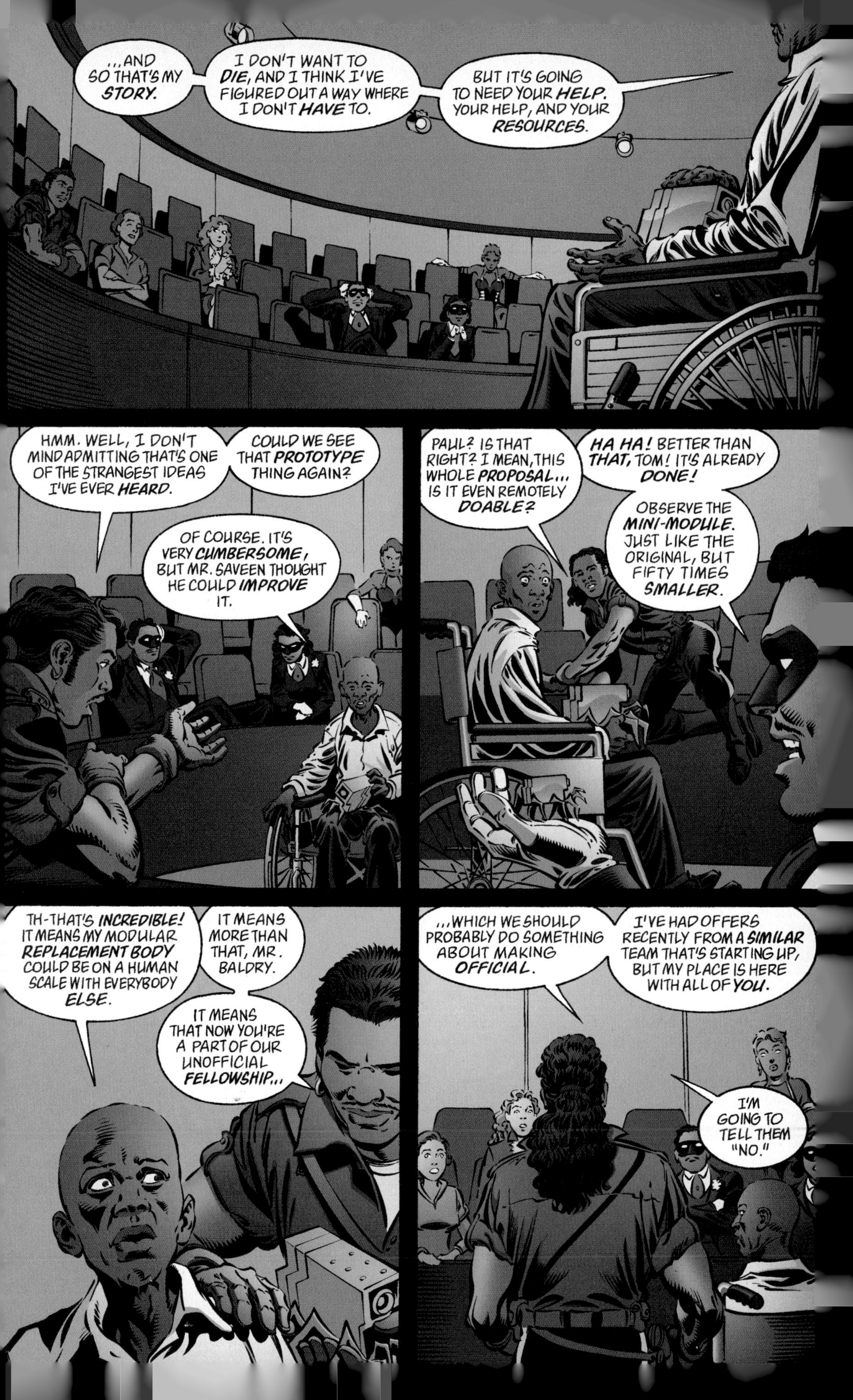
...AND SO THAT'S MY STORY.
I DON'T WANT TO DIE, AND I THINK I'VE FIGURED OUT A WAY WHERE I DON'T HAVE TO.
BUT IT'S GOING TO NEED YOUR HELP. YOUR HELP, AND YOUR RESOURCES.
HMM. WELL, I DON'T MIND ADMITTING THAT'S ONE OF THE STRANGEST IDEAS I'VE EVER HEARD.
COULD WE SEE THAT PROTOTYPE THING AGAIN?
OF COURSE. IT'S VERY CUMBERSOME, BUT MR. SAVEEN THOUGHT HE COULD IMPROVE IT.
PAUL? IS THAT RIGHT? I MEAN, THIS WHOLE PROPOSAL... IS IT EVEN REMOTELY DOABLE?
HA HA! BETTER THAN THAT, TOM! IT'S ALREADY DONE!
OBSERVE THE MINI-MODULE. JUST LIKE THE ORIGINAL, BUT FIFTY TIMES SMALLER.
TH-THAT'S INCREDIBLE! IT MEANS MY MODULAR REPLACEMENT BODY COULD BE ON A HUMAN SCALE WITH EVERYBODY ELSE.
IT MEANS MORE THAN THAT, MR. BALDRY.
IT MEANS THAT NOW YOU'RE A PART OF OUR UNOFFICIAL FELLOWSHIP...
...WHICH WE SHOULD PROBABLY DO SOMETHING ABOUT MAKING OFFICIAL.
I'VE HAD OFFERS RECENTLY FROM A SIMILAR TEAM THAT'S STARTING UP, BUT MY PLACE IS HERE WITH ALL OF YOU.
I'M GOING TO TELL THEM "NO."

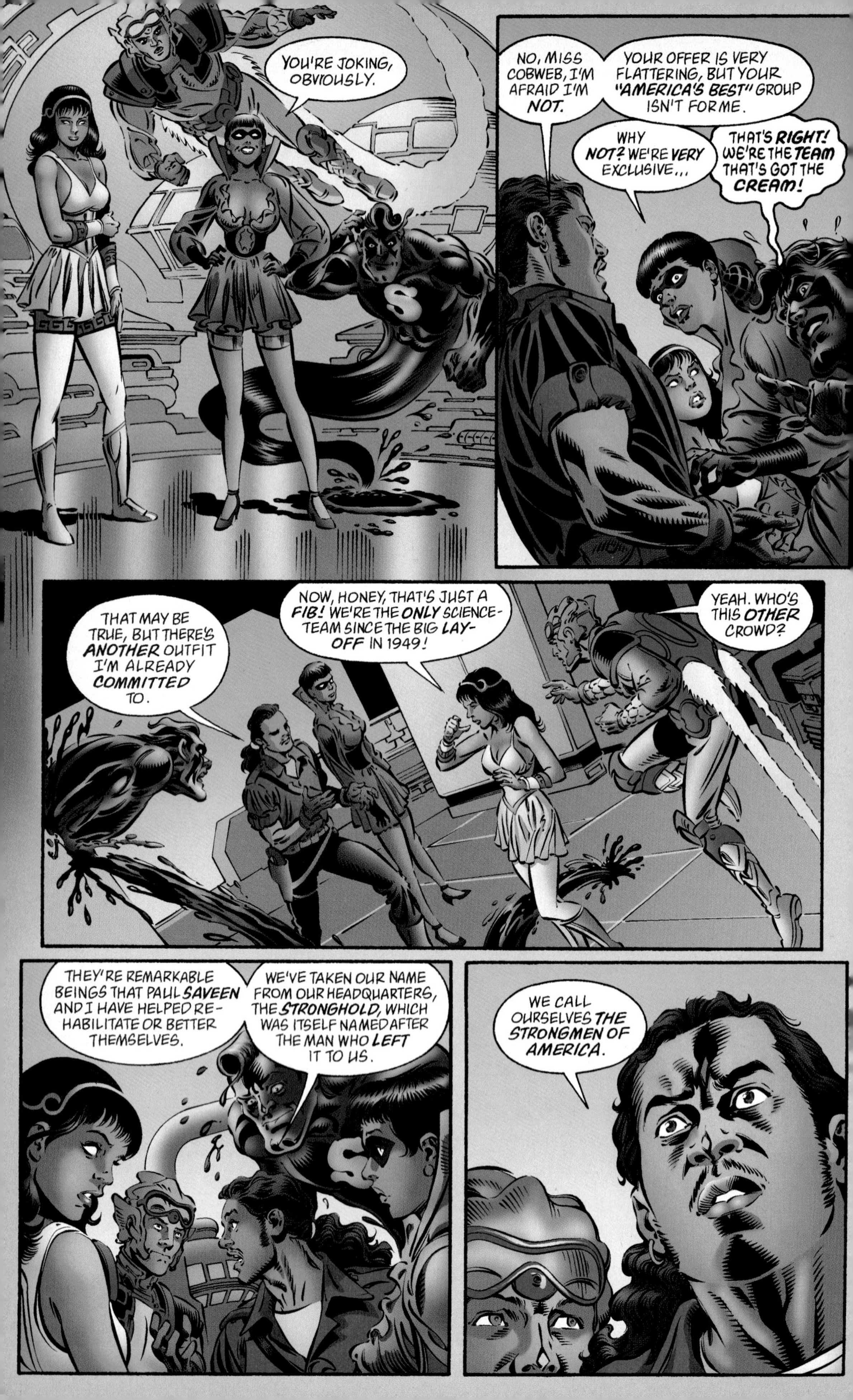
YOU'RE JOKING, OBVIOUSLY.
NO, MISS COBWEB, I'M AFRAID I'M NOT.
YOUR OFFER IS VERY FLATTERING, BUT YOUR "AMERICA'S BEST" GROUP ISN'T FOR ME.
WHY NOT? WE'RE VERY EXCLUSIVE...
THAT'S RIGHT! WE'RE THE TEAM THAT'S GOT THE CREAM!
THAT MAY BE TRUE, BUT THERE'S ANOTHER OUTFIT I'M ALREADY COMMITTED TO.
NOW, HONEY, THAT'S JUST A FIB! WE'RE THE ONLY SCIENCE-TEAM SINCE THE BIG LAY-OFF IN 1949!
YEAH. WHO'S THIS OTHER CROWD?
THEY'RE REMARKABLE BEINGS THAT PAUL SAVEEN AND I HAVE HELPED RE-HABILITATE OR BETTER THEMSELVES.
WE'VE TAKEN OUR NAME FROM OUR HEADQUARTERS, THE STRONGHOLD, WHICH WAS ITSELF NAMED AFTER THE MAN WHO LEFT IT TO US.
WE CALL OURSELVES THE STRONGMEN OF AMERICA.

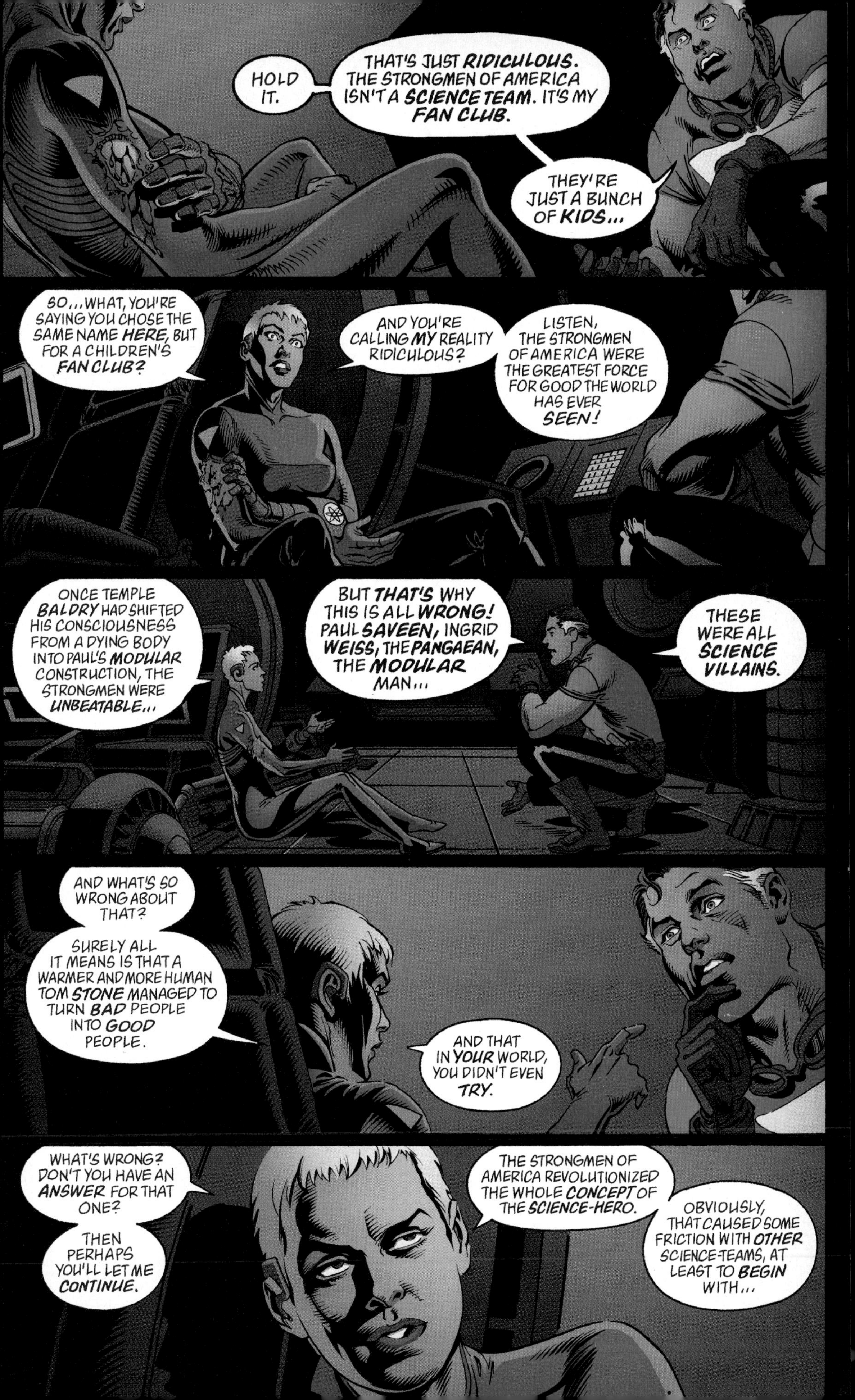
HOLD IT.
THAT'S JUST RIDICULOUS. THE STRONGMEN OF AMERICA ISN'T A SCIENCE TEAM. IT'S MY FAN CLUB.
THEY'RE JUST A BUNCH OF KIDS...
SO...WHAT, YOU'RE SAYING YOU CHOSE THE SAME NAME HERE, BUT FOR A CHILDREN'S FAN CLUB?
AND YOU'RE CALLING MY REALITY RIDICULOUS?
LISTEN, THE STRONGMEN OF AMERICA WERE THE GREATEST FORCE FOR GOOD THE WORLD HAS EVER SEEN!
ONCE TEMPLE BALDRY HAD SHIFTED HIS CONSCIOUSNESS FROM A DYING BODY INTO PAUL'S MODULAR CONSTRUCTION, THE STRONGMEN WERE UNBEATABLE...
BUT THAT'S WHY THIS IS ALL WRONG! PAUL SAVEEN, INGRID WEISS, THE PANGAEAN, THE MODULAR MAN...
THESE WERE ALL SCIENCE VILLAINS.
AND WHAT'S SO WRONG ABOUT THAT?
SURELY ALL IT MEANS IS THAT A WARMER AND MORE HUMAN TOM STONE MANAGED TO TURN BAD PEOPLE INTO GOOD PEOPLE.
AND THAT IN YOUR WORLD, YOU DIDN'T EVEN TRY.
WHAT'S WRONG? DON'T YOU HAVE AN ANSWER FOR THAT ONE?
THEN PERHAPS YOU'LL LET ME CONTINUE.
THE STRONGMEN OF AMERICA REVOLUTIONIZED THE WHOLE CONCEPT OF THE SCIENCE-HERO.
OBVIOUSLY, THAT CAUSED SOME FRICTION WITH OTHER SCIENCE-TEAMS, AT LEAST TO BEGIN WITH...

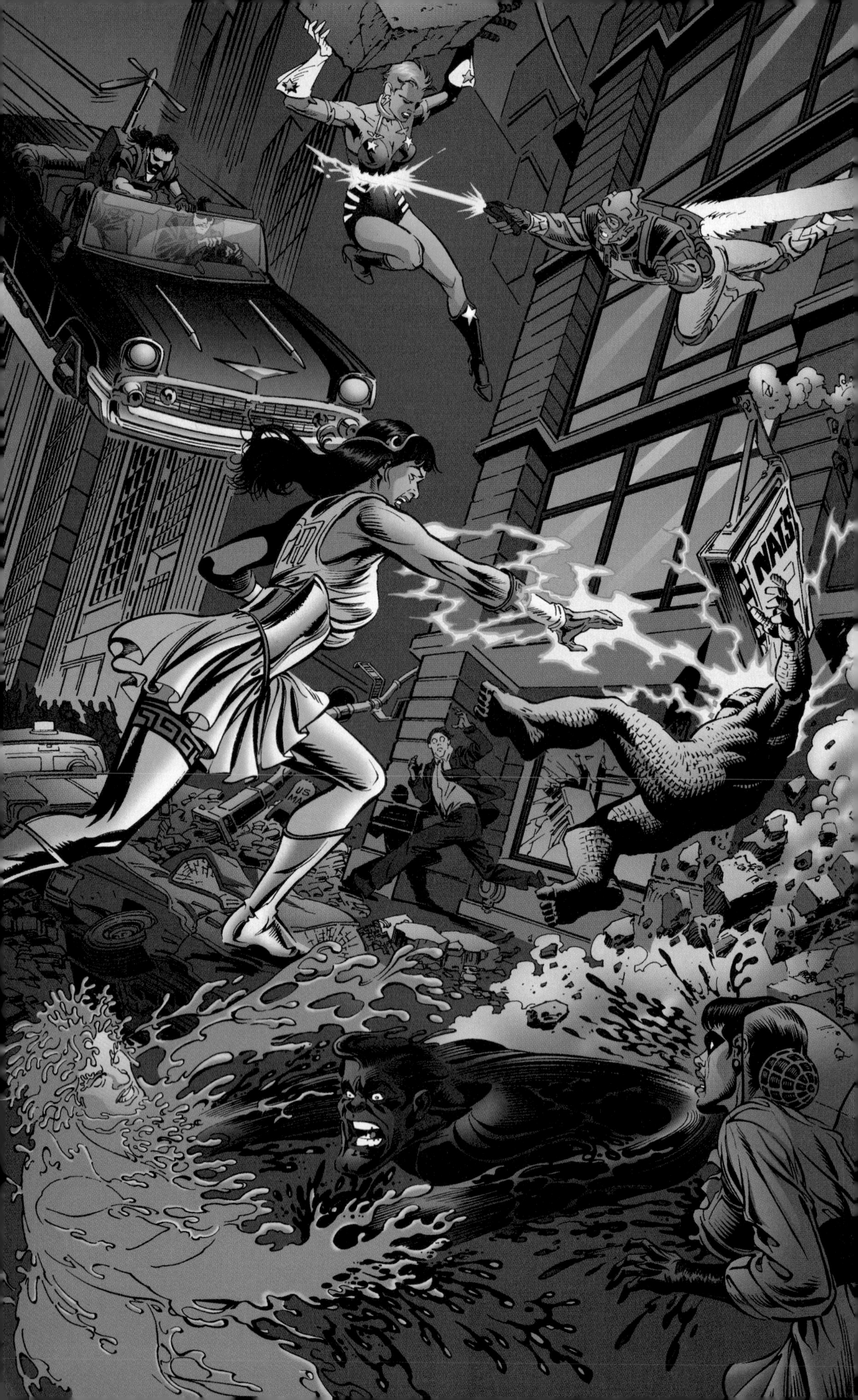

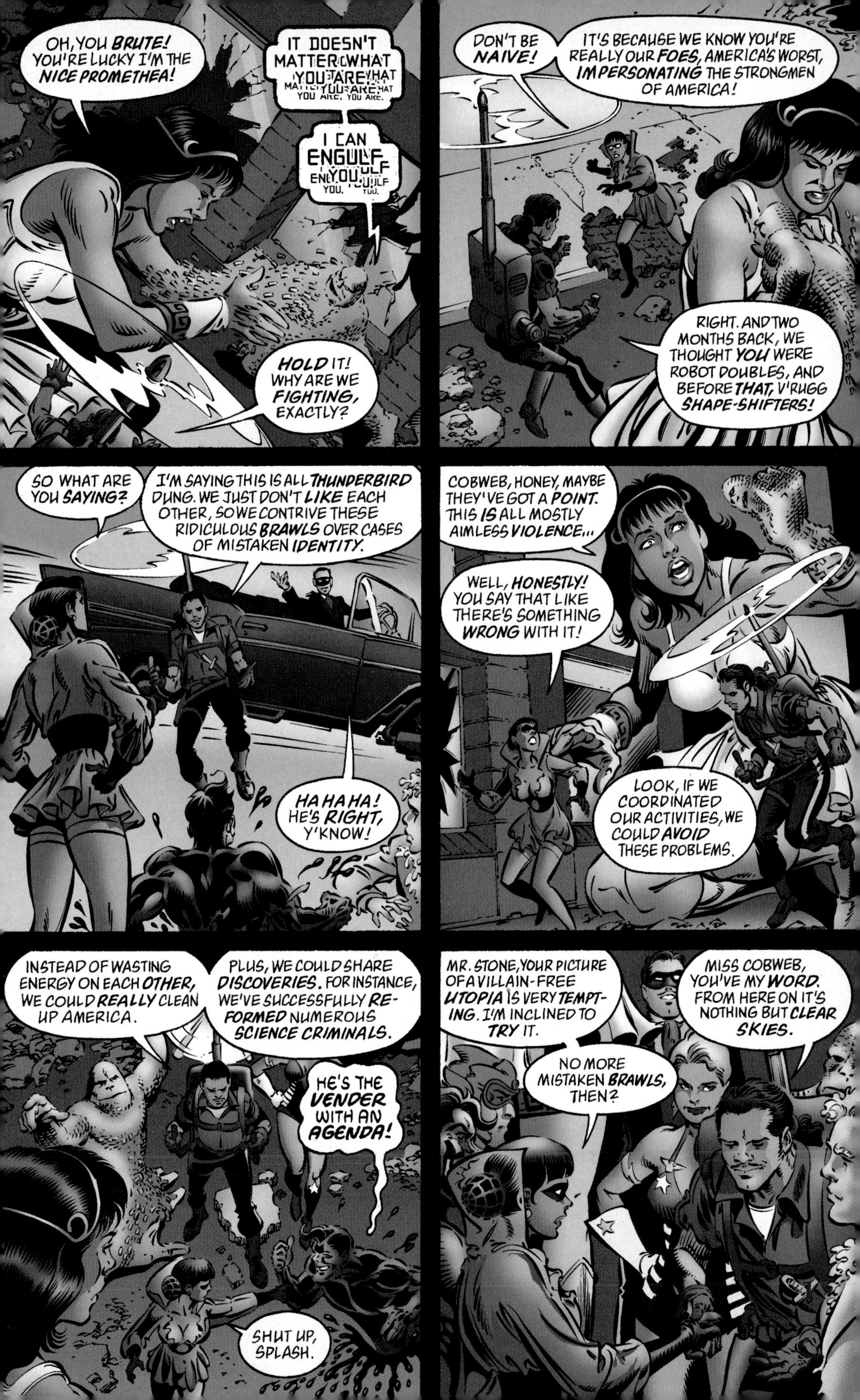
OH, YOU BRUTE! YOU'RE LUCKY I'M THE NICE PROMETHEA!
IT DOESN'T MATTER WHAT YOU ARE.
I CAN ENGULF YOU.
HOLD IT! WHY ARE WE FIGHTING, EXACTLY?
DON'T BE NAIVE!
IT'S BECAUSE WE KNOW YOU'RE REALLY OUR FOES, AMERICA'S WORST, IMPERSONATING THE STRONGMEN OF AMERICA!
RIGHT. AND TWO MONTHS BACK, WE THOUGHT YOU WERE ROBOT DOUBLES, AND BEFORE THAT, V'RUGG SHAPE-SHIFTERS!
SO WHAT ARE YOU SAYING?
I'M SAYING THIS IS ALL THUNDERBIRD DUNG. WE JUST DON'T LIKE EACH OTHER, SO WE CONTRIVE THESE RIDICULOUS BRAWLS OVER CASES OF MISTAKEN IDENTITY.
HA HA HA! HE'S RIGHT, Y'KNOW!
COBWEB, HONEY, MAYBE THEY'VE GOT A POINT. THIS IS ALL MOSTLY AIMLESS VIOLENCE...
WELL, HONESTLY! YOU SAY THAT LIKE THERE'S SOMETHING WRONG WITH IT!
LOOK, IF WE COORDINATED OUR ACTIVITIES, WE COULD AVOID THESE PROBLEMS.
INSTEAD OF WASTING ENERGY ON EACH OTHER, WE COULD REALLY CLEAN UP AMERICA.
PLUS, WE COULD SHARE DISCOVERIES. FOR INSTANCE, WE'VE SUCCESSFULLY RE-FORMED NUMEROUS SCIENCE CRIMINALS.
HE'S THE VENDER WITH AN AGENDA!
SHUT UP, SPLASH.
MR. STONE, YOUR PICTURE OF A VILLAIN-FREE UTOPIA IS VERY TEMPTING. I'M INCLINED TO TRY IT.
MISS COBWEB, YOU'VE MY WORD. FROM HERE ON IT'S NOTHING BUT CLEAR SKIES.
NO MORE MISTAKEN BRAWLS, THEN?

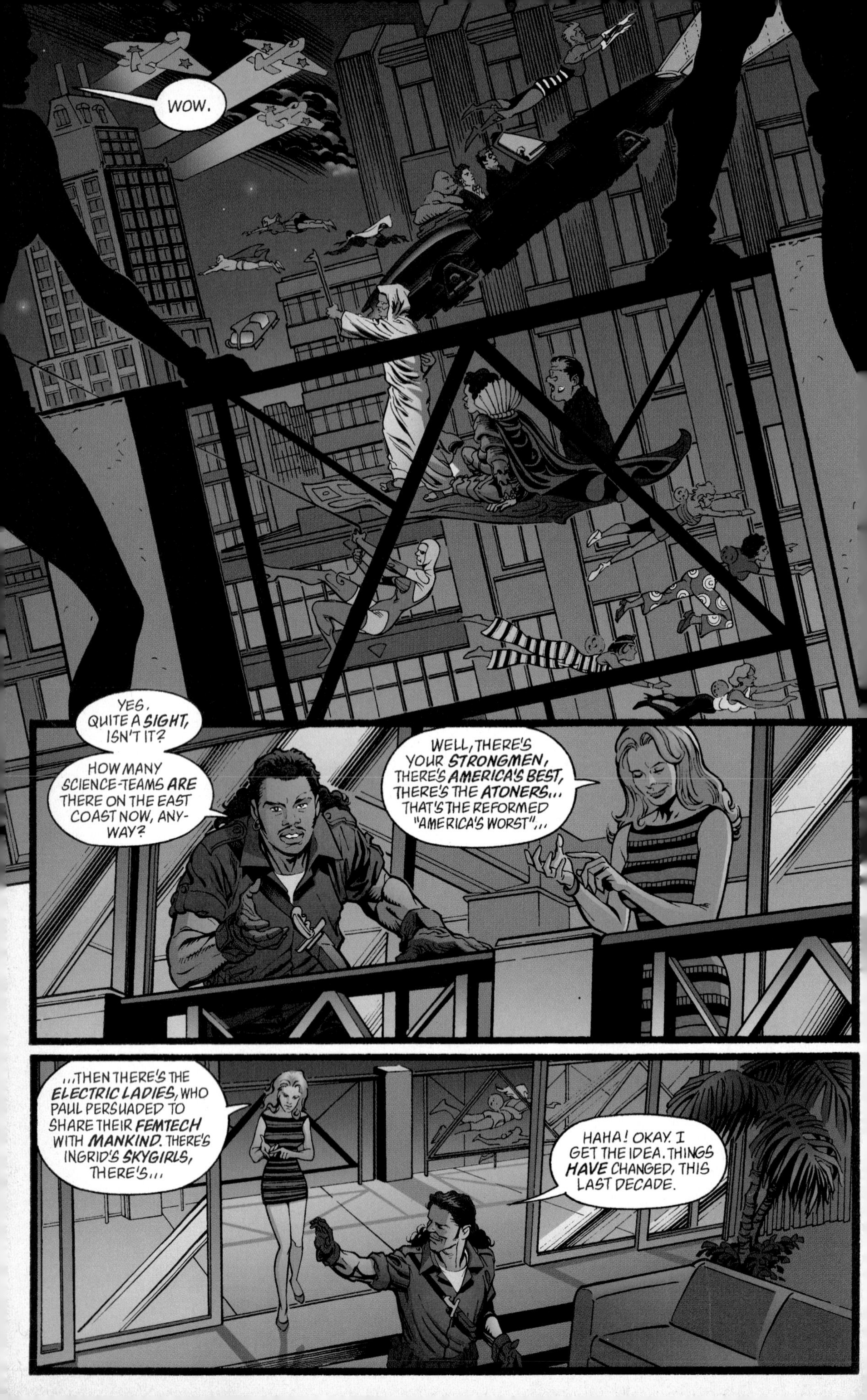
WOW.
YES. QUITE A SIGHT, ISN'T IT?
HOW MANY SCIENCE-TEAMS ARE THERE ON THE EAST COAST NOW, ANYWAY?
WELL, THERE'S YOUR STRONGMEN, THERE'S AMERICA'S BEST, THERE'S THE ATONERS... THAT'S THE REFORMED "AMERICA'S WORST"...
...THEN THERE'S THE ELECTRIC LADIES, WHO PAUL PERSUADED TO SHARE THEIR FEMTECH WITH MANKIND. THERE'S INGRID'S SKYGIRLS, THERE'S...
HAHA! OKAY. I GET THE IDEA. THINGS HAVE CHANGED, THIS LAST DECADE.

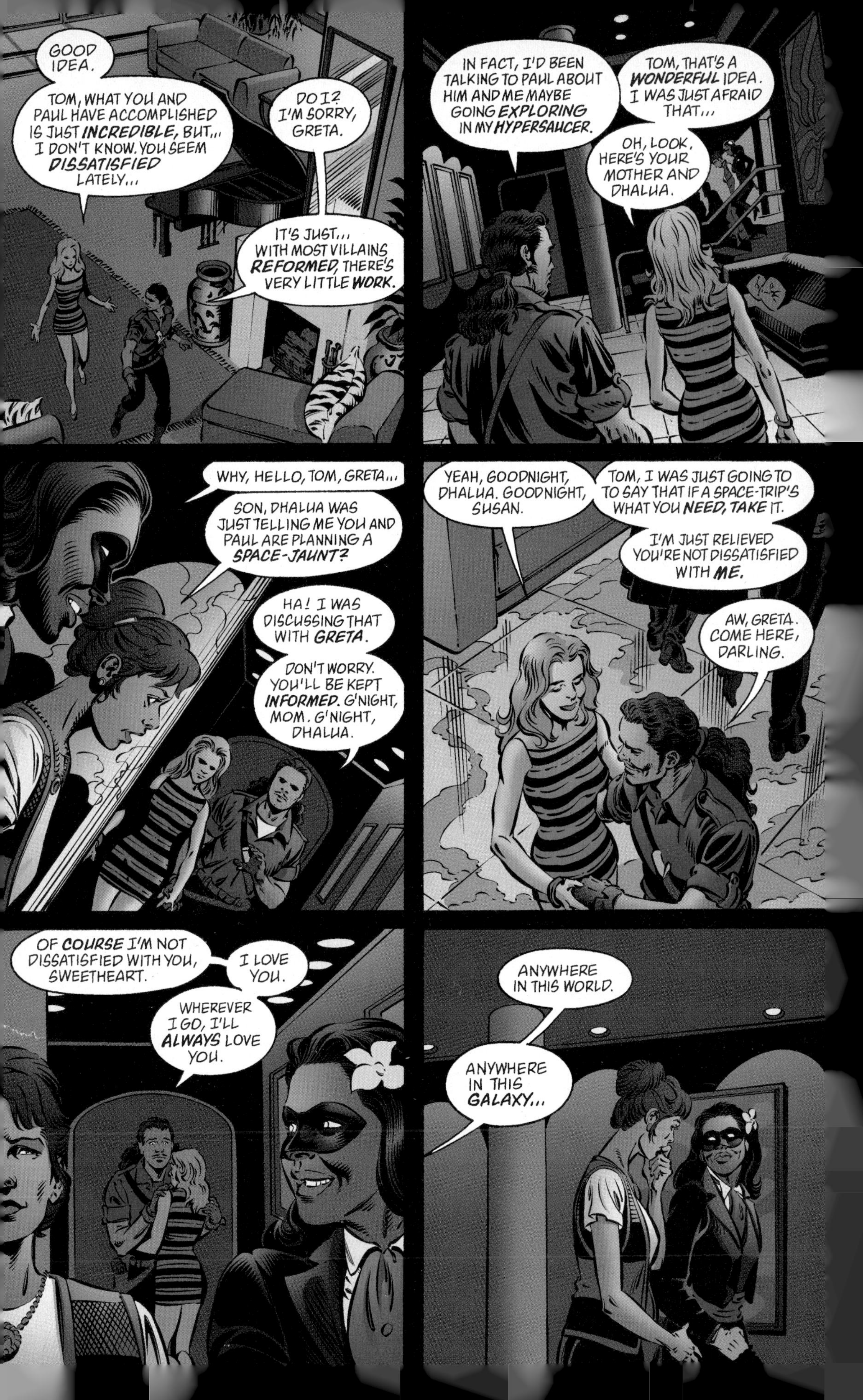
GOOD IDEA.
TOM, WHAT YOU AND PAUL HAVE ACCOMPLISHED IS JUST INCREDIBLE, BUT... I DON'T KNOW. YOU SEEM DISSATISFIED LATELY...
DO I? I'M SORRY, GRETA.
IT'S JUST... WITH MOST VILLAINS REFORMED, THERE'S VERY LITTLE WORK.
IN FACT, I'D BEEN TALKING TO PAUL ABOUT HIM AND ME MAYBE GOING EXPLORING IN MY HYPERSAUCER.
TOM, THAT'S A WONDERFUL IDEA. I WAS JUST AFRAID THAT...
OH, LOOK. HERE'S YOUR MOTHER AND DHALUA.
WHY, HELLO, TOM, GRETA...
SON, DHALUA WAS JUST TELLING ME YOU AND PAUL ARE PLANNING A SPACE-JAUNT?
HA! I WAS DISCUSSING THAT WITH GRETA.
DON'T WORRY. YOU'LL BE KEPT INFORMED. G'NIGHT, MOM. G'NIGHT, DHALUA.
YEAH, GOODNIGHT, DHALUA. GOODNIGHT, SUSAN.
TOM, I WAS JUST GOING TO TO SAY THAT IF A SPACE-TRIP'S WHAT YOU NEED, TAKE IT.
I'M JUST RELIEVED YOU'RE NOT DISSATISFIED WITH ME.
AW, GRETA. COME HERE, DARLING.
OF COURSE I'M NOT DISSATISFIED WITH YOU, SWEETHEART.
I LOVE YOU.
WHEREVER I GO, I'LL ALWAYS LOVE YOU.
ANYWHERE IN THIS WORLD.
ANYWHERE IN THIS GALAXY...

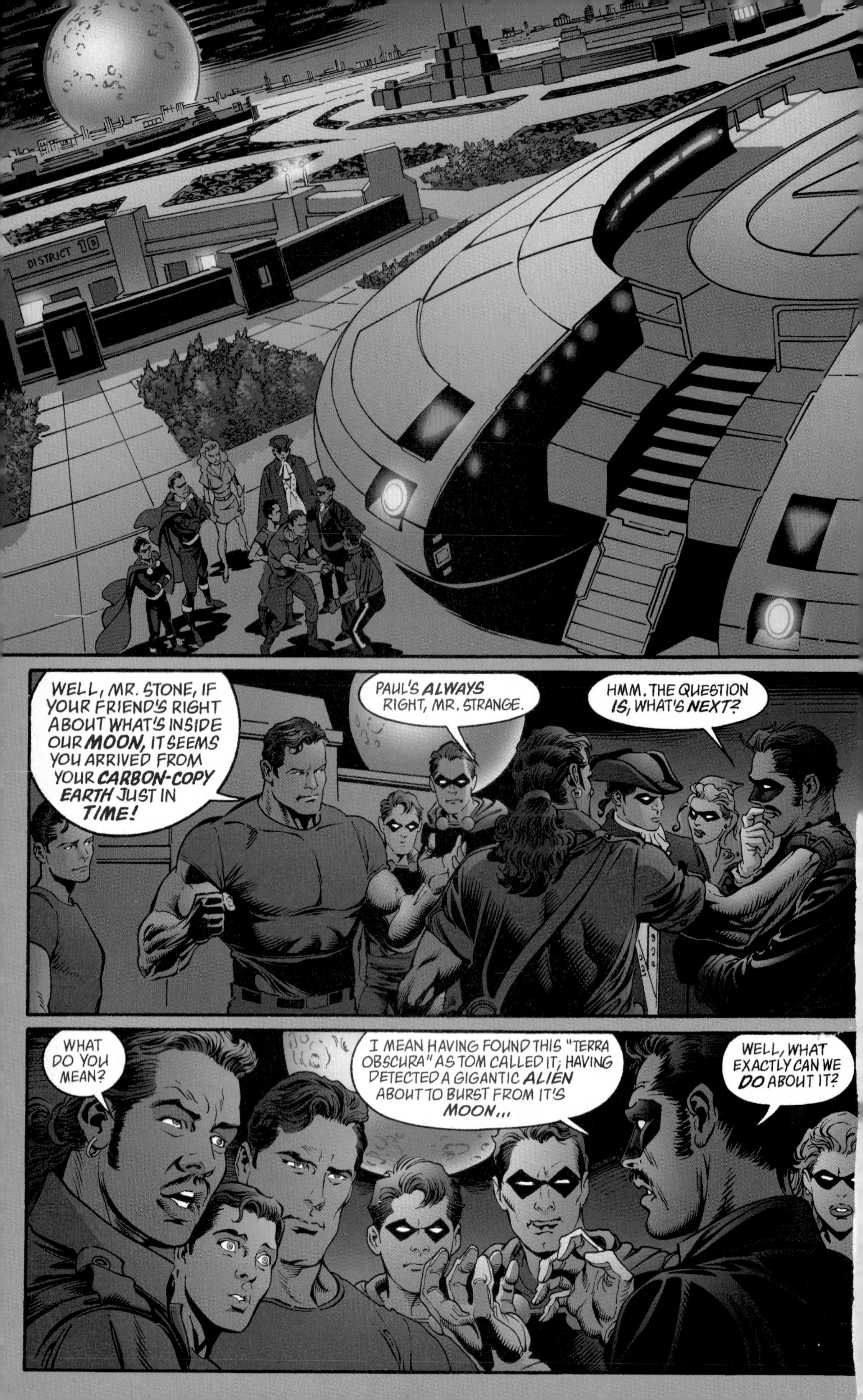
DISTRICT 10
WELL, MR. STONE, IF YOUR FRIEND'S RIGHT ABOUT WHAT'S INSIDE OUR MOON, IT SEEMS YOU ARRIVED FROM YOUR CARBON-COPY EARTH JUST IN TIME!
PAUL'S ALWAYS RIGHT, MR. STRANGE.
HMM. THE QUESTION IS, WHAT'S NEXT?
WHAT DO YOU MEAN?
I MEAN HAVING FOUND THIS "TERRA OBSCURA" AS TOM CALLED IT; HAVING DETECTED A GIGANTIC ALIEN ABOUT TO BURST FROM IT'S MOON...
WELL, WHAT EXACTLY CAN WE DO ABOUT IT?

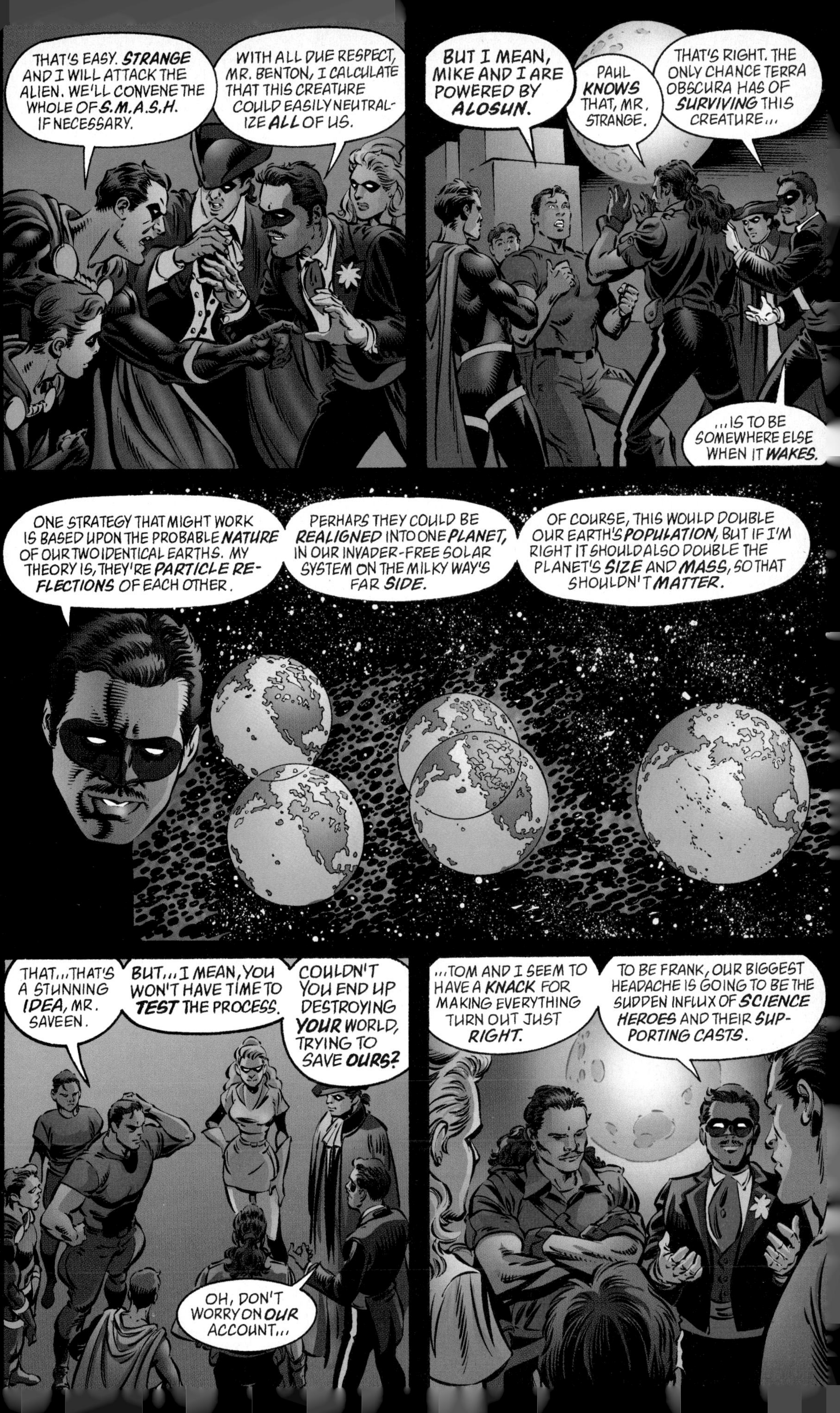

THAT'S EASY. STRANGE AND I WILL ATTACK THE ALIEN. WE'LL CONVENE THE WHOLE OF S.M.A.S.H. IF NECESSARY.
WITH ALL DUE RESPECT, MR. BENTON, I CALCULATE THAT THIS CREATURE COULD EASILY NEUTRALIZE ALL OF US.
BUT I MEAN, MIKE AND I ARE POWERED BY ALOSUN.
PAUL KNOWS THAT, MR. STRANGE.
THAT'S RIGHT. THE ONLY CHANCE TERRA OBSCURA HAS OF SURVIVING THIS CREATURE...
...IS TO BE SOMEWHERE ELSE WHEN IT WAKES.
ONE STRATEGY THAT MIGHT WORK IS BASED UPON THE PROBABLE NATURE OF OUR TWO IDENTICAL EARTHS. MY THEORY IS, THEY'RE PARTICLE REFLECTIONS OF EACH OTHER.
PERHAPS THEY COULD BE REALIGNED INTO ONE PLANET, IN OUR INVADER-FREE SOLAR SYSTEM ON THE MILKY WAY'S FAR SIDE.
OF COURSE, THIS WOULD DOUBLE OUR EARTH'S POPULATION, BUT IF I'M RIGHT IT SHOULD ALSO DOUBLE THE PLANET'S SIZE AND MASS, SO THAT SHOULDN'T MATTER.
THAT...THAT'S A STUNNING IDEA, MR. SAVEEN.
BUT...I MEAN, YOU WON'T HAVE TIME TO TEST THE PROCESS.
COULDN'T YOU END UP DESTROYING YOUR WORLD, TRYING TO SAVE OURS?
OH, DON'T WORRY ON OUR ACCOUNT...
...TOM AND I SEEM TO HAVE A KNACK FOR MAKING EVERYTHING TURN OUT JUST RIGHT.
TO BE FRANK, OUR BIGGEST HEADACHE IS GOING TO BE THE SUDDEN INFLUX OF SCIENCE HEROES AND THEIR SUPPORTING CASTS.

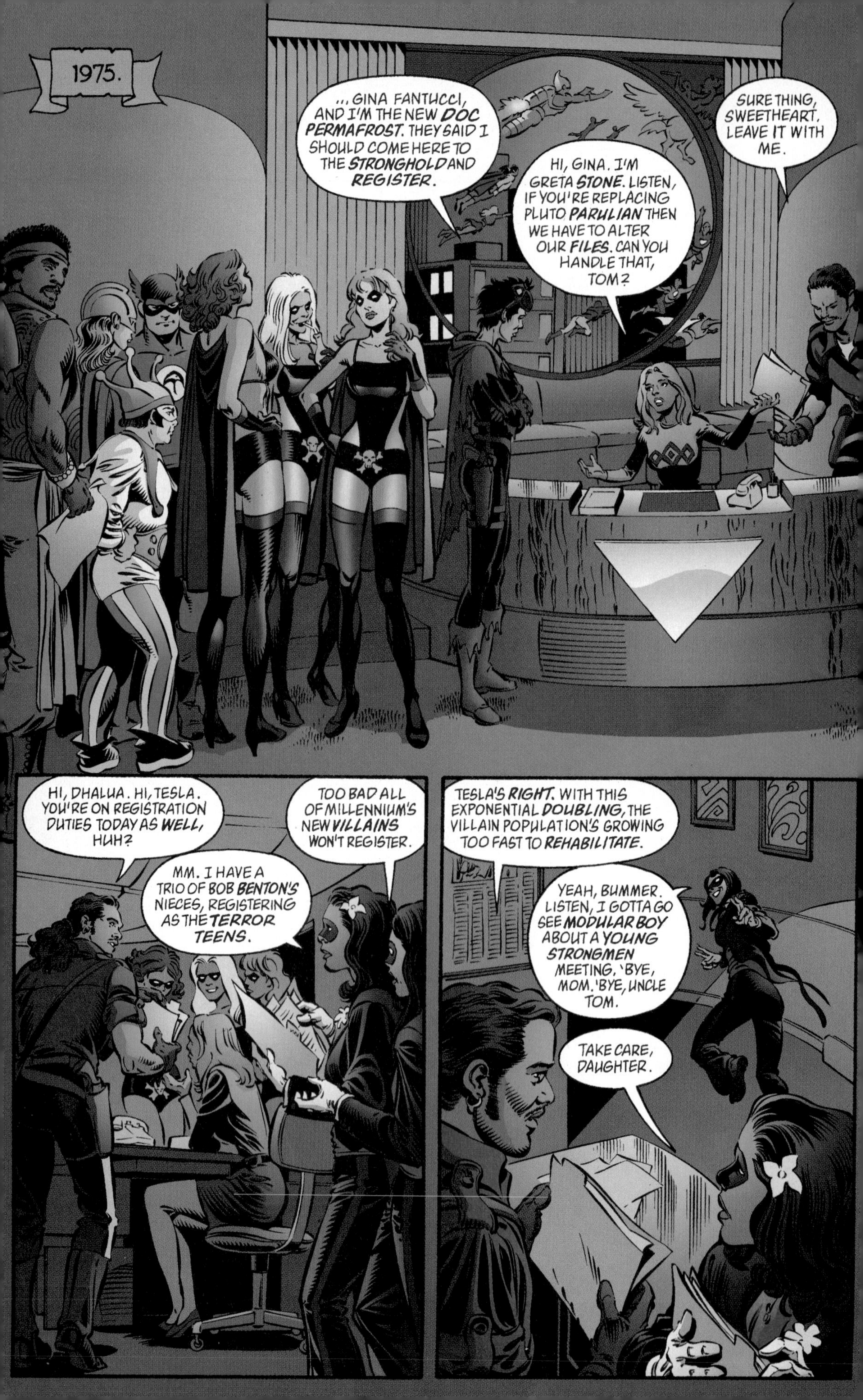
1975.
...GINA FANTUCCI, AND I'M THE NEW DOC PERMAFROST. THEY SAID I SHOULD COME HERE TO THE STRONGHOLD AND REGISTER.
HI, GINA. I'M GRETA STONE. LISTEN, IF YOU'RE REPLACING PLUTO PARULIAN THEN WE HAVE TO ALTER OUR FILES. CAN YOU HANDLE THAT, TOM?
SURE THING, SWEETHEART. LEAVE IT WITH ME.
HI, DHALUA. HI, TESLA. YOU'RE ON REGISTRATION DUTIES TODAY AS WELL, HUH?
MM. I HAVE A TRIO OF BOB BENTON'S NIECES, REGISTERING AS THE TERROR TEENS.
TOO BAD ALL OF MILLENNIUM'S NEW VILLAINS WON'T REGISTER.
TESLA'S RIGHT. WITH THIS EXPONENTIAL DOUBLING, THE VILLAIN POPULATION'S GROWING TOO FAST TO REHABILITATE.
YEAH, BUMMER. LISTEN, I GOTTA GO SEE MODULAR BOY ABOUT A YOUNG STRONGMEN MEETING. 'BYE, MOM. 'BYE, UNCLE TOM.
TAKE CARE, DAUGHTER.

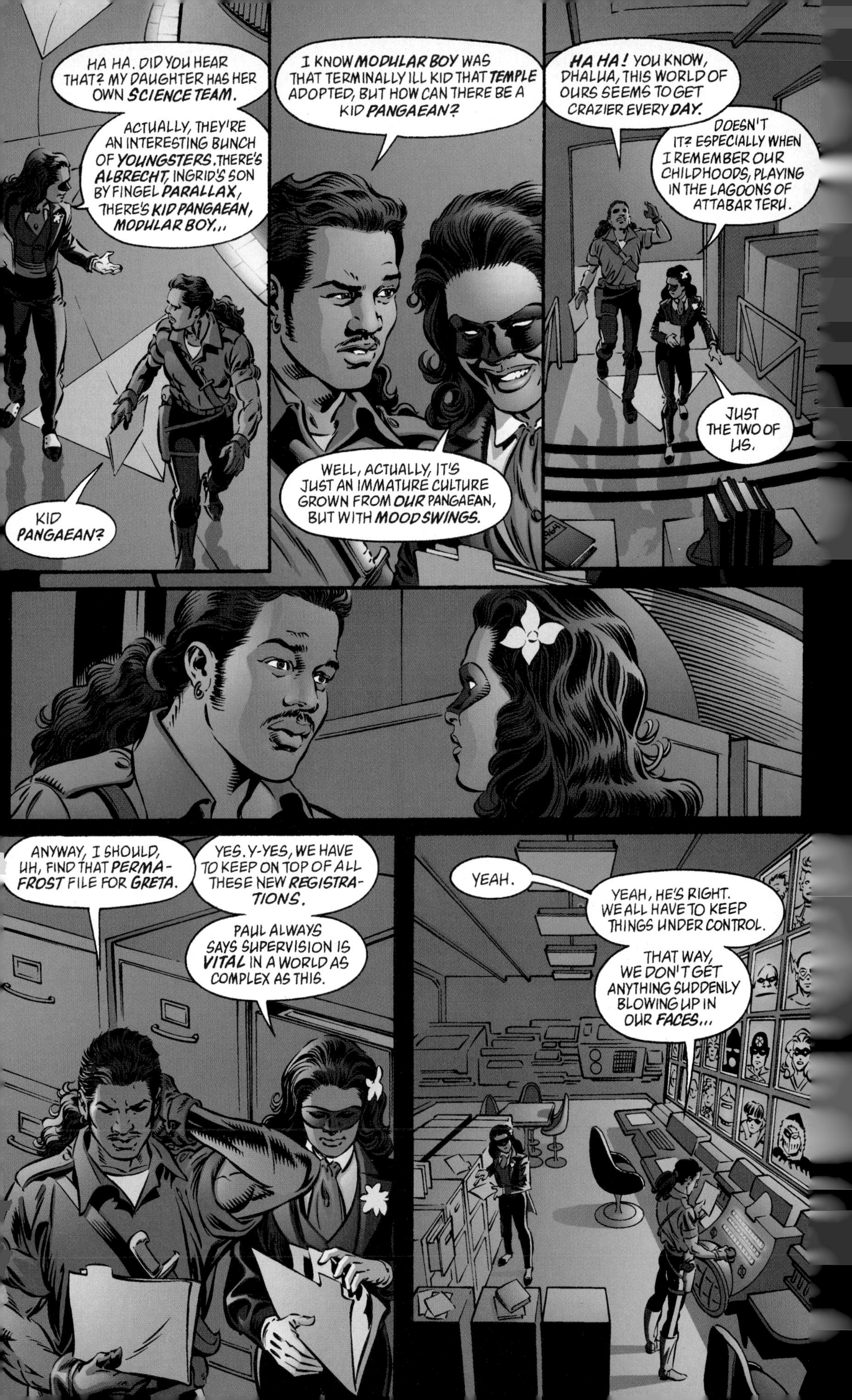
HA HA. DID YOU HEAR THAT? MY DAUGHTER HAS HER OWN SCIENCE TEAM.
ACTUALLY, THEY'RE AN INTERESTING BUNCH OF YOUNGSTERS. THERE'S ALBRECHT, INGRID'S SON BY FINGEL PARALLAX, THERE'S KID PANGAEAN, MODULAR BOY...
KID PANGAEAN?
I KNOW MODULAR BOY WAS THAT TERMINALLY ILL KID THAT TEMPLE ADOPTED, BUT HOW CAN THERE BE A KID PANGAEAN?
WELL, ACTUALLY, IT'S JUST AN IMMATURE CULTURE GROWN FROM OUR PANGAEAN, BUT WITH MOOD SWINGS.
HA HA! YOU KNOW, DHALUA, THIS WORLD OF OURS SEEMS TO GET CRAZIER EVERY DAY.
DOESN'T IT? ESPECIALLY WHEN I REMEMBER OUR CHILDHOODS, PLAYING IN THE LAGOONS OF ATTABAR TERU.
JUST THE TWO OF US.
ANYWAY, I SHOULD, UH, FIND THAT PERMA-FROST FILE FOR GRETA.
YES. Y-YES, WE HAVE TO KEEP ON TOP OF ALL THESE NEW REGISTRA-TIONS.
PAUL ALWAYS SAYS SUPERVISION IS VITAL IN A WORLD AS COMPLEX AS THIS.
YEAH.
YEAH, HE'S RIGHT. WE ALL HAVE TO KEEP THINGS UNDER CONTROL.
THAT WAY, WE DON'T GET ANYTHING SUDDENLY BLOWING UP IN OUR FACES...

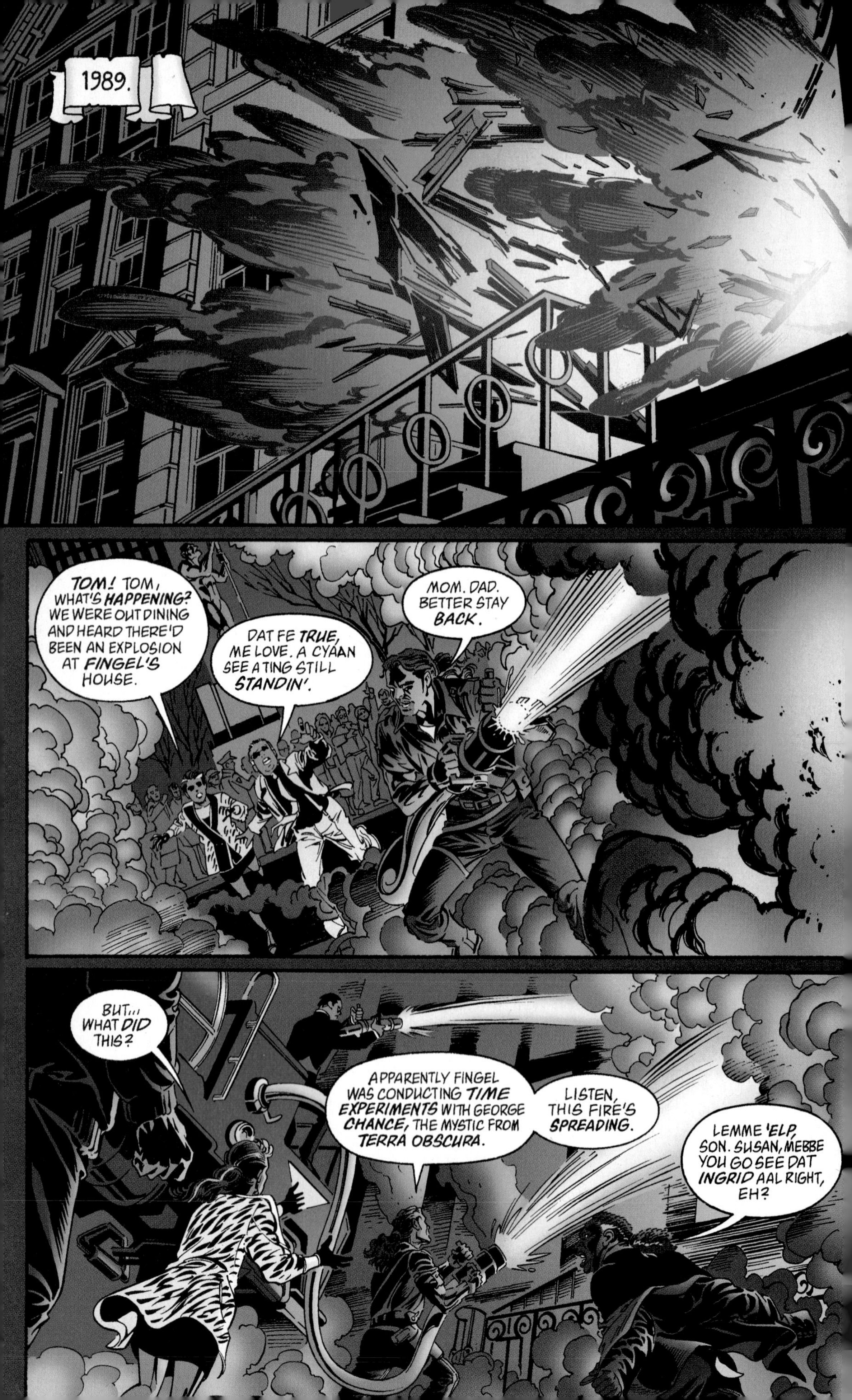
1989.
TOM! TOM, WHAT'S HAPPENING? WE WERE OUT DINING AND HEARD THERE'D BEEN AN EXPLOSION AT FINGEL'S HOUSE.
DAT FE TRUE, ME LOVE. A CYAAN SEE A TING STILL STANDIN'.
MOM. DAD. BETTER STAY BACK.
BUT... WHAT DID THIS?
APPARENTLY FINGEL WAS CONDUCTING TIME EXPERIMENTS WITH GEORGE CHANCE, THE MYSTIC FROM TERRA OBSCURA.
LISTEN, THIS FIRE'S SPREADING.
LEMME 'ELP, SON. SUSAN, MEBBE YOU GO SEE DAT INGRID AAL RIGHT, EH?

I JUST GOT HERE. I--IS FINGEL...?

HE'S IN *THERE*! MY *DAD'S* IN THERE! MOM, LET ME *GO*!

ALBRECHT, MY *DARLING*, HE'S *DEAD*. YOUR FATHER IS DEAD. THERE IS NO *POINT*...

CHUKULTEH. SUSAN, THIS IS *TERRIBLE*.

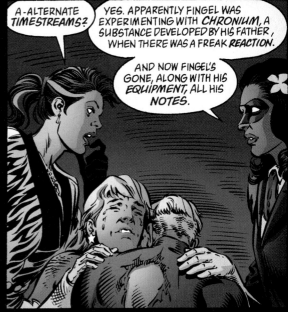

WH-WHAT *HAPPENED*? TOM MENTIONED GEORGE *CHANCE*, THE *GHOST*...

FROM WHAT INGRID RE-MEMBERS, CHANCE AND FINGEL WERE INVESTIGAT-ING ALTERNATE *TIMESTREAMS* WHEN SOMETHING HAPPENED.

INGRID AND ALBRECHT GOT OUT OKAY, BEING SUPER-HUMANS. FINGEL AND CHANCE *DIDN'T*.

A-ALTERNATE *TIMESTREAMS?*

YES. APPARENTLY FINGEL WAS EXPERIMENTING WITH *CHRONIUM*, A SUBSTANCE DEVELOPED BY HIS FATHER, WHEN THERE WAS A FREAK *REACTION*.

AND NOW FINGEL'S GONE, ALONG WITH HIS *EQUIPMENT*, ALL HIS *NOTES*.

EVERYTHING'S GONE? B-BUT,...DOESN'T THAT MEAN THAT *TIME TRAVEL* IS...?

AFTER TONIGHT, SUSAN, TIME TRAVEL IS *IMPOSSIBLE*.

THE *PANGAEAN* CAN'T EVER RETURN TO HIS OWN *PERIOD*. IN FACT, *NOBODY* CAN TRAVEL INTO THE PAST AGAIN.

NOT FOR *ANY* REASON.

I GUESS WE ALL BETTER HOPE THAT WE NEVER HAVE *NEED* TO.

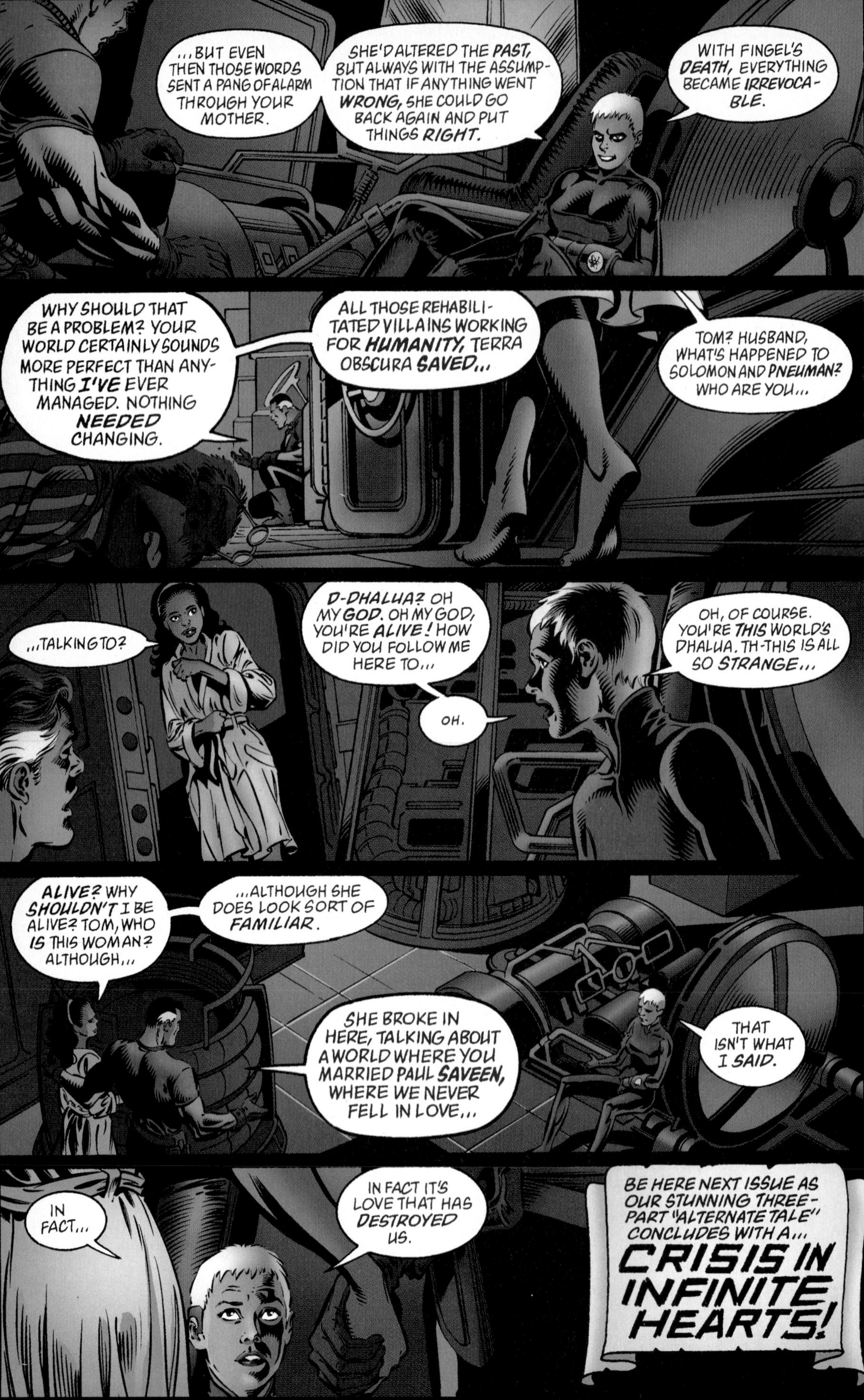
...BUT EVEN THEN THOSE WORDS SENT A PANG OF ALARM THROUGH YOUR MOTHER.
SHE'D ALTERED THE PAST, BUT ALWAYS WITH THE ASSUMPTION THAT IF ANYTHING WENT WRONG, SHE COULD GO BACK AGAIN AND PUT THINGS RIGHT.
WITH FINGEL'S DEATH, EVERYTHING BECAME IRREVOCABLE.
WHY SHOULD THAT BE A PROBLEM? YOUR WORLD CERTAINLY SOUNDS MORE PERFECT THAN ANYTHING I'VE EVER MANAGED. NOTHING NEEDED CHANGING.
ALL THOSE REHABILITATED VILLAINS WORKING FOR HUMANITY, TERRA OBSCURA SAVED...
TOM? HUSBAND, WHAT'S HAPPENED TO SOLOMON AND PNEUMAN? WHO ARE YOU...
...TALKING TO?
D-DHALUA? OH MY GOD. OH MY GOD, YOU'RE ALIVE! HOW DID YOU FOLLOW ME HERE TO...
OH.
OH, OF COURSE. YOU'RE THIS WORLD'S DHALUA. TH-THIS IS ALL SO STRANGE...
ALIVE? WHY SHOULDN'T I BE ALIVE? TOM, WHO IS THIS WOMAN? ALTHOUGH...
...ALTHOUGH SHE DOES LOOK SORT OF FAMILIAR.
SHE BROKE IN HERE, TALKING ABOUT A WORLD WHERE YOU MARRIED PAUL SAVEEN, WHERE WE NEVER FELL IN LOVE...
THAT ISN'T WHAT I SAID.
IN FACT...
IN FACT IT'S LOVE THAT HAS DESTROYED US.
BE HERE NEXT ISSUE AS OUR STUNNING THREE-PART "ALTERNATE TALE" CONCLUDES WITH A...
CRISIS IN INFINITE HEARTS!

# CHAPTER THREE

**In which a tragic romance is revealed, friendships and alliances are broken, and Tom Strong must make a change.**

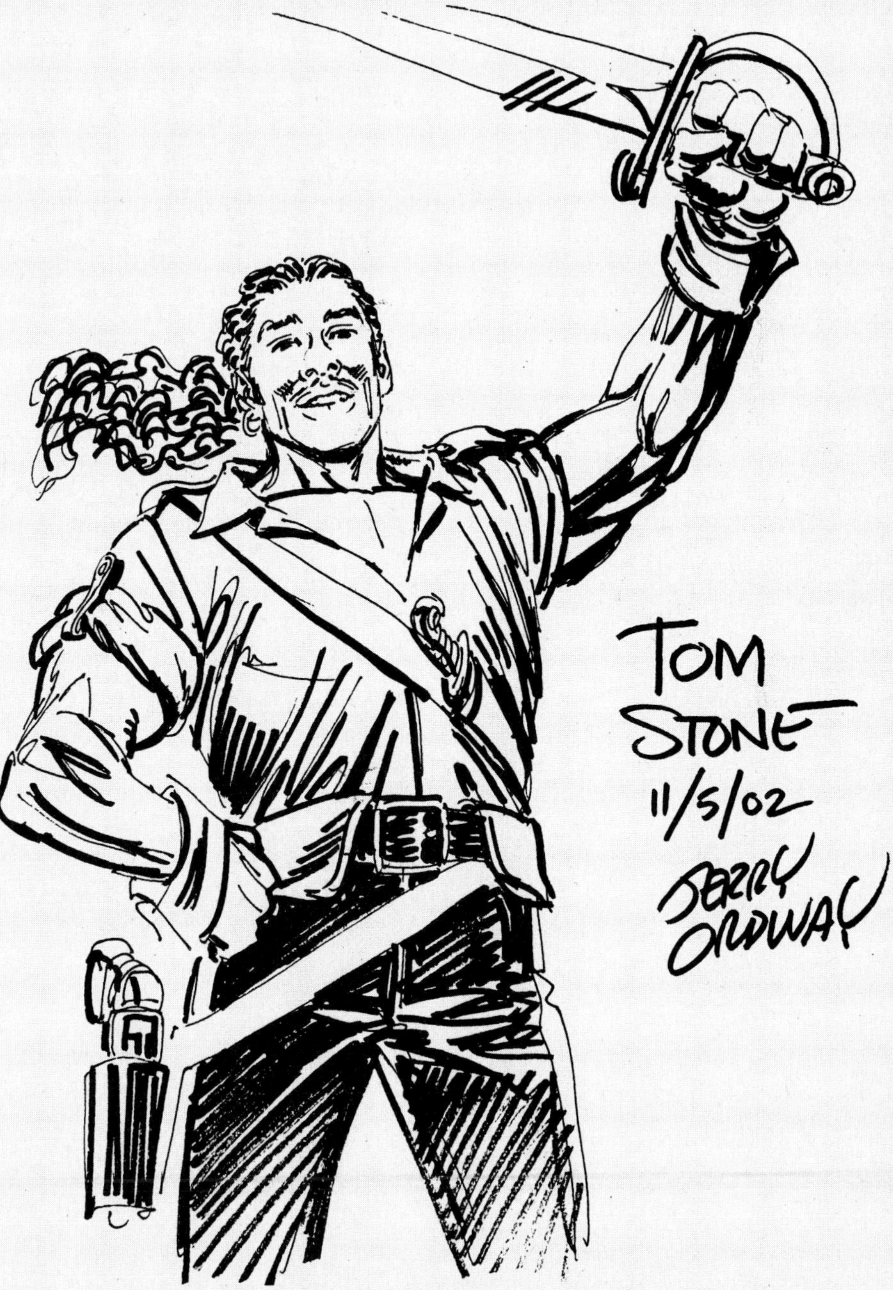
TOM STONE
11/5/02
JERRY ORDWAY

**Cover art:**
**Chris Sprouse and Karl Story**

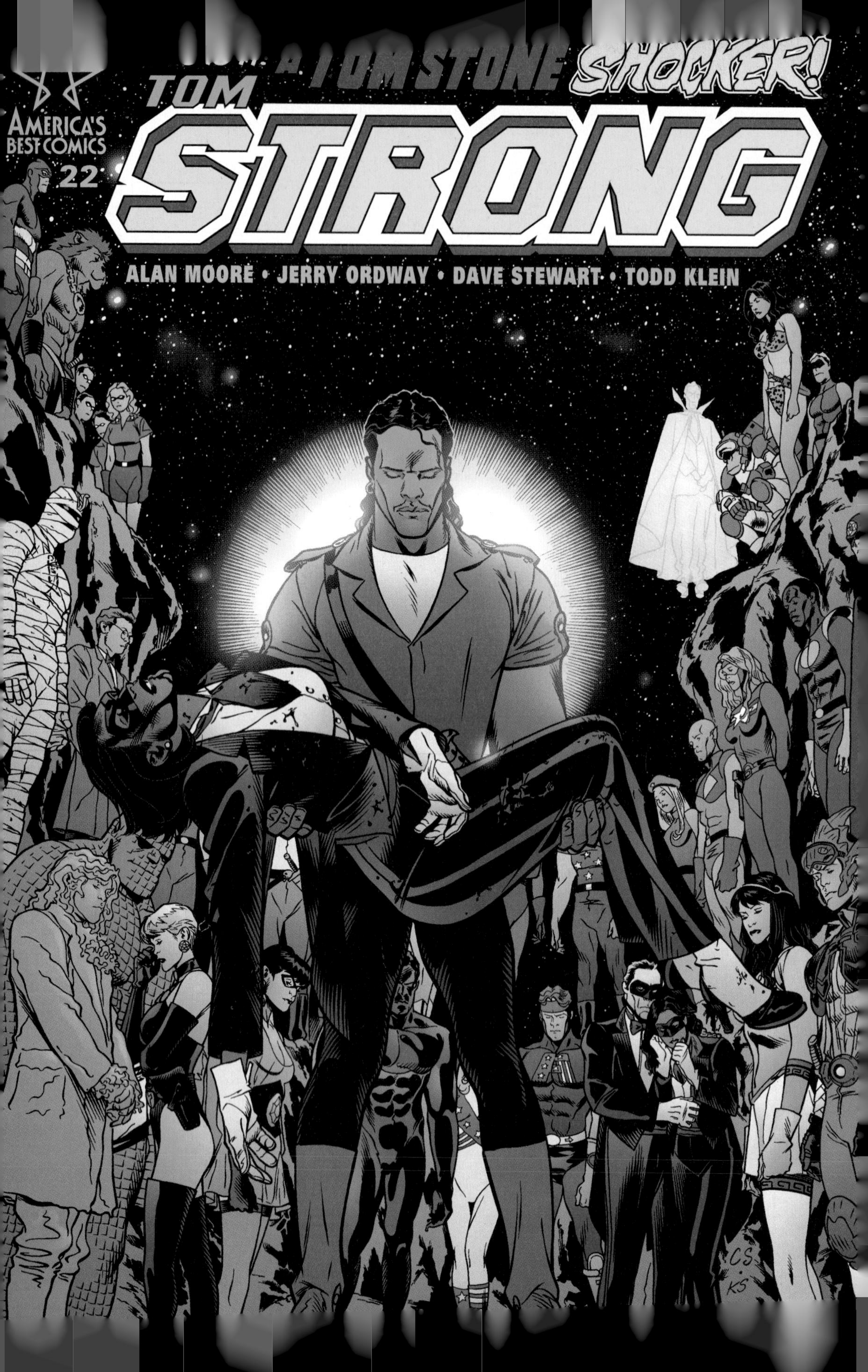

A TOMSTONE SHOCKER!
AMERICA'S BEST COMICS
22
TOM STRONG
ALAN MOORE • JERRY ORDWAY • DAVE STEWART • TODD KLEIN
CS
KS

SO, LET'S *SEE:*

WHERE YOU'RE FROM, A BRIEF DELAY ON MY MOTHER'S PART IN 1899 BROUGHT AN ENTIRELY DIFFERENT *WORLD* INTO BEING...

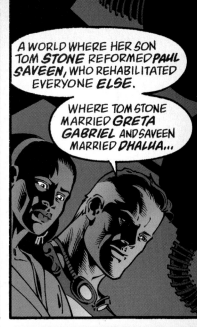

A WORLD WHERE HER SON TOM *STONE* REFORMED *PAUL SAVEEN,* WHO REHABILITATED EVERYONE *ELSE.*

WHERE TOM STONE MARRIED *GRETA GABRIEL* AND SAVEEN MARRIED *DHALUA...*

A WORLD SO WONDERFUL THAT MOTHER USED A *TIME APPARATUS* TO GO BACK AND *CAUSE* THE FATEFUL DELAY *HERSELF...*

...CEMENTING HER *UTOPIA* IN PLACE *FOREVER.*

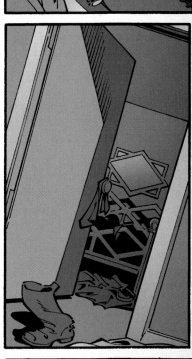

YES. SHE DID.

BUT IT WASN'T UNTIL FINGEL PARALLAX AND HIS TIME MACHINES WERE *DESTROYED* IN 1989 THAT WHAT SHE'D DONE BECAME *IRREVERSIBLE...*

...AND BY THEN, THE CRACKS IN HER UTOPIA WERE WIDENING INTO A *CHASM.*

AND THAT CHASM WOULD EVENTUALLY SWALLOW EVERY-THING.

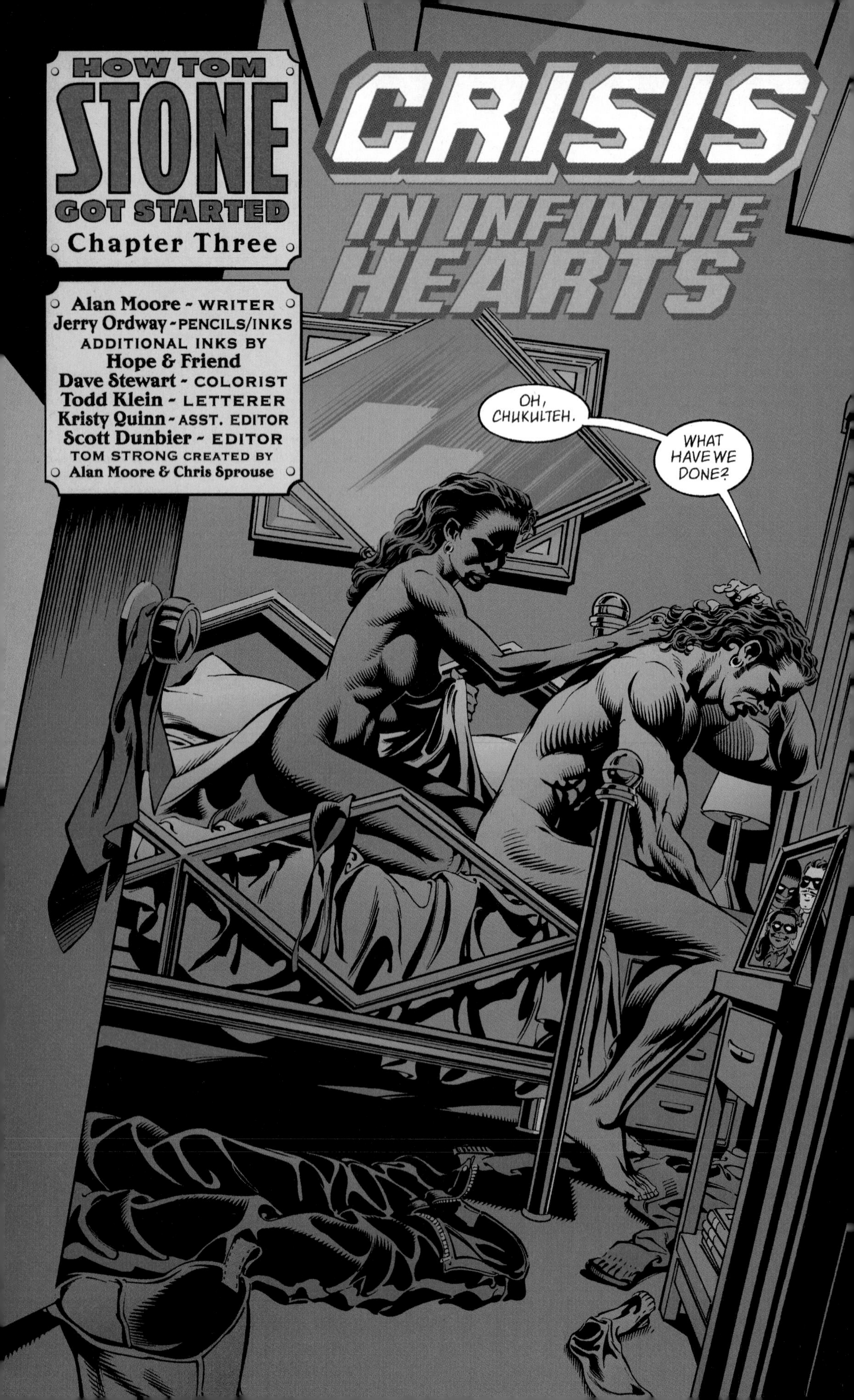
HOW TOM STONE GOT STARTED
Chapter Three
CRISIS IN INFINITE HEARTS
Alan Moore - WRITER
Jerry Ordway - PENCILS/INKS
ADDITIONAL INKS BY
Hope & Friend
Dave Stewart - COLORIST
Todd Klein - LETTERER
Kristy Quinn - ASST. EDITOR
Scott Dunbier - EDITOR
TOM STRONG CREATED BY
Alan Moore & Chris Sprouse
OH, CHUKULTEH.
WHAT HAVE WE DONE?

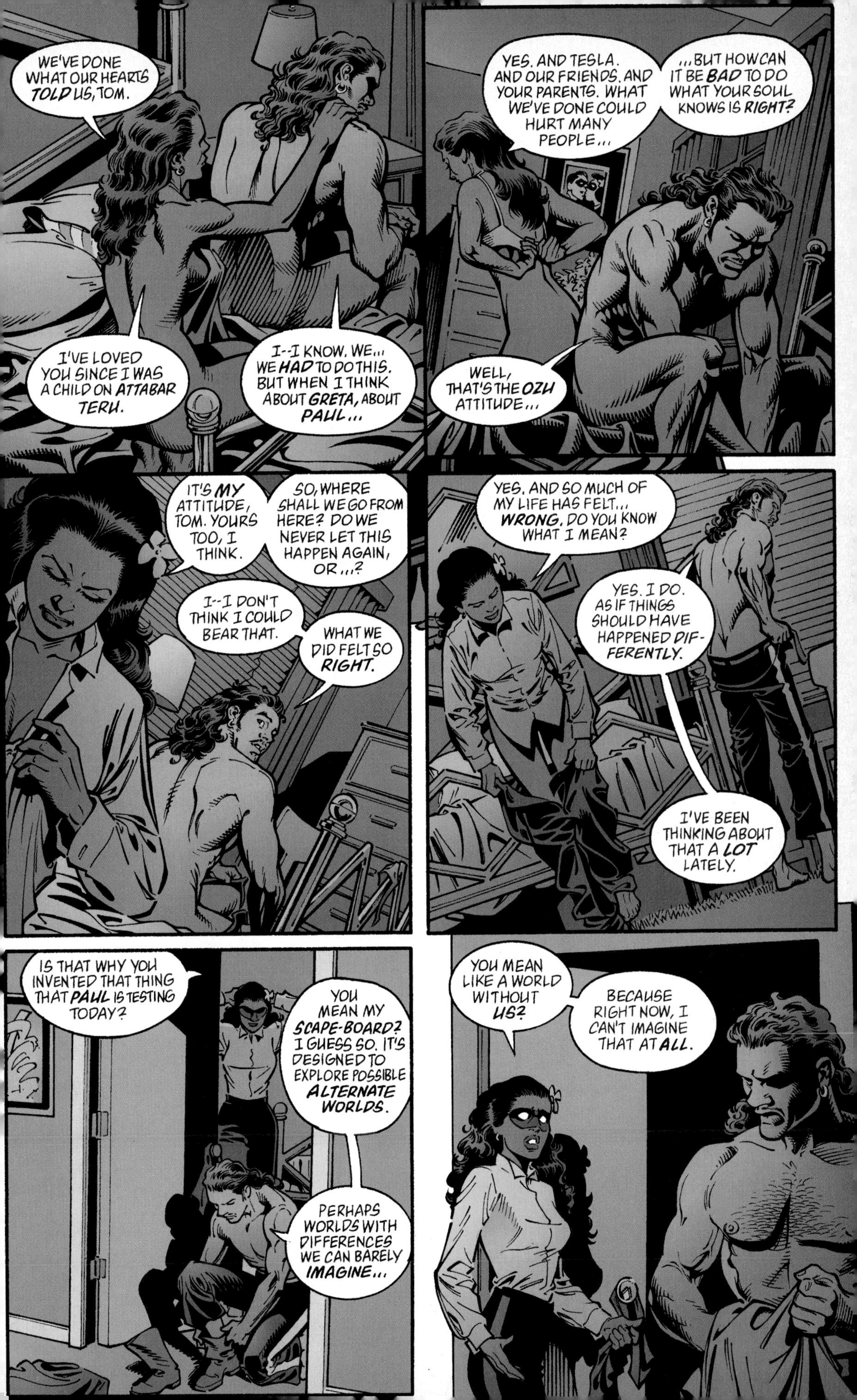
WE'VE DONE WHAT OUR HEARTS TOLD US, TOM.
I'VE LOVED YOU SINCE I WAS A CHILD ON ATTABAR TERU.
I--I KNOW. WE... WE HAD TO DO THIS. BUT WHEN I THINK ABOUT GRETA, ABOUT PAUL...
YES. AND TESLA. AND OUR FRIENDS. AND YOUR PARENTS. WHAT WE'VE DONE COULD HURT MANY PEOPLE...
...BUT HOW CAN IT BE BAD TO DO WHAT YOUR SOUL KNOWS IS RIGHT?
WELL, THAT'S THE OZU ATTITUDE...
IT'S MY ATTITUDE, TOM. YOURS TOO, I THINK.
SO, WHERE SHALL WE GO FROM HERE? DO WE NEVER LET THIS HAPPEN AGAIN, OR...?
I--I DON'T THINK I COULD BEAR THAT.
WHAT WE DID FELT SO RIGHT.
YES. AND SO MUCH OF MY LIFE HAS FELT... WRONG. DO YOU KNOW WHAT I MEAN?
YES. I DO. AS IF THINGS SHOULD HAVE HAPPENED DIF-FERENTLY.
I'VE BEEN THINKING ABOUT THAT A LOT LATELY.
IS THAT WHY YOU INVENTED THAT THING THAT PAUL IS TESTING TODAY?
YOU MEAN MY SCAPE-BOARD? I GUESS SO. IT'S DESIGNED TO EXPLORE POSSIBLE ALTERNATE WORLDS.
PERHAPS WORLDS WITH DIFFERENCES WE CAN BARELY IMAGINE...
YOU MEAN LIKE A WORLD WITHOUT US?
BECAUSE RIGHT NOW, I CAN'T IMAGINE THAT AT ALL.

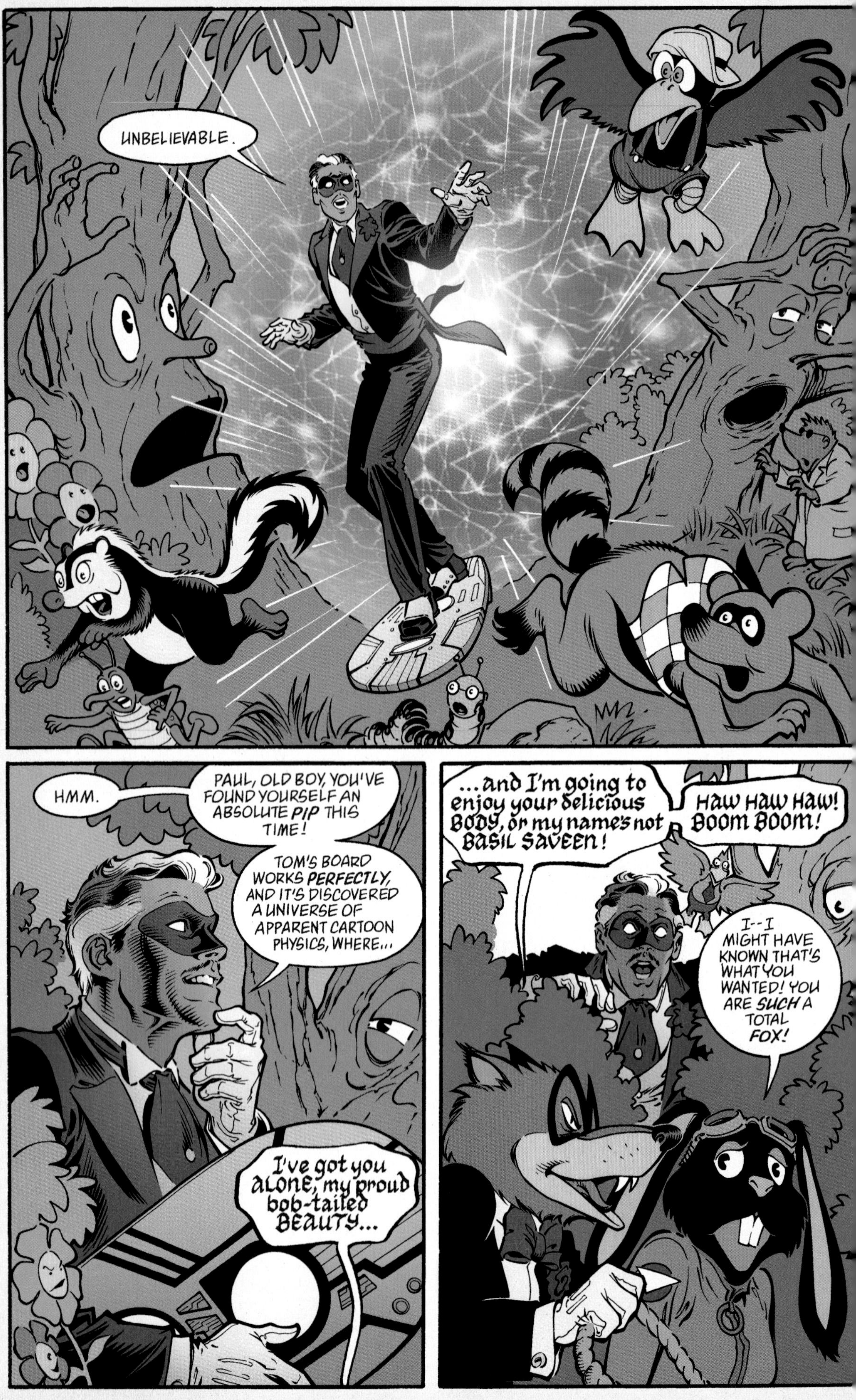
UNBELIEVABLE.
HMM.
PAUL, OLD BOY, YOU'VE FOUND YOURSELF AN ABSOLUTE PIP THIS TIME!
TOM'S BOARD WORKS PERFECTLY, AND IT'S DISCOVERED A UNIVERSE OF APPARENT CARTOON PHYSICS, WHERE...
I've got you ALONE, my proud bob-tailed BEAUTY...
...and I'm going to enjoy your delicious BODY, or my name's not BASIL SAVEEN!
HAW HAW HAW! BOOM BOOM!
I--I MIGHT HAVE KNOWN THAT'S WHAT YOU WANTED! YOU ARE SUCH A TOTAL FOX!

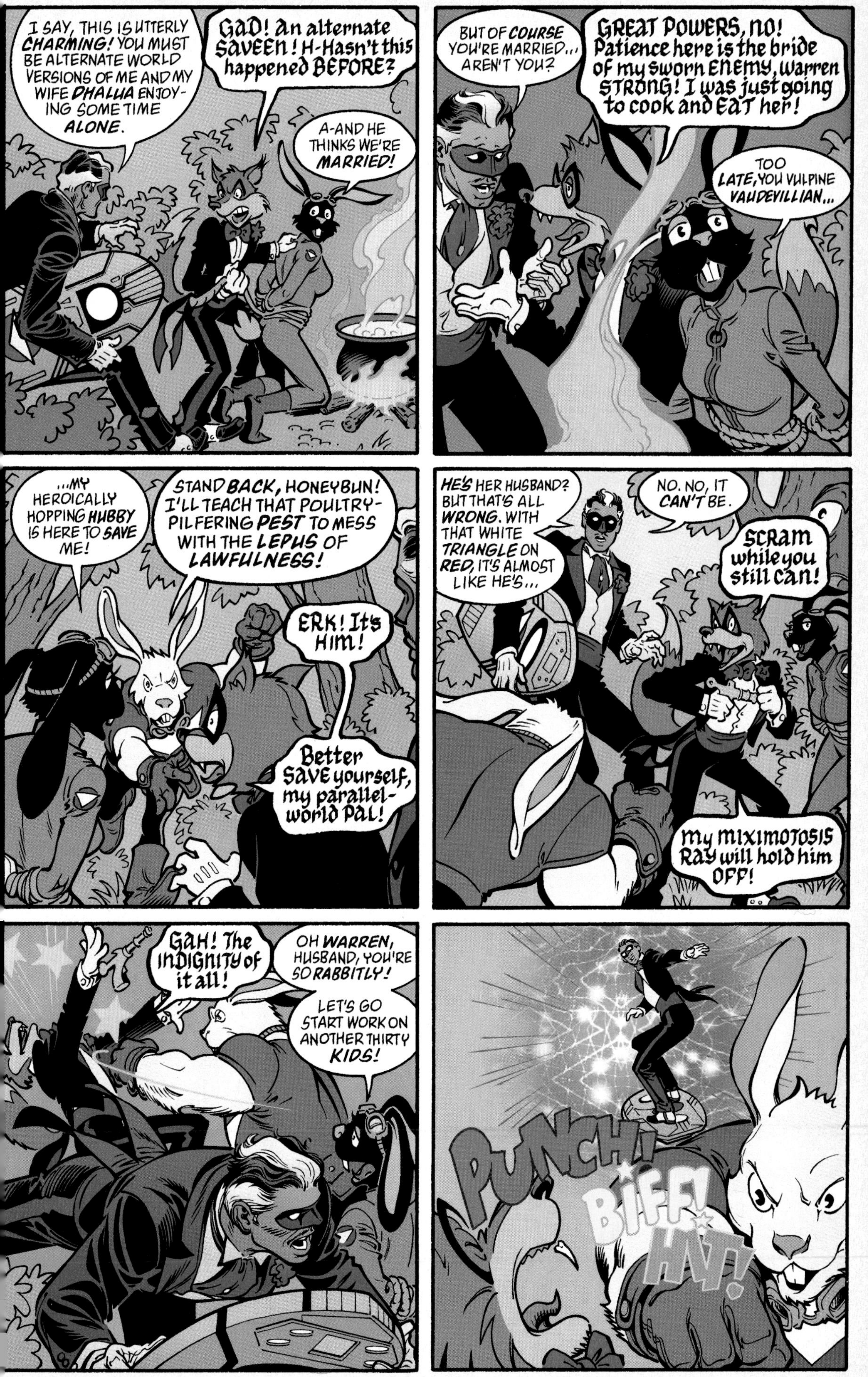
I SAY, THIS IS UTTERLY CHARMING! YOU MUST BE ALTERNATE WORLD VERSIONS OF ME AND MY WIFE DHALUA ENJOYING SOME TIME ALONE.
GAD! An alternate SAVEEN! H-Hasn't this happened BEFORE?
A-AND HE THINKS WE'RE MARRIED!
BUT OF COURSE YOU'RE MARRIED... AREN'T YOU?
GREAT POWERS, NO! Patience here is the bride of my sworn ENEMY, Warren STRONG! I was just going to cook and EAT her!
TOO LATE, YOU VULPINE VAUDEVILLIAN...
...MY HEROICALLY HOPPING HUBBY IS HERE TO SAVE ME!
STAND BACK, HONEYBUN! I'LL TEACH THAT POULTRY-PILFERING PEST TO MESS WITH THE LEPUS OF LAWFULNESS!
ERK! It's HIM!
Better SAVE yourself, my parallel-world PAL!
HE'S HER HUSBAND? BUT THAT'S ALL WRONG. WITH THAT WHITE TRIANGLE ON RED, IT'S ALMOST LIKE HE'S...
NO. NO, IT CAN'T BE.
SCRAM while you still can!
My MIXIMOTOSIS RAY will hold him OFF!
GAH! The INDIGNITY of it all!
OH WARREN, HUSBAND, YOU'RE SO RABBITLY!
LET'S GO START WORK ON ANOTHER THIRTY KIDS!
PUNCH! BIFF! HAT!

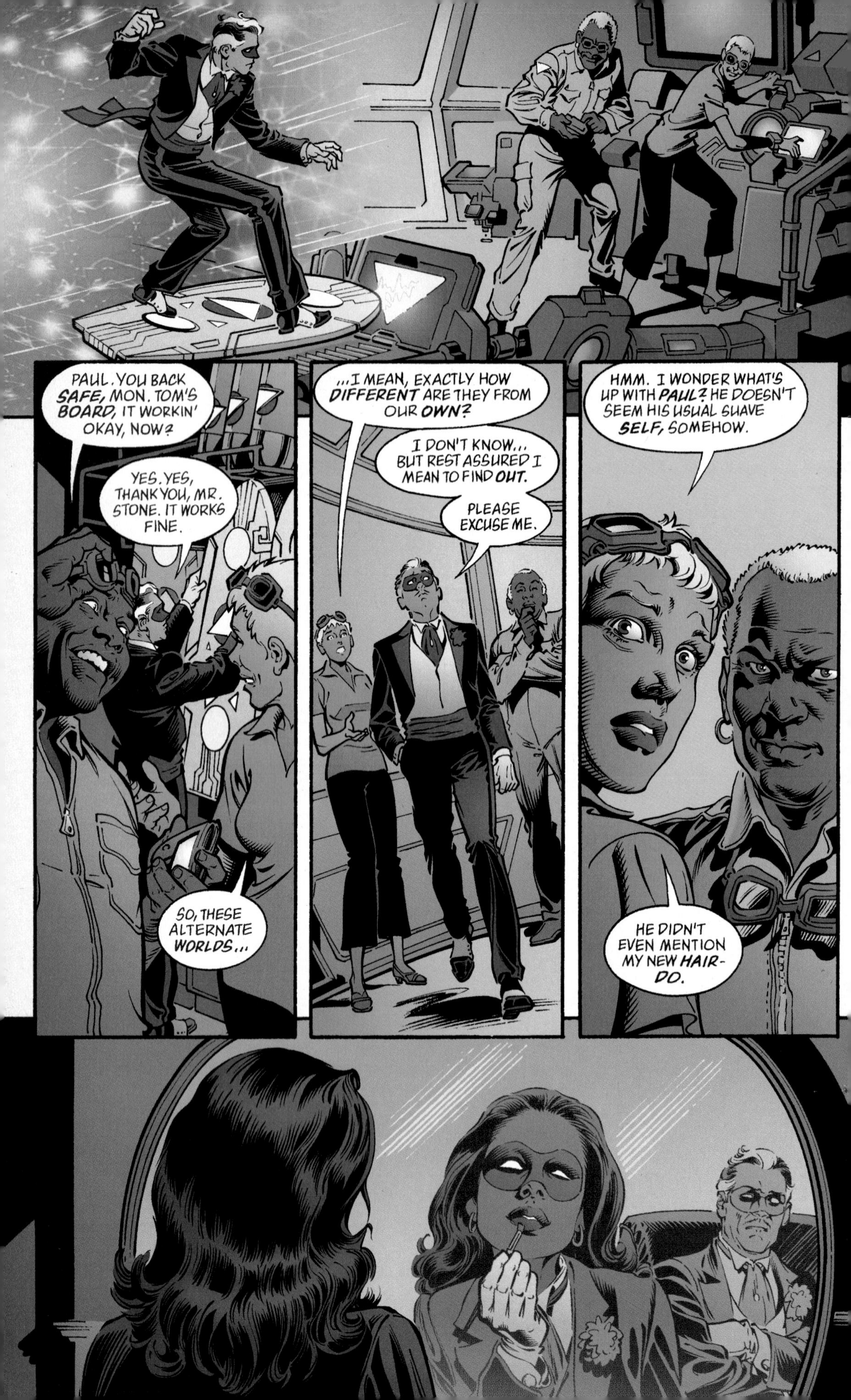
PAUL. YOU BACK SAFE, MON. TOM'S BOARD, IT WORKIN' OKAY, NOW?
YES. YES, THANK YOU, MR. STONE. IT WORKS FINE.
SO, THESE ALTERNATE WORLDS...
...I MEAN, EXACTLY HOW DIFFERENT ARE THEY FROM OUR OWN?
I DON'T KNOW... BUT REST ASSURED I MEAN TO FIND OUT.
PLEASE EXCUSE ME.
HMM. I WONDER WHAT'S UP WITH PAUL? HE DOESN'T SEEM HIS USUAL SUAVE SELF, SOMEHOW.
HE DIDN'T EVEN MENTION MY NEW HAIR-DO.

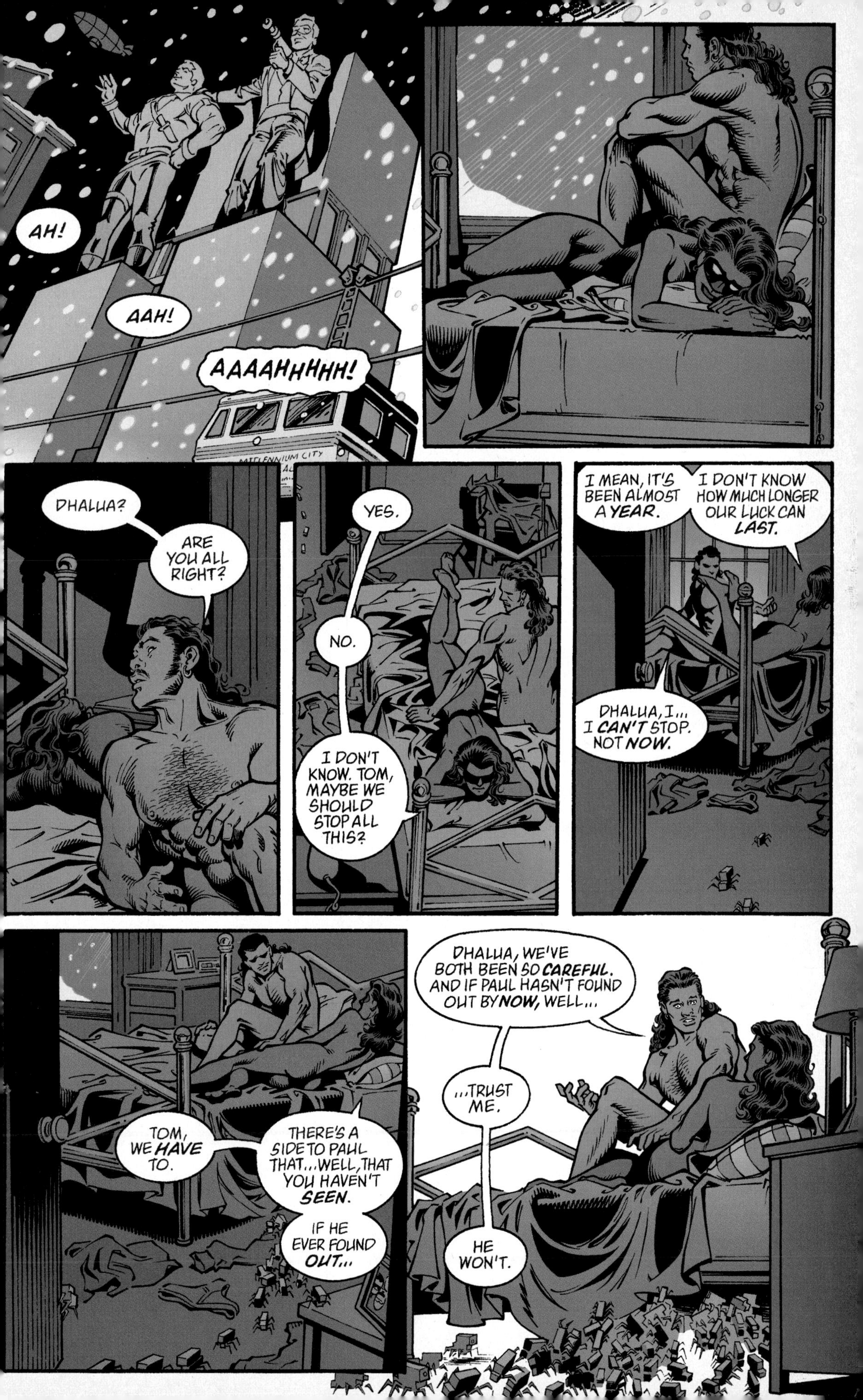
AH!
AAH!
AAAAHHHHH!
MILLENNIUM CITY
DHALUA?
ARE YOU ALL RIGHT?
YES.
NO.
I DON'T KNOW. TOM, MAYBE WE SHOULD STOP ALL THIS?
I MEAN, IT'S BEEN ALMOST A YEAR.
I DON'T KNOW HOW MUCH LONGER OUR LUCK CAN LAST.
DHALUA, I... I CAN'T STOP. NOT NOW.
TOM, WE HAVE TO.
THERE'S A SIDE TO PAUL THAT...WELL, THAT YOU HAVEN'T SEEN.
IF HE EVER FOUND OUT...
DHALUA, WE'VE BOTH BEEN SO CAREFUL. AND IF PAUL HASN'T FOUND OUT BY NOW, WELL...
...TRUST ME.
HE WON'T.

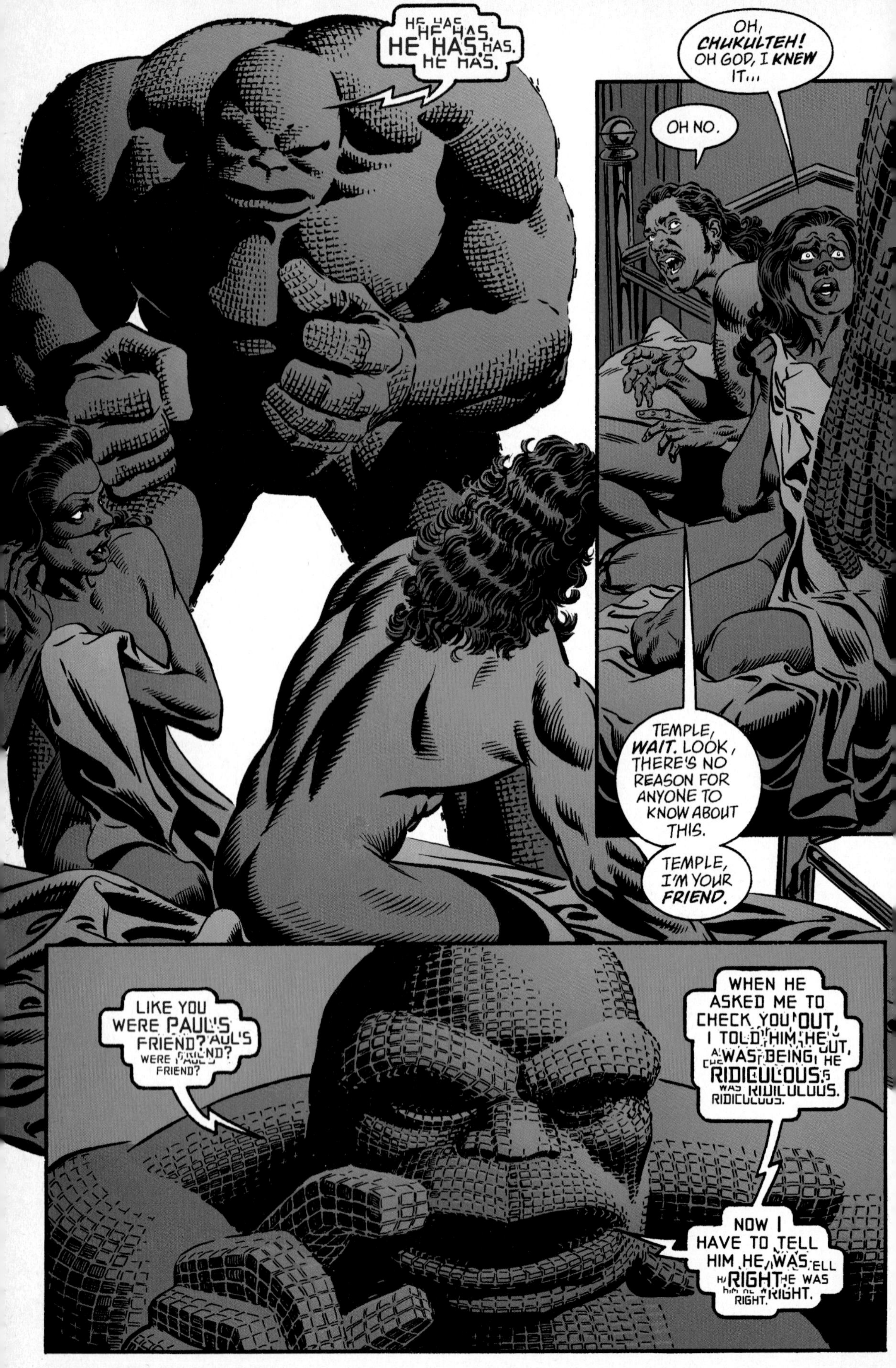
HE HAS. HE HAS. HE HAS.
OH, CHUKULTEH! OH GOD, I KNEW IT...
OH NO.
TEMPLE, WAIT. LOOK, THERE'S NO REASON FOR ANYONE TO KNOW ABOUT THIS.
TEMPLE, I'M YOUR FRIEND.
LIKE YOU WERE PAUL'S FRIEND?
WHEN HE ASKED ME TO CHECK YOU OUT, I TOLD HIM HE WAS BEING RIDICULOUS.
NOW I HAVE TO TELL HIM HE WAS RIGHT.

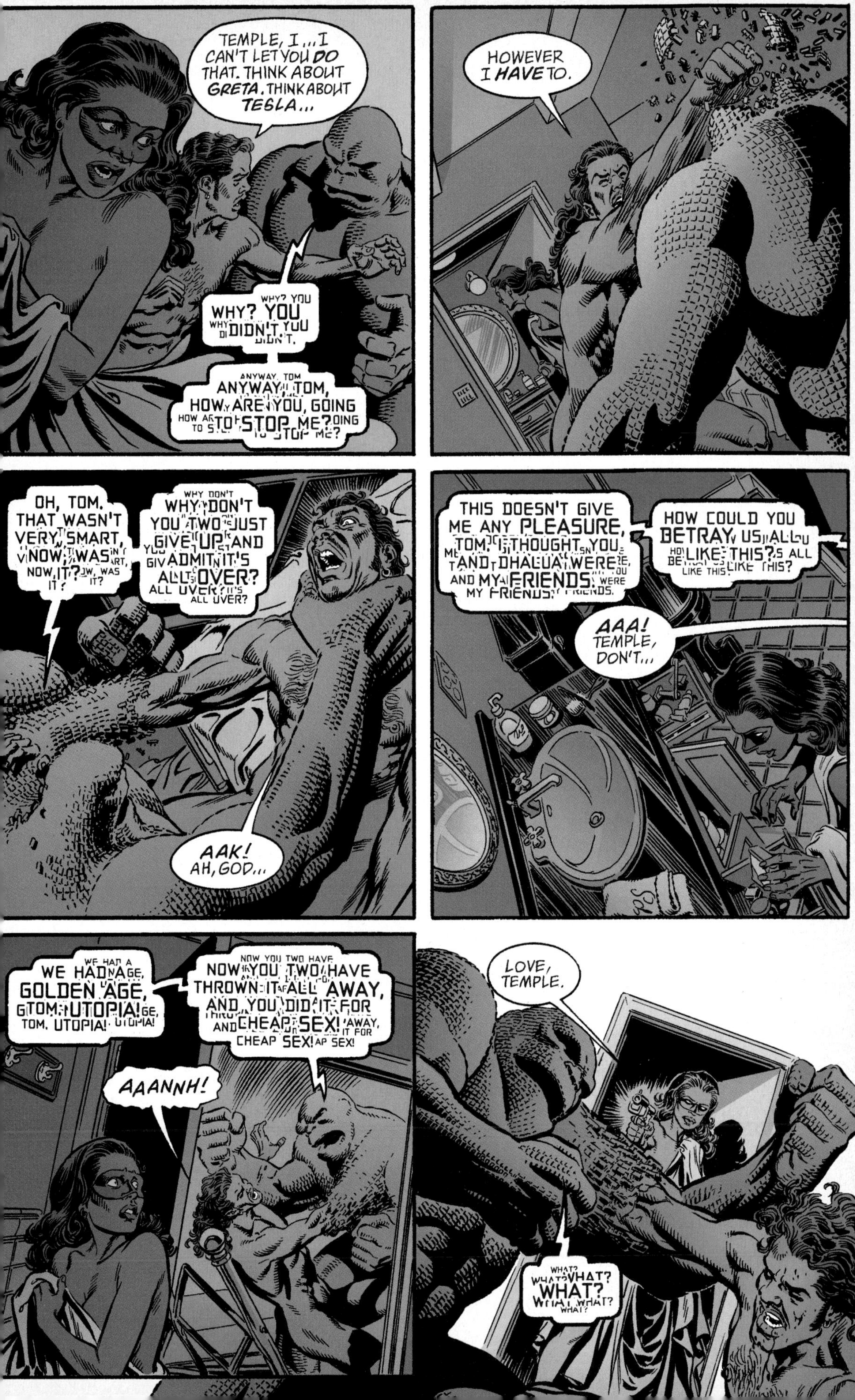
TEMPLE, I...I CAN'T LET YOU DO THAT. THINK ABOUT GRETA. THINK ABOUT TESLA...
WHY? YOU DIDN'T.
ANYWAY, TOM, HOW ARE YOU GOING TO STOP ME?
HOWEVER I HAVE TO.
OH, TOM. THAT WASN'T VERY SMART, NOW, WAS IT?
WHY DON'T YOU TWO JUST GIVE UP AND ADMIT IT'S ALL OVER?
AAK! AH, GOD...
THIS DOESN'T GIVE ME ANY PLEASURE, TOM. I THOUGHT YOU AND DHALUA WERE MY FRIENDS.
HOW COULD YOU BETRAY US ALL LIKE THIS?
AAA! TEMPLE, DON'T...
WE HAD A GOLDEN AGE, TOM. UTOPIA!
NOW YOU TWO HAVE THROWN IT ALL AWAY, AND YOU DID IT FOR CHEAP SEX!
AAANNH!
LOVE, TEMPLE.
WHAT? WHAT?

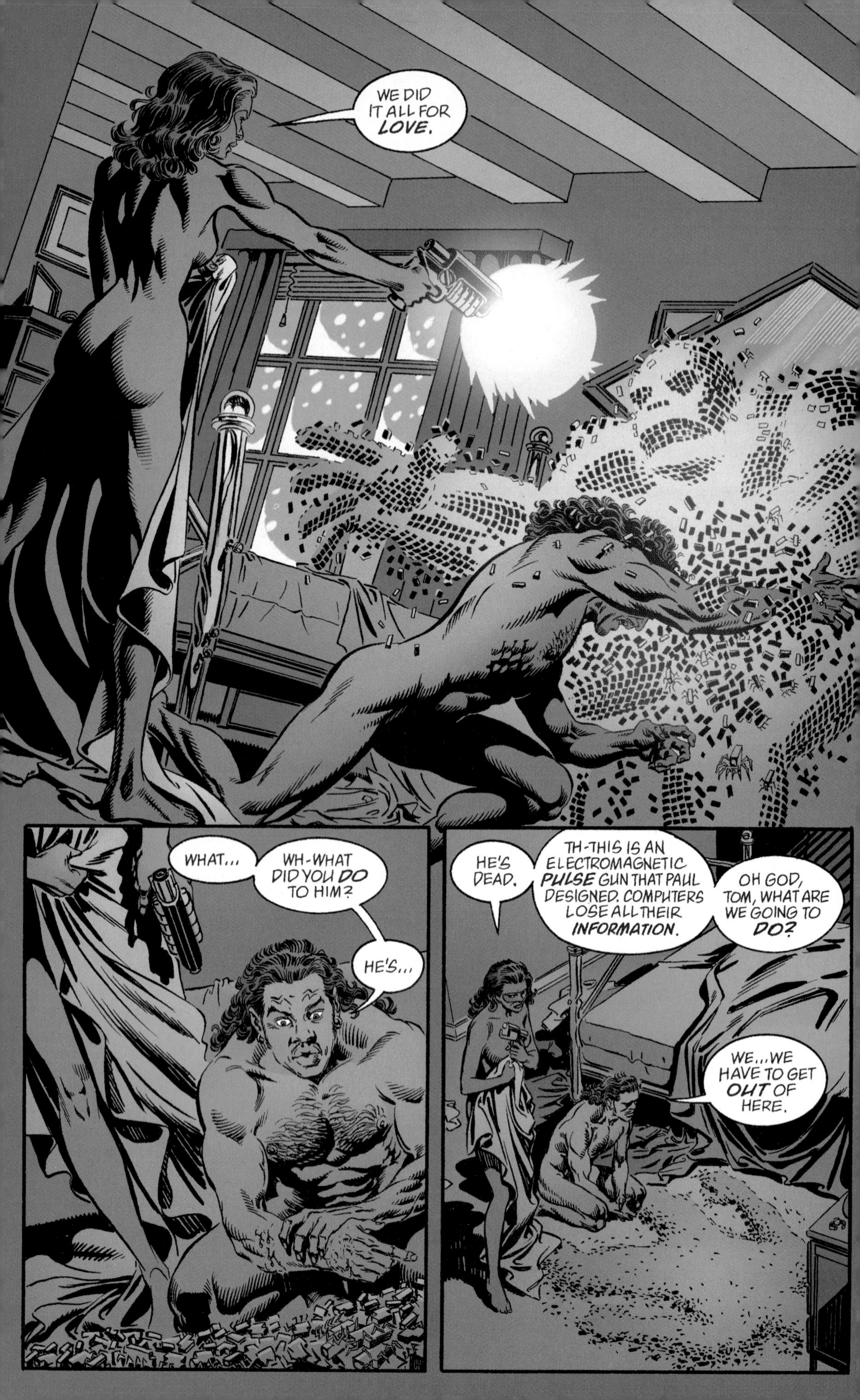
WE DID IT ALL FOR LOVE.
WHAT...
WH-WHAT DID YOU DO TO HIM?
HE'S...
HE'S DEAD.
TH-THIS IS AN ELECTROMAGNETIC PULSE GUN THAT PAUL DESIGNED. COMPUTERS LOSE ALL THEIR INFORMATION.
OH GOD, TOM, WHAT ARE WE GOING TO DO?
WE...WE HAVE TO GET OUT OF HERE.

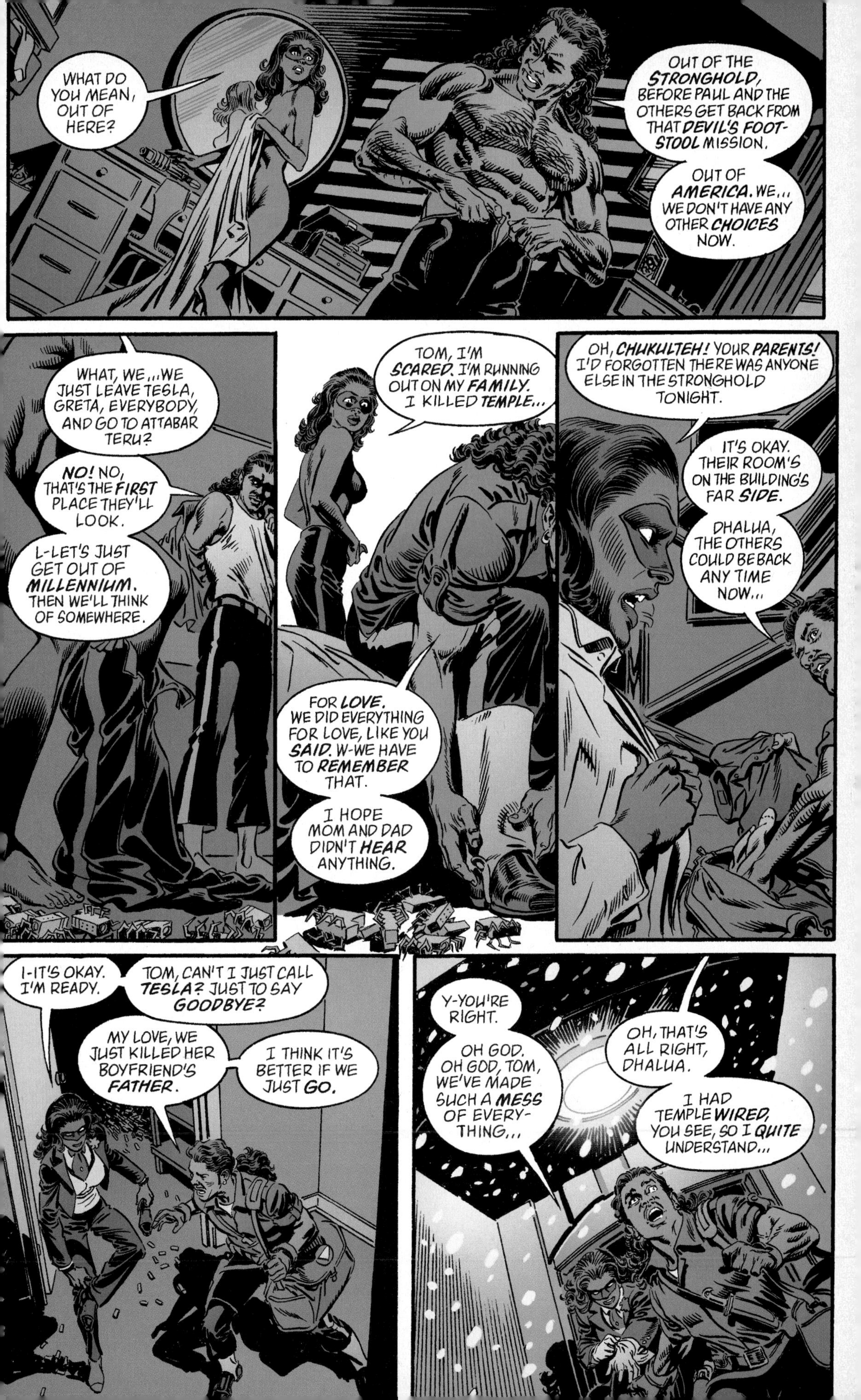
WHAT DO YOU MEAN, OUT OF HERE?
OUT OF THE STRONGHOLD, BEFORE PAUL AND THE OTHERS GET BACK FROM THAT DEVIL'S FOOT-STOOL MISSION.
OUT OF AMERICA. WE... WE DON'T HAVE ANY OTHER CHOICES NOW.
WHAT, WE,...WE JUST LEAVE TESLA, GRETA, EVERYBODY, AND GO TO ATTABAR TERU?
NO! NO, THAT'S THE FIRST PLACE THEY'LL LOOK.
L-LET'S JUST GET OUT OF MILLENNIUM. THEN WE'LL THINK OF SOMEWHERE.
TOM, I'M SCARED. I'M RUNNING OUT ON MY FAMILY. I KILLED TEMPLE...
FOR LOVE. WE DID EVERYTHING FOR LOVE, LIKE YOU SAID. W-WE HAVE TO REMEMBER THAT.
I HOPE MOM AND DAD DIDN'T HEAR ANYTHING.
OH, CHUKULTEH! YOUR PARENTS! I'D FORGOTTEN THERE WAS ANYONE ELSE IN THE STRONGHOLD TONIGHT.
IT'S OKAY. THEIR ROOM'S ON THE BUILDING'S FAR SIDE.
DHALUA, THE OTHERS COULD BE BACK ANY TIME NOW...
I-IT'S OKAY. I'M READY.
TOM, CAN'T I JUST CALL TESLA? JUST TO SAY GOODBYE?
MY LOVE, WE JUST KILLED HER BOYFRIEND'S FATHER.
I THINK IT'S BETTER IF WE JUST GO.
Y-YOU'RE RIGHT.
OH GOD. OH GOD, TOM, WE'VE MADE SUCH A MESS OF EVERY-THING...
OH, THAT'S ALL RIGHT, DHALUA.
I HAD TEMPLE WIRED, YOU SEE, SO I QUITE UNDERSTAND...

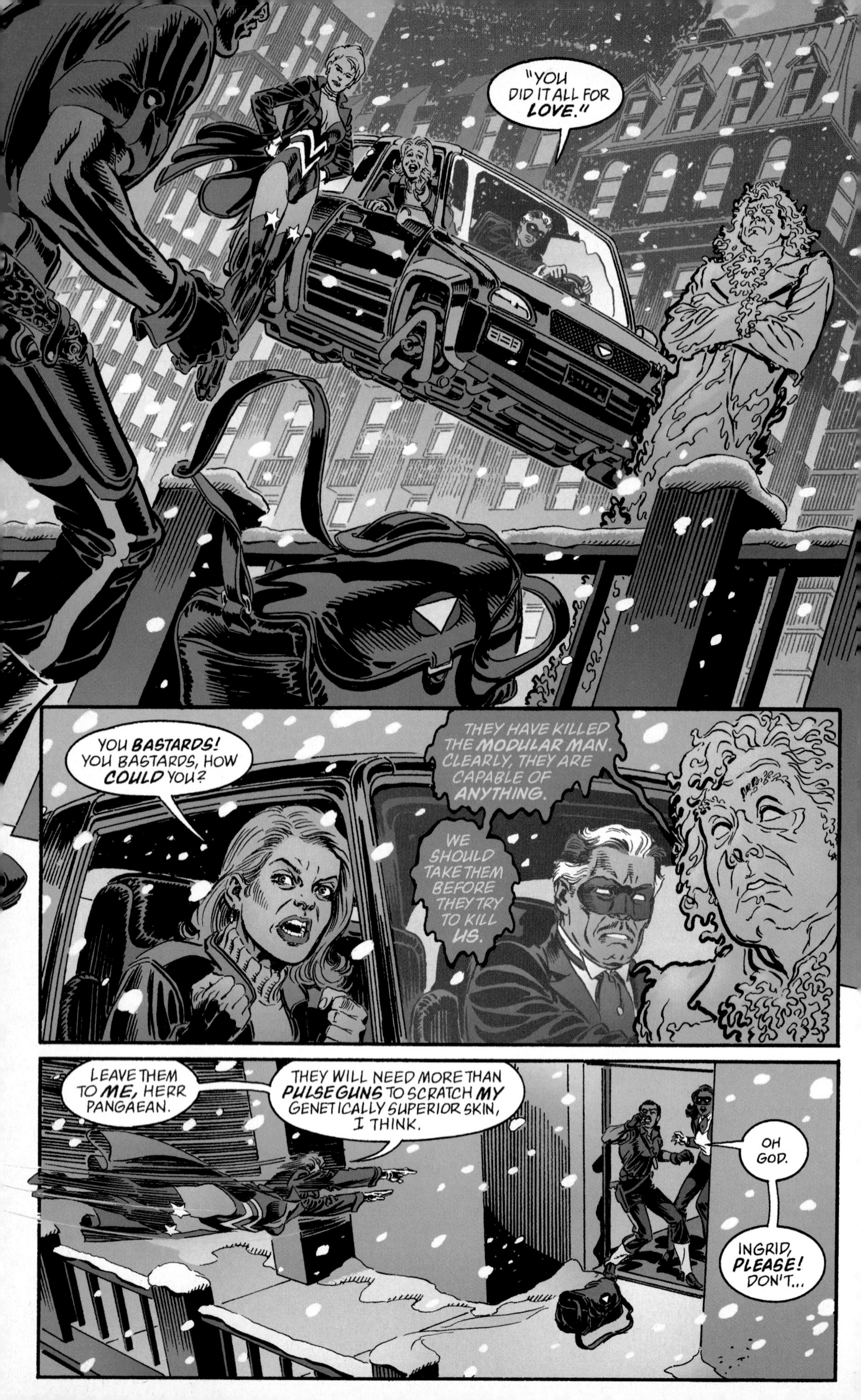
"YOU DID IT ALL FOR LOVE."
YOU BASTARDS! YOU BASTARDS, HOW COULD YOU?
THEY HAVE KILLED THE MODULAR MAN. CLEARLY, THEY ARE CAPABLE OF ANYTHING.
WE SHOULD TAKE THEM BEFORE THEY TRY TO KILL US.
LEAVE THEM TO ME, HERR PANGAEAN.
THEY WILL NEED MORE THAN PULSEGUNS TO SCRATCH MY GENETICALLY SUPERIOR SKIN, I THINK.
OH GOD.
INGRID, PLEASE! DON'T...

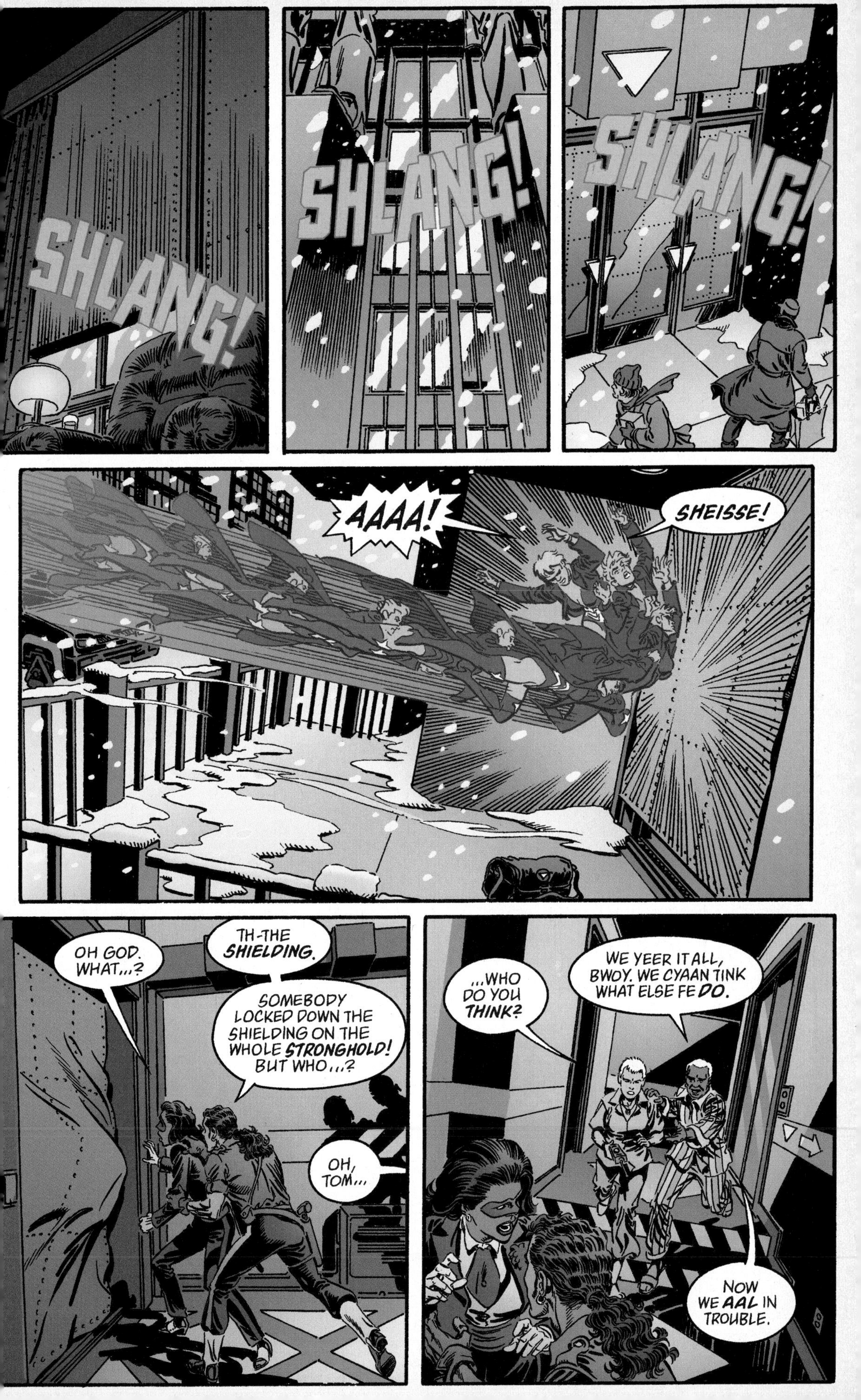
SHLANG!
SHLANG!
SHLANG!
AAAA!
SHEISSE!
OH GOD. WHAT...?
TH-THE SHIELDING.
SOMEBODY LOCKED DOWN THE SHIELDING ON THE WHOLE STRONGHOLD! BUT WHO...?
OH, TOM...
...WHO DO YOU THINK?
WE YEER IT ALL, BWOY. WE CYAAN TINK WHAT ELSE FE DO.
NOW WE AAL IN TROUBLE.

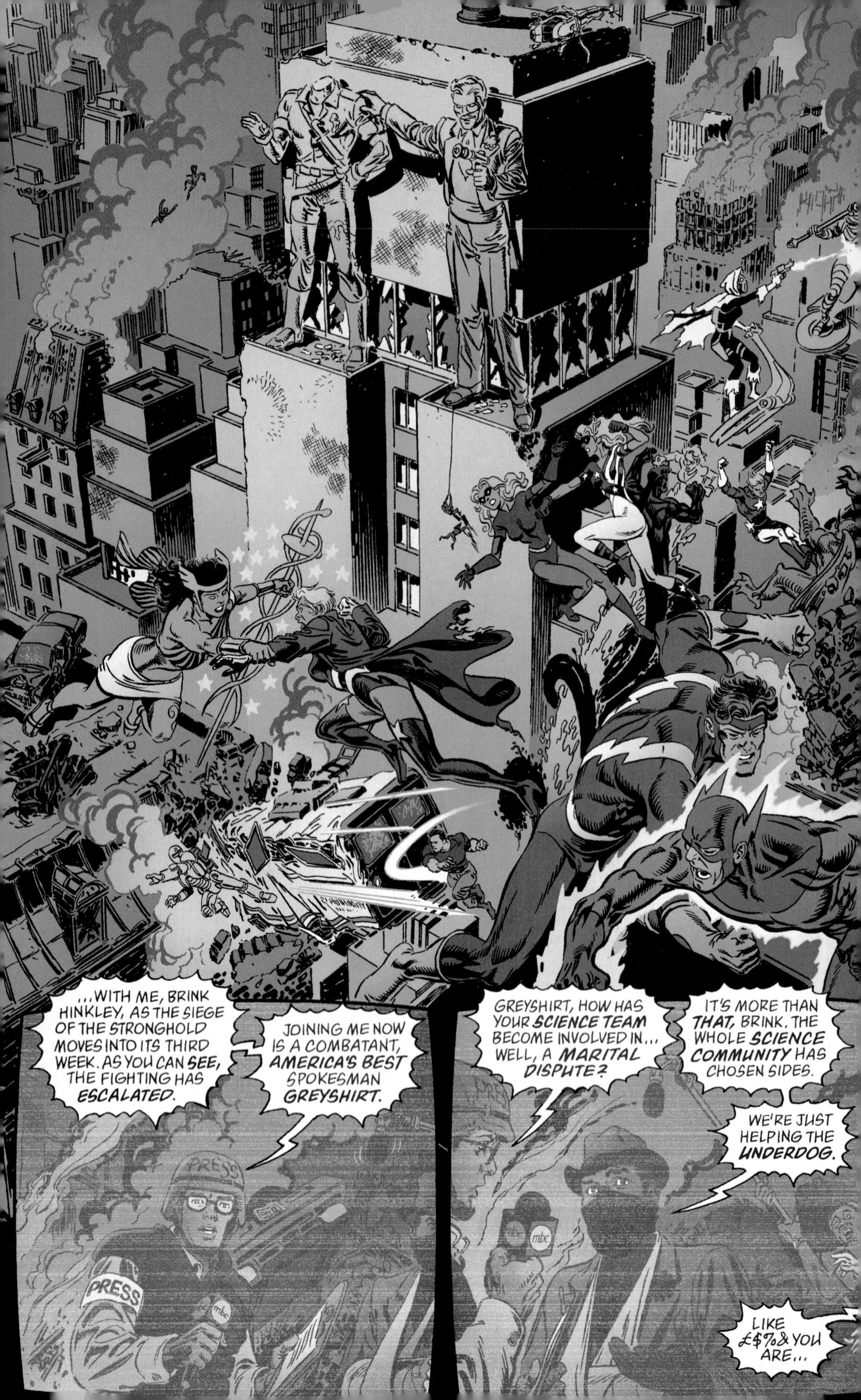
...WITH ME, BRINK HINKLEY, AS THE SIEGE OF THE STRONGHOLD MOVES INTO ITS THIRD WEEK. AS YOU CAN **SEE**, THE FIGHTING HAS **ESCALATED**.
JOINING ME NOW IS A COMBATANT, **AMERICA'S BEST** SPOKESMAN **GREYSHIRT**.
GREYSHIRT, HOW HAS YOUR **SCIENCE TEAM** BECOME INVOLVED IN... WELL, A **MARITAL DISPUTE**?
IT'S MORE THAN **THAT**, BRINK. THE WHOLE **SCIENCE COMMUNITY** HAS CHOSEN SIDES.
WE'RE JUST HELPING THE **UNDERDOG**.
LIKE £$%& YOU ARE...
PRESS
PRESS

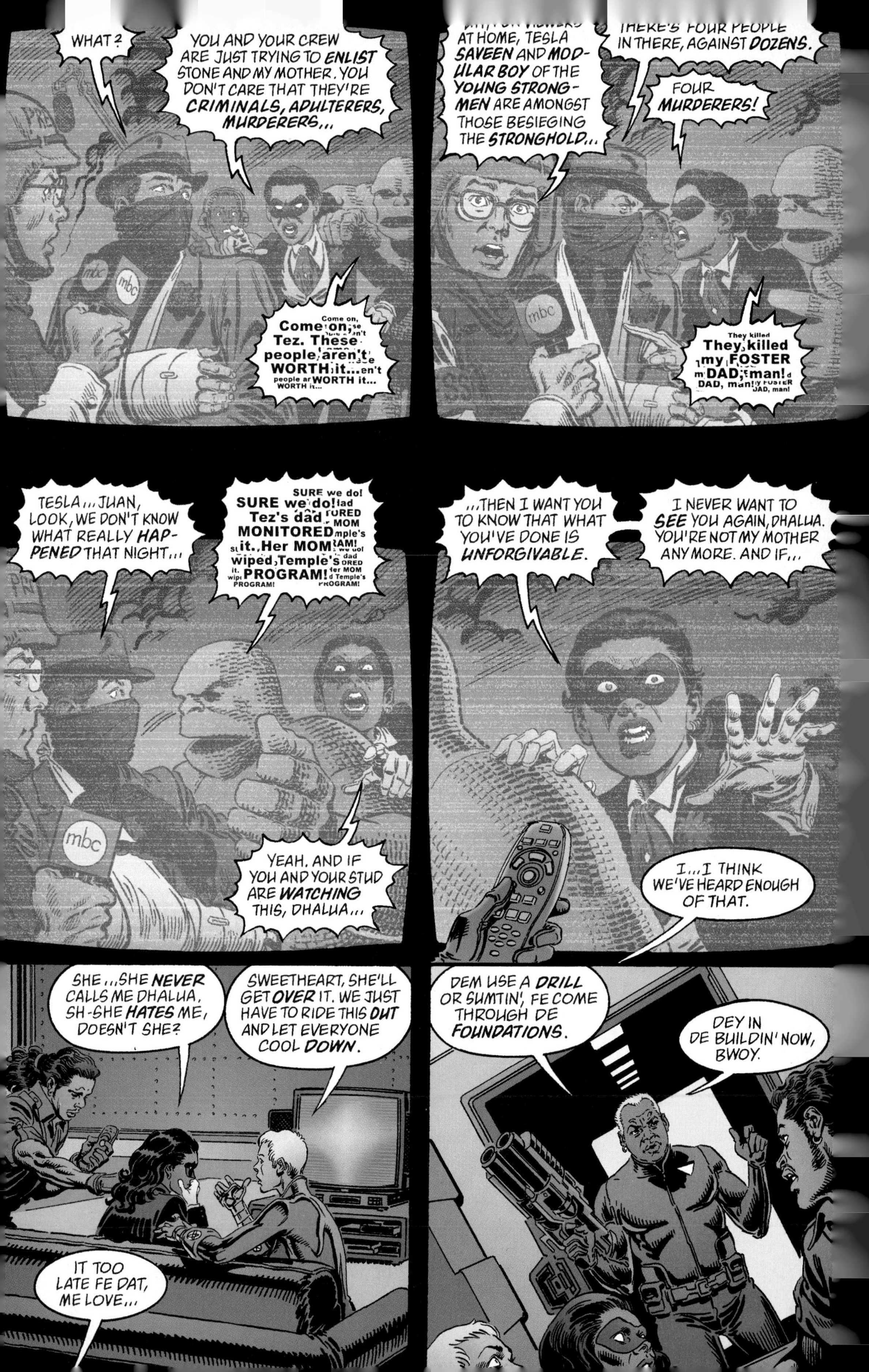
WHAT?
YOU AND YOUR CREW ARE JUST TRYING TO ENLIST STONE AND MY MOTHER. YOU DON'T CARE THAT THEY'RE CRIMINALS, ADULTERERS, MURDERERS...
Come on, Tez. These people aren't WORTH it...
AT HOME, TESLA SAVEEN AND MODULAR BOY OF THE YOUNG STRONGMEN ARE AMONGST THOSE BESIEGING THE STRONGHOLD...
THERE'S FOUR PEOPLE IN THERE, AGAINST DOZENS.
FOUR MURDERERS!
They killed my FOSTER DAD, man!
TESLA... JUAN, LOOK, WE DON'T KNOW WHAT REALLY HAPPENED THAT NIGHT...
SURE we do! Tez's dad MONITORED it. Her MOM wiped Temple's PROGRAM!
YEAH. AND IF YOU AND YOUR STUD ARE WATCHING THIS, DHALUA...
...THEN I WANT YOU TO KNOW THAT WHAT YOU'VE DONE IS UNFORGIVABLE.
I NEVER WANT TO SEE YOU AGAIN, DHALUA. YOU'RE NOT MY MOTHER ANYMORE. AND IF...
I... I THINK WE'VE HEARD ENOUGH OF THAT.
SHE... SHE NEVER CALLS ME DHALUA. SH-SHE HATES ME, DOESN'T SHE?
SWEETHEART, SHE'LL GET OVER IT. WE JUST HAVE TO RIDE THIS OUT AND LET EVERYONE COOL DOWN.
IT TOO LATE FE DAT, ME LOVE...
DEM USE A DRILL OR SUMTIN', FE COME THROUGH DE FOUNDATIONS.
DEY IN DE BUILDIN' NOW, BWOY.

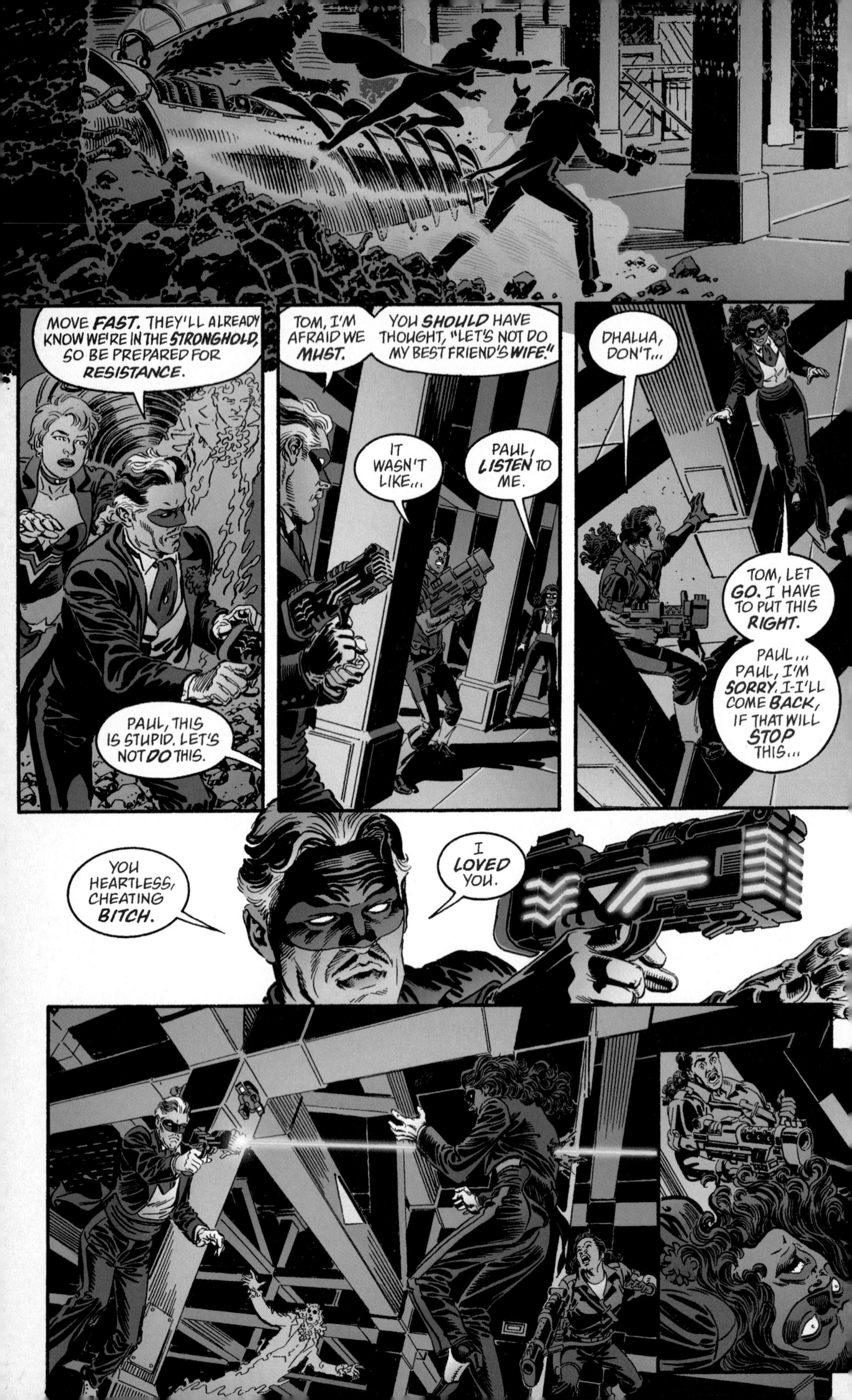
MOVE FAST. THEY'LL ALREADY KNOW WE'RE IN THE STRONGHOLD, SO BE PREPARED FOR RESISTANCE.
PAUL, THIS IS STUPID. LET'S NOT DO THIS.
TOM, I'M AFRAID WE MUST.
YOU SHOULD HAVE THOUGHT, "LET'S NOT DO MY BEST FRIEND'S WIFE."
IT WASN'T LIKE...
PAUL, LISTEN TO ME.
DHALUA, DON'T...
TOM, LET GO. I HAVE TO PUT THIS RIGHT.
PAUL... PAUL, I'M SORRY. I-I'LL COME BACK, IF THAT WILL STOP THIS...
YOU HEARTLESS, CHEATING BITCH.
I LOVED YOU.

YOU *KILLED* HER! SAVEEN, YOU BASTARD, YOU KILLED *DHALUA!*

RRAAAAAAGH!!

OH GOD, TOMAS. THEY'RE ALL GOING TO *KILL* EACH OTHER!

THIS IS ALL MY FAULT.

SUSAN, ME LOVE, WHAT YOU SAYIN'? YOU DONE NUTHIN' WRONG, WOMAN.

YES I HAVE. I ALTERED *TIME.*

I ALTERED TIME AND DIDN'T *TELL* ANYONE.

ALTERED *TIME?*

YES, USING FINGEL'S *MACHINE.* I--I WANTED A LIFE WITH *YOU,* RATHER THAN AN EARLY DEATH WITH *SINCLAIR.*

BUT EVERYTHING'S GONE *WRONG...*

...AND WITH FINGEL'S TIME EQUIPMENT *DESTROYED,* THERE'S NO WAY TO PUT IT *RIGHT.*

N-NOT UNLESS...

WHAT IS IT, SUSAN? WHAT YOU PLANNIN', NOW?

LEVEL 5

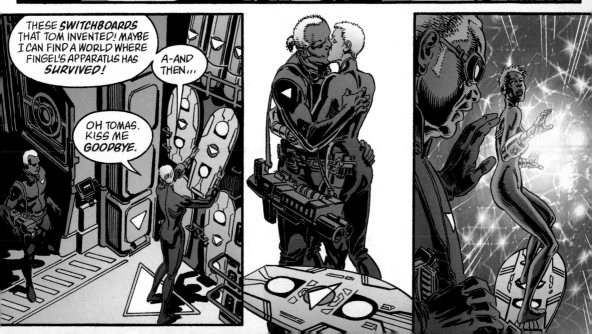

THESE *SWITCHBOARDS* THAT TOM INVENTED! MAYBE I CAN FIND A WORLD WHERE FINGEL'S APPARATUS HAS *SURVIVED!*

A-AND THEN...

OH TOMAS. KISS ME *GOODBYE.*

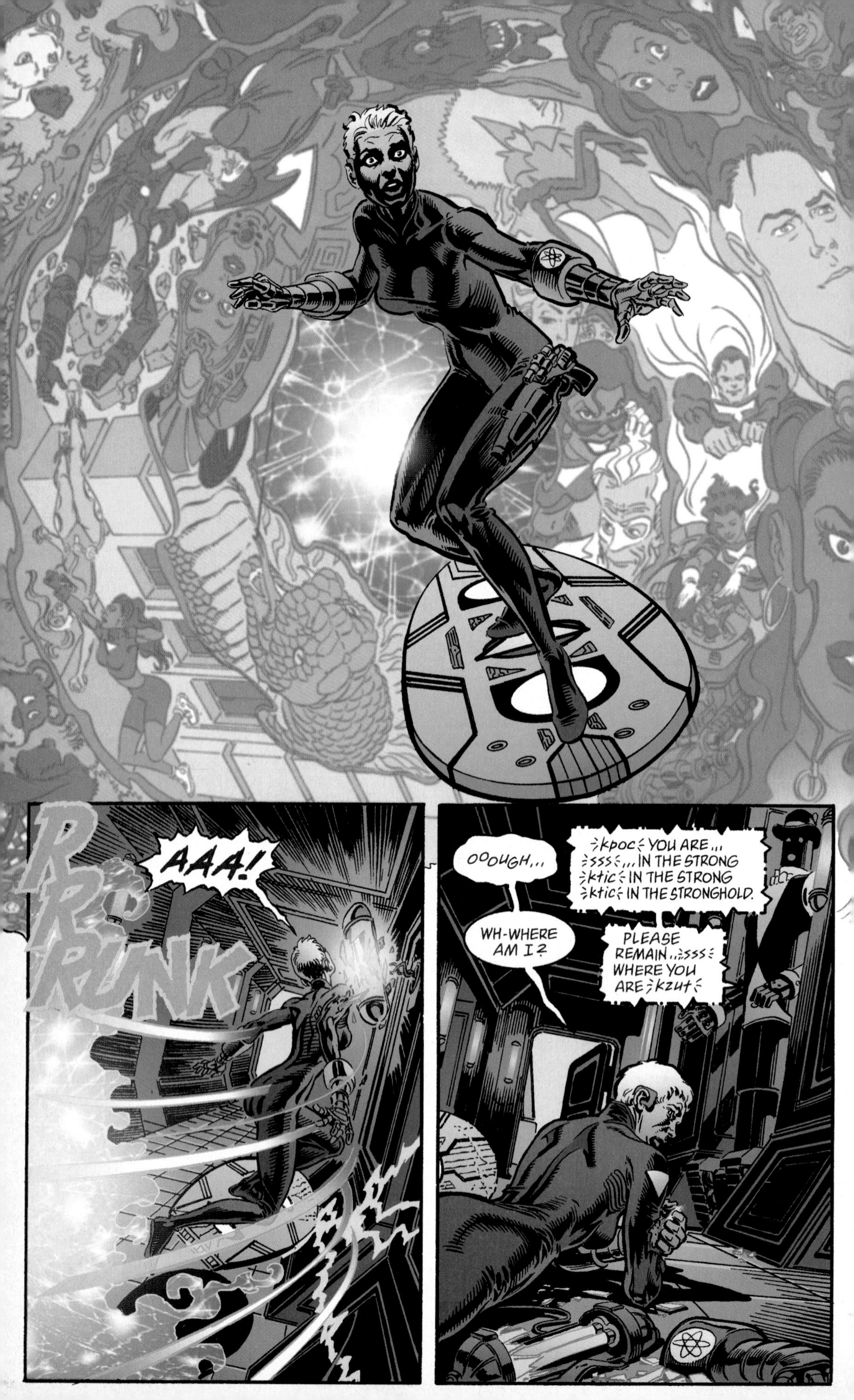
R-RUNK
AAA!
OOOUGH...
ᛃkpocᛃ YOU ARE... ᛃsssᛃ... IN THE STRONG ᛃkticᛃ IN THE STRONG ᛃkticᛃ IN THE STRONGHOLD.
WH-WHERE AM I?
PLEASE REMAIN... ᛃsssᛃ WHERE YOU ARE ᛃkzutᛃ

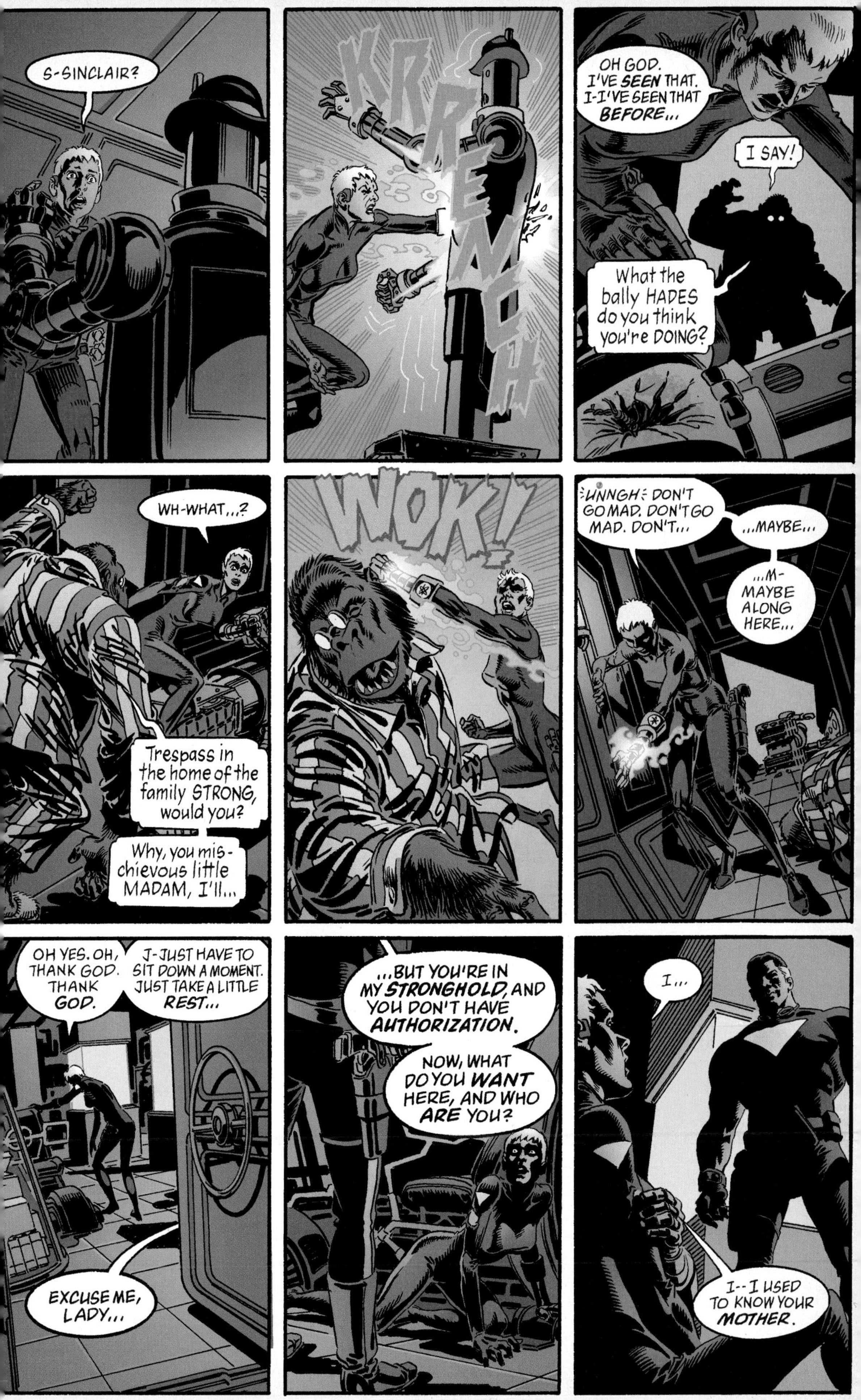
S-SINCLAIR?
KRRRENCHH
OH GOD. I'VE SEEN THAT. I-I'VE SEEN THAT BEFORE...
I SAY!
What the bally HADES do you think you're DOING?
WH-WHAT...?
Trespass in the home of the family STRONG, would you?
Why, you mis-chievous little MADAM, I'll...
WOK!
UNNGH: DON'T GO MAD. DON'T GO MAD. DON'T...
...MAYBE...
...M-MAYBE ALONG HERE...
OH YES. OH, THANK GOD. THANK GOD.
J-JUST HAVE TO SIT DOWN A MOMENT. JUST TAKE A LITTLE REST...
EXCUSE ME, LADY...
...BUT YOU'RE IN MY STRONGHOLD, AND YOU DON'T HAVE AUTHORIZATION.
NOW, WHAT DO YOU WANT HERE, AND WHO ARE YOU?
I...
I-- I USED TO KNOW YOUR MOTHER.

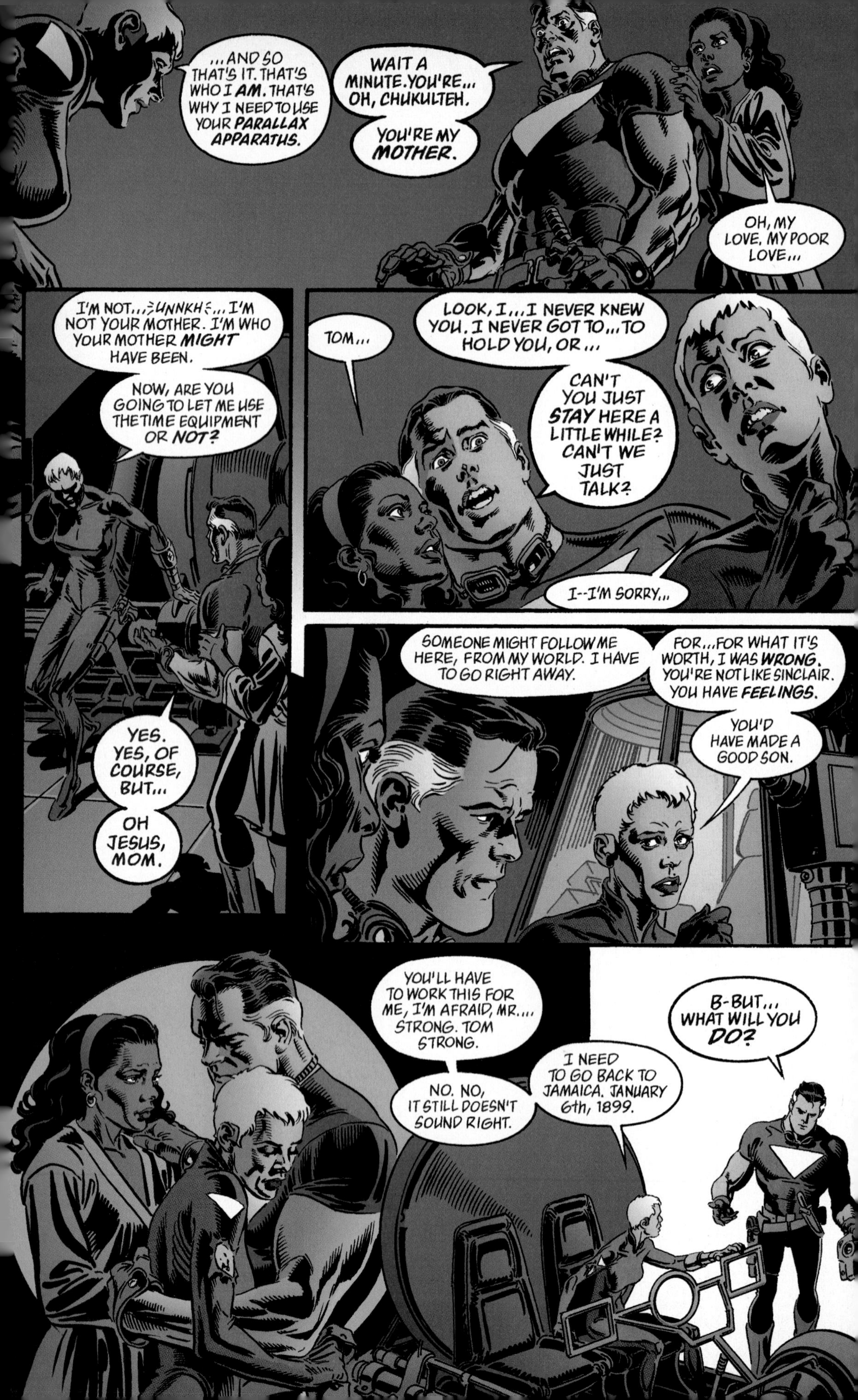
...AND SO THAT'S IT. THAT'S WHO I AM. THAT'S WHY I NEED TO USE YOUR PARALLAX APPARATUS.
WAIT A MINUTE. YOU'RE... OH, CHUKULTEH.
YOU'RE MY MOTHER.
OH, MY LOVE, MY POOR LOVE...
I'M NOT... UNNKH ... I'M NOT YOUR MOTHER. I'M WHO YOUR MOTHER MIGHT HAVE BEEN.
NOW, ARE YOU GOING TO LET ME USE THE TIME EQUIPMENT OR NOT?
YES. YES, OF COURSE, BUT...
OH JESUS, MOM.
TOM...
LOOK, I... I NEVER KNEW YOU. I NEVER GOT TO... TO HOLD YOU, OR...
CAN'T YOU JUST STAY HERE A LITTLE WHILE? CAN'T WE JUST TALK?
I--I'M SORRY...
SOMEONE MIGHT FOLLOW ME HERE, FROM MY WORLD. I HAVE TO GO RIGHT AWAY.
FOR... FOR WHAT IT'S WORTH, I WAS WRONG. YOU'RE NOT LIKE SINCLAIR. YOU HAVE FEELINGS.
YOU'D HAVE MADE A GOOD SON.
YOU'LL HAVE TO WORK THIS FOR ME, I'M AFRAID, MR.... STRONG. TOM STRONG.
NO. NO, IT STILL DOESN'T SOUND RIGHT.
I NEED TO GO BACK TO JAMAICA. JANUARY 6th, 1899.
B-BUT... WHAT WILL YOU DO?

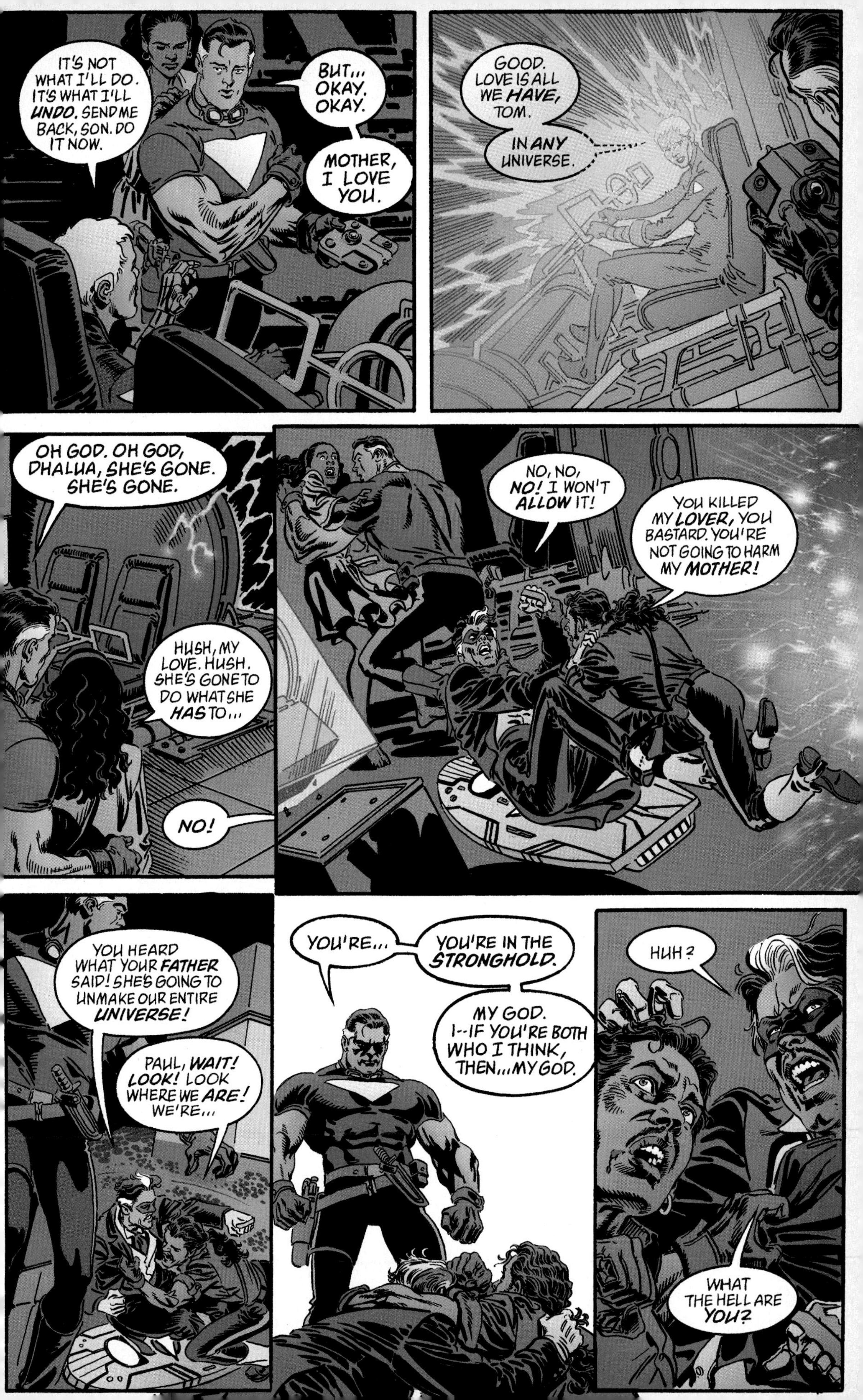
IT'S NOT WHAT I'LL DO. IT'S WHAT I'LL UNDO. SEND ME BACK, SON. DO IT NOW.
BUT... OKAY. OKAY.
MOTHER, I LOVE YOU.
GOOD. LOVE IS ALL WE HAVE, TOM.
IN ANY UNIVERSE.
OH GOD. OH GOD, DHALUA, SHE'S GONE. SHE'S GONE.
HUSH, MY LOVE. HUSH. SHE'S GONE TO DO WHAT SHE HAS TO...
NO!
NO, NO, NO! I WON'T ALLOW IT!
YOU KILLED MY LOVER, YOU BASTARD. YOU'RE NOT GOING TO HARM MY MOTHER!
YOU HEARD WHAT YOUR FATHER SAID! SHE'S GOING TO UNMAKE OUR ENTIRE UNIVERSE!
PAUL, WAIT! LOOK! LOOK WHERE WE ARE! WE'RE...
YOU'RE...
YOU'RE IN THE STRONGHOLD.
MY GOD. I--IF YOU'RE BOTH WHO I THINK, THEN... MY GOD.
HUH?
WHAT THE HELL ARE YOU?

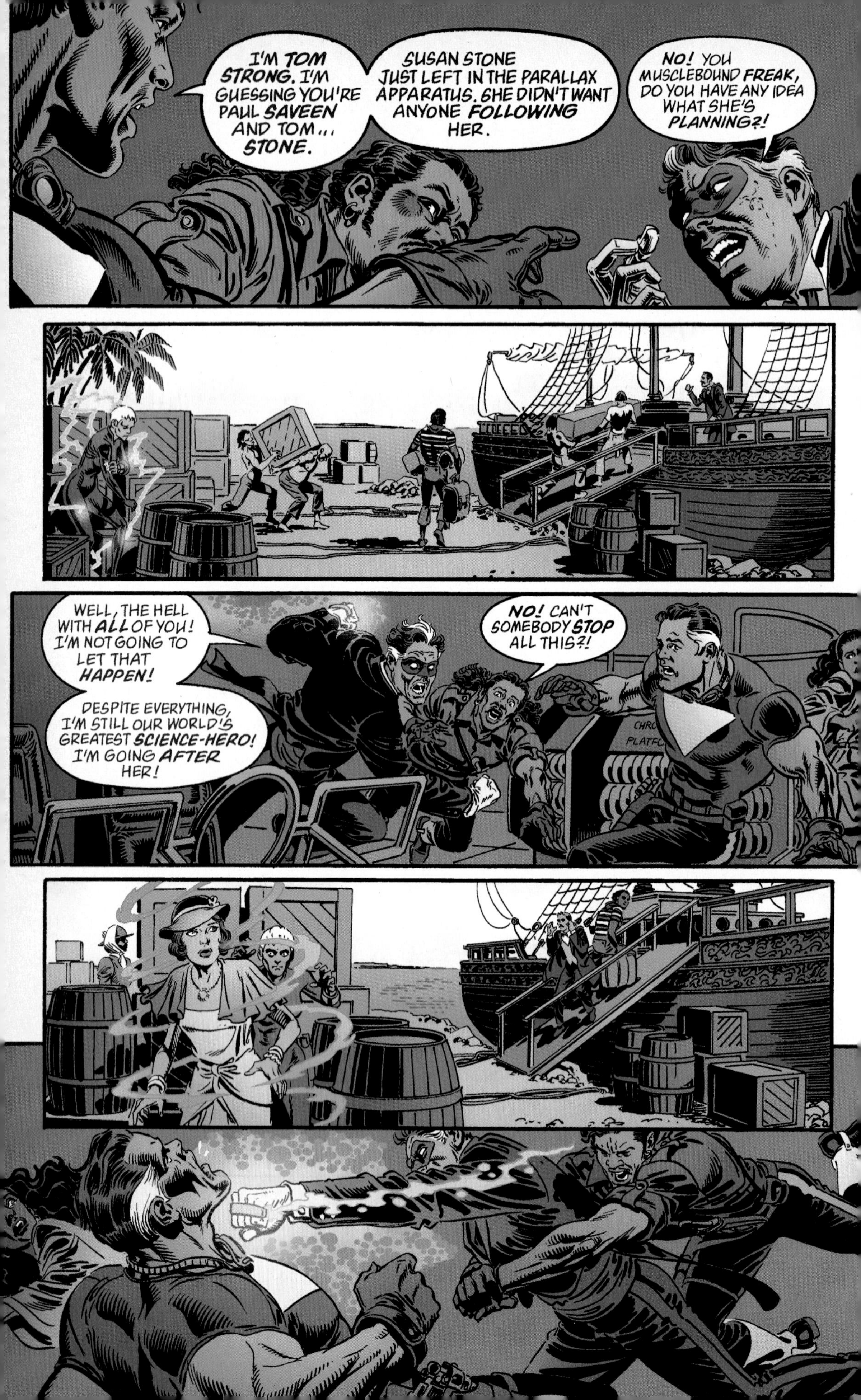
I'M TOM STRONG. I'M GUESSING YOU'RE PAUL SAVEEN AND TOM... STONE.
SUSAN STONE JUST LEFT IN THE PARALLAX APPARATUS. SHE DIDN'T WANT ANYONE FOLLOWING HER.
NO! YOU MUSCLEBOUND FREAK, DO YOU HAVE ANY IDEA WHAT SHE'S PLANNING?!
WELL, THE HELL WITH ALL OF YOU! I'M NOT GOING TO LET THAT HAPPEN!
DESPITE EVERYTHING, I'M STILL OUR WORLD'S GREATEST SCIENCE-HERO! I'M GOING AFTER HER!
NO! CAN'T SOMEBODY STOP ALL THIS?!

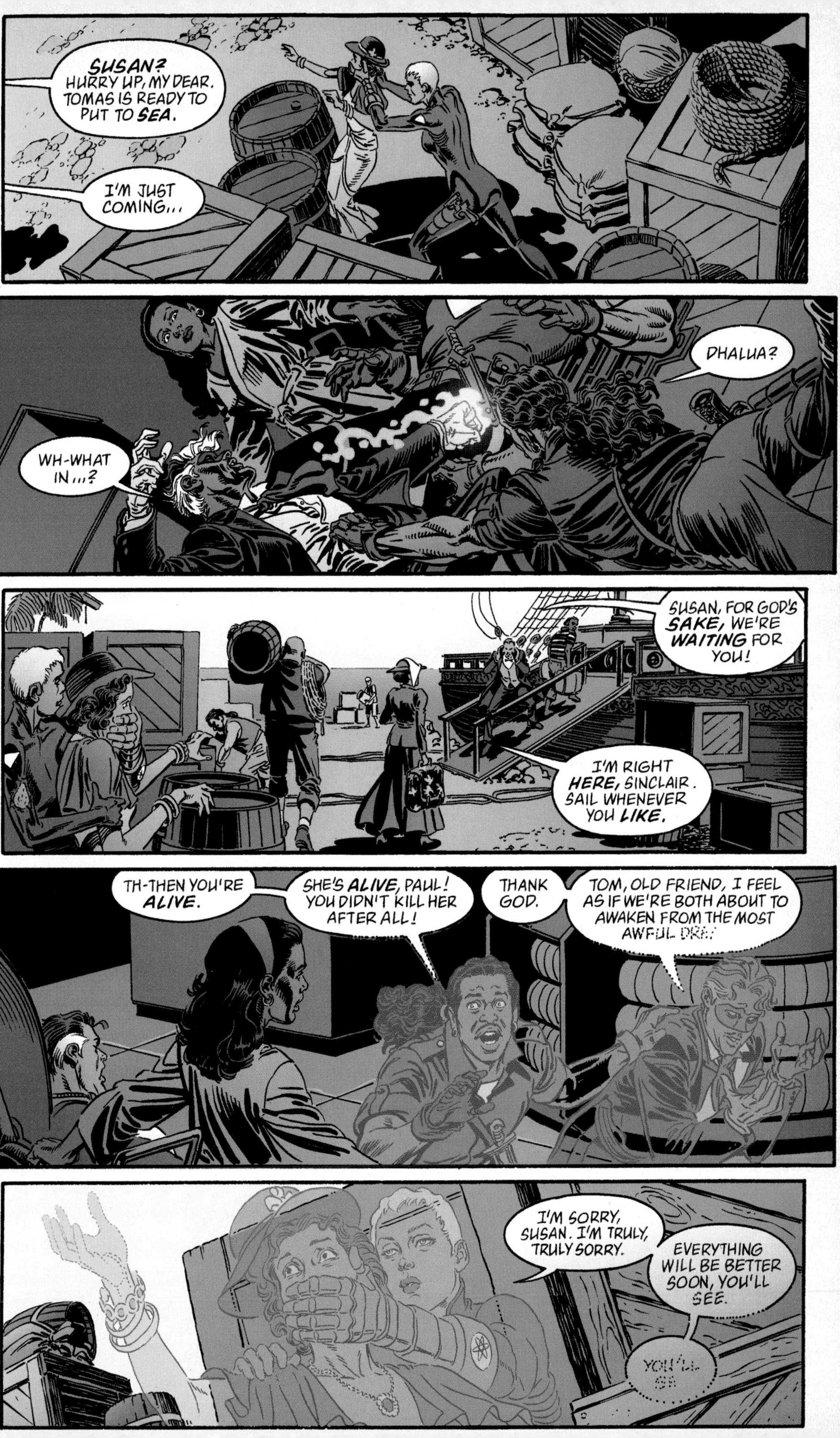
SUSAN? HURRY UP, MY DEAR. TOMAS IS READY TO PUT TO SEA.
I'M JUST COMING...
DHALUA?
WH-WHAT IN...?
SUSAN, FOR GOD'S SAKE, WE'RE WAITING FOR YOU!
I'M RIGHT HERE, SINCLAIR. SAIL WHENEVER YOU LIKE.
TH-THEN YOU'RE ALIVE.
SHE'S ALIVE, PAUL! YOU DIDN'T KILL HER AFTER ALL!
THANK GOD.
TOM, OLD FRIEND, I FEEL AS IF WE'RE BOTH ABOUT TO AWAKEN FROM THE MOST AWFUL
I'M SORRY, SUSAN. I'M TRULY, TRULY SORRY.
EVERYTHING WILL BE BETTER SOON, YOU'LL SEE.
YOU'LL

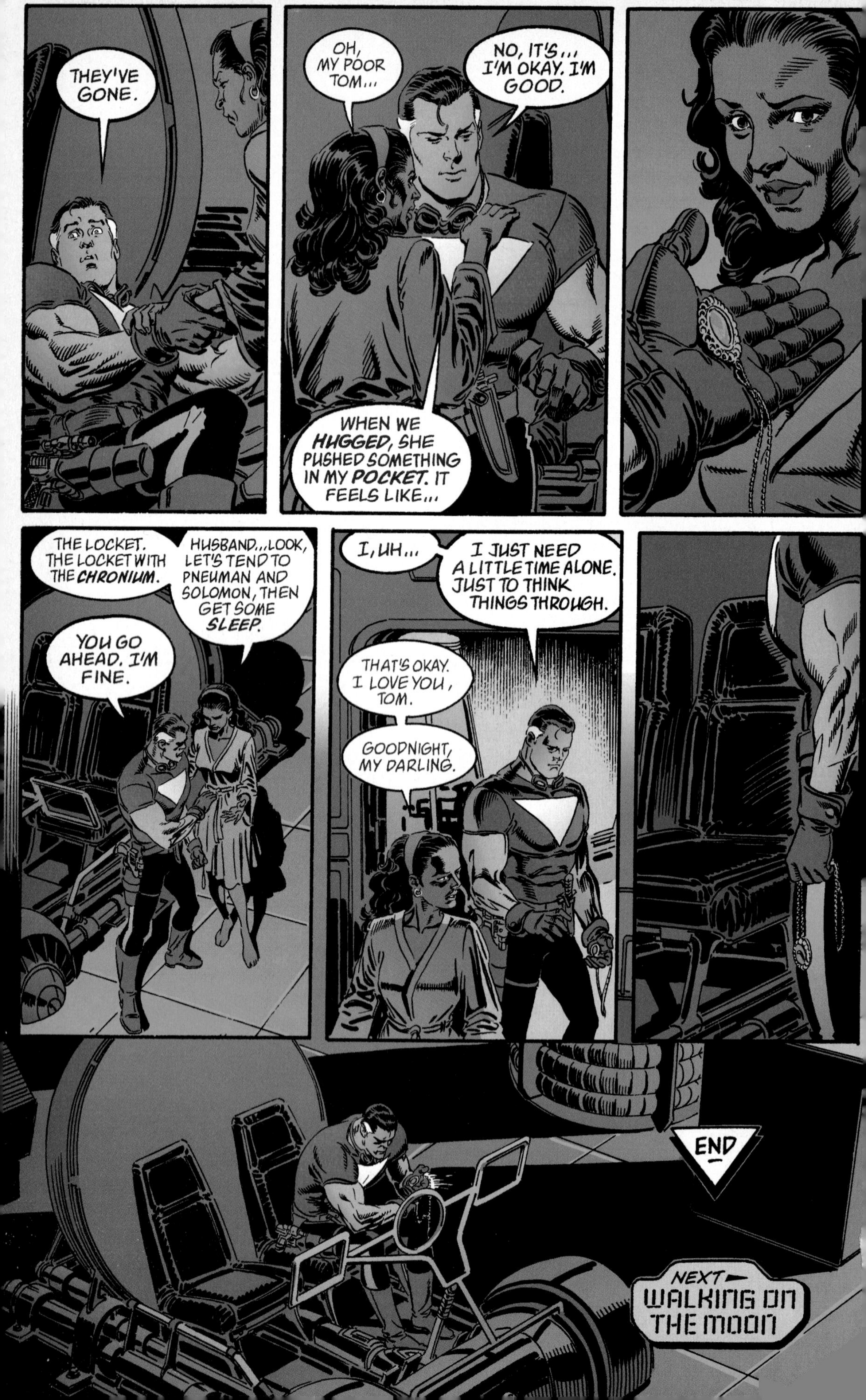
THEY'VE GONE.
OH, MY POOR TOM...
NO, IT'S... I'M OKAY. I'M GOOD.
WHEN WE HUGGED, SHE PUSHED SOMETHING IN MY POCKET. IT FEELS LIKE...
THE LOCKET. THE LOCKET WITH THE CHRONIUM.
HUSBAND... LOOK, LET'S TEND TO PNEUMAN AND SOLOMON, THEN GET SOME SLEEP.
YOU GO AHEAD. I'M FINE.
I, UH...
I JUST NEED A LITTLE TIME ALONE. JUST TO THINK THINGS THROUGH.
THAT'S OKAY. I LOVE YOU, TOM.
GOODNIGHT, MY DARLING.
END
NEXT
WALKING ON THE MOON

# CHAPTER FOUR

**In which Svetlana X asks Tom for help,
Tesla and Val get carried away,
and the Moon reveals a secret.**

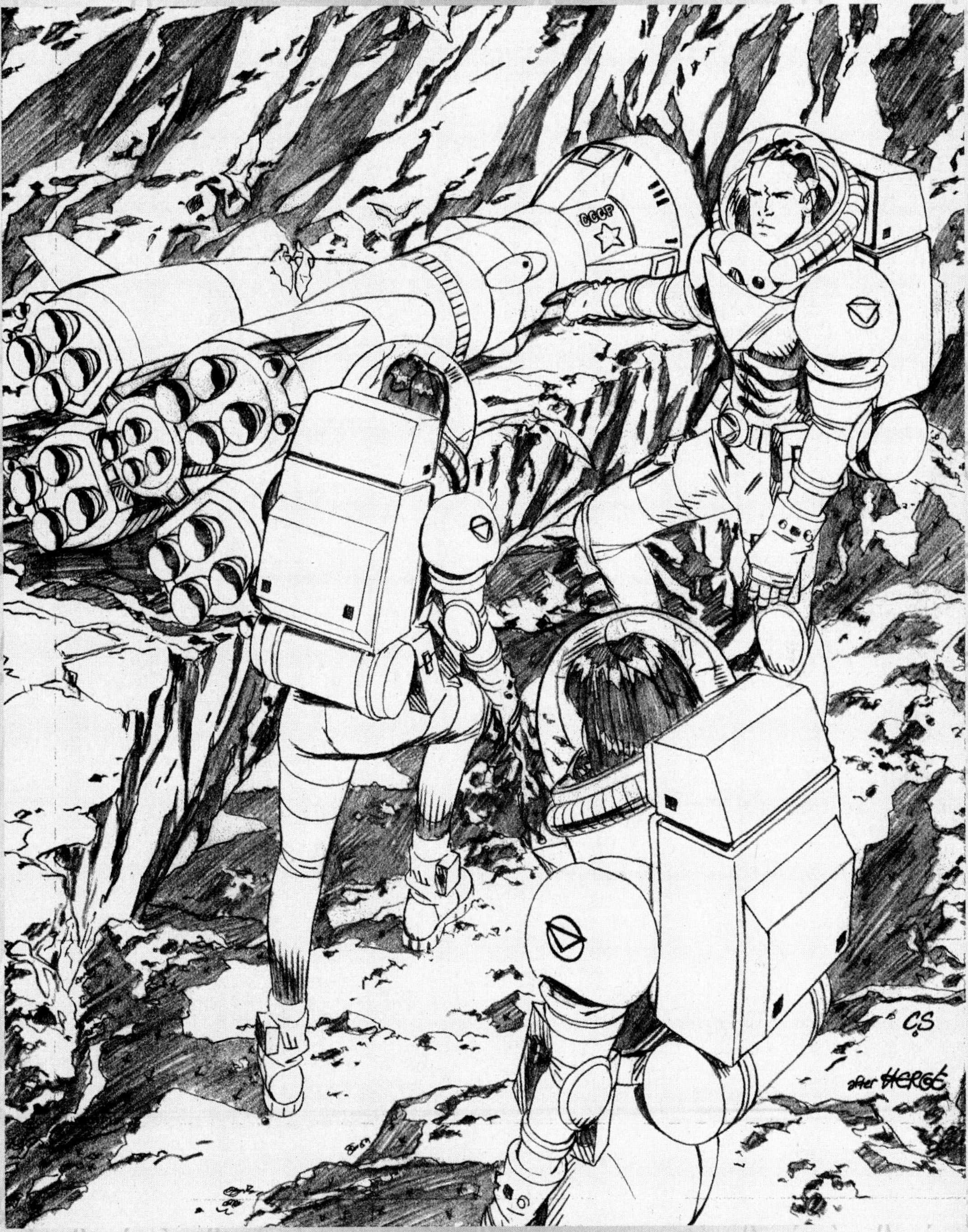
CCCP
CS
after HERGÉ

**Cover art:
Chris Sprouse and Karl Story**

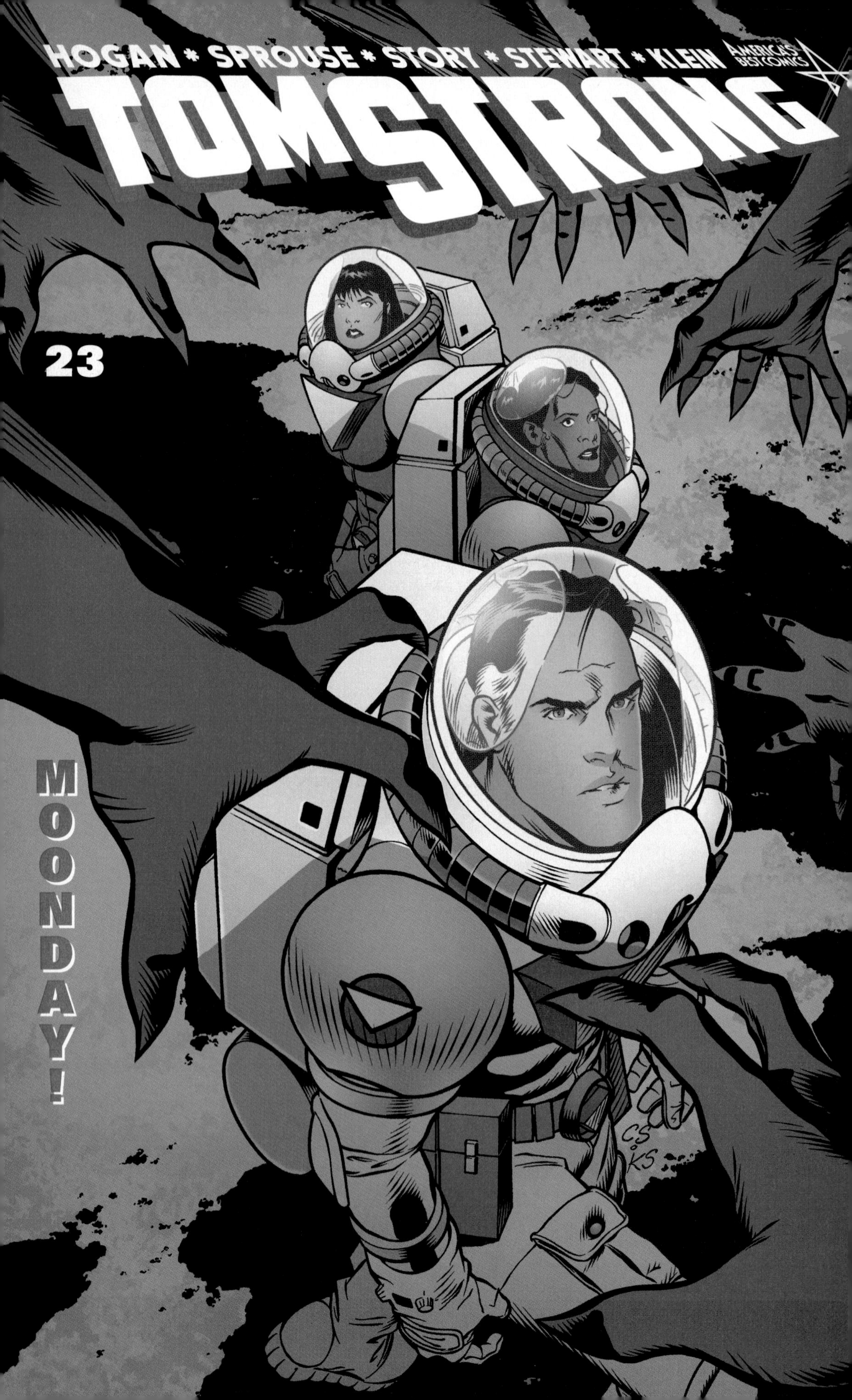
HOGAN * SPROUSE * STORY * STEWART * KLEIN
AMERICA'S BEST COMICS
TOM STRONG
23
MOONDAY!
CS
KS

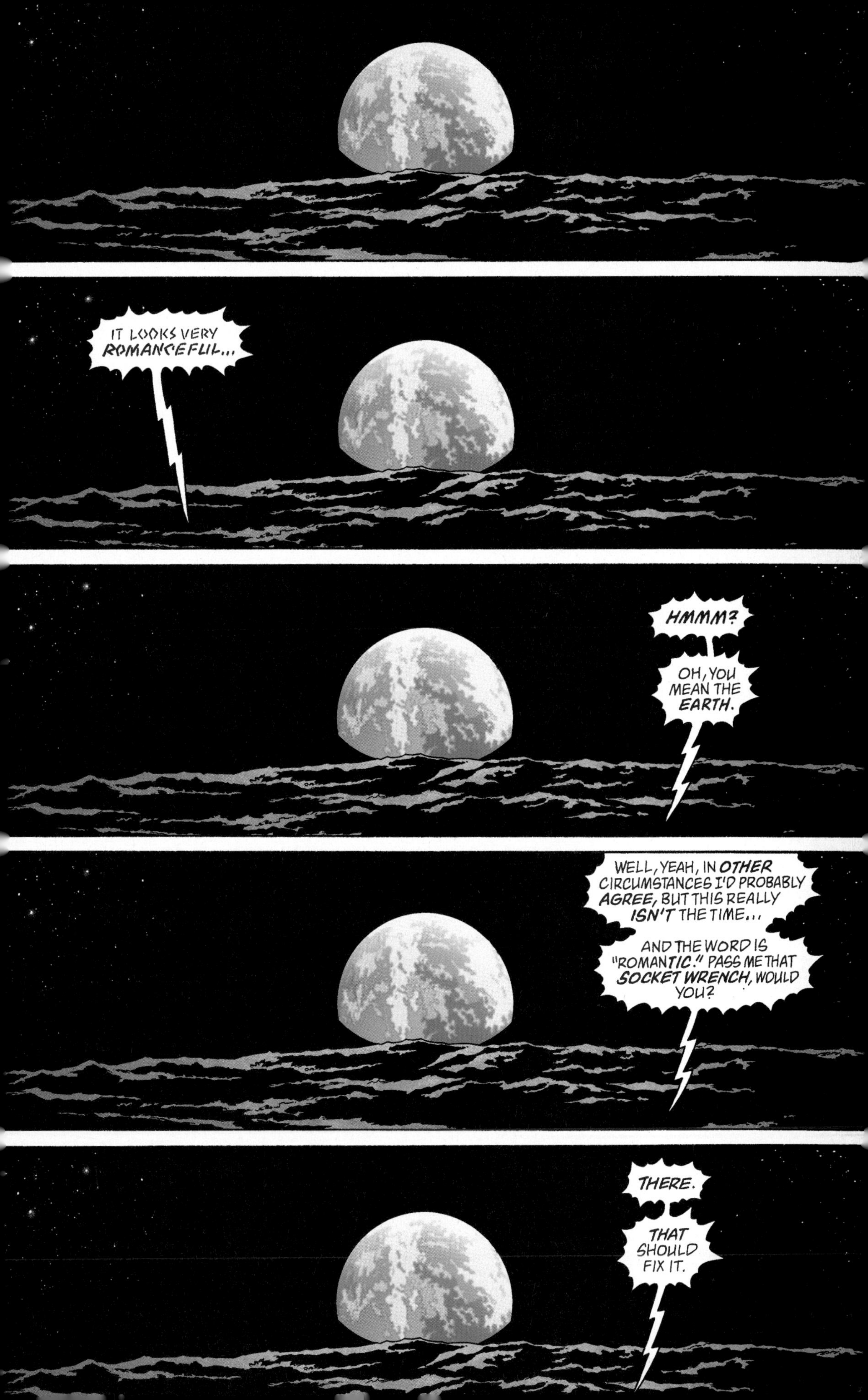
IT LOOKS VERY ROMANCEFUL...
HMMM?
OH, YOU MEAN THE EARTH.
WELL, YEAH, IN OTHER CIRCUMSTANCES I'D PROBABLY AGREE, BUT THIS REALLY ISN'T THE TIME...
AND THE WORD IS "ROMANTIC." PASS ME THAT SOCKET WRENCH, WOULD YOU?
THERE.
THAT SHOULD FIX IT.

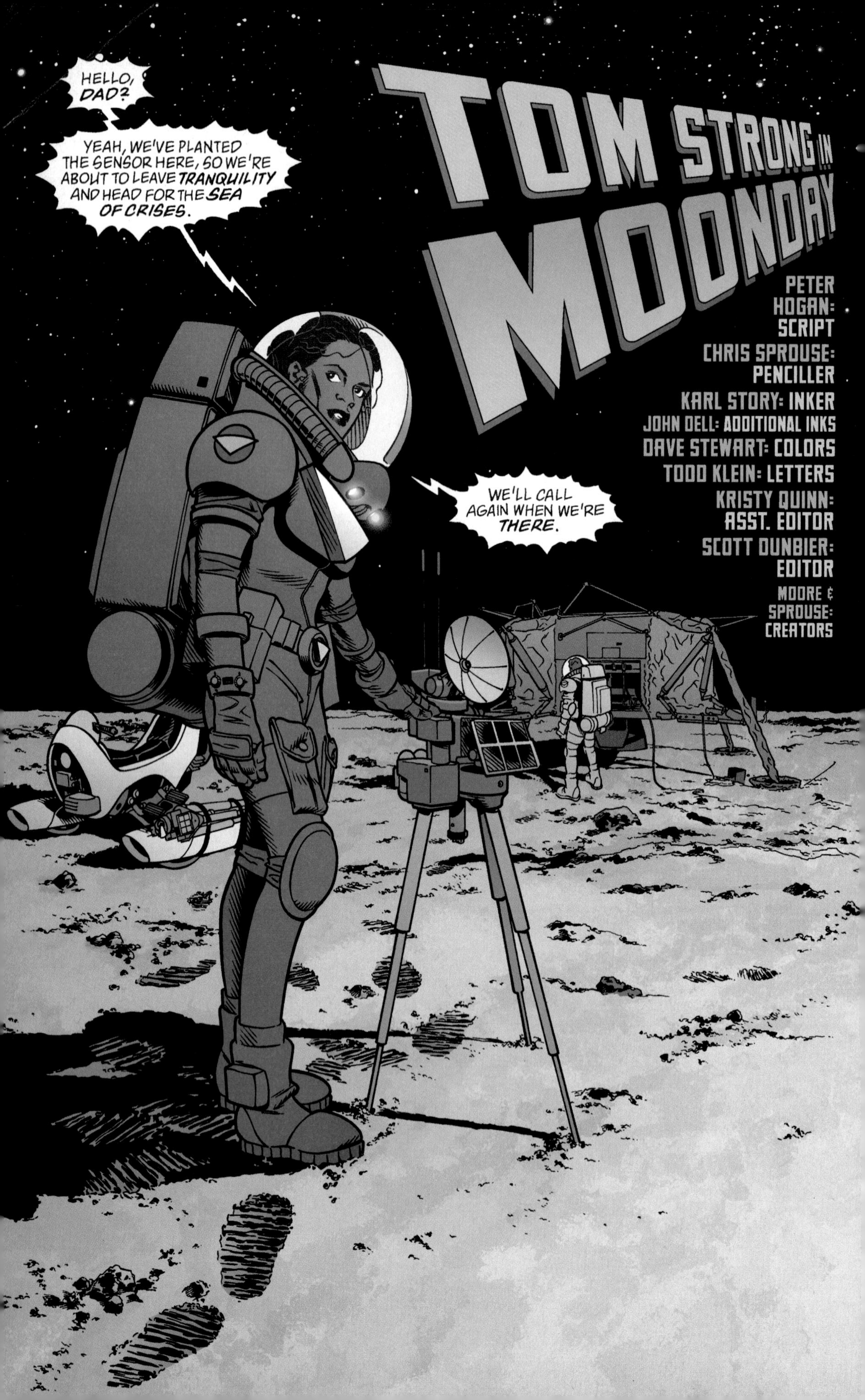

HELLO, DAD?
YEAH, WE'VE PLANTED THE SENSOR HERE, SO WE'RE ABOUT TO LEAVE TRANQUILITY AND HEAD FOR THE SEA OF CRISES.
TOM STRONG IN... MOONDAY
PETER HOGAN: SCRIPT
CHRIS SPROUSE: PENCILLER
KARL STORY: INKER
JOHN DELL: ADDITIONAL INKS
DAVE STEWART: COLORS
TODD KLEIN: LETTERS
KRISTY QUINN: ASST. EDITOR
SCOTT DUNBIER: EDITOR
MOORE & SPROUSE: CREATORS
WE'LL CALL AGAIN WHEN WE'RE THERE.

WHY ARE THEY CALLED *SEAS* WHEN THERE IS NO *WATER?*

BECAUSE THEY LOOK *DARK* FROM THE EARTH, SO ANCIENT ASTRONOMERS THOUGHT THEY MIGHT *BE* SEAS.

I GUESS THE NAME JUST *STUCK.*

AND *THESE* WORDS... THEY ARE *TRUE?*

HERE MEN FROM THE PLANET EARTH FIRST SET FOOT UPON THE MOON JULY 1969, A.D. WE CAME IN PEACE FOR ALL MANKIND

Neil A. Armstrong
NEIL A. ARMSTRONG
ASTRONAUT

Michael Collins
MICHAEL A. COLLINS
ASTRONAUT

Edwin E. Aldrin Jr
EDWIN E. ALDRIN, JR
ASTRONAUT

Richard Nixon
RICHARD NIXON
UNITED STATES OF AM

YEAH, KIND OF...

OF COURSE, *DAD* WAS HERE TWENTY YEARS *EARLIER,* BUT THAT WAS A *SECRET...* AND ANYWAY, IT DOESN'T TAKE ANYTHING AWAY FROM WHAT *THESE* GUYS DID.

THEY FLEW UP HERE IN THIS LIKE, REALLY PRIMITIVE *BUCKET.* IT MUST HAVE TAKEN REAL *GUTS...*

*BUCKET* IS LIKE *ROCKET?*

I JUST MEANT THEY KIND OF *ROUGHED* IT.

OKAY, *ENOUGH* TOURIST STUFF--WE'D BETTER GET *MOVING.*

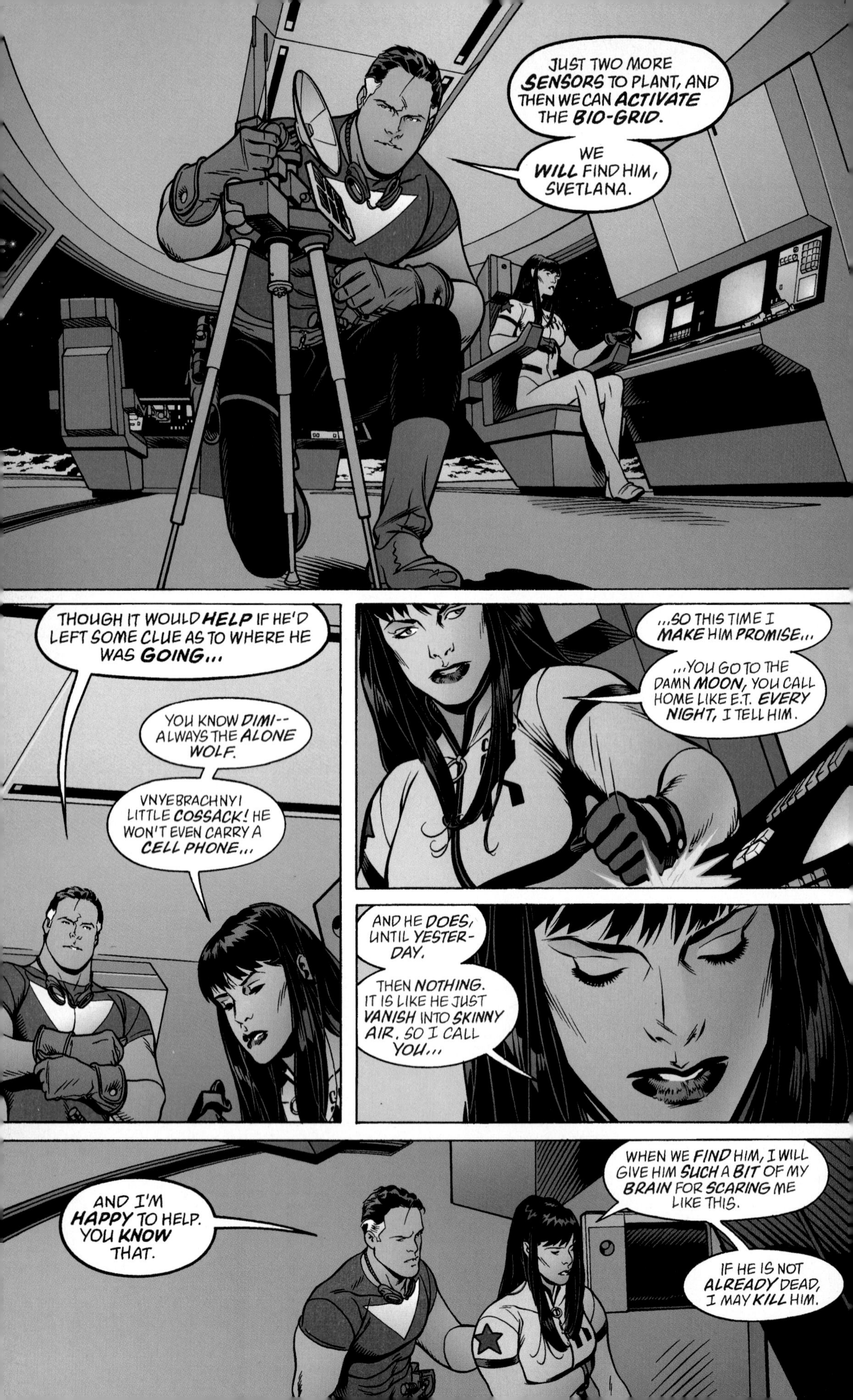
JUST TWO MORE SENSORS TO PLANT, AND THEN WE CAN ACTIVATE THE BIO-GRID.
WE WILL FIND HIM, SVETLANA.
THOUGH IT WOULD HELP IF HE'D LEFT SOME CLUE AS TO WHERE HE WAS GOING...
YOU KNOW DIMI-- ALWAYS THE ALONE WOLF.
VNYEBRACHNYI LITTLE COSSACK! HE WON'T EVEN CARRY A CELL PHONE...
...SO THIS TIME I MAKE HIM PROMISE...
...YOU GO TO THE DAMN MOON, YOU CALL HOME LIKE E.T. EVERY NIGHT, I TELL HIM.
AND HE DOES, UNTIL YESTER-DAY.
THEN NOTHING. IT IS LIKE HE JUST VANISH INTO SKINNY AIR. SO I CALL YOU...
AND I'M HAPPY TO HELP. YOU KNOW THAT.
WHEN WE FIND HIM, I WILL GIVE HIM SUCH A BIT OF MY BRAIN FOR SCARING ME LIKE THIS.
IF HE IS NOT ALREADY DEAD, I MAY KILL HIM.

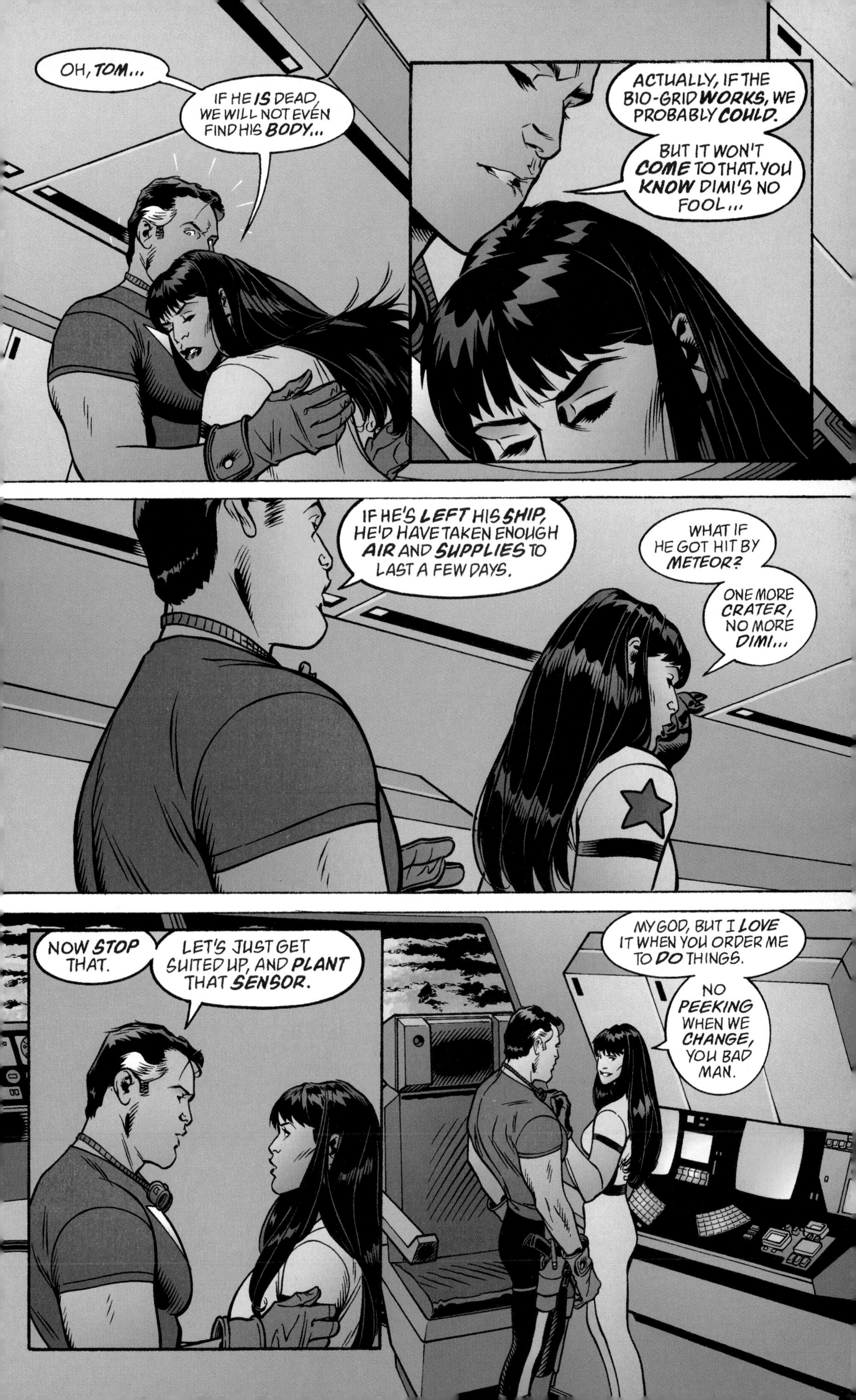
OH, TOM...
IF HE IS DEAD, WE WILL NOT EVEN FIND HIS BODY...
ACTUALLY, IF THE BIO-GRID WORKS, WE PROBABLY COULD.
BUT IT WON'T COME TO THAT. YOU KNOW DIMI'S NO FOOL...
IF HE'S LEFT HIS SHIP, HE'D HAVE TAKEN ENOUGH AIR AND SUPPLIES TO LAST A FEW DAYS.
WHAT IF HE GOT HIT BY METEOR?
ONE MORE CRATER, NO MORE DIMI...
NOW STOP THAT.
LET'S JUST GET SUITED UP, AND PLANT THAT SENSOR.
MY GOD, BUT I LOVE IT WHEN YOU ORDER ME TO DO THINGS.
NO PEEKING WHEN WE CHANGE, YOU BAD MAN.

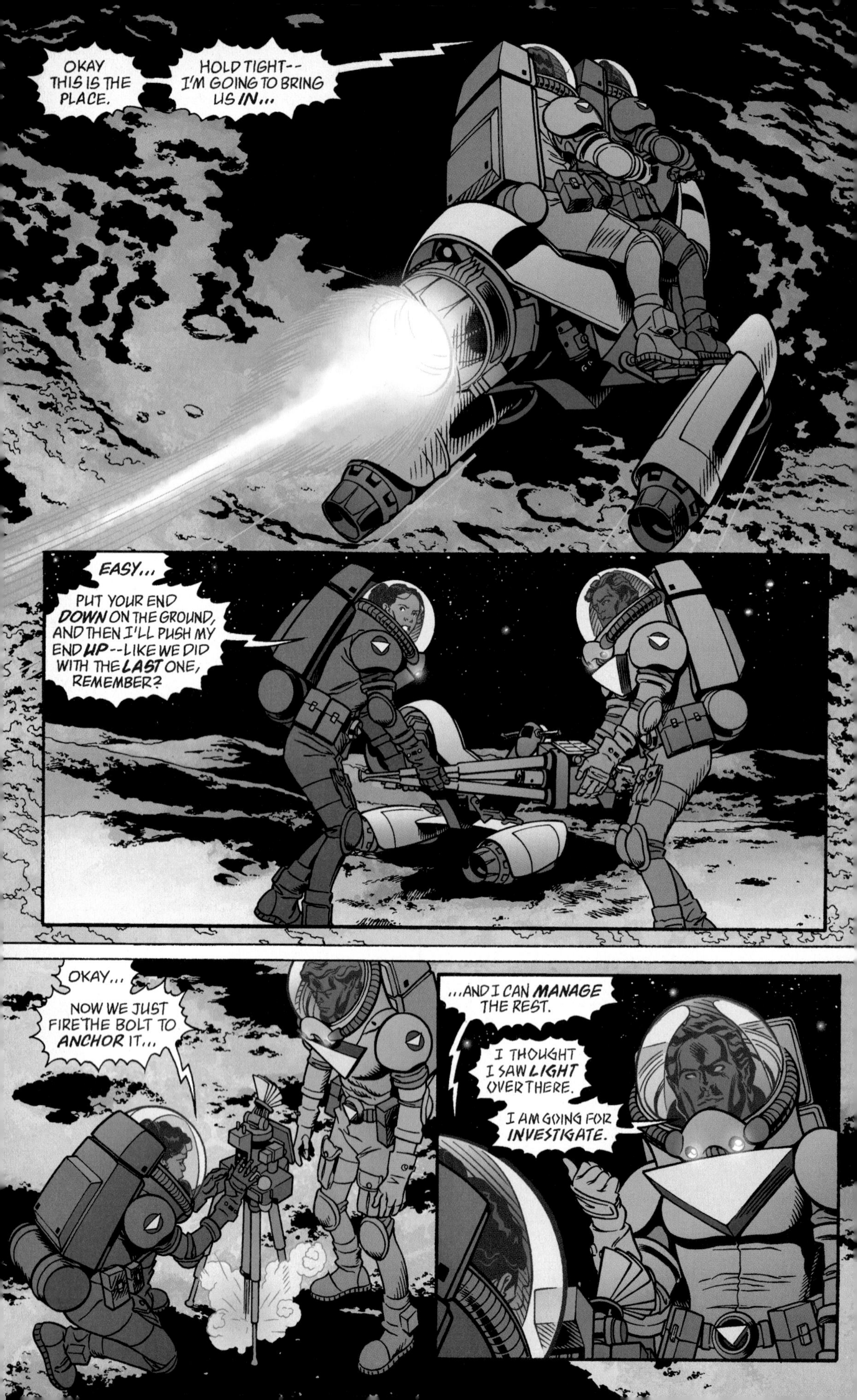
OKAY THIS IS THE PLACE.
HOLD TIGHT-- I'M GOING TO BRING US IN...
EASY...
PUT YOUR END DOWN ON THE GROUND, AND THEN I'LL PUSH MY END UP--LIKE WE DID WITH THE LAST ONE, REMEMBER?
OKAY...
NOW WE JUST FIRE THE BOLT TO ANCHOR IT...
...AND I CAN MANAGE THE REST.
I THOUGHT I SAW LIGHT OVER THERE.
I AM GOING FOR INVESTIGATE.

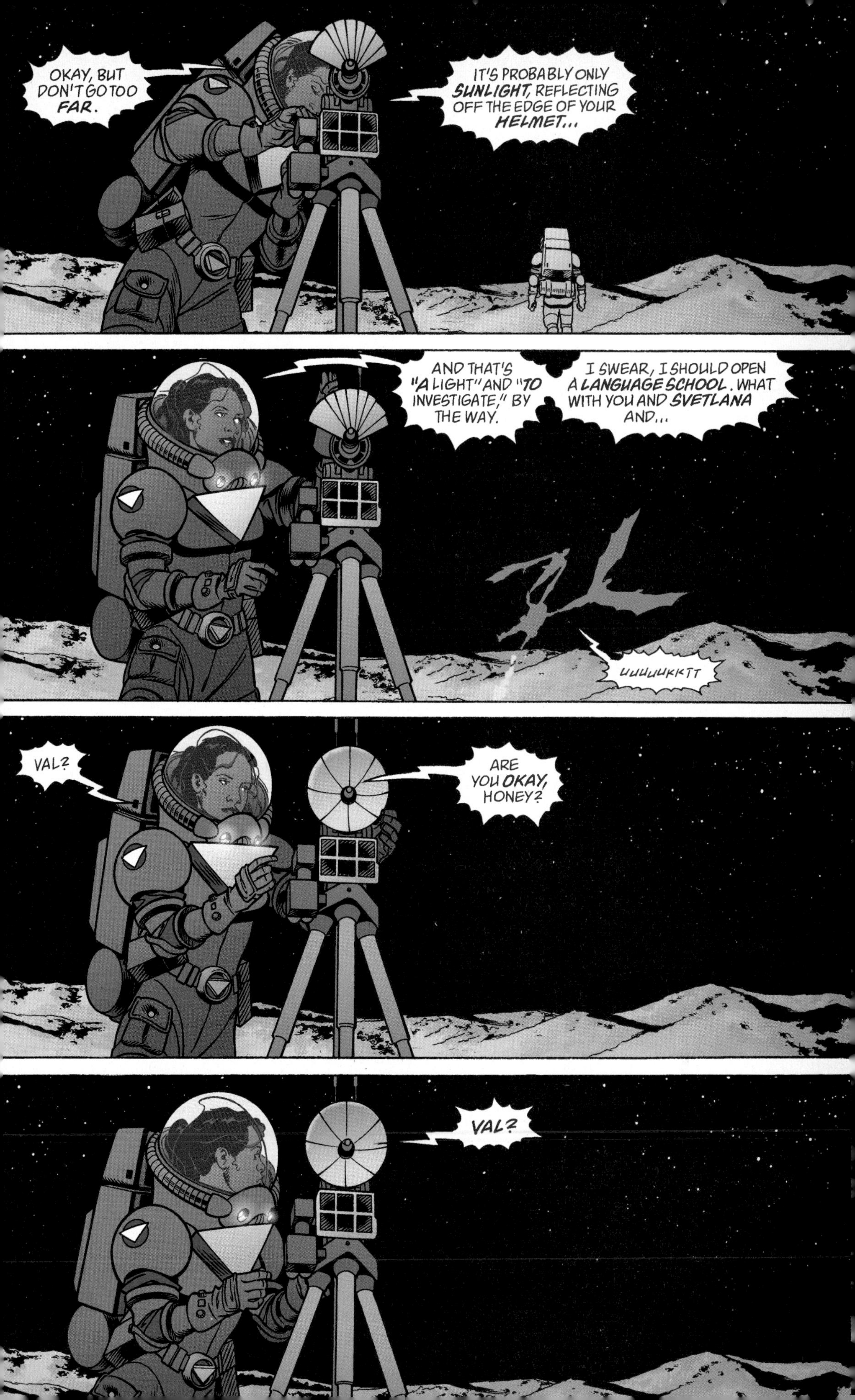
OKAY, BUT DON'T GO TOO FAR.
IT'S PROBABLY ONLY SUNLIGHT, REFLECTING OFF THE EDGE OF YOUR HELMET...
AND THAT'S "A LIGHT" AND "TO INVESTIGATE," BY THE WAY.
I SWEAR, I SHOULD OPEN A LANGUAGE SCHOOL. WHAT WITH YOU AND SVETLANA AND...
UUUUUKKTT
VAL?
ARE YOU OKAY, HONEY?
VAL?

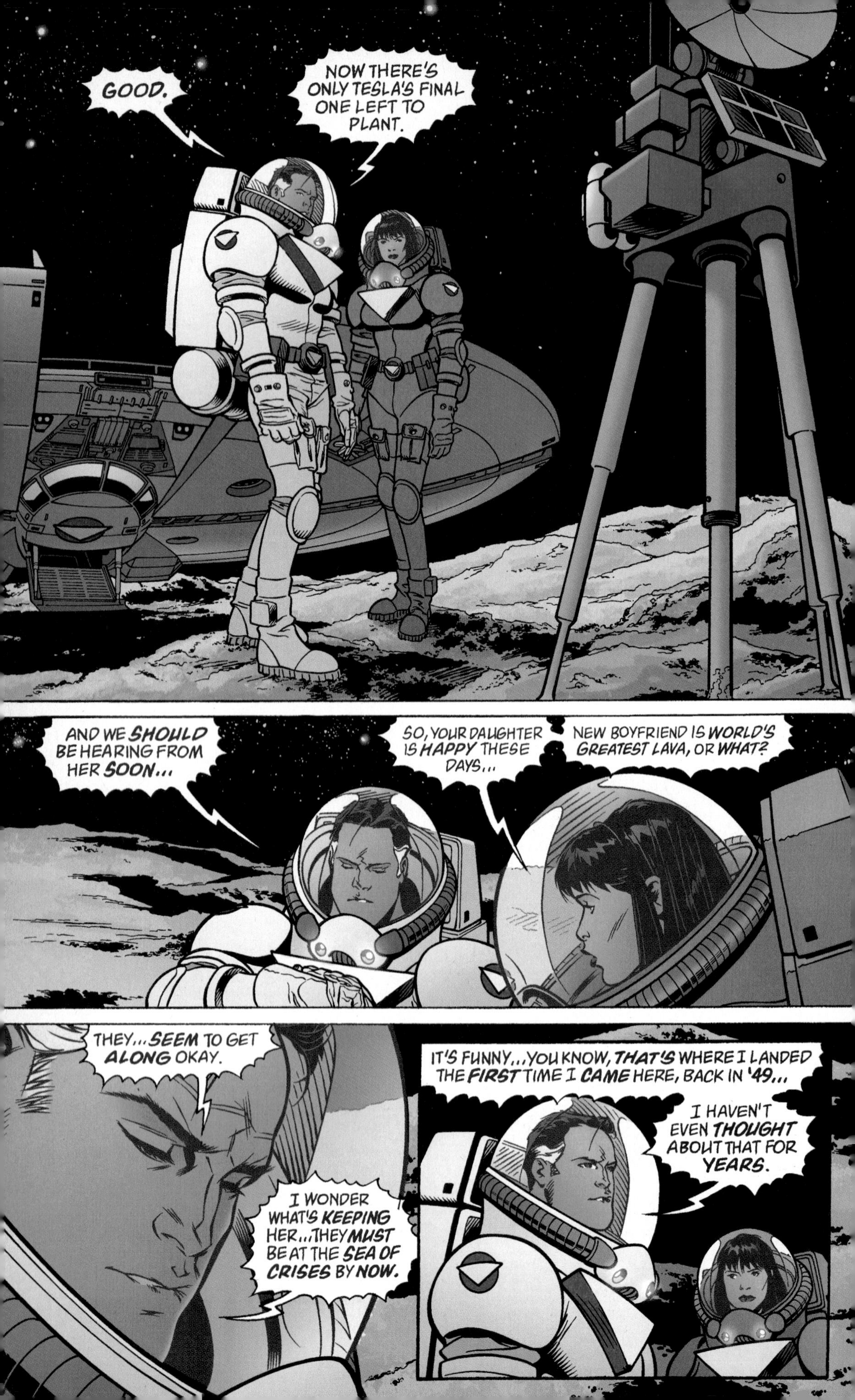
GOOD.
NOW THERE'S ONLY TESLA'S FINAL ONE LEFT TO PLANT.
AND WE SHOULD BE HEARING FROM HER SOON...
SO, YOUR DAUGHTER IS HAPPY THESE DAYS...
NEW BOYFRIEND IS WORLD'S GREATEST LAVA, OR WHAT?
THEY... SEEM TO GET ALONG OKAY.
I WONDER WHAT'S KEEPING HER... THEY MUST BE AT THE SEA OF CRISES BY NOW.
IT'S FUNNY... YOU KNOW, THAT'S WHERE I LANDED THE FIRST TIME I CAME HERE, BACK IN '49...
I HAVEN'T EVEN THOUGHT ABOUT THAT FOR YEARS.

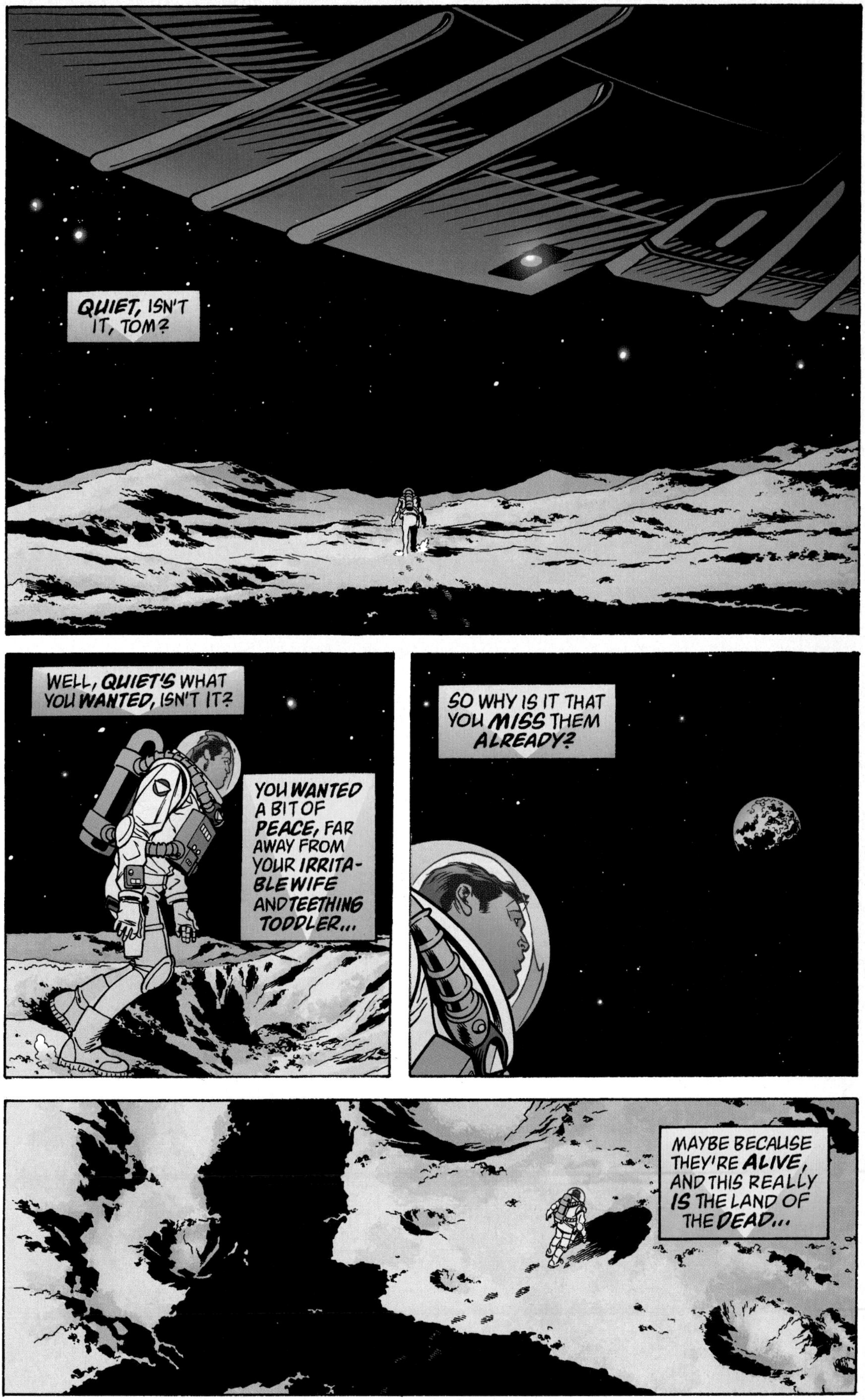
QUIET, ISN'T IT, TOM?
WELL, QUIET'S WHAT YOU WANTED, ISN'T IT?
YOU WANTED A BIT OF PEACE, FAR AWAY FROM YOUR IRRITA-BLE WIFE AND TEETHING TODDLER...
SO WHY IS IT THAT YOU MISS THEM ALREADY?
MAYBE BECAUSE THEY'RE ALIVE, AND THIS REALLY IS THE LAND OF THE DEAD...

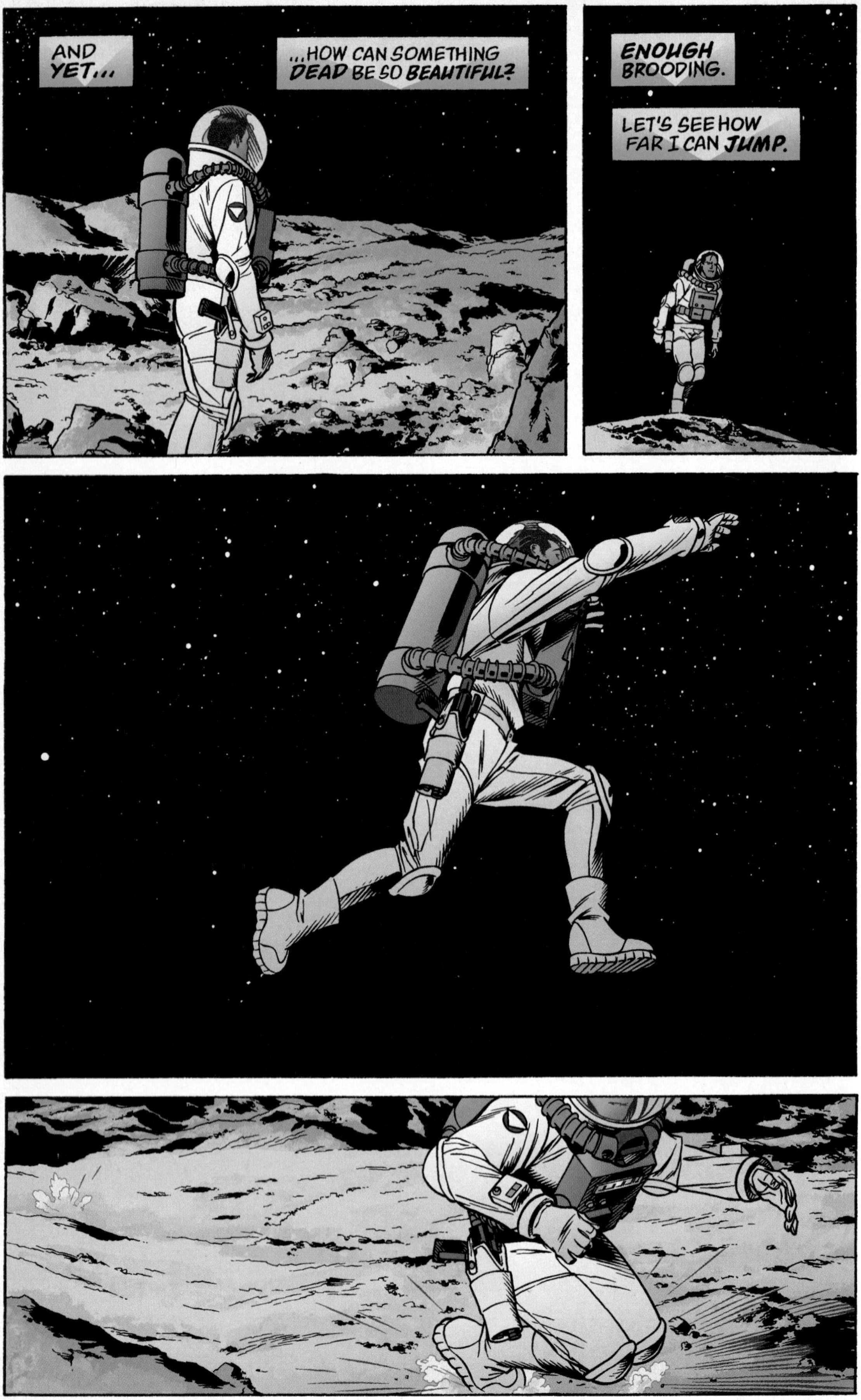
AND YET...
...HOW CAN SOMETHING DEAD BE SO BEAUTIFUL?
ENOUGH BROODING.
LET'S SEE HOW FAR I CAN JUMP.

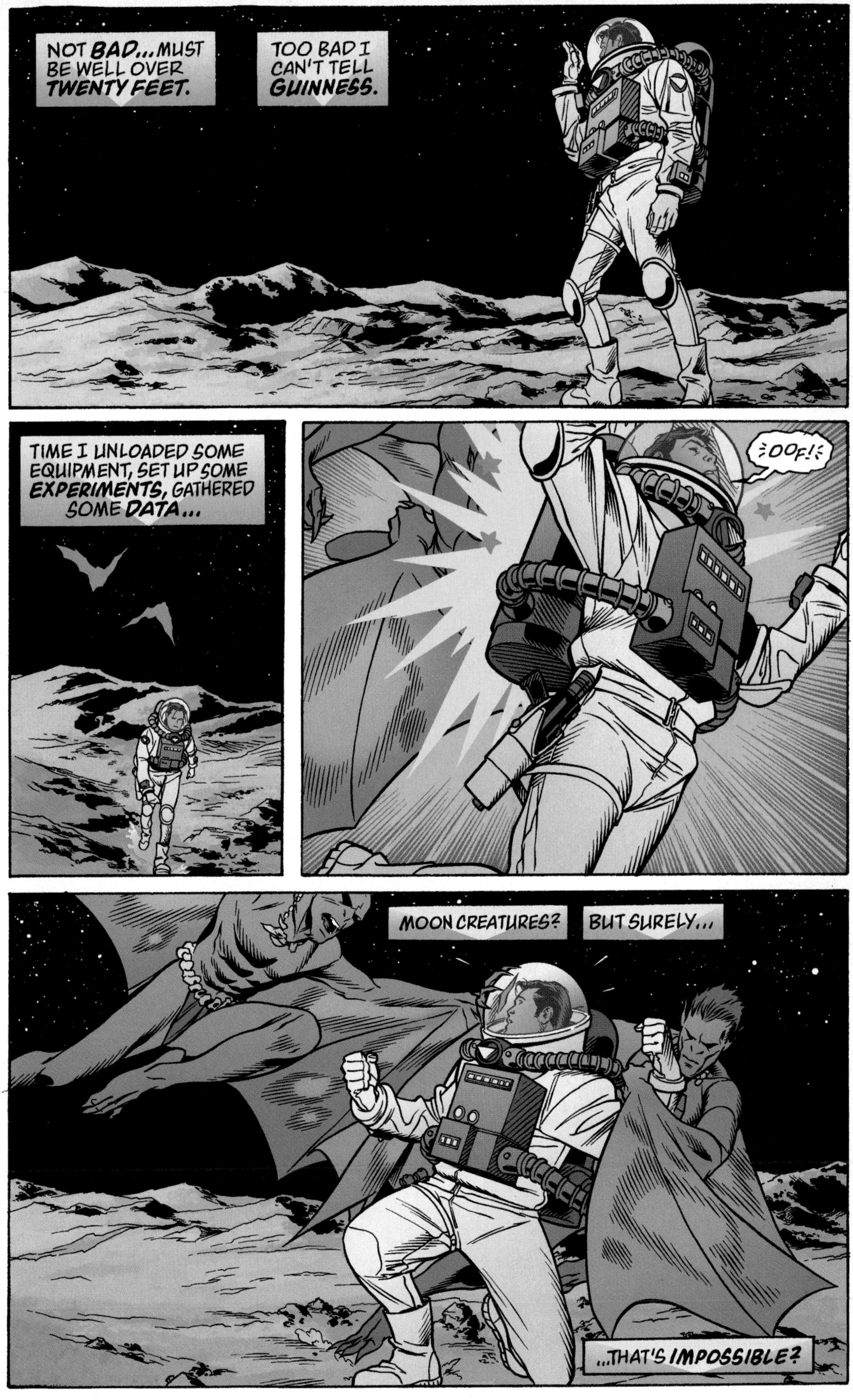
NOT BAD... MUST BE WELL OVER TWENTY FEET.
TOO BAD I CAN'T TELL GUINNESS.
TIME I UNLOADED SOME EQUIPMENT, SET UP SOME EXPERIMENTS, GATHERED SOME DATA...
OOF!
MOON CREATURES?
BUT SURELY...
...THAT'S IMPOSSIBLE?

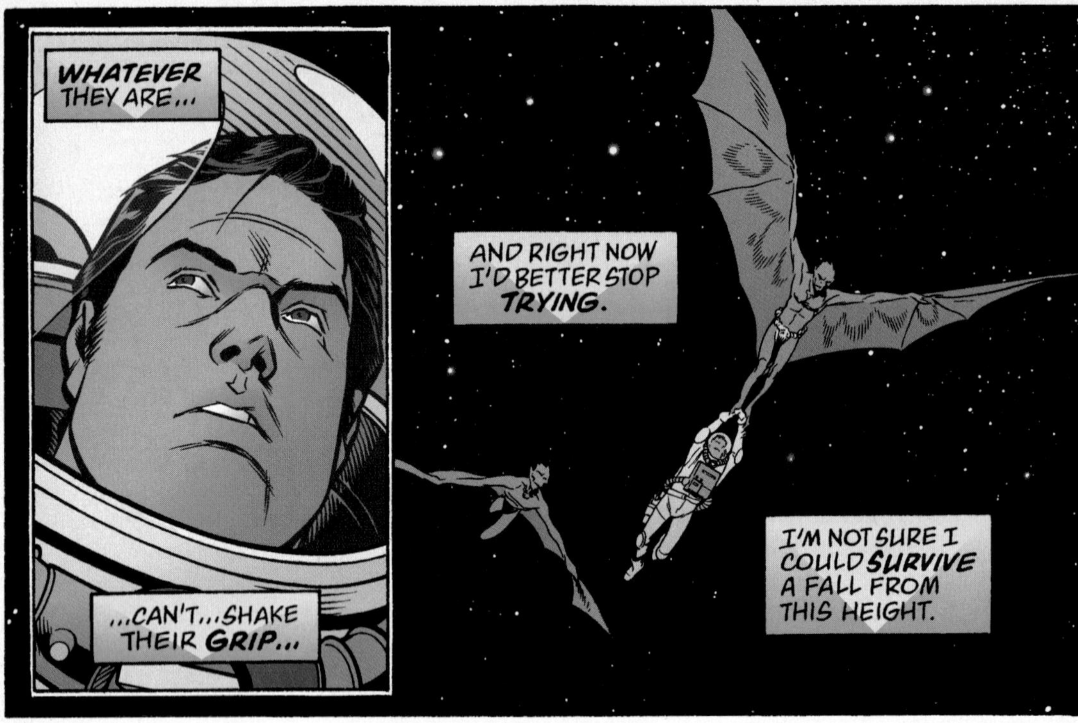
WHATEVER THEY ARE...
...CAN'T...SHAKE THEIR GRIP...
AND RIGHT NOW I'D BETTER STOP TRYING.
I'M NOT SURE I COULD SURVIVE A FALL FROM THIS HEIGHT.

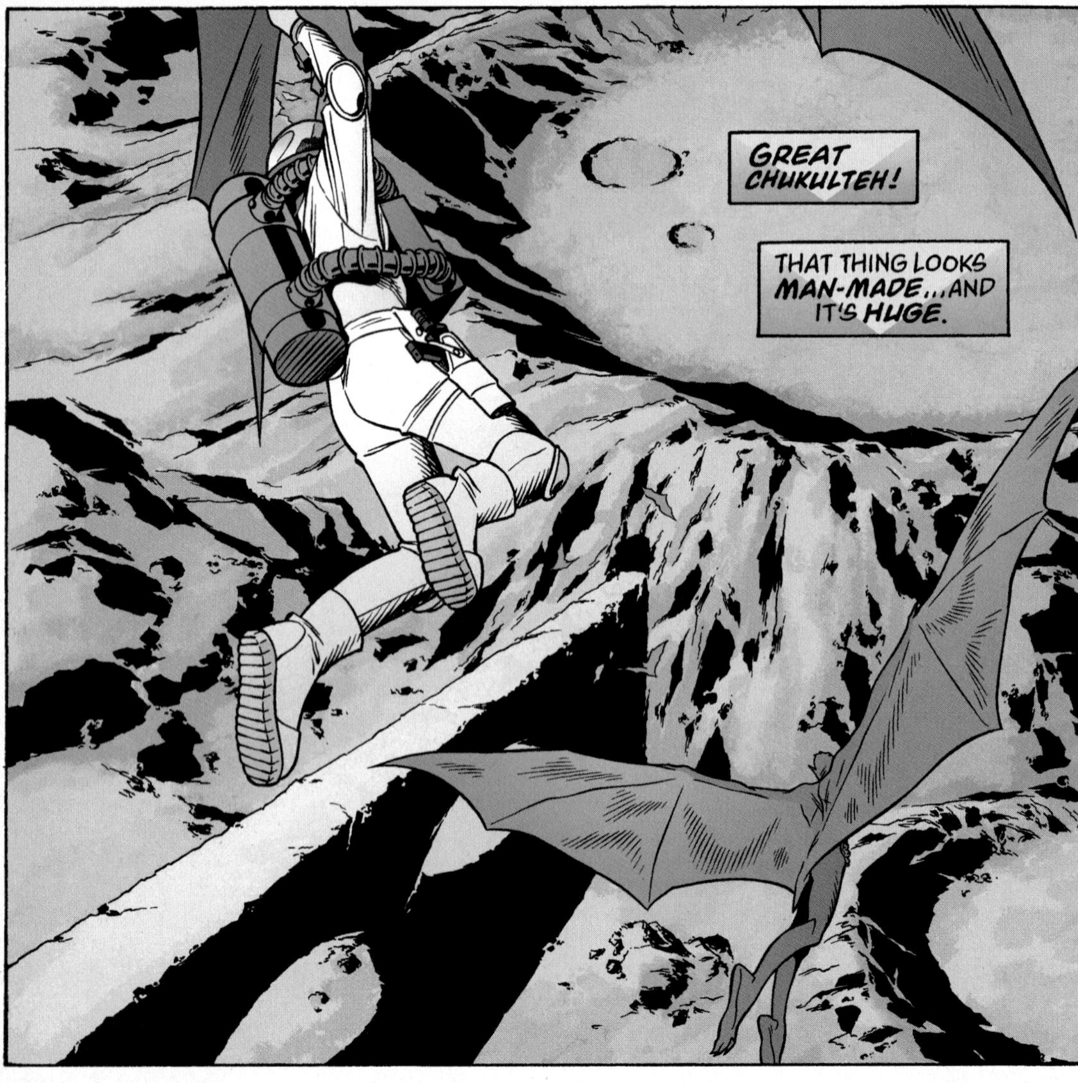
GREAT CHUKULTEH!
THAT THING LOOKS MAN-MADE...AND IT'S HUGE.

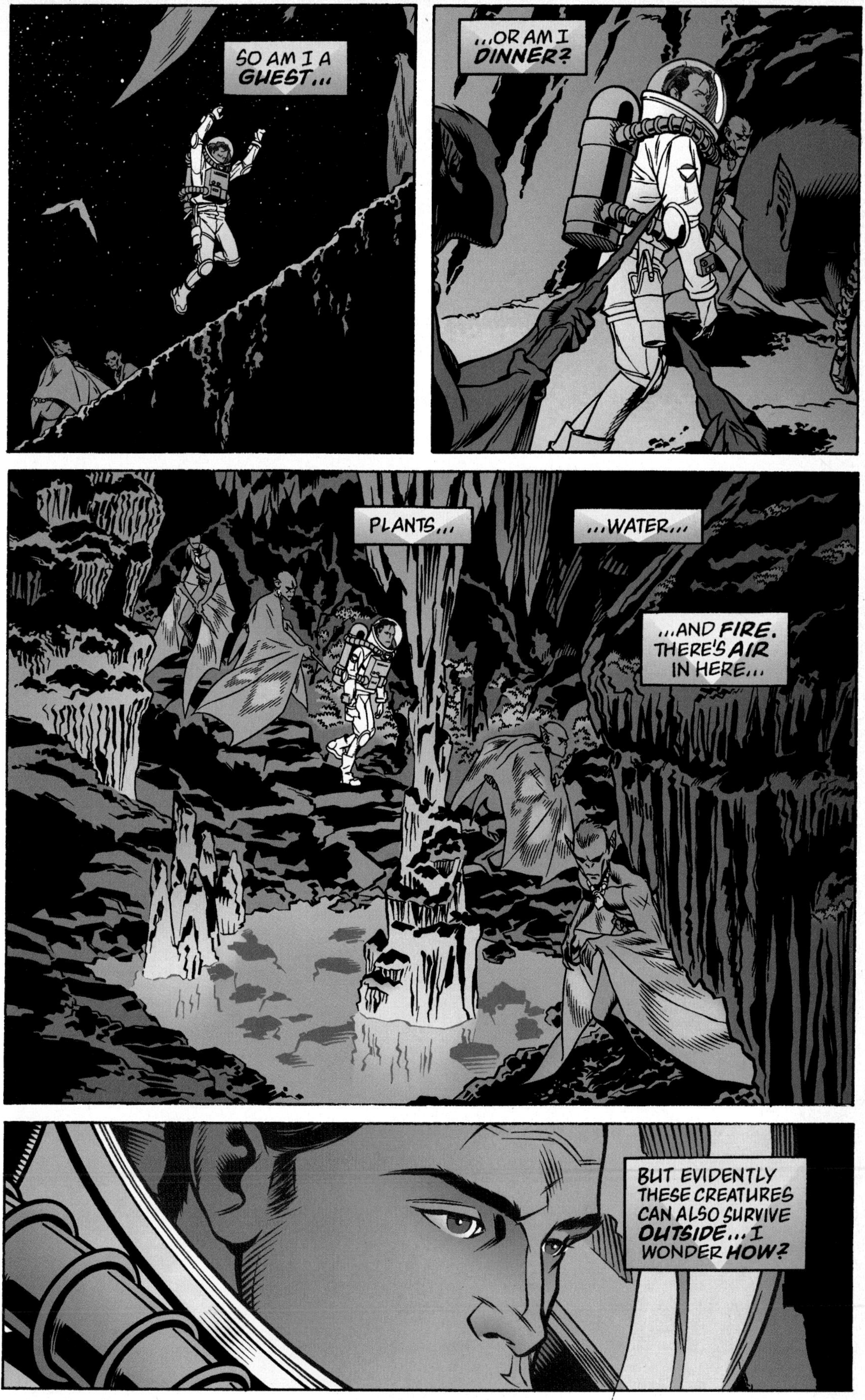
SO AM I A GUEST...
...OR AM I DINNER?
PLANTS...
...WATER...
...AND FIRE. THERE'S AIR IN HERE...
BUT EVIDENTLY THESE CREATURES CAN ALSO SURVIVE OUTSIDE... I WONDER HOW?

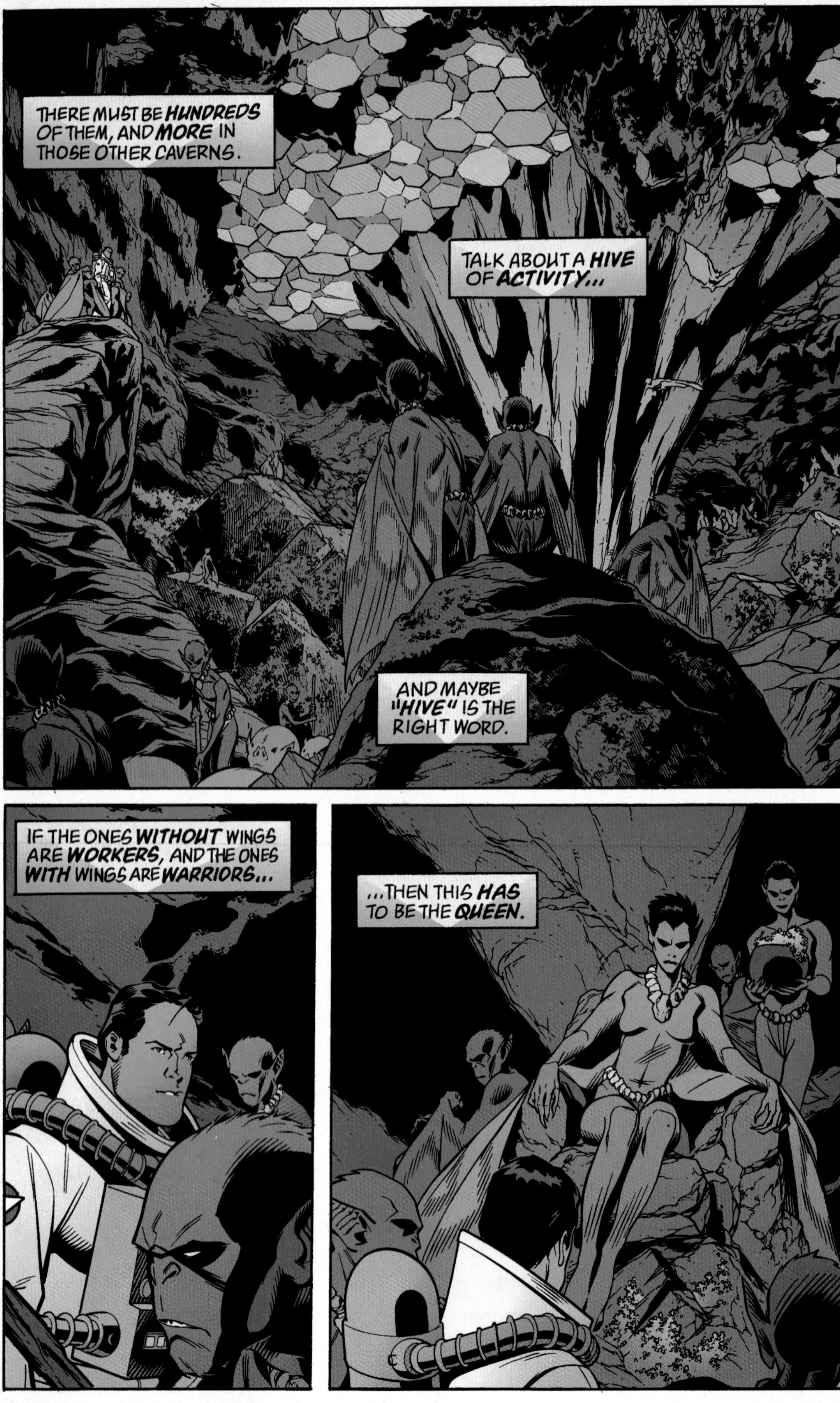
THERE MUST BE HUNDREDS OF THEM, AND MORE IN THOSE OTHER CAVERNS.
TALK ABOUT A HIVE OF ACTIVITY...
AND MAYBE "HIVE" IS THE RIGHT WORD.
IF THE ONES WITHOUT WINGS ARE WORKERS, AND THE ONES WITH WINGS ARE WARRIORS...
...THEN THIS HAS TO BE THE QUEEN.

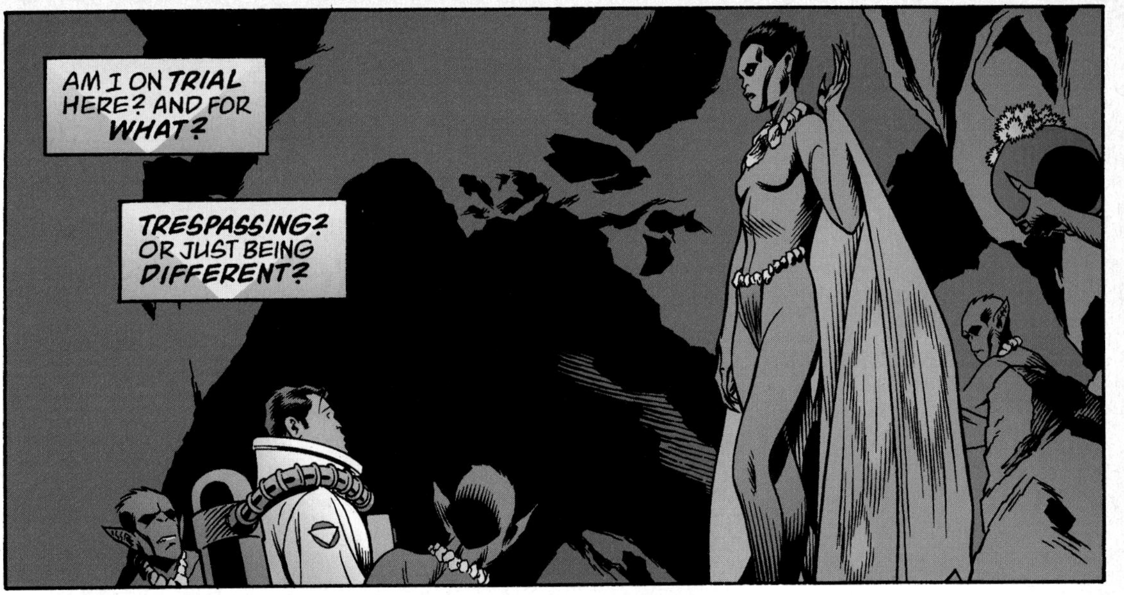
AM I ON TRIAL HERE? AND FOR WHAT?
TRESPASSING? OR JUST BEING DIFFERENT?

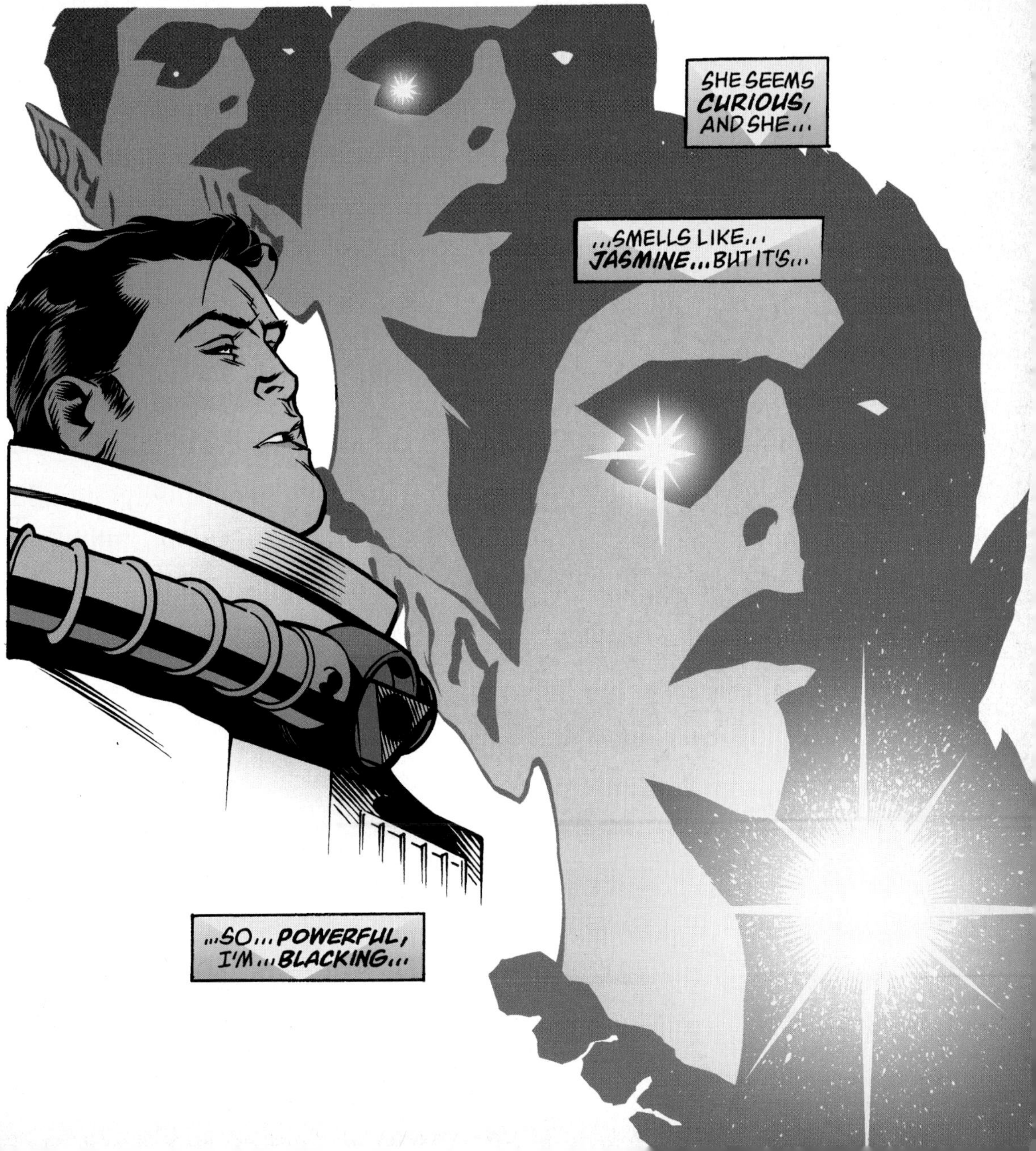
SHE SEEMS CURIOUS, AND SHE...
...SMELLS LIKE... JASMINE... BUT IT'S...
...SO... POWERFUL, I'M... BLACKING...

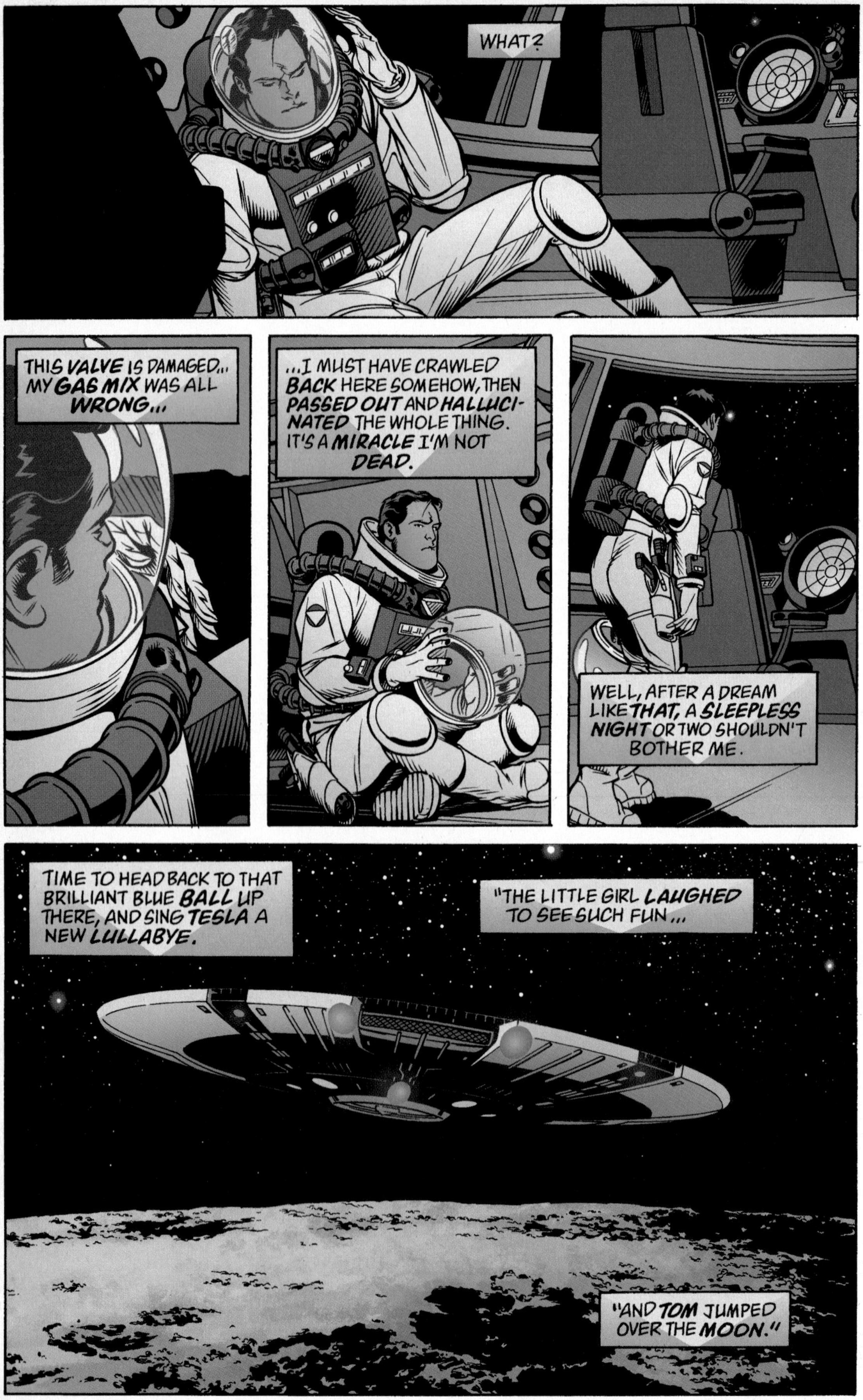

WHAT?
THIS VALVE IS DAMAGED... MY GAS MIX WAS ALL WRONG...
...I MUST HAVE CRAWLED BACK HERE SOMEHOW, THEN PASSED OUT AND HALLUCINATED THE WHOLE THING. IT'S A MIRACLE I'M NOT DEAD.
WELL, AFTER A DREAM LIKE THAT, A SLEEPLESS NIGHT OR TWO SHOULDN'T BOTHER ME.
TIME TO HEAD BACK TO THAT BRILLIANT BLUE BALL UP THERE, AND SING TESLA A NEW LULLABYE.
"THE LITTLE GIRL LAUGHED TO SEE SUCH FUN...
"AND TOM JUMPED OVER THE MOON."

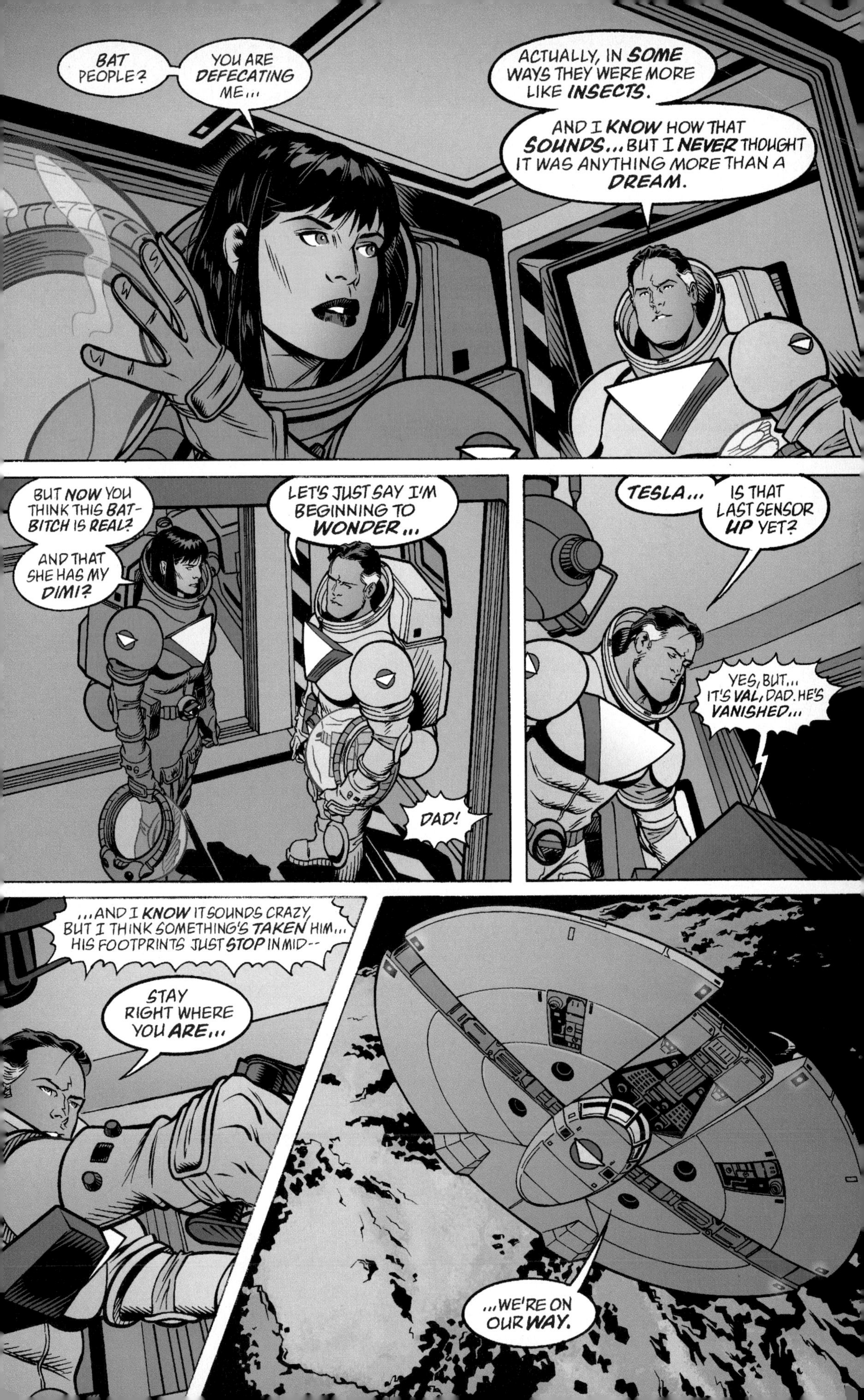
BAT PEOPLE?
YOU ARE DEFECATING ME...
ACTUALLY, IN SOME WAYS THEY WERE MORE LIKE INSECTS.
AND I KNOW HOW THAT SOUNDS... BUT I NEVER THOUGHT IT WAS ANYTHING MORE THAN A DREAM.
BUT NOW YOU THINK THIS BAT-BITCH IS REAL?
AND THAT SHE HAS MY DIMI?
LET'S JUST SAY I'M BEGINNING TO WONDER...
DAD!
TESLA...
IS THAT LAST SENSOR UP YET?
YES, BUT... IT'S VAL, DAD. HE'S VANISHED...
...AND I KNOW IT SOUNDS CRAZY, BUT I THINK SOMETHING'S TAKEN HIM... HIS FOOTPRINTS JUST STOP IN MID--
STAY RIGHT WHERE YOU ARE...
...WE'RE ON OUR WAY.

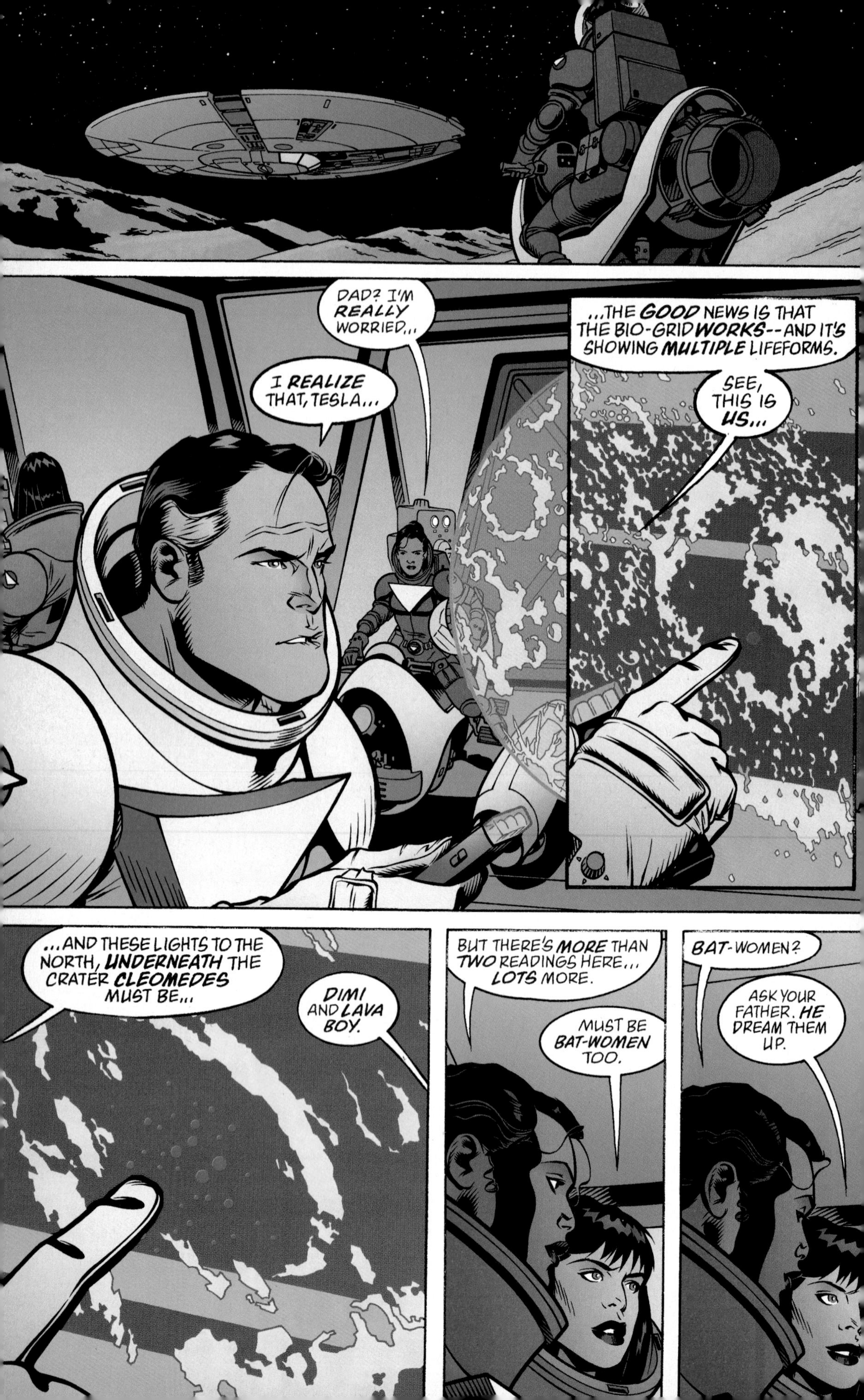
DAD? I'M REALLY WORRIED...
I REALIZE THAT, TESLA...
...THE GOOD NEWS IS THAT THE BIO-GRID WORKS--AND IT'S SHOWING MULTIPLE LIFEFORMS.
SEE, THIS IS US...
...AND THESE LIGHTS TO THE NORTH, UNDERNEATH THE CRATER CLEOMEDES MUST BE...
DIMI AND LAVA BOY.
BUT THERE'S MORE THAN TWO READINGS HERE... LOTS MORE.
MUST BE BAT-WOMEN TOO.
BAT-WOMEN?
ASK YOUR FATHER. HE DREAM THEM UP.

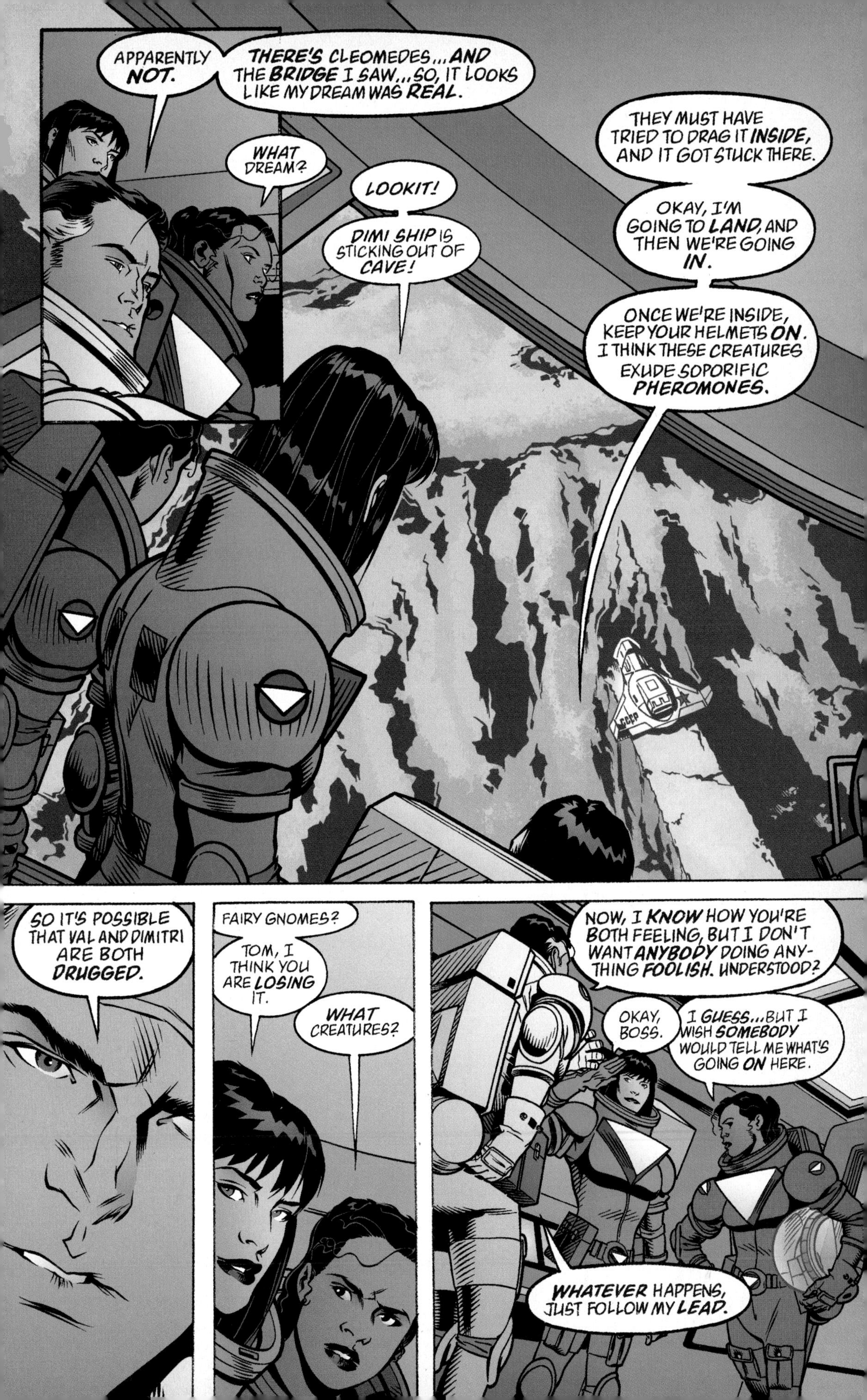
APPARENTLY NOT.
THERE'S CLEOMEDES... AND THE BRIDGE I SAW... SO, IT LOOKS LIKE MY DREAM WAS REAL.
WHAT DREAM?
LOOKIT!
DIMI SHIP IS STICKING OUT OF CAVE!
THEY MUST HAVE TRIED TO DRAG IT INSIDE, AND IT GOT STUCK THERE.
OKAY, I'M GOING TO LAND, AND THEN WE'RE GOING IN.
ONCE WE'RE INSIDE, KEEP YOUR HELMETS ON. I THINK THESE CREATURES EXUDE SOPORIFIC PHEROMONES.
CCCP
SO IT'S POSSIBLE THAT VAL AND DIMITRI ARE BOTH DRUGGED.
FAIRY GNOMES?
TOM, I THINK YOU ARE LOSING IT.
WHAT CREATURES?
NOW, I KNOW HOW YOU'RE BOTH FEELING, BUT I DON'T WANT ANYBODY DOING ANYTHING FOOLISH. UNDERSTOOD?
OKAY, BOSS.
I GUESS... BUT I WISH SOMEBODY WOULD TELL ME WHAT'S GOING ON HERE.
WHATEVER HAPPENS, JUST FOLLOW MY LEAD.

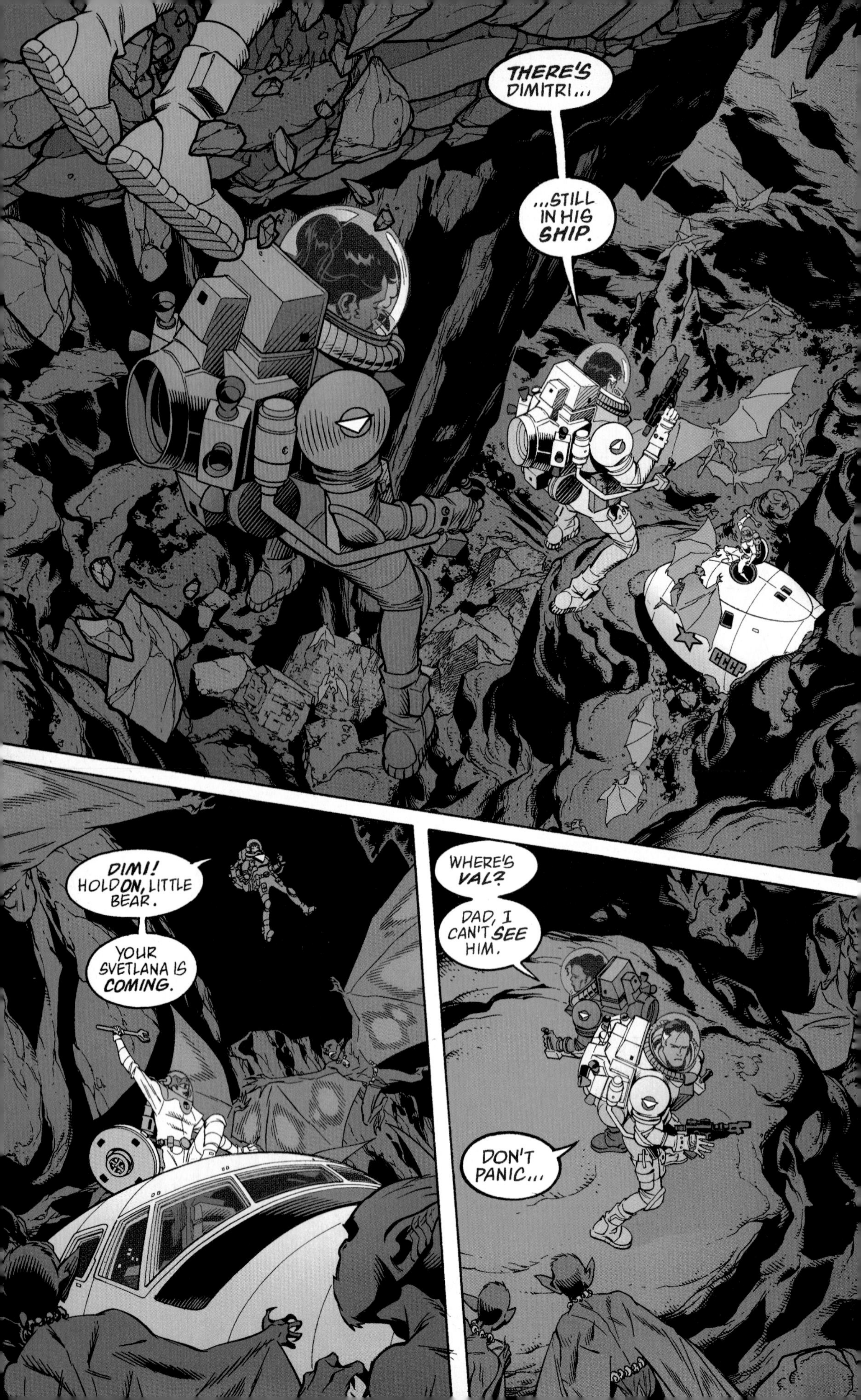
THERE'S DIMITRI...
...STILL IN HIS SHIP.
DIMI! HOLD ON, LITTLE BEAR.
YOUR SVETLANA IS COMING.
WHERE'S VAL?
DAD, I CAN'T SEE HIM.
DON'T PANIC...

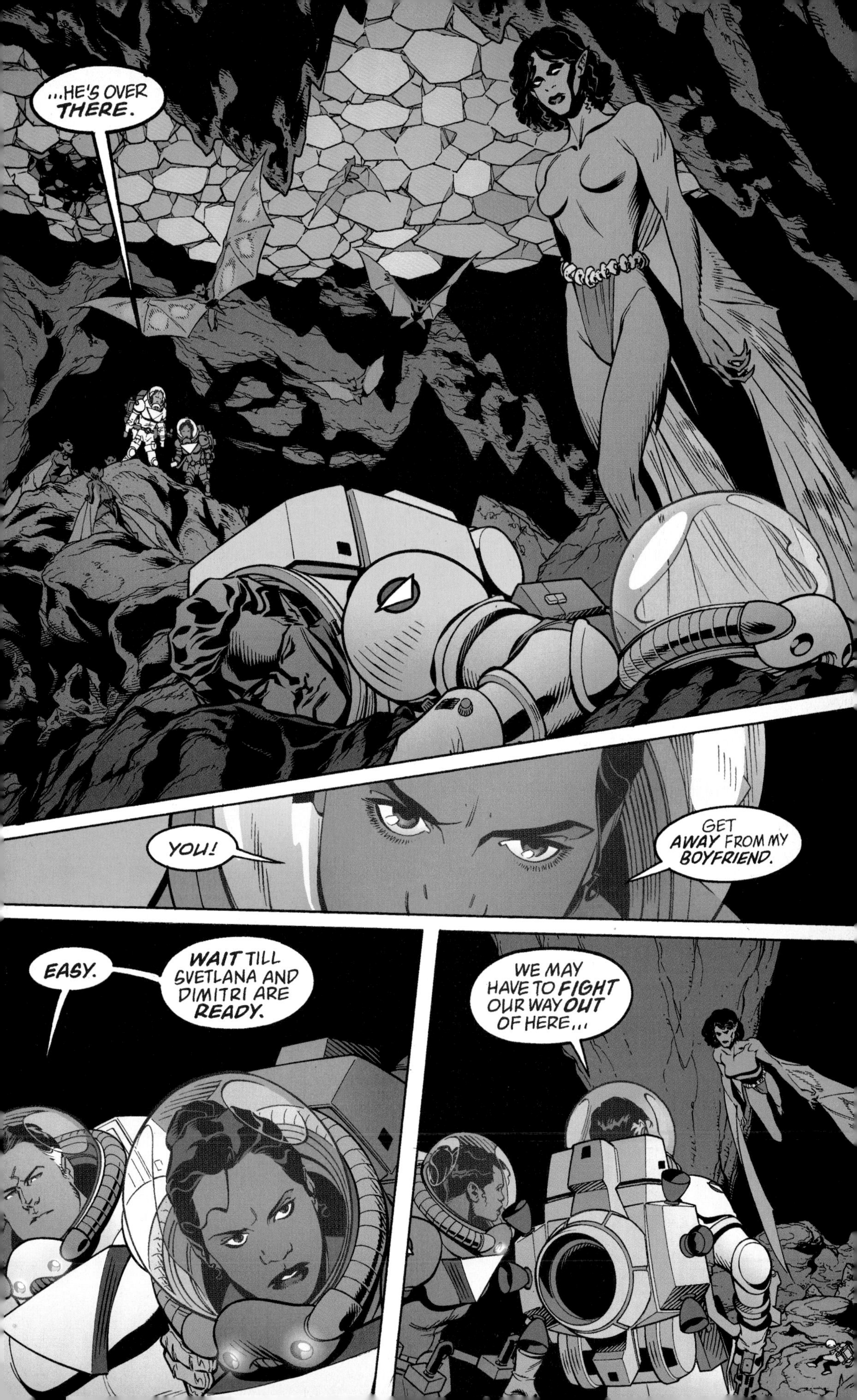
...HE'S OVER THERE.
YOU!
GET AWAY FROM MY BOYFRIEND.
EASY.
WAIT TILL SVETLANA AND DIMITRI ARE READY.
WE MAY HAVE TO FIGHT OUR WAY OUT OF HERE...

OR MAYBE NOT...

DAD? WHAT'S GOING *ON* HERE?

I'M NOT SURE...

...BUT I *THINK* SHE'S SAYING WE CAN *LEAVE.*

PUT VAL'S *HELMET* ON, AND GET HIM *MOVING.*

*DIMITRI?* YOU *OKAY?*

IF MY WIFE DOES NOT *CRUSH* ME TO *DEATH,* YES.

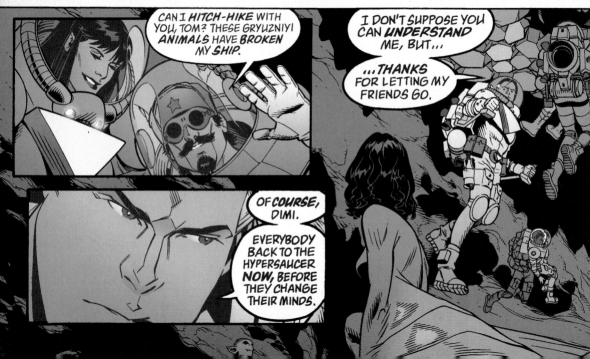

CAN I *HITCH-HIKE* WITH YOU, TOM? THESE *GRYUZNIYI* ANIMALS HAVE *BROKEN* MY *SHIP.*

I DON'T SUPPOSE YOU CAN *UNDERSTAND* ME, BUT...

...*THANKS* FOR LETTING MY FRIENDS GO.

OF *COURSE,* DIMI.

EVERYBODY BACK TO THE HYPERSAUCER *NOW,* BEFORE THEY CHANGE THEIR MINDS.

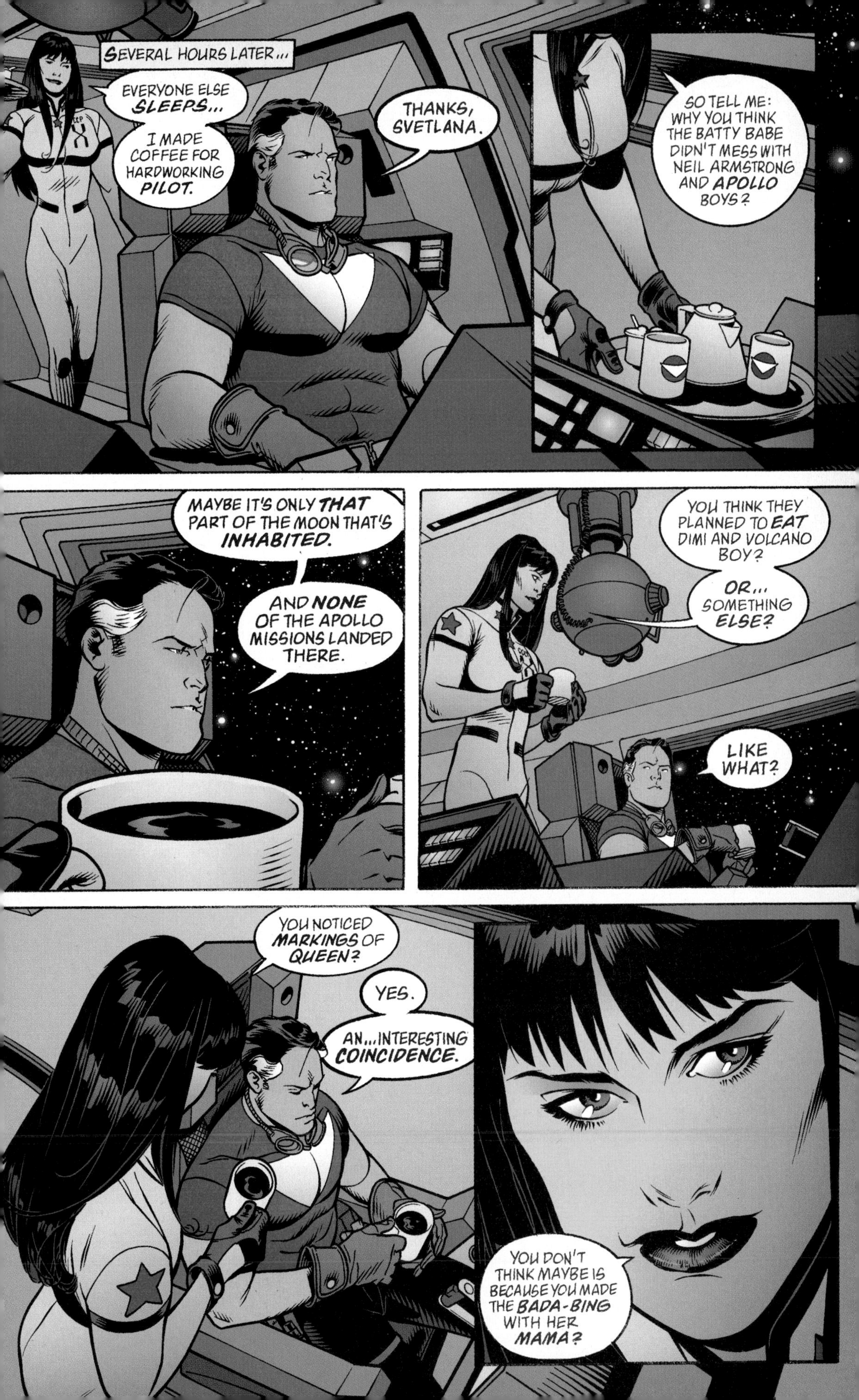
SEVERAL HOURS LATER...
EVERYONE ELSE SLEEPS...
I MADE COFFEE FOR HARDWORKING PILOT.
THANKS, SVETLANA.
SO TELL ME: WHY YOU THINK THE BATTY BABE DIDN'T MESS WITH NEIL ARMSTRONG AND APOLLO BOYS?
MAYBE IT'S ONLY THAT PART OF THE MOON THAT'S INHABITED.
AND NONE OF THE APOLLO MISSIONS LANDED THERE.
YOU THINK THEY PLANNED TO EAT DIMI AND VOLCANO BOY?
OR... SOMETHING ELSE?
LIKE WHAT?
YOU NOTICED MARKINGS OF QUEEN?
YES.
AN...INTERESTING COINCIDENCE.
YOU DON'T THINK MAYBE IS BECAUSE YOU MADE THE BADA-BING WITH HER MAMA?

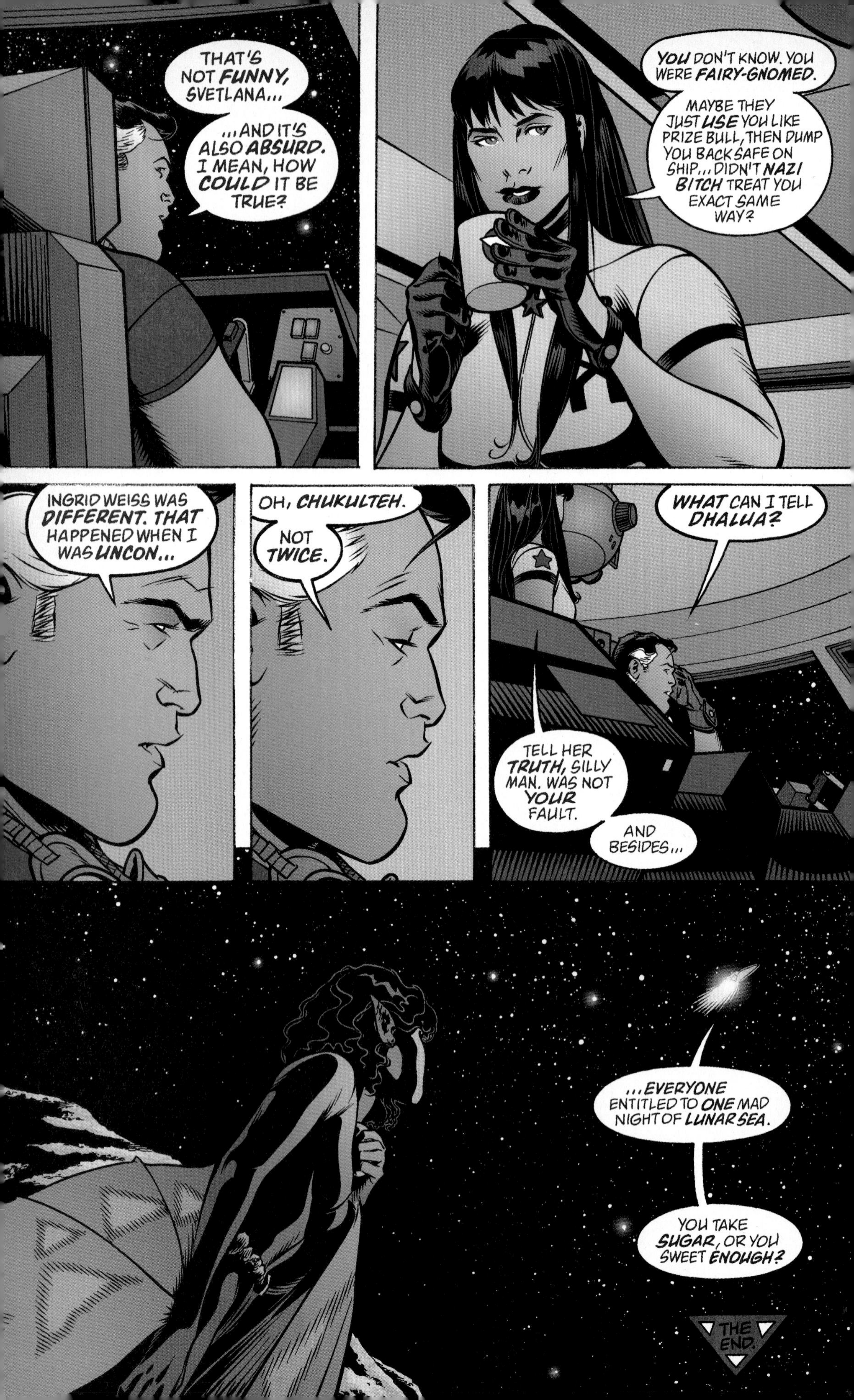
THAT'S NOT FUNNY, SVETLANA...
...AND IT'S ALSO ABSURD. I MEAN, HOW COULD IT BE TRUE?
YOU DON'T KNOW. YOU WERE FAIRY-GNOMED.
MAYBE THEY JUST USE YOU LIKE PRIZE BULL, THEN DUMP YOU BACK SAFE ON SHIP... DIDN'T NAZI BITCH TREAT YOU EXACT SAME WAY?
INGRID WEISS WAS DIFFERENT. THAT HAPPENED WHEN I WAS UNCON...
OH, CHUKULTEH.
NOT TWICE.
WHAT CAN I TELL DHALUA?
TELL HER TRUTH, SILLY MAN. WAS NOT YOUR FAULT.
AND BESIDES...
...EVERYONE ENTITLED TO ONE MAD NIGHT OF LUNAR SEA.
YOU TAKE SUGAR, OR YOU SWEET ENOUGH?
THE END.

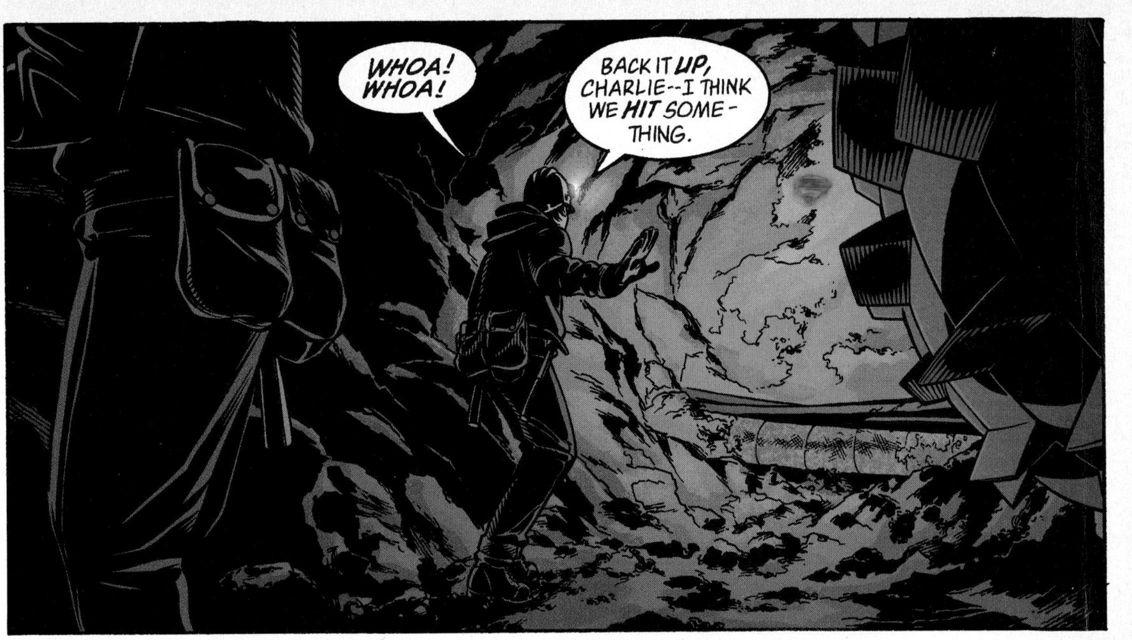
WHOA! WHOA!
BACK IT UP, CHARLIE--I THINK WE HIT SOME-THING.

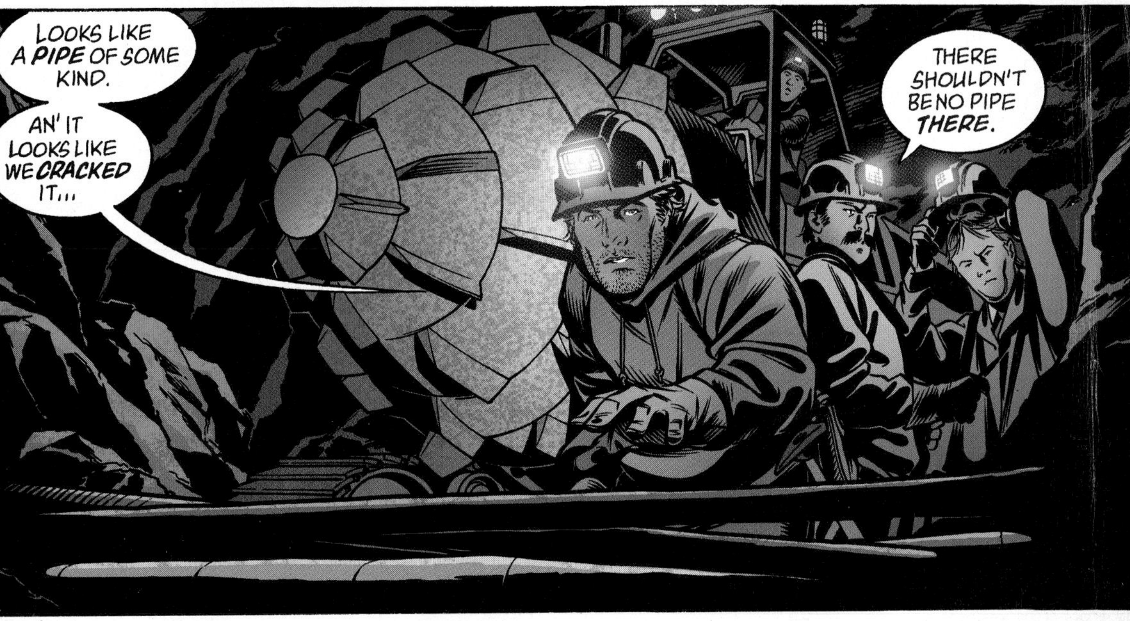
LOOKS LIKE A PIPE OF SOME KIND.
AN' IT LOOKS LIKE WE CRACKED IT...
THERE SHOULDN'T BE NO PIPE THERE.

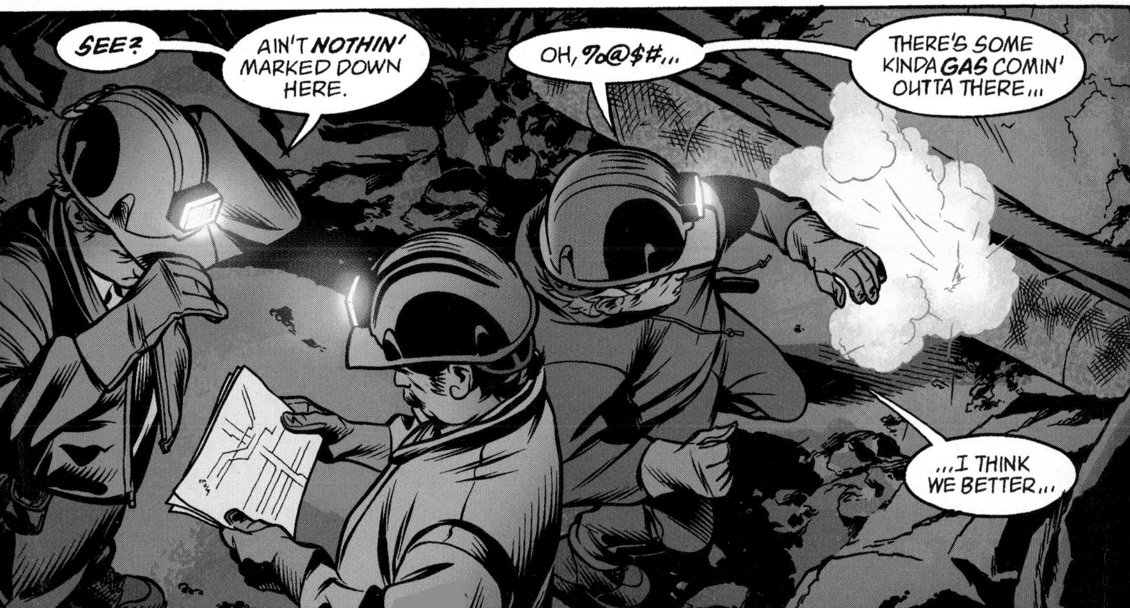
SEE?
AIN'T NOTHIN' MARKED DOWN HERE.
OH, %@$#...
THERE'S SOME KINDA GAS COMIN' OUTTA THERE...
...I THINK WE BETTER...

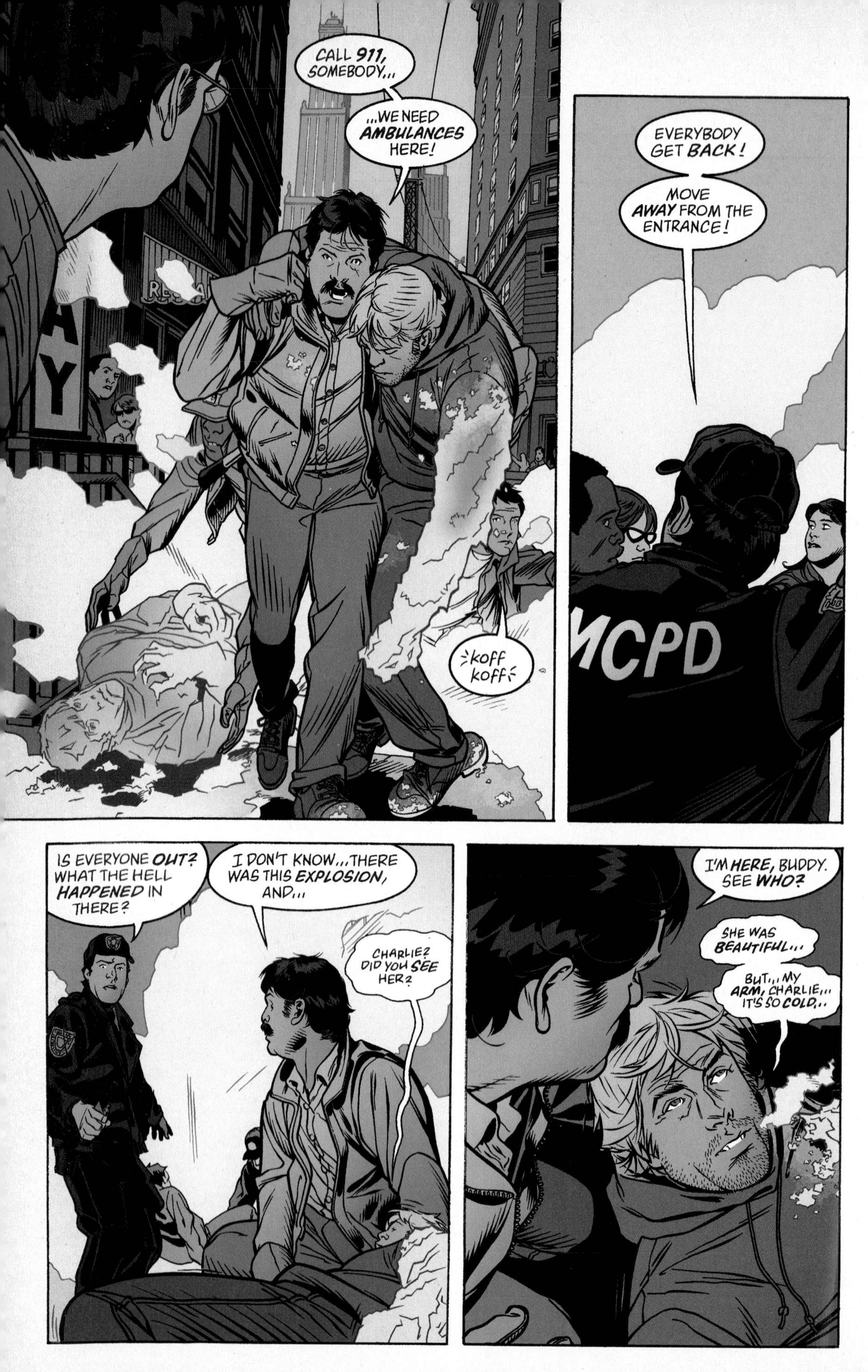
CALL 911, SOMEBODY...
...WE NEED AMBULANCES HERE!
koff koff
EVERYBODY GET BACK!
MOVE AWAY FROM THE ENTRANCE!
MCPD
IS EVERYONE OUT? WHAT THE HELL HAPPENED IN THERE?
I DON'T KNOW... THERE WAS THIS EXPLOSION, AND...
CHARLIE? DID YOU SEE HER?
I'M HERE, BUDDY. SEE WHO?
SHE WAS BEAUTIFUL...
BUT... MY ARM, CHARLIE... IT'S SO COLD...

# CHAPTER FIVE

In which an old, cold flame is reborn,
a deceased foe has a last shot at revenge,
and Tom tries to make things right.

**Cover art:**
**Chris Sprouse and Karl Story**

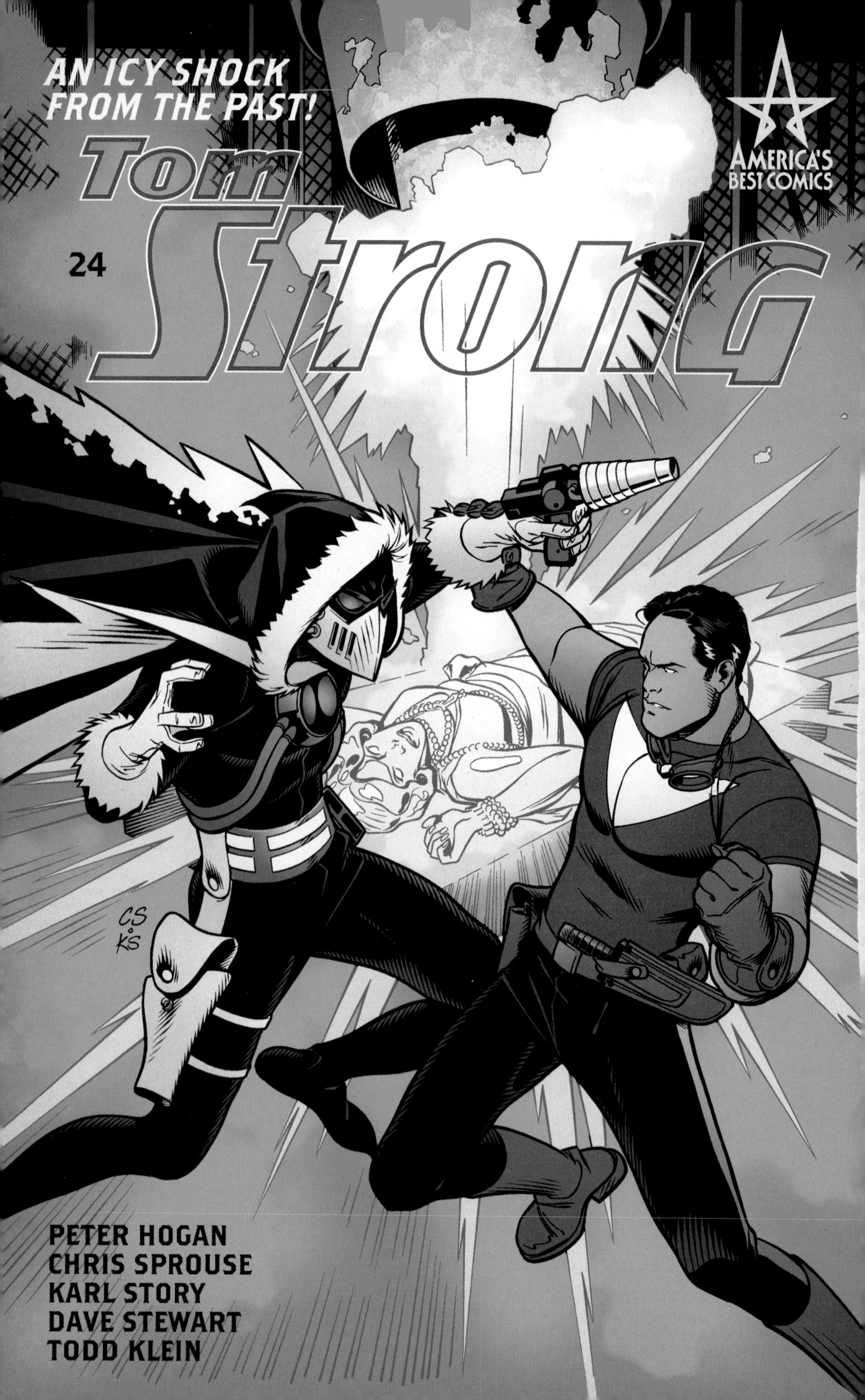
AN ICY SHOCK FROM THE PAST!
Tom Strong
24
AMERICA'S BEST COMICS
CS KS
PETER HOGAN
CHRIS SPROUSE
KARL STORY
DAVE STEWART
TODD KLEIN

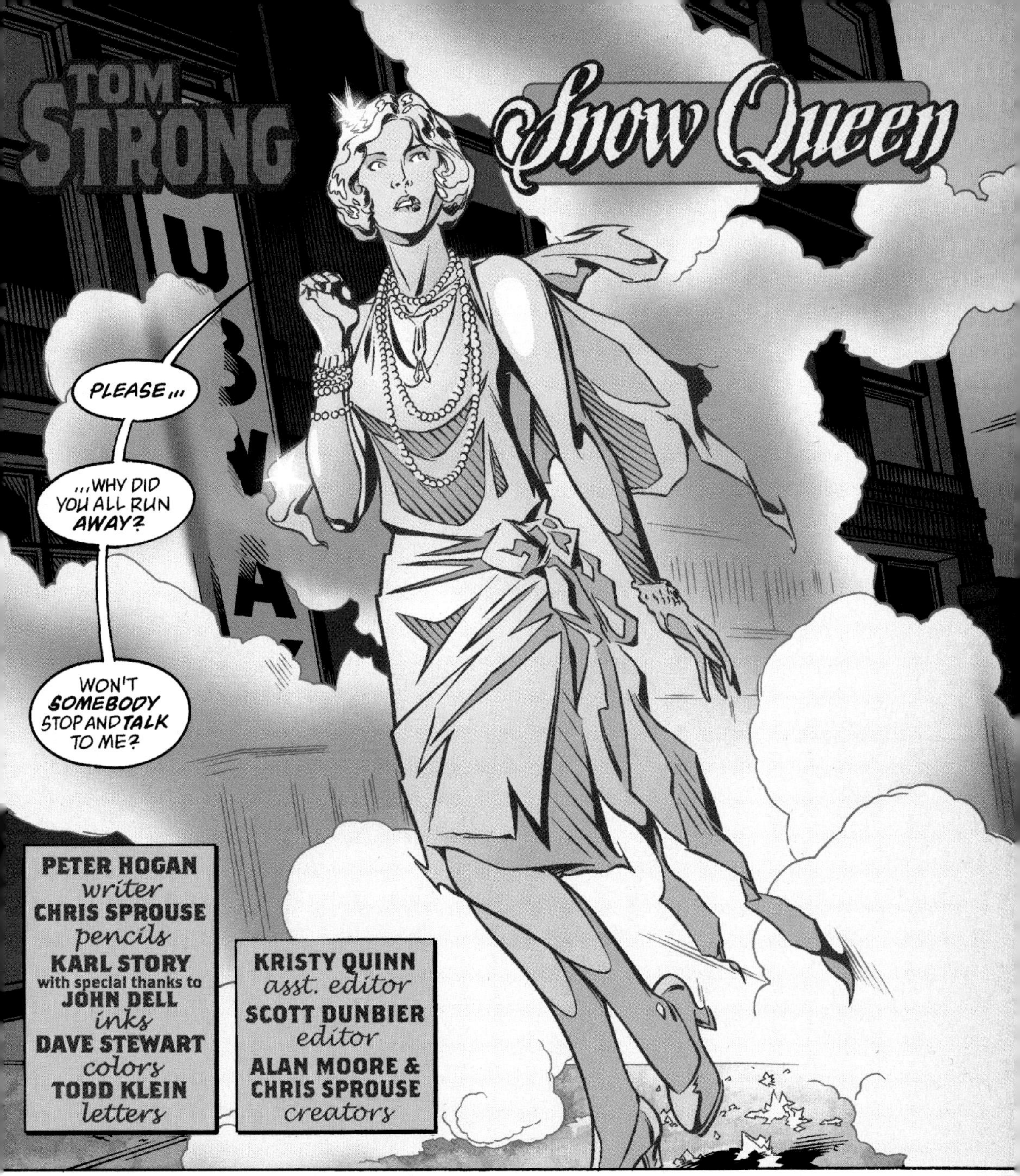
TOM STRONG
Snow Queen
PLEASE...
...WHY DID YOU ALL RUN AWAY?
WON'T SOMEBODY STOP AND TALK TO ME?
PETER HOGAN writer
CHRIS SPROUSE pencils
KARL STORY with special thanks to JOHN DELL inks
DAVE STEWART colors
TODD KLEIN letters
KRISTY QUINN asst. editor
SCOTT DUNBIER editor
ALAN MOORE & CHRIS SPROUSE creators

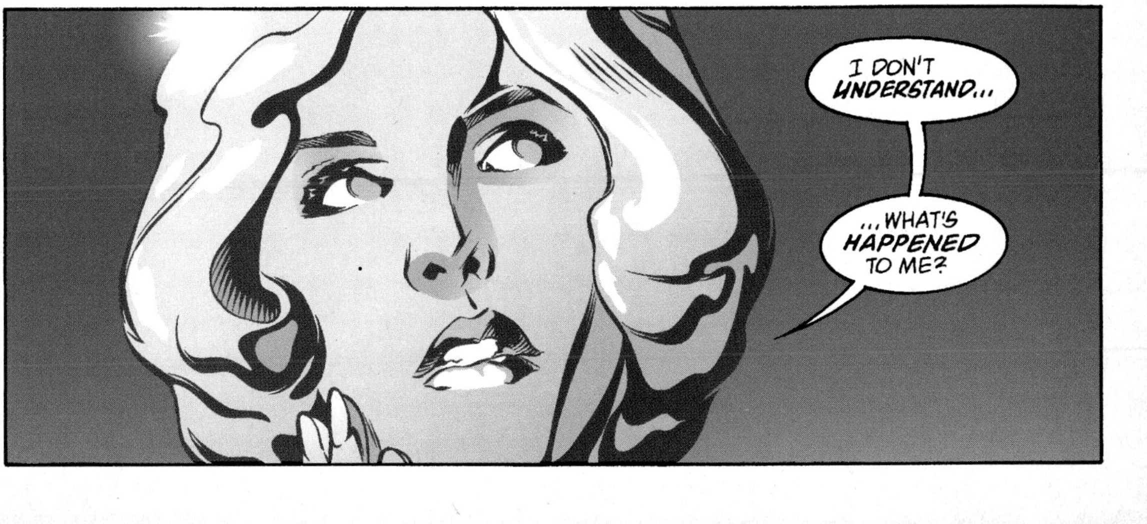
I DON'T UNDERSTAND...
...WHAT'S HAPPENED TO ME?

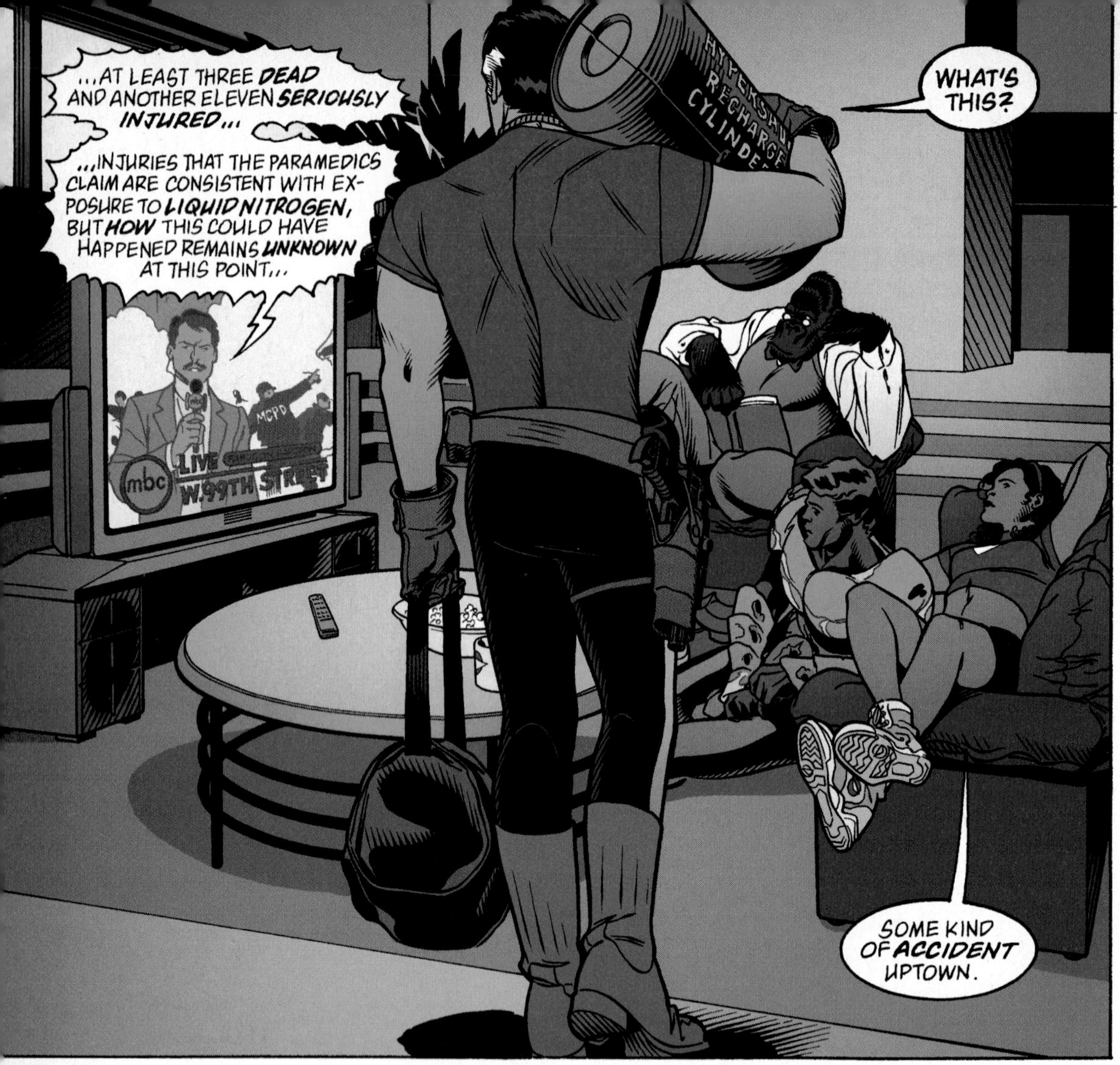
...AT LEAST THREE DEAD AND ANOTHER ELEVEN SERIOUSLY INJURED...
...INJURIES THAT THE PARAMEDICS CLAIM ARE CONSISTENT WITH EXPOSURE TO LIQUID NITROGEN, BUT HOW THIS COULD HAVE HAPPENED REMAINS UNKNOWN AT THIS POINT...
mbc
LIVE
W.99TH STREET
MCPD
WHAT'S THIS?
SOME KIND OF ACCIDENT UPTOWN.

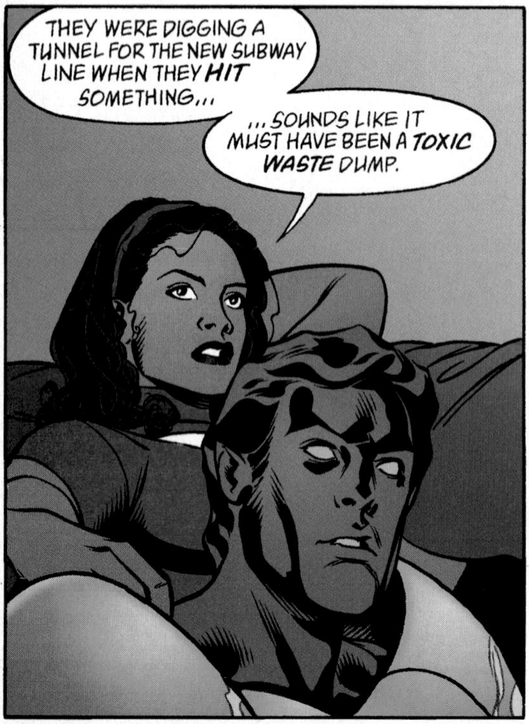
THEY WERE DIGGING A TUNNEL FOR THE NEW SUBWAY LINE WHEN THEY HIT SOMETHING...
...SOUNDS LIKE IT MUST HAVE BEEN A TOXIC WASTE DUMP.

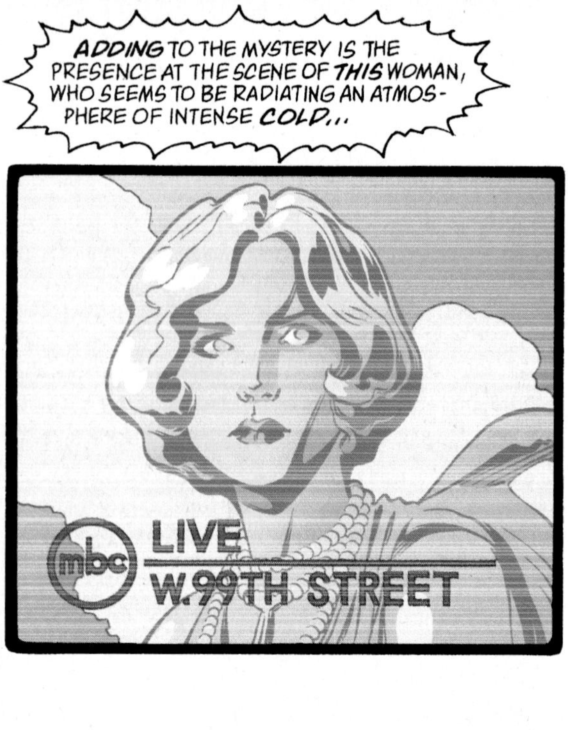
ADDING TO THE MYSTERY IS THE PRESENCE AT THE SCENE OF THIS WOMAN, WHO SEEMS TO BE RADIATING AN ATMOSPHERE OF INTENSE COLD...
mbc
LIVE
W.99TH STREET

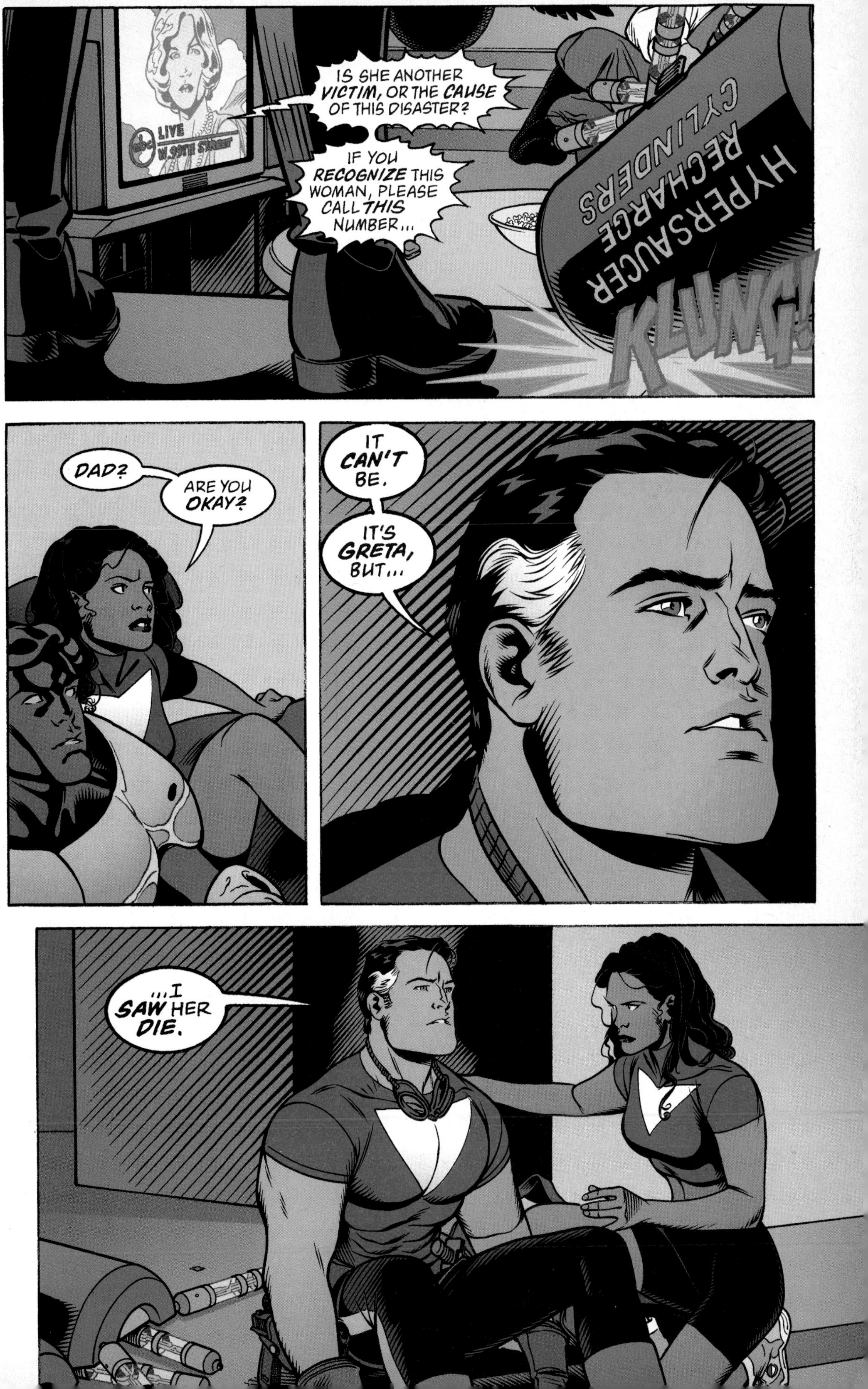
IS SHE ANOTHER VICTIM, OR THE CAUSE OF THIS DISASTER?
LIVE W. 99TH STREET
IF YOU RECOGNIZE THIS WOMAN, PLEASE CALL THIS NUMBER...
HYPERSAUCER RECHARGE CYLINDERS
KLUNG!
DAD?
ARE YOU OKAY?
IT CAN'T BE.
IT'S GRETA, BUT...
...I SAW HER DIE.

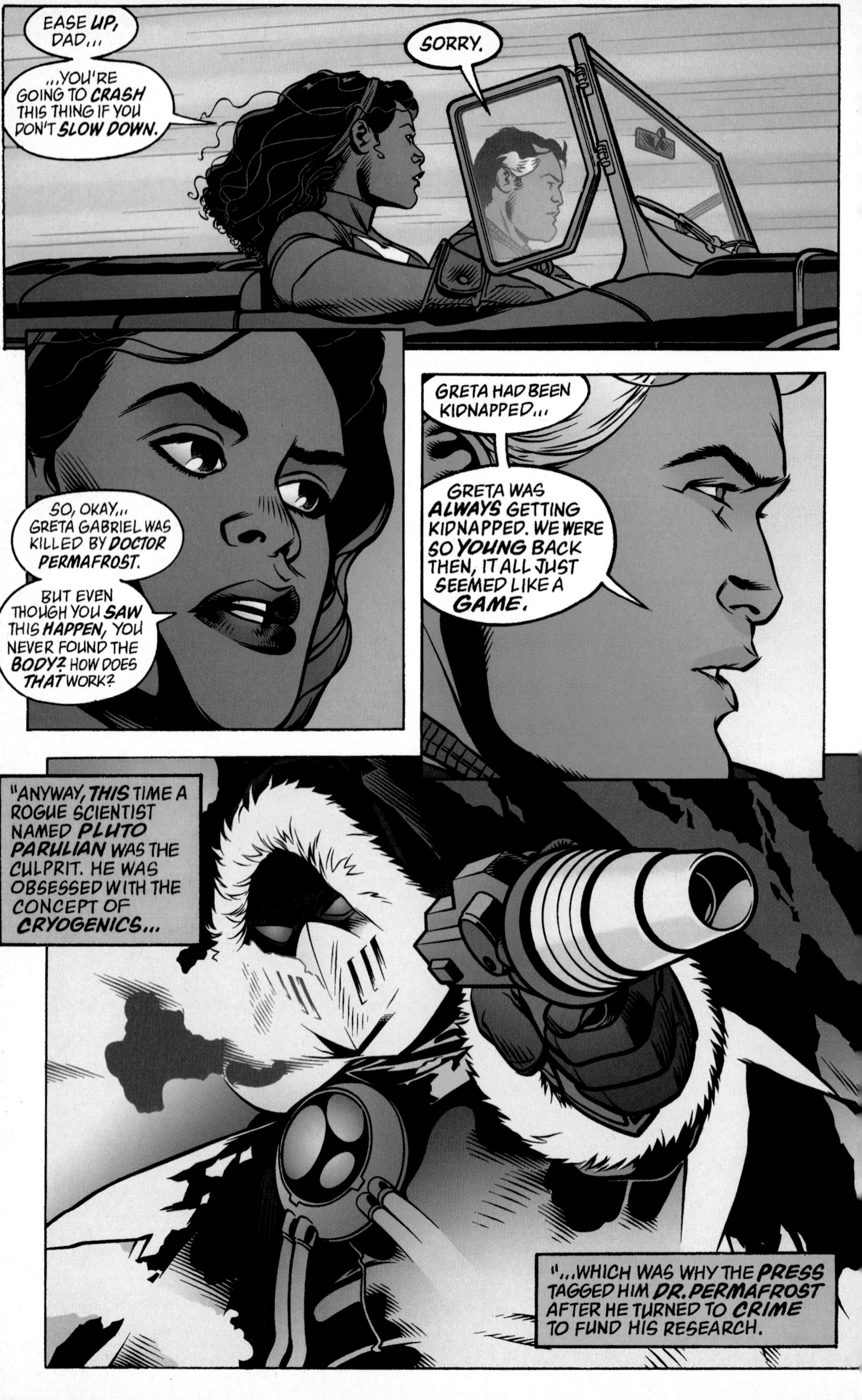
EASE UP, DAD...
...YOU'RE GOING TO CRASH THIS THING IF YOU DON'T SLOW DOWN.
SORRY.
SO, OKAY... GRETA GABRIEL WAS KILLED BY DOCTOR PERMAFROST.
BUT EVEN THOUGH YOU SAW THIS HAPPEN, YOU NEVER FOUND THE BODY? HOW DOES THAT WORK?
GRETA HAD BEEN KIDNAPPED...
GRETA WAS ALWAYS GETTING KIDNAPPED. WE WERE SO YOUNG BACK THEN, IT ALL JUST SEEMED LIKE A GAME.
"ANYWAY, THIS TIME A ROGUE SCIENTIST NAMED PLUTO PARULIAN WAS THE CULPRIT. HE WAS OBSESSED WITH THE CONCEPT OF CRYOGENICS...
"...WHICH WAS WHY THE PRESS TAGGED HIM DR. PERMAFROST AFTER HE TURNED TO CRIME TO FUND HIS RESEARCH.

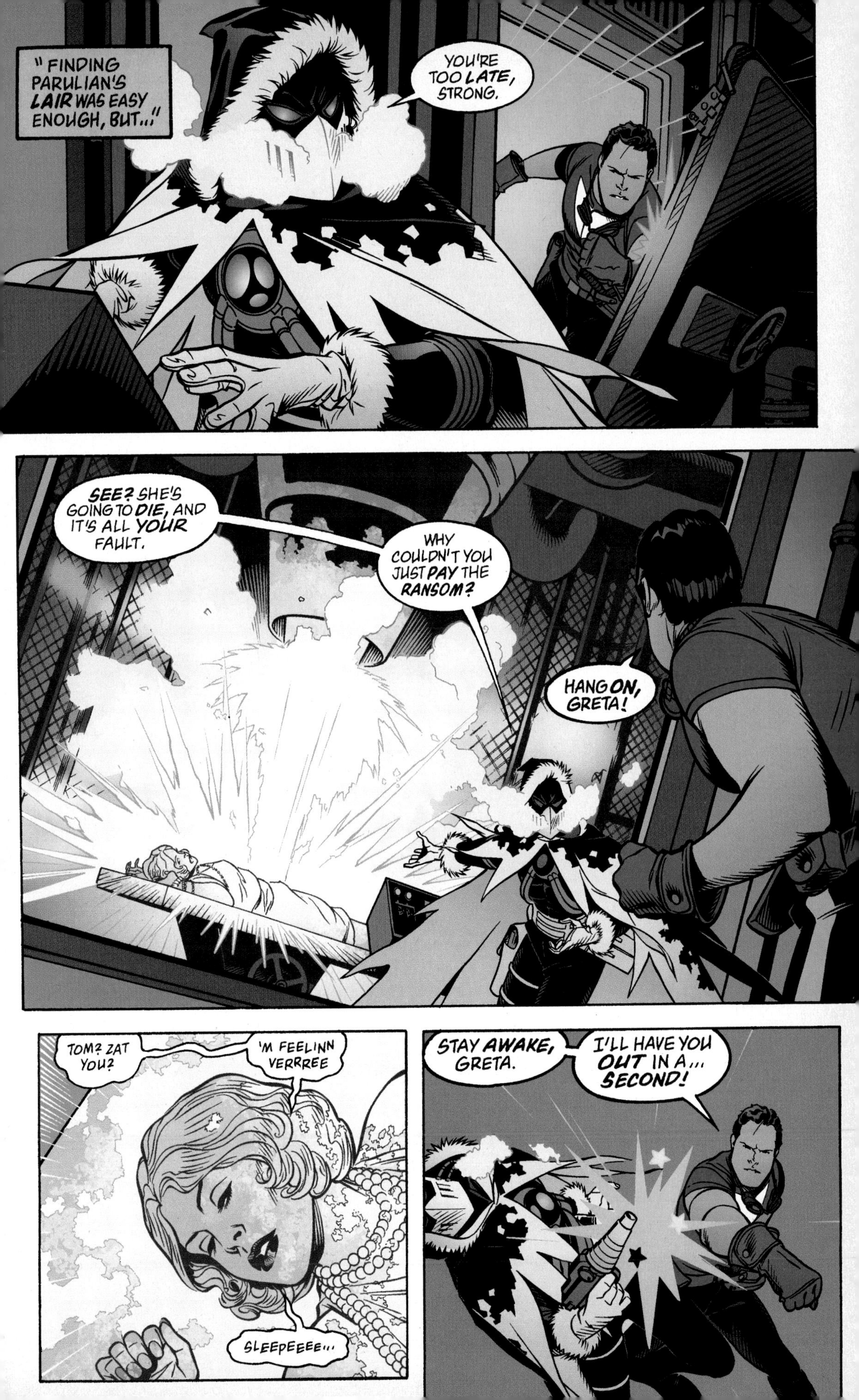
"FINDING PARULIAN'S LAIR WAS EASY ENOUGH, BUT..."
YOU'RE TOO LATE, STRONG.
SEE? SHE'S GOING TO DIE, AND IT'S ALL YOUR FAULT.
WHY COULDN'T YOU JUST PAY THE RANSOM?
HANG ON, GRETA!
TOM? ZAT YOU?
'M FEELINN VERRREE
SLEEPEEEE...
STAY AWAKE, GRETA.
I'LL HAVE YOU OUT IN A... SECOND!

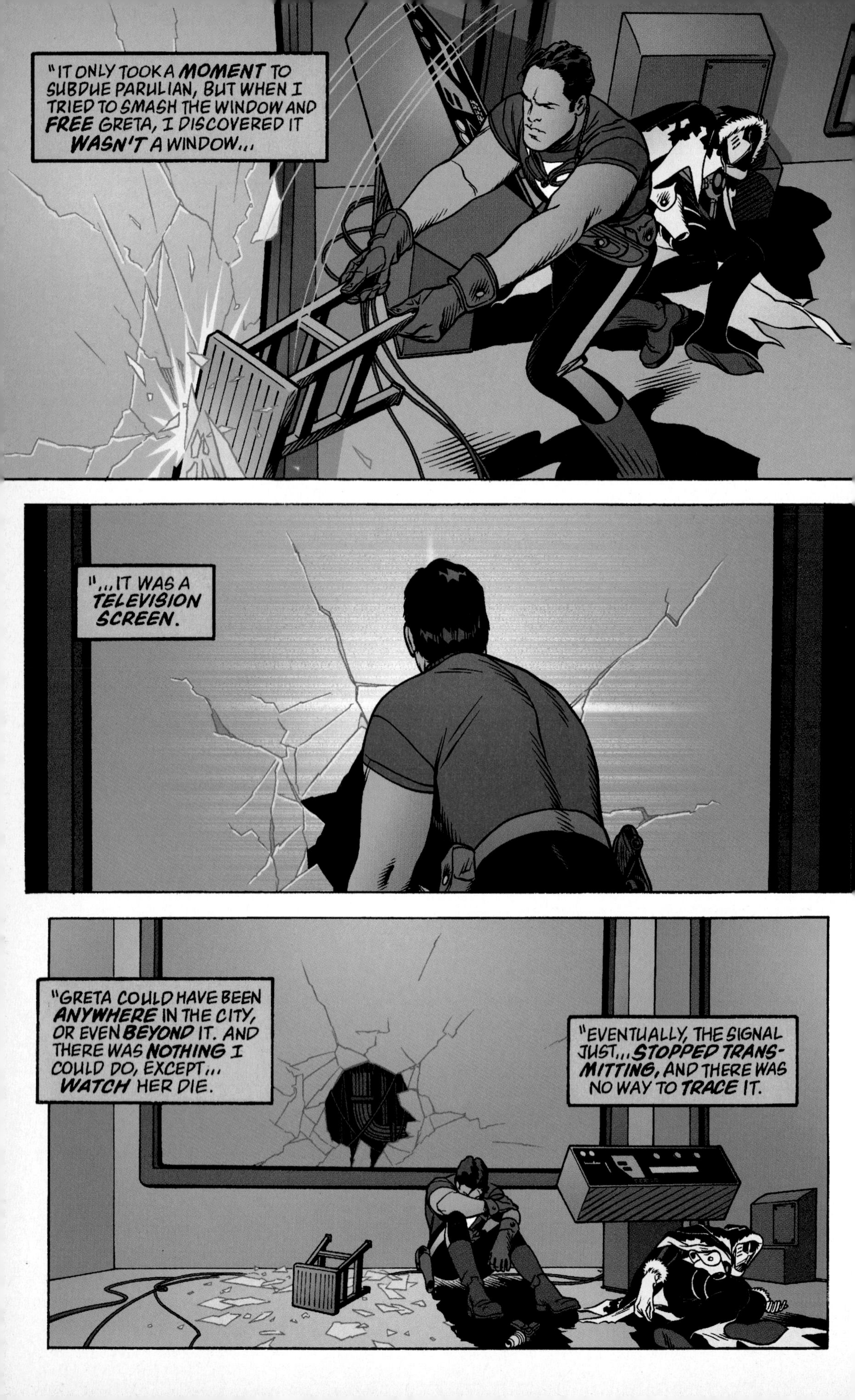
"IT ONLY TOOK A MOMENT TO SUBDUE PARULIAN, BUT WHEN I TRIED TO SMASH THE WINDOW AND FREE GRETA, I DISCOVERED IT WASN'T A WINDOW...
"...IT WAS A TELEVISION SCREEN.
"GRETA COULD HAVE BEEN ANYWHERE IN THE CITY, OR EVEN BEYOND IT. AND THERE WAS NOTHING I COULD DO, EXCEPT... WATCH HER DIE.
"EVENTUALLY, THE SIGNAL JUST... STOPPED TRANS-MITTING, AND THERE WAS NO WAY TO TRACE IT.

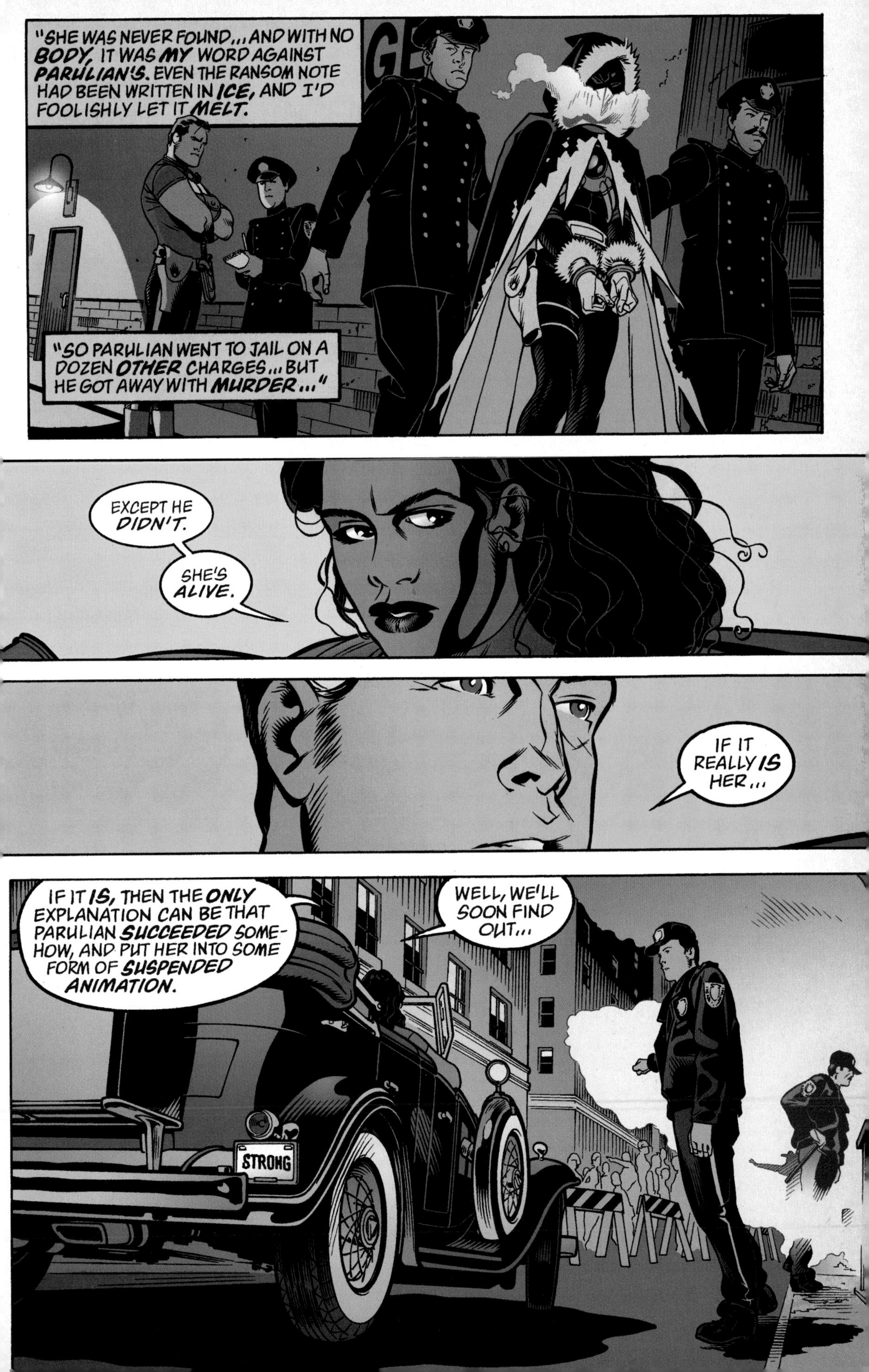
"SHE WAS NEVER FOUND... AND WITH NO BODY, IT WAS MY WORD AGAINST PARULIAN'S. EVEN THE RANSOM NOTE HAD BEEN WRITTEN IN ICE, AND I'D FOOLISHLY LET IT MELT.
"SO PARULIAN WENT TO JAIL ON A DOZEN OTHER CHARGES... BUT HE GOT AWAY WITH MURDER..."
EXCEPT HE DIDN'T.
SHE'S ALIVE.
IF IT REALLY IS HER...
IF IT IS, THEN THE ONLY EXPLANATION CAN BE THAT PARULIAN SUCCEEDED SOME-HOW, AND PUT HER INTO SOME FORM OF SUSPENDED ANIMATION.
WELL, WE'LL SOON FIND OUT...
STRONG

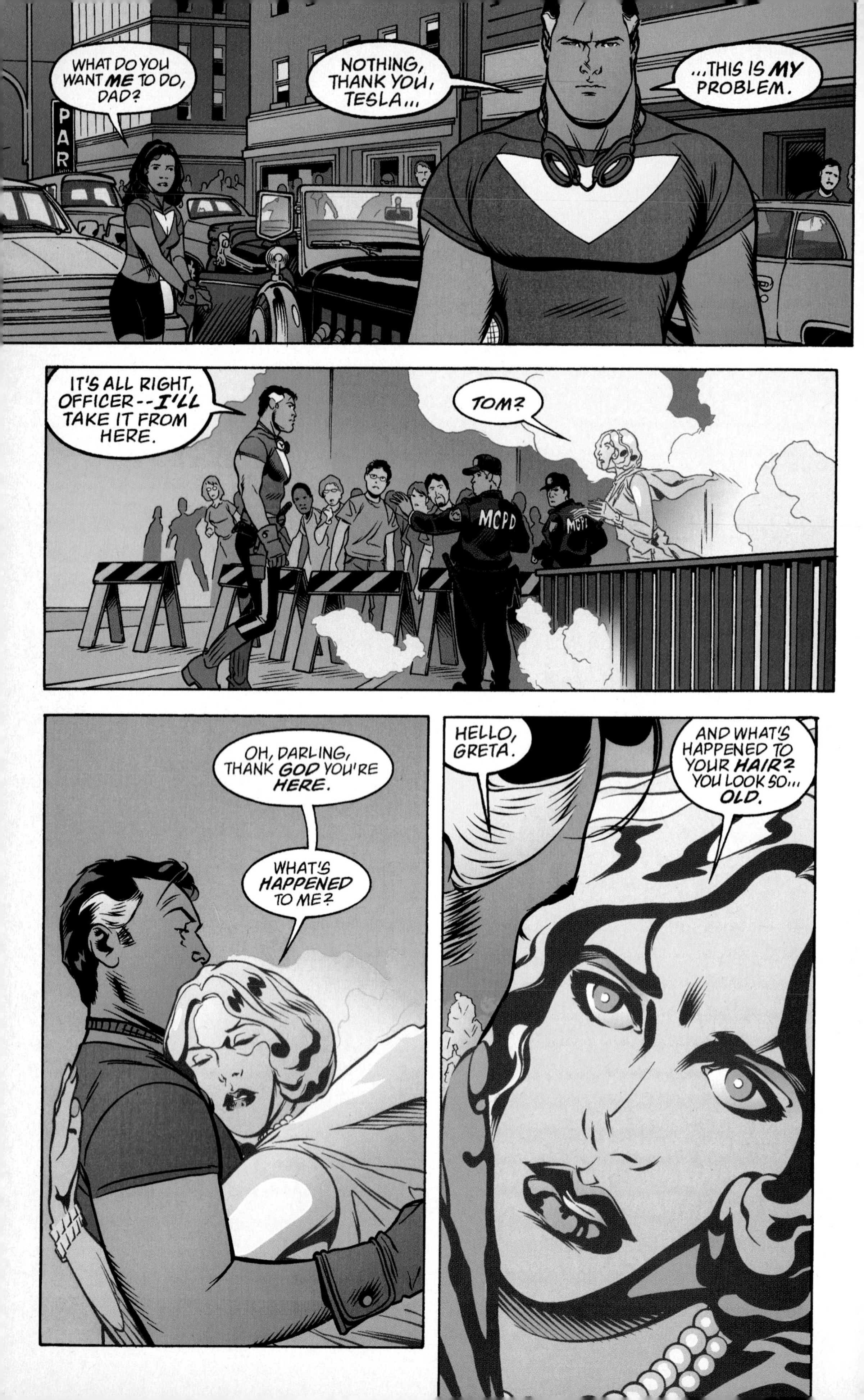
WHAT DO YOU WANT ME TO DO, DAD?
NOTHING, THANK YOU, TESLA...
...THIS IS MY PROBLEM.
PAR
IT'S ALL RIGHT, OFFICER--I'LL TAKE IT FROM HERE.
TOM?
MCPD
OH, DARLING, THANK GOD YOU'RE HERE.
WHAT'S HAPPENED TO ME?
HELLO, GRETA.
AND WHAT'S HAPPENED TO YOUR HAIR? YOU LOOK SO... OLD.

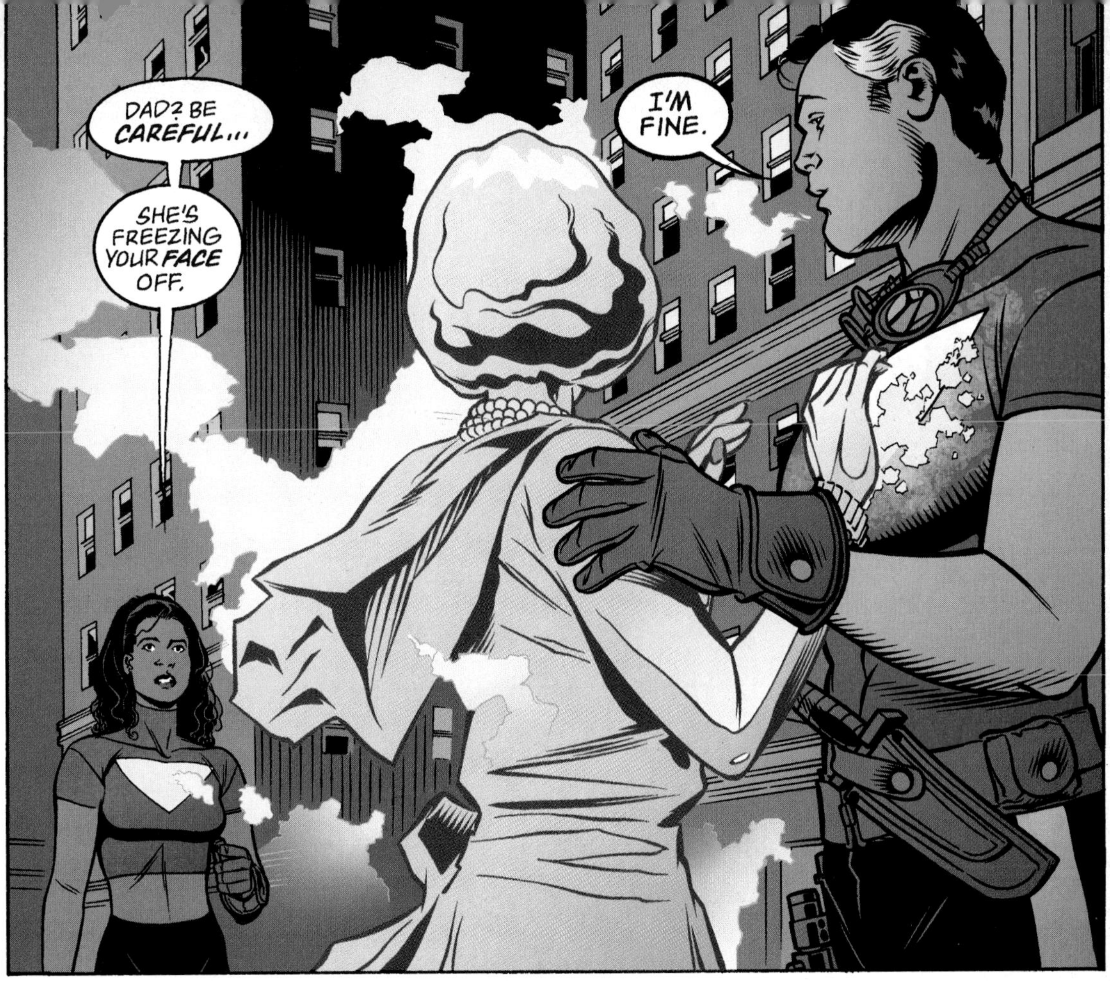
DAD? BE CAREFUL...
SHE'S FREEZING YOUR FACE OFF.
I'M FINE.

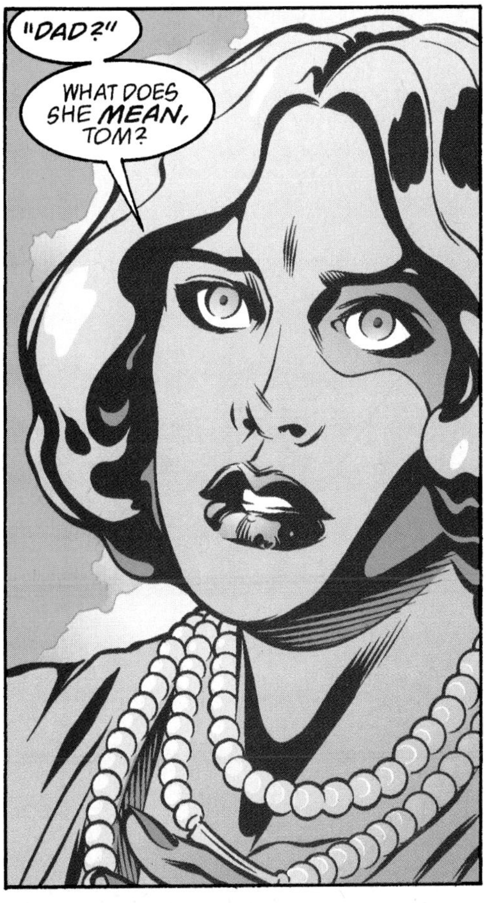
"DAD?"
WHAT DOES SHE MEAN, TOM?

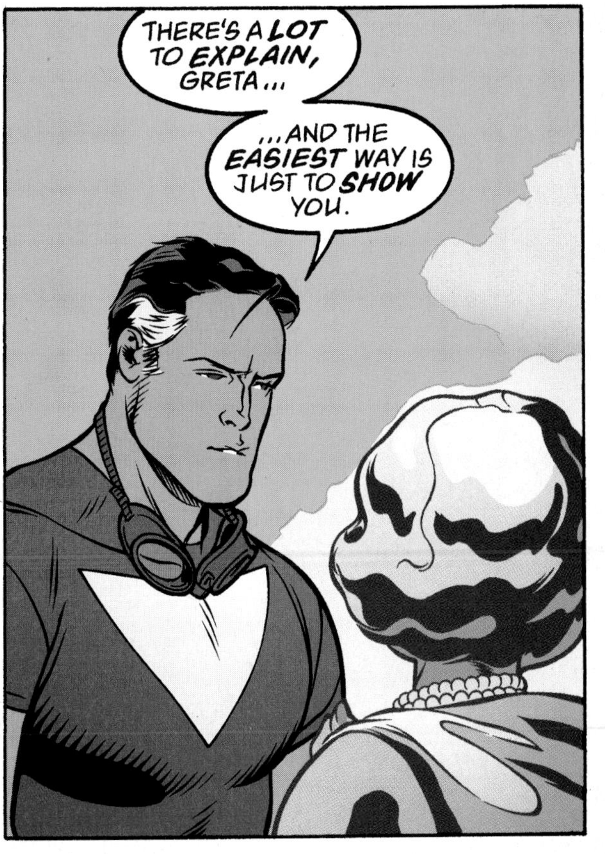
THERE'S A LOT TO EXPLAIN, GRETA...
...AND THE EASIEST WAY IS JUST TO SHOW YOU.

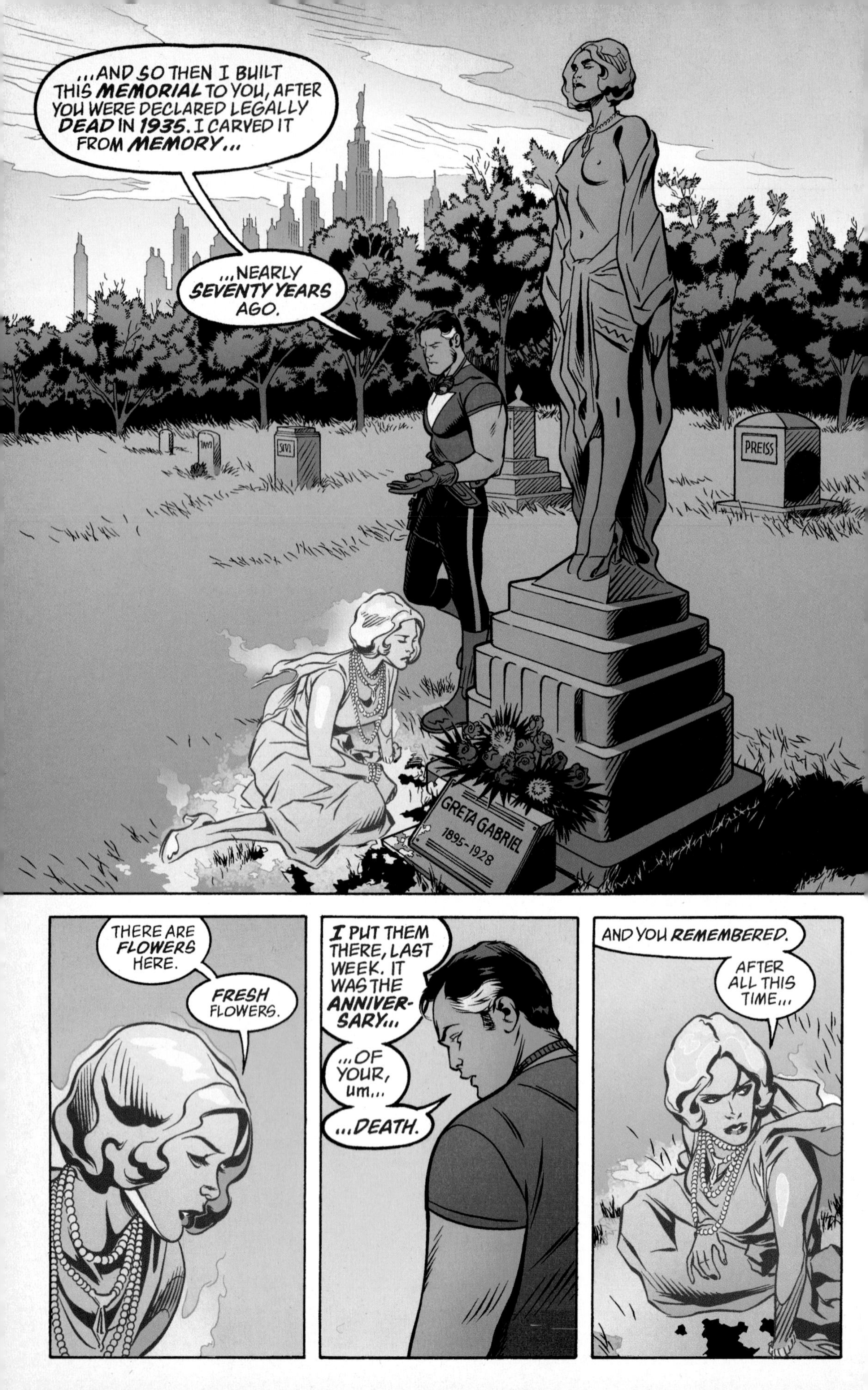
...AND SO THEN I BUILT THIS MEMORIAL TO YOU, AFTER YOU WERE DECLARED LEGALLY DEAD IN 1935. I CARVED IT FROM MEMORY...
...NEARLY SEVENTY YEARS AGO.
PREISS
GRETA GABRIEL 1895-1928
THERE ARE FLOWERS HERE.
FRESH FLOWERS.
I PUT THEM THERE, LAST WEEK. IT WAS THE ANNIVERSARY...
...OF YOUR, um...
...DEATH.
AND YOU REMEMBERED.
AFTER ALL THIS TIME...

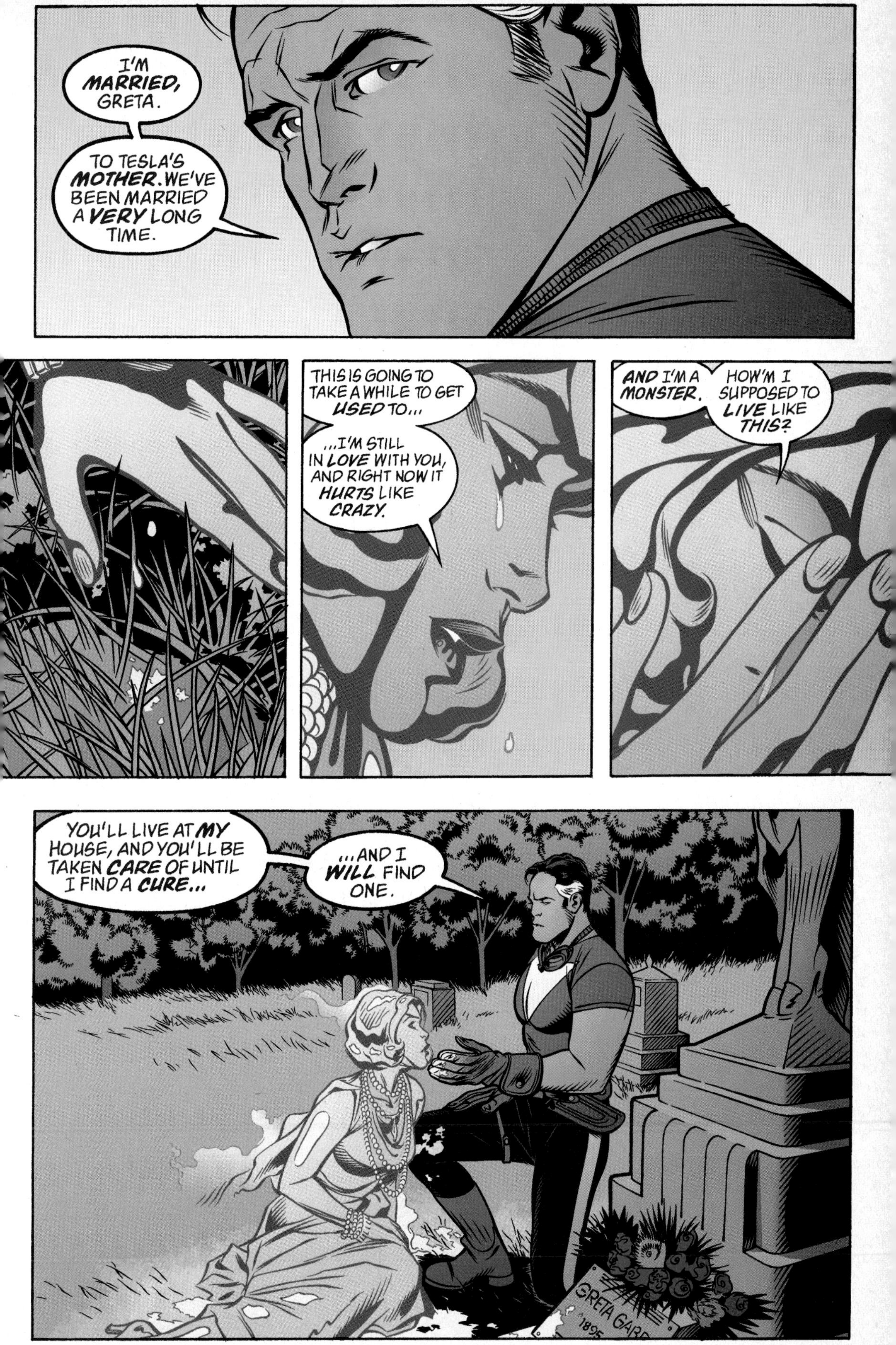
I'M MARRIED, GRETA.
TO TESLA'S MOTHER. WE'VE BEEN MARRIED A VERY LONG TIME.
THIS IS GOING TO TAKE A WHILE TO GET USED TO...
...I'M STILL IN LOVE WITH YOU, AND RIGHT NOW IT HURTS LIKE CRAZY.
AND I'M A MONSTER.
HOW'M I SUPPOSED TO LIVE LIKE THIS?
YOU'LL LIVE AT MY HOUSE, AND YOU'LL BE TAKEN CARE OF UNTIL I FIND A CURE...
...AND I WILL FIND ONE.

YOUR ⋗ptic⋖ SUPPER, MISS GABRIEL.

AND MAY I SAY WHAT A ⋗ssss⋖ PLEASURE IT IS TO ⋗ktik⋖ TO ⋗ptoc⋖ SEE YOU AGAIN.

THANK YOU, PNEUMAN.

IT'S GOOD TO SEE YOU, TOO.

I TRUST THESE ⋗ptang⋖ QUARTERS ARE ⋗tuk tuk⋖ QUARTERS ARE ⋗ssss⋖ SATISFACTORY?

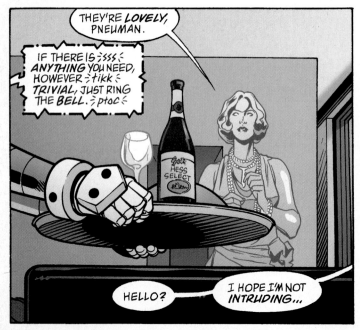

THEY'RE LOVELY, PNEUMAN.

IF THERE IS ⋗sss⋖ ANYTHING YOU NEED, HOWEVER ⋗tikk⋖ TRIVIAL, JUST RING THE BELL. ⋗ptoc⋖

HESS SELECT

HELLO?

I HOPE I'M NOT INTRUDING...

I JUST WANTED TO WELCOME YOU TO MY HOME.

I'M DHALUA.

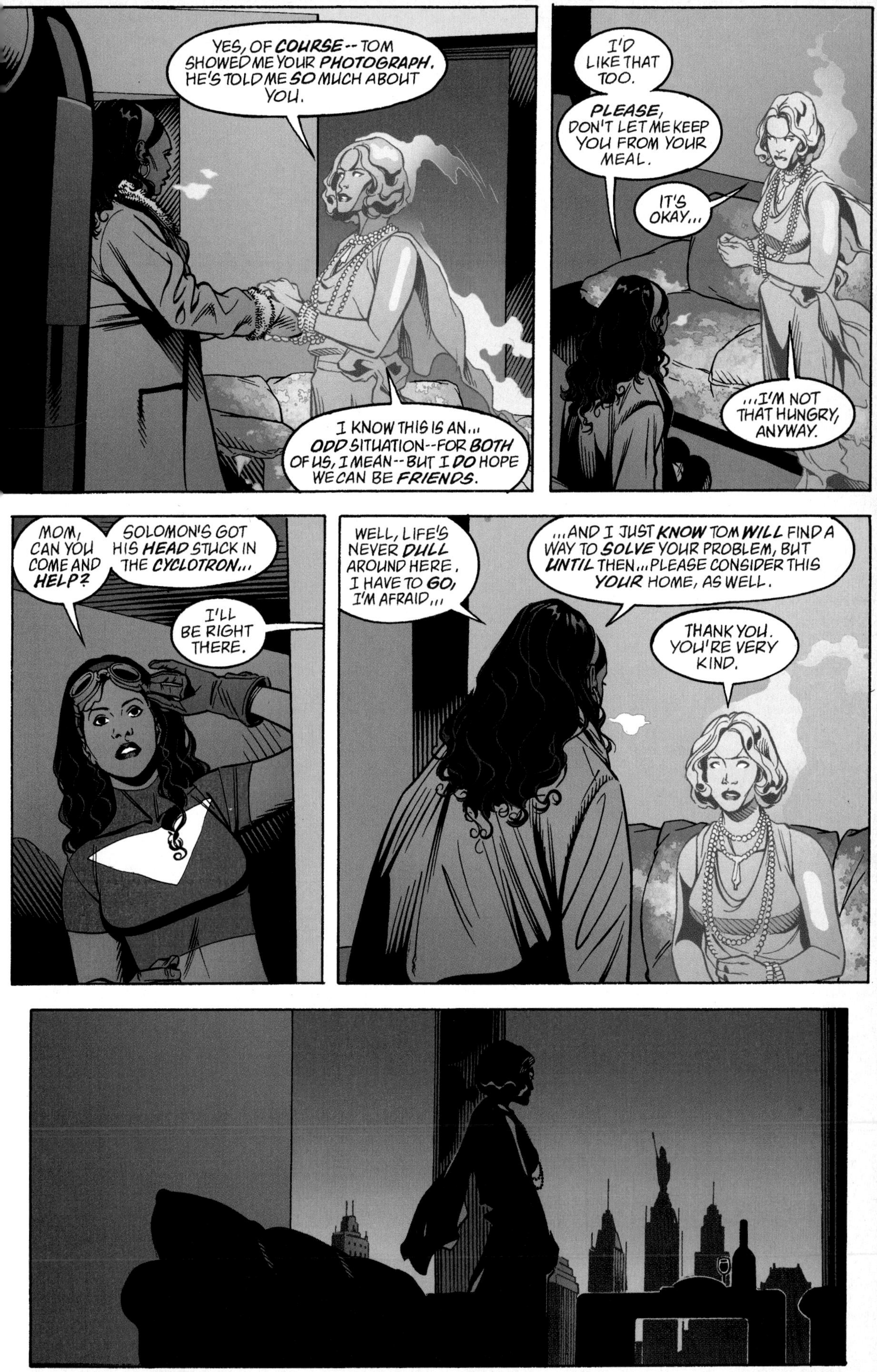
YES, OF COURSE -- TOM SHOWED ME YOUR PHOTOGRAPH. HE'S TOLD ME SO MUCH ABOUT YOU.
I KNOW THIS IS AN... ODD SITUATION--FOR BOTH OF US, I MEAN -- BUT I DO HOPE WE CAN BE FRIENDS.
I'D LIKE THAT TOO.
PLEASE, DON'T LET ME KEEP YOU FROM YOUR MEAL.
IT'S OKAY...
...I'M NOT THAT HUNGRY, ANYWAY.
MOM, CAN YOU COME AND HELP?
SOLOMON'S GOT HIS HEAD STUCK IN THE CYCLOTRON...
I'LL BE RIGHT THERE.
WELL, LIFE'S NEVER DULL AROUND HERE. I HAVE TO GO, I'M AFRAID...
...AND I JUST KNOW TOM WILL FIND A WAY TO SOLVE YOUR PROBLEM, BUT UNTIL THEN... PLEASE CONSIDER THIS YOUR HOME, AS WELL.
THANK YOU. YOU'RE VERY KIND.

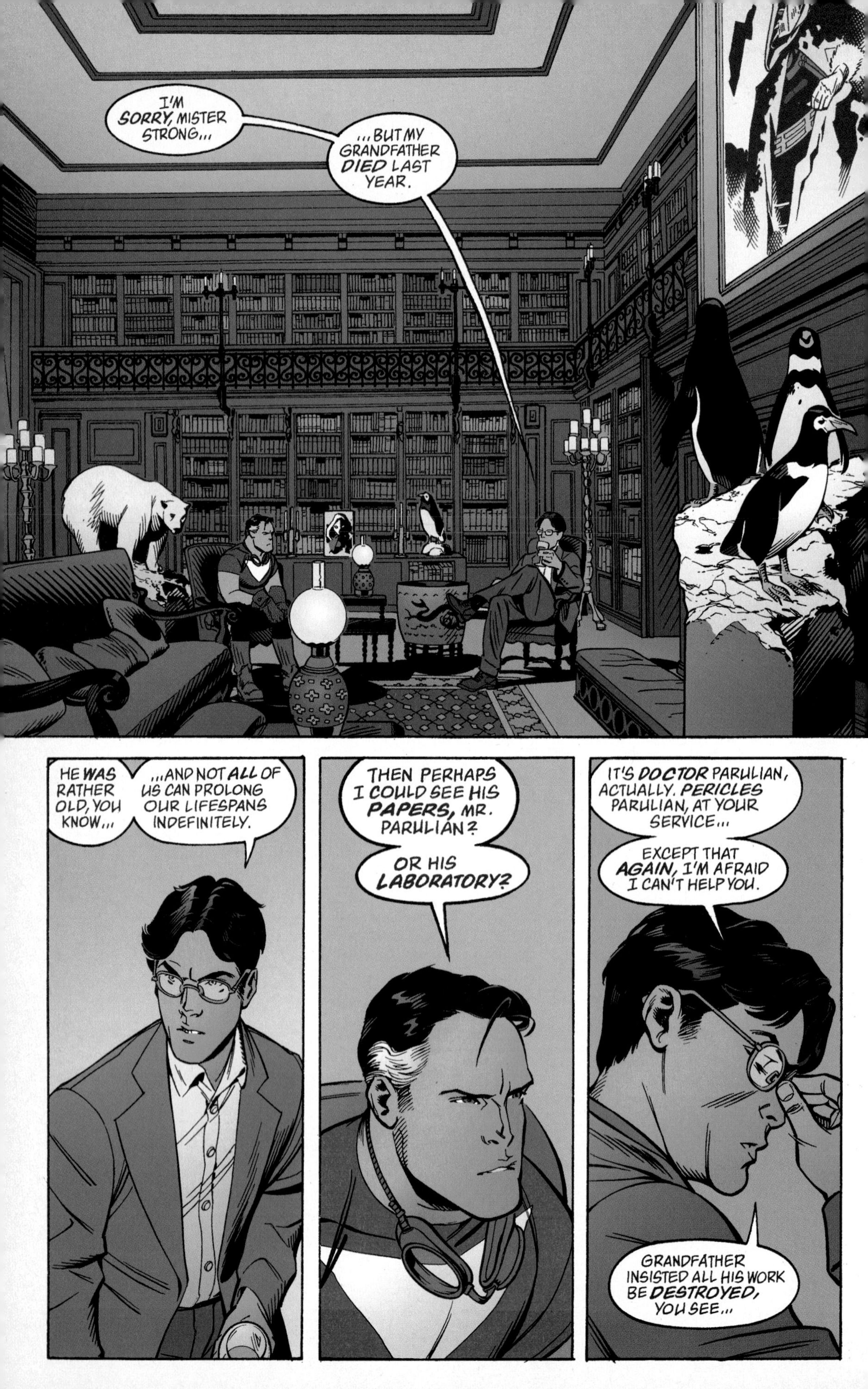
I'M SORRY, MISTER STRONG...
...BUT MY GRANDFATHER DIED LAST YEAR.
HE WAS RATHER OLD, YOU KNOW...
...AND NOT ALL OF US CAN PROLONG OUR LIFESPANS INDEFINITELY.
THEN PERHAPS I COULD SEE HIS PAPERS, MR. PARULIAN?
OR HIS LABORATORY?
IT'S DOCTOR PARULIAN, ACTUALLY. PERICLES PARULIAN, AT YOUR SERVICE...
EXCEPT THAT AGAIN, I'M AFRAID I CAN'T HELP YOU.
GRANDFATHER INSISTED ALL HIS WORK BE DESTROYED, YOU SEE...

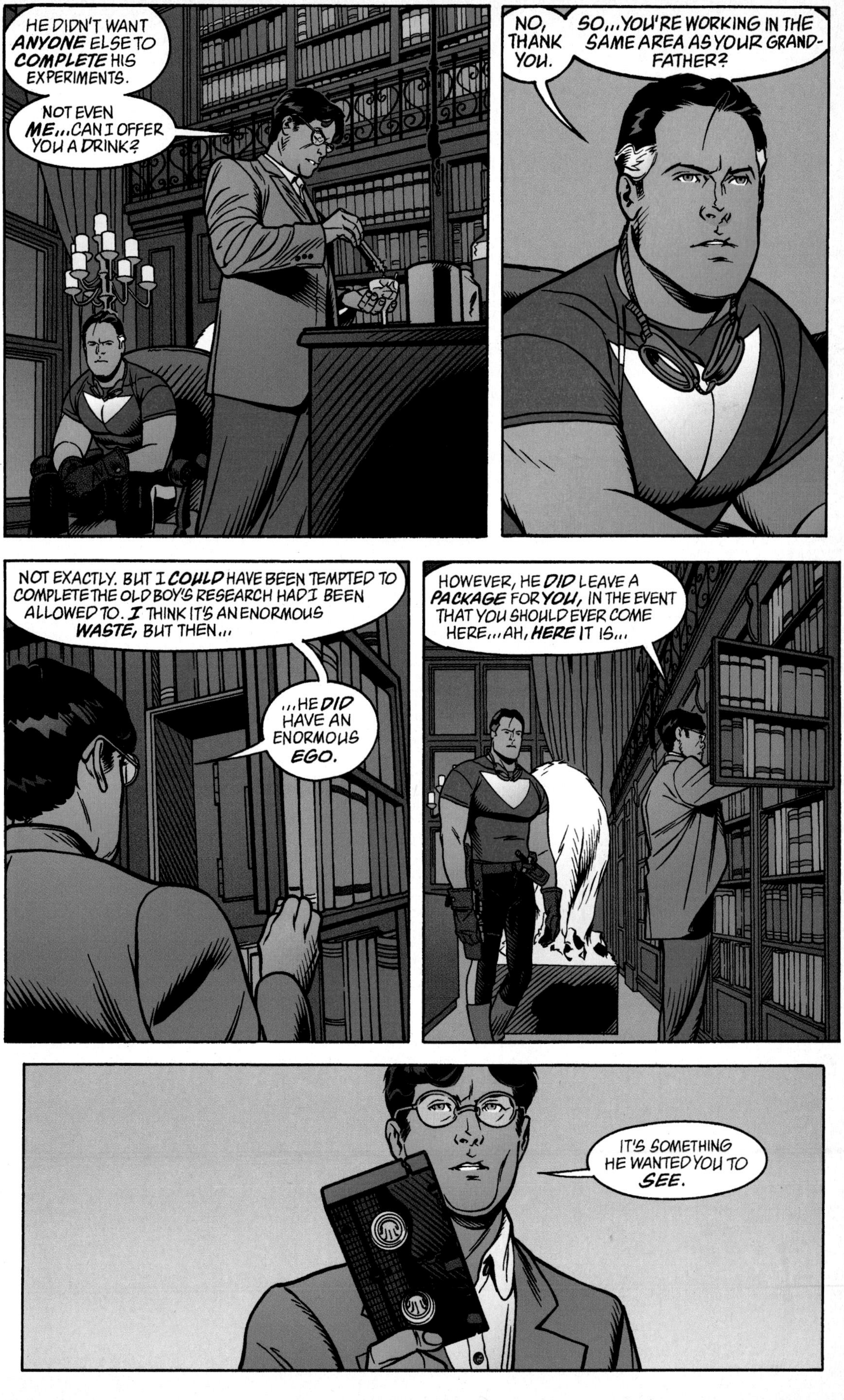
HE DIDN'T WANT ANYONE ELSE TO COMPLETE HIS EXPERIMENTS.
NOT EVEN ME...CAN I OFFER YOU A DRINK?
NO, THANK YOU.
SO...YOU'RE WORKING IN THE SAME AREA AS YOUR GRAND-FATHER?
NOT EXACTLY. BUT I COULD HAVE BEEN TEMPTED TO COMPLETE THE OLD BOY'S RESEARCH HAD I BEEN ALLOWED TO. I THINK IT'S AN ENORMOUS WASTE, BUT THEN...
...HE DID HAVE AN ENORMOUS EGO.
HOWEVER, HE DID LEAVE A PACKAGE FOR YOU, IN THE EVENT THAT YOU SHOULD EVER COME HERE...AH, HERE IT IS...
IT'S SOMETHING HE WANTED YOU TO SEE.

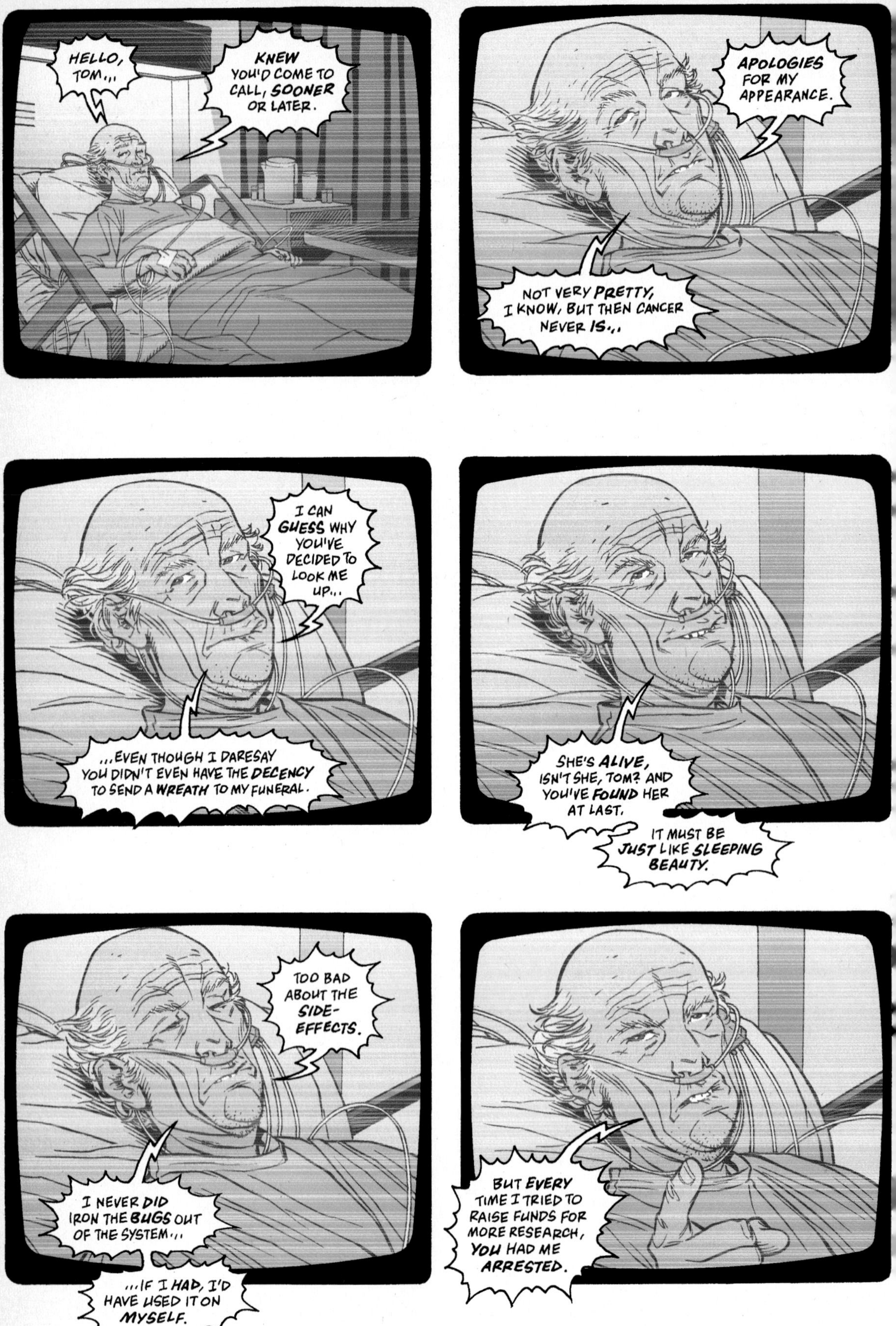
HELLO, TOM...
KNEW YOU'D COME TO CALL, SOONER OR LATER.
APOLOGIES FOR MY APPEARANCE.
NOT VERY PRETTY, I KNOW, BUT THEN CANCER NEVER IS...
I CAN GUESS WHY YOU'VE DECIDED TO LOOK ME UP...
...EVEN THOUGH I DARESAY YOU DIDN'T EVEN HAVE THE DECENCY TO SEND A WREATH TO MY FUNERAL.
SHE'S ALIVE, ISN'T SHE, TOM? AND YOU'VE FOUND HER AT LAST.
IT MUST BE JUST LIKE SLEEPING BEAUTY.
TOO BAD ABOUT THE SIDE-EFFECTS.
I NEVER DID IRON THE BUGS OUT OF THE SYSTEM...
...IF I HAD, I'D HAVE USED IT ON MYSELF.
BUT EVERY TIME I TRIED TO RAISE FUNDS FOR MORE RESEARCH, YOU HAD ME ARRESTED.

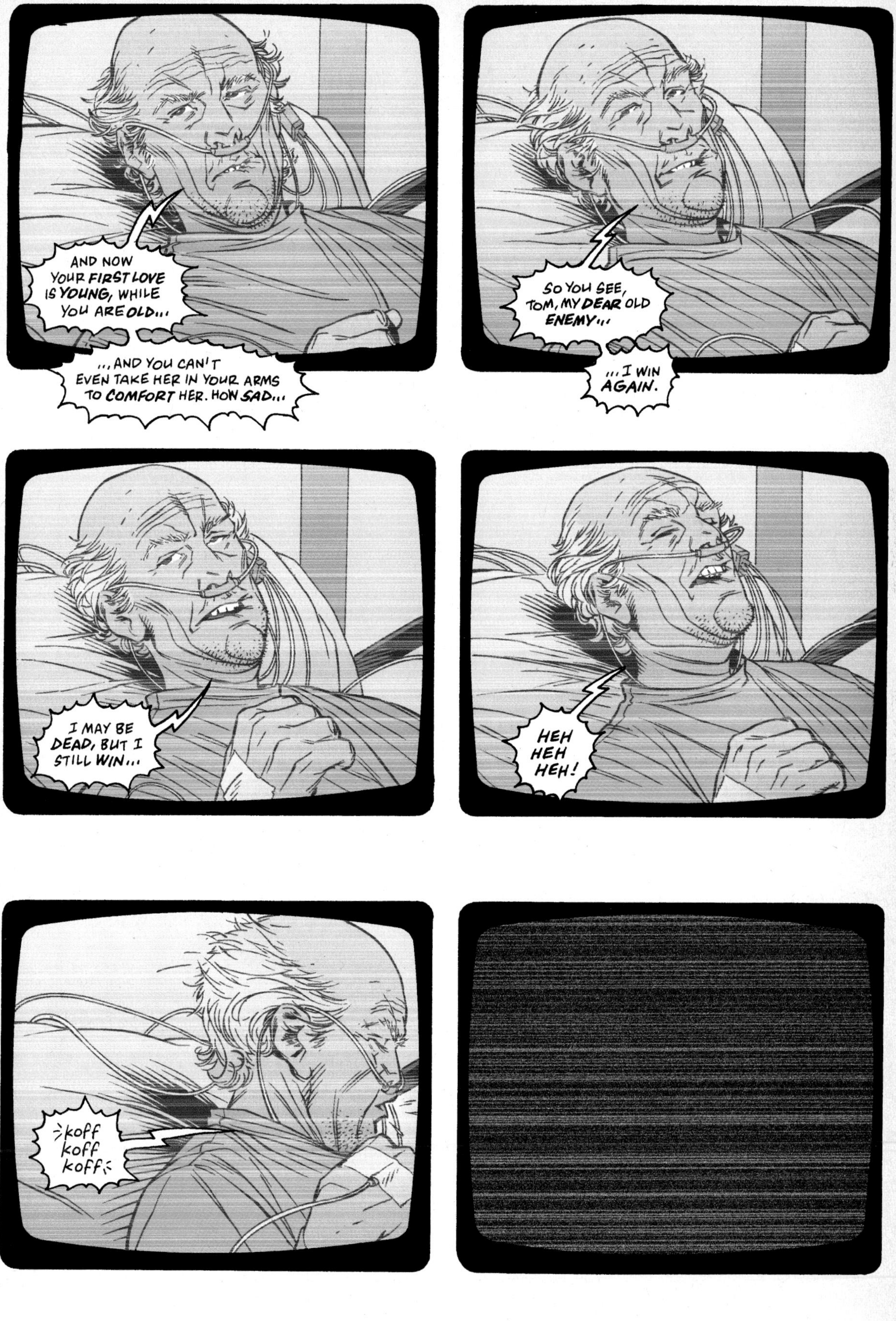
AND NOW YOUR FIRST LOVE IS YOUNG, WHILE YOU ARE OLD...
...AND YOU CAN'T EVEN TAKE HER IN YOUR ARMS TO COMFORT HER. HOW SAD...
SO YOU SEE, TOM, MY DEAR OLD ENEMY...
...I WIN AGAIN.
I MAY BE DEAD, BUT I STILL WIN...
HEH HEH HEH!
koff koff koff

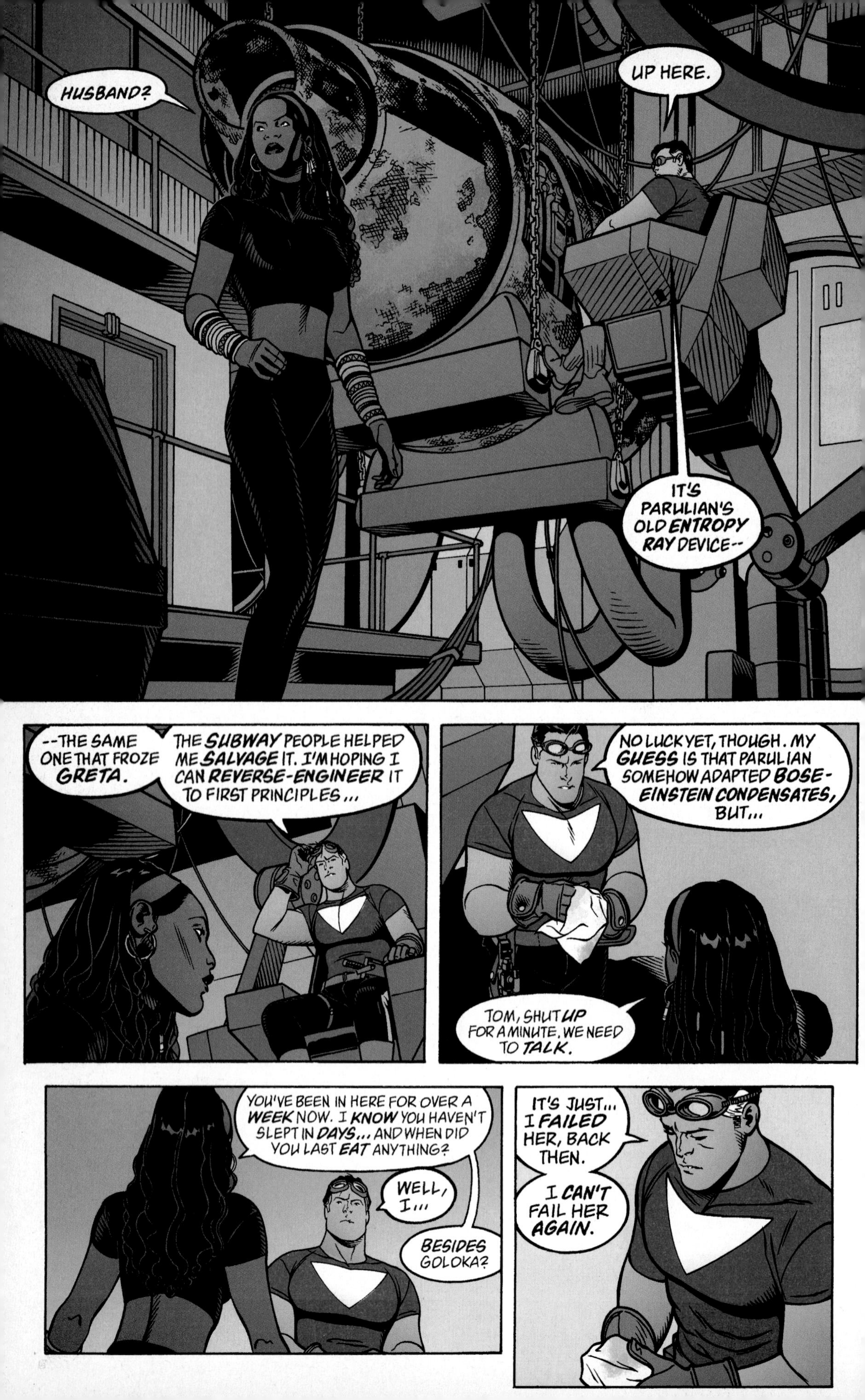
HUSBAND?
UP HERE.
IT'S PARULIAN'S OLD ENTROPY RAY DEVICE--
--THE SAME ONE THAT FROZE GRETA.
THE SUBWAY PEOPLE HELPED ME SALVAGE IT. I'M HOPING I CAN REVERSE-ENGINEER IT TO FIRST PRINCIPLES...
NO LUCK YET, THOUGH. MY GUESS IS THAT PARULIAN SOMEHOW ADAPTED BOSE-EINSTEIN CONDENSATES, BUT...
TOM, SHUT UP FOR A MINUTE. WE NEED TO TALK.
YOU'VE BEEN IN HERE FOR OVER A WEEK NOW. I KNOW YOU HAVEN'T SLEPT IN DAYS... AND WHEN DID YOU LAST EAT ANYTHING?
WELL, I...
BESIDES GOLOKA?
IT'S JUST... I FAILED HER, BACK THEN.
I CAN'T FAIL HER AGAIN.

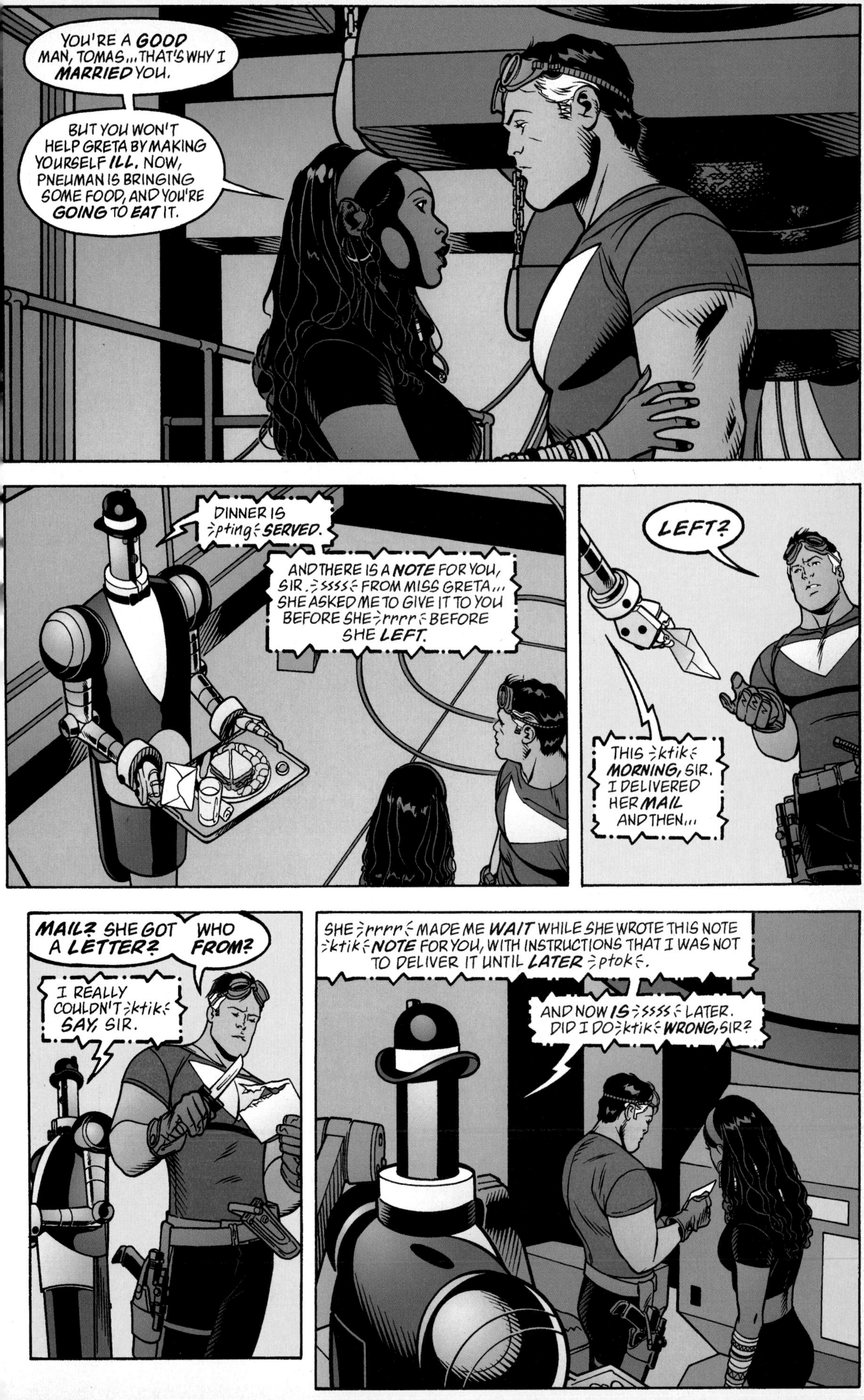
YOU'RE A GOOD MAN, TOMAS... THAT'S WHY I MARRIED YOU.
BUT YOU WON'T HELP GRETA BY MAKING YOURSELF ILL. NOW, PNEUMAN IS BRINGING SOME FOOD, AND YOU'RE GOING TO EAT IT.
DINNER IS ⁕pting⁕ SERVED.
AND THERE IS A NOTE FOR YOU, SIR. ⁕ssss⁕ FROM MISS GRETA... SHE ASKED ME TO GIVE IT TO YOU BEFORE SHE ⁕rrrr⁕ BEFORE SHE LEFT.
LEFT?
THIS ⁕ktik⁕ MORNING, SIR. I DELIVERED HER MAIL AND THEN...
MAIL? SHE GOT A LETTER?
WHO FROM?
I REALLY COULDN'T ⁕ktik⁕ SAY, SIR.
SHE ⁕rrrr⁕ MADE ME WAIT WHILE SHE WROTE THIS NOTE ⁕ktik⁕ NOTE FOR YOU, WITH INSTRUCTIONS THAT I WAS NOT TO DELIVER IT UNTIL LATER ⁕ptok⁕.
AND NOW IS ⁕ssss⁕ LATER. DID I DO ⁕ktik⁕ WRONG, SIR?

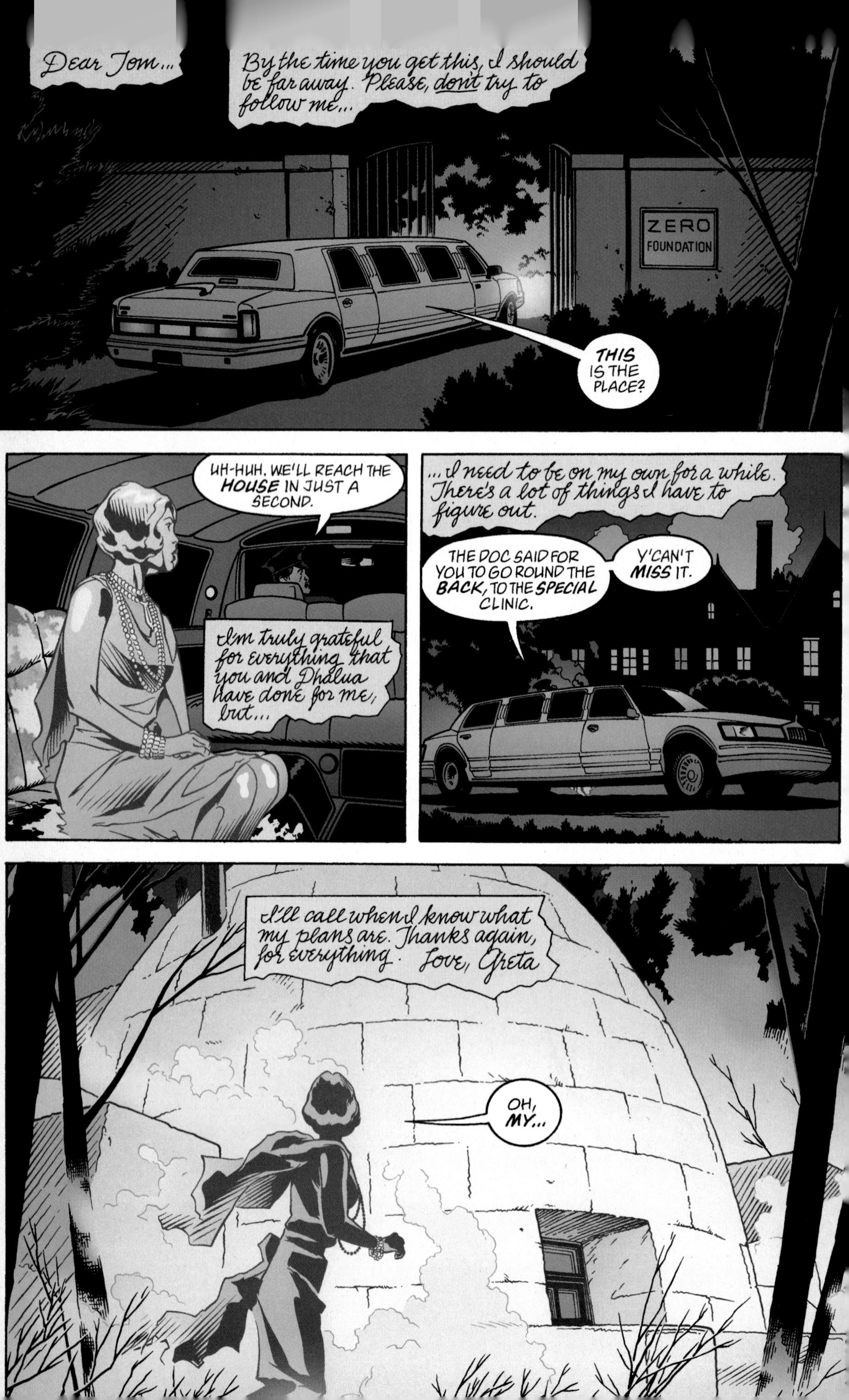
Dear Tom...
By the time you get this, I should be far away. Please, don't try to follow me...
ZERO FOUNDATION
THIS IS THE PLACE?
UH-HUH. WE'LL REACH THE HOUSE IN JUST A SECOND.
I'm truly grateful for everything that you and Dhalua have done for me, but...
...I need to be on my own for a while. There's a lot of things I have to figure out.
THE DOC SAID FOR YOU TO GO ROUND THE BACK, TO THE SPECIAL CLINIC.
Y'CAN'T MISS IT.
I'll call when I know what my plans are. Thanks again, for everything. Love, Greta
OH, MY...

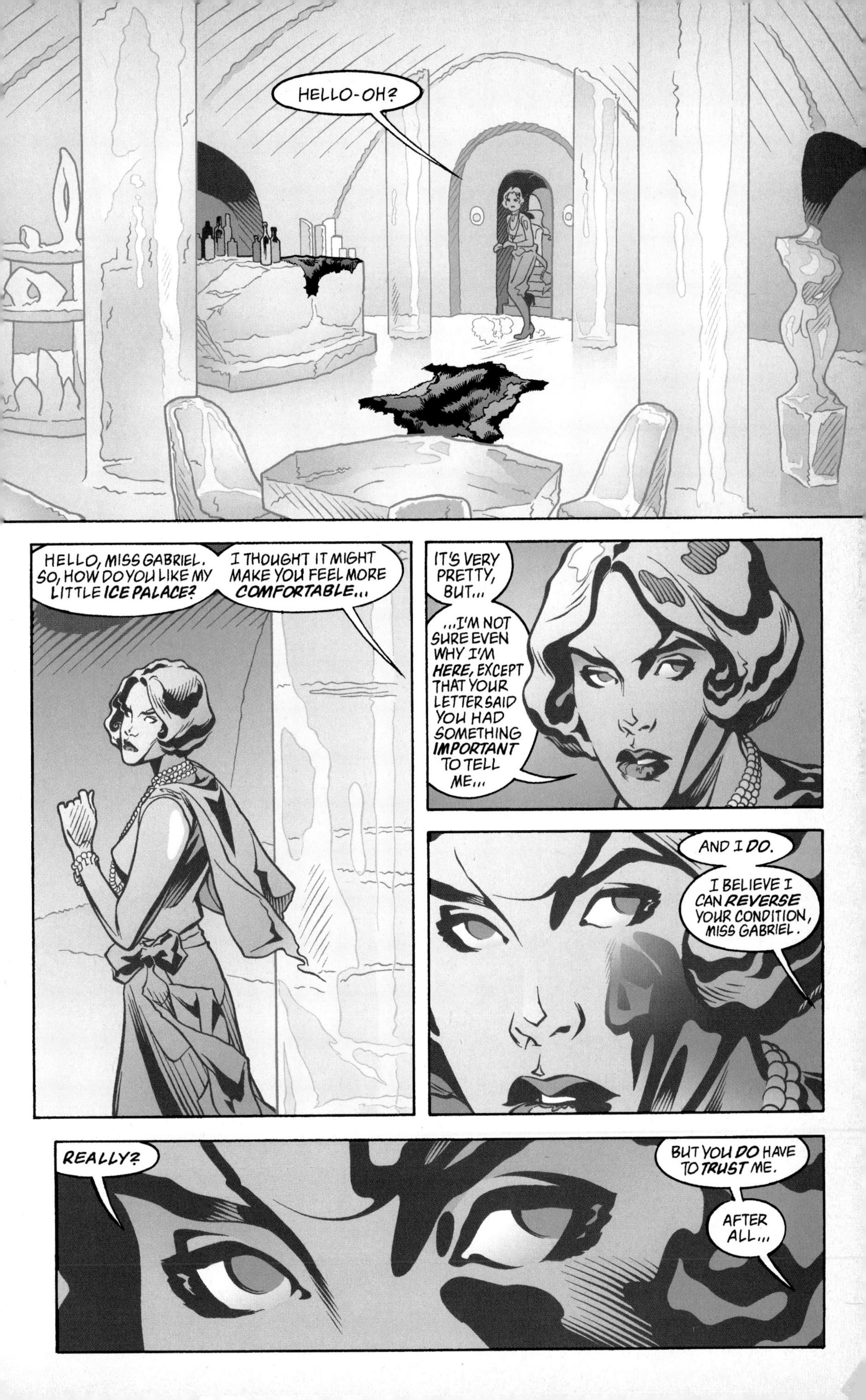
HELLO-OH?
HELLO, MISS GABRIEL. SO, HOW DO YOU LIKE MY LITTLE ICE PALACE?
I THOUGHT IT MIGHT MAKE YOU FEEL MORE COMFORTABLE...
IT'S VERY PRETTY, BUT...
...I'M NOT SURE EVEN WHY I'M HERE, EXCEPT THAT YOUR LETTER SAID YOU HAD SOMETHING IMPORTANT TO TELL ME...
AND I DO.
I BELIEVE I CAN REVERSE YOUR CONDITION, MISS GABRIEL.
REALLY?
BUT YOU DO HAVE TO TRUST ME.
AFTER ALL...

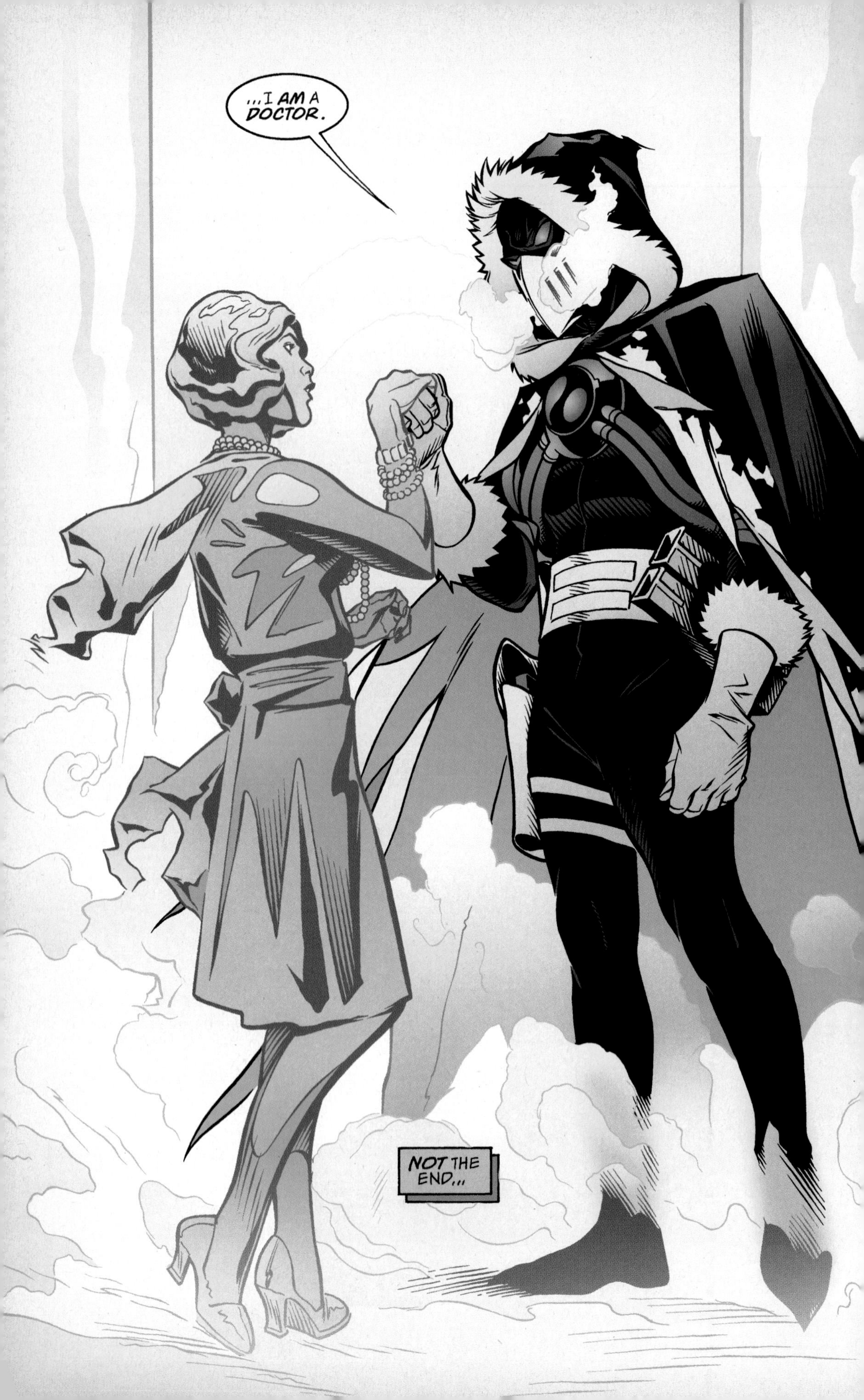
...I AM A DOCTOR.
NOT THE END...

# CHAPTER SIX

**In which Tom meets his number one fan, things go awry across Millennium City, and it all comes down to a photo finish.**

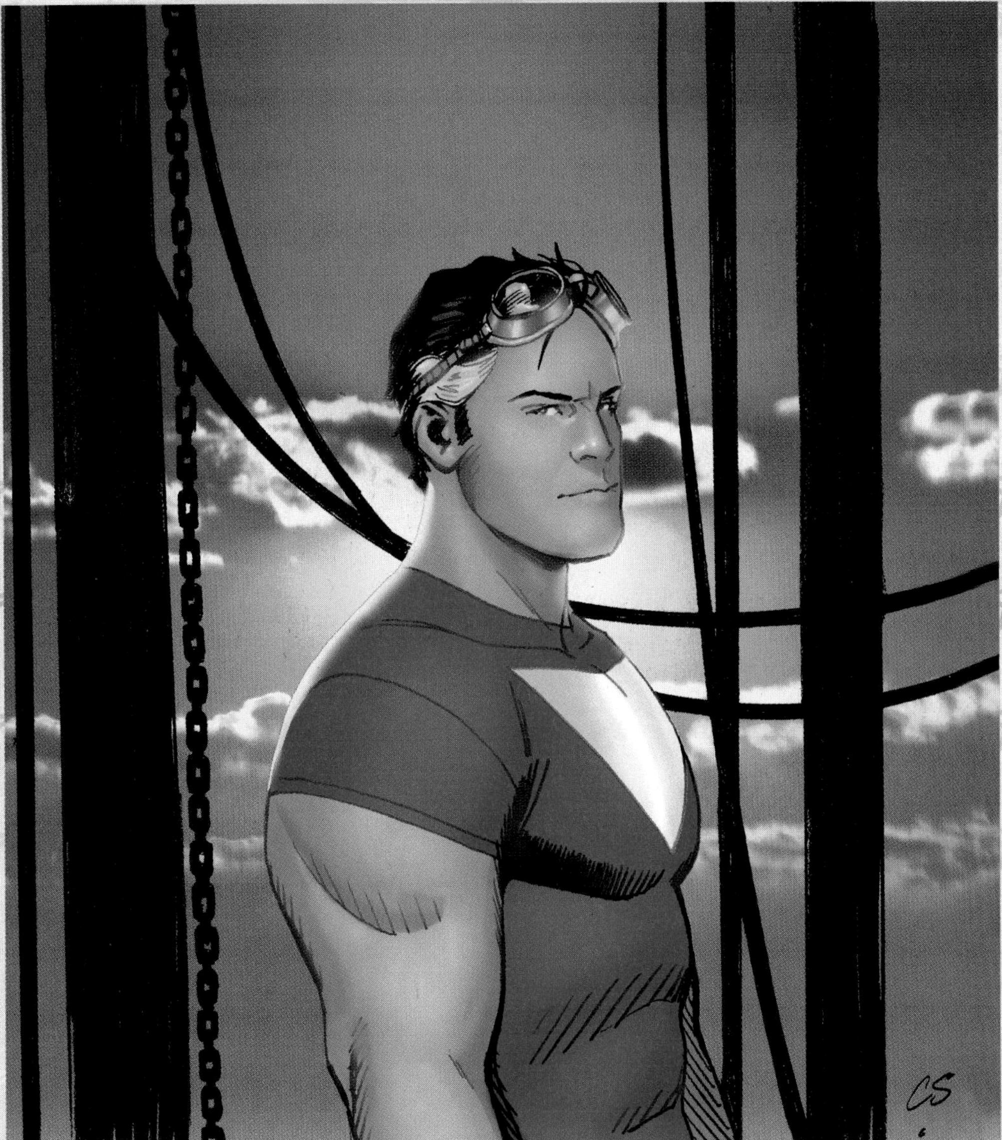
CS
&
JV

**Cover art:**
**Chris Sprouse and Karl Story**

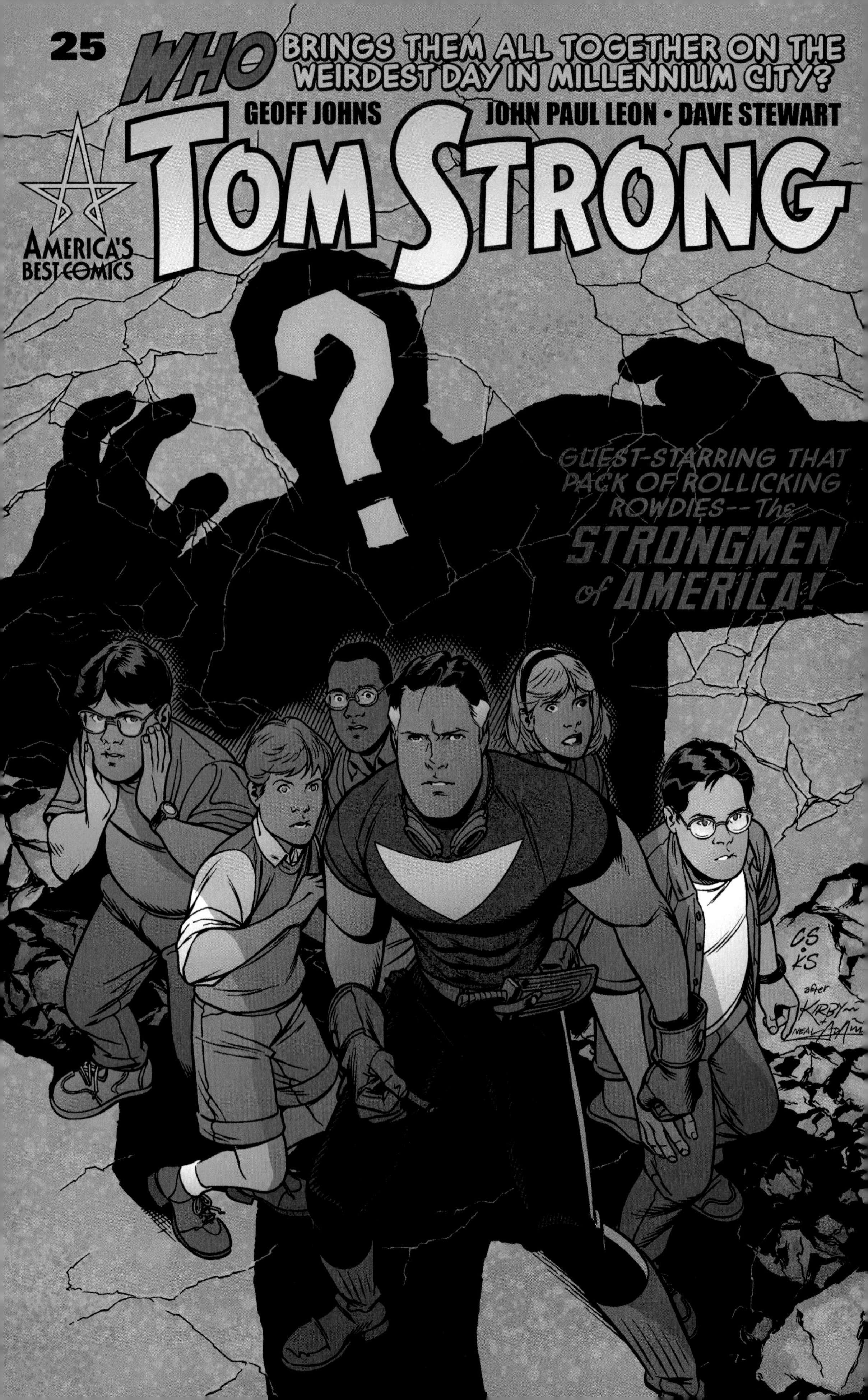
25
WHO BRINGS THEM ALL TOGETHER ON THE WEIRDEST DAY IN MILLENNIUM CITY?
GEOFF JOHNS
JOHN PAUL LEON • DAVE STEWART
TOM STRONG
AMERICA'S BEST COMICS
GUEST-STARRING THAT PACK OF ROLLICKING ROWDIES-- The STRONGMEN of AMERICA!
C.S. K.S. after KIRBY + NEAL ADAMS

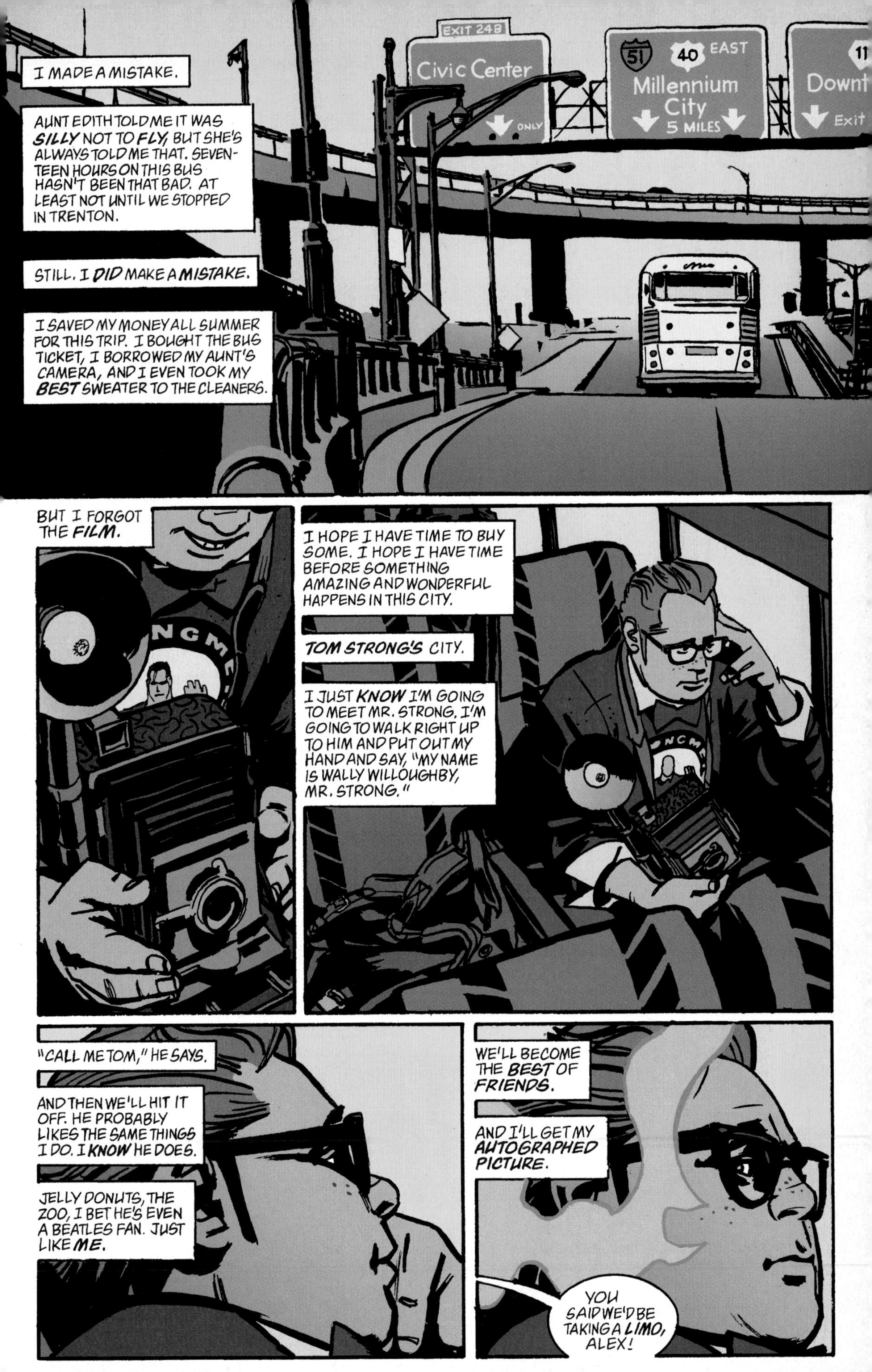
I MADE A MISTAKE.
AUNT EDITH TOLD ME IT WAS SILLY NOT TO FLY, BUT SHE'S ALWAYS TOLD ME THAT. SEVENTEEN HOURS ON THIS BUS HASN'T BEEN THAT BAD. AT LEAST NOT UNTIL WE STOPPED IN TRENTON.
STILL. I DID MAKE A MISTAKE.
I SAVED MY MONEY ALL SUMMER FOR THIS TRIP. I BOUGHT THE BUS TICKET, I BORROWED MY AUNT'S CAMERA, AND I EVEN TOOK MY BEST SWEATER TO THE CLEANERS.
EXIT 24B
Civic Center
ONLY
51
40 EAST
Millennium City
5 MILES
Downt
Exit
BUT I FORGOT THE FILM.
I HOPE I HAVE TIME TO BUY SOME. I HOPE I HAVE TIME BEFORE SOMETHING AMAZING AND WONDERFUL HAPPENS IN THIS CITY.
TOM STRONG'S CITY.
I JUST KNOW I'M GOING TO MEET MR. STRONG. I'M GOING TO WALK RIGHT UP TO HIM AND PUT OUT MY HAND AND SAY, "MY NAME IS WALLY WILLOUGHBY, MR. STRONG."
"CALL ME TOM," HE SAYS.
AND THEN WE'LL HIT IT OFF. HE PROBABLY LIKES THE SAME THINGS I DO. I KNOW HE DOES.
JELLY DONUTS, THE ZOO, I BET HE'S EVEN A BEATLES FAN. JUST LIKE ME.
WE'LL BECOME THE BEST OF FRIENDS.
AND I'LL GET MY AUTOGRAPHED PICTURE.
YOU SAID WE'D BE TAKING A LIMO, ALEX!

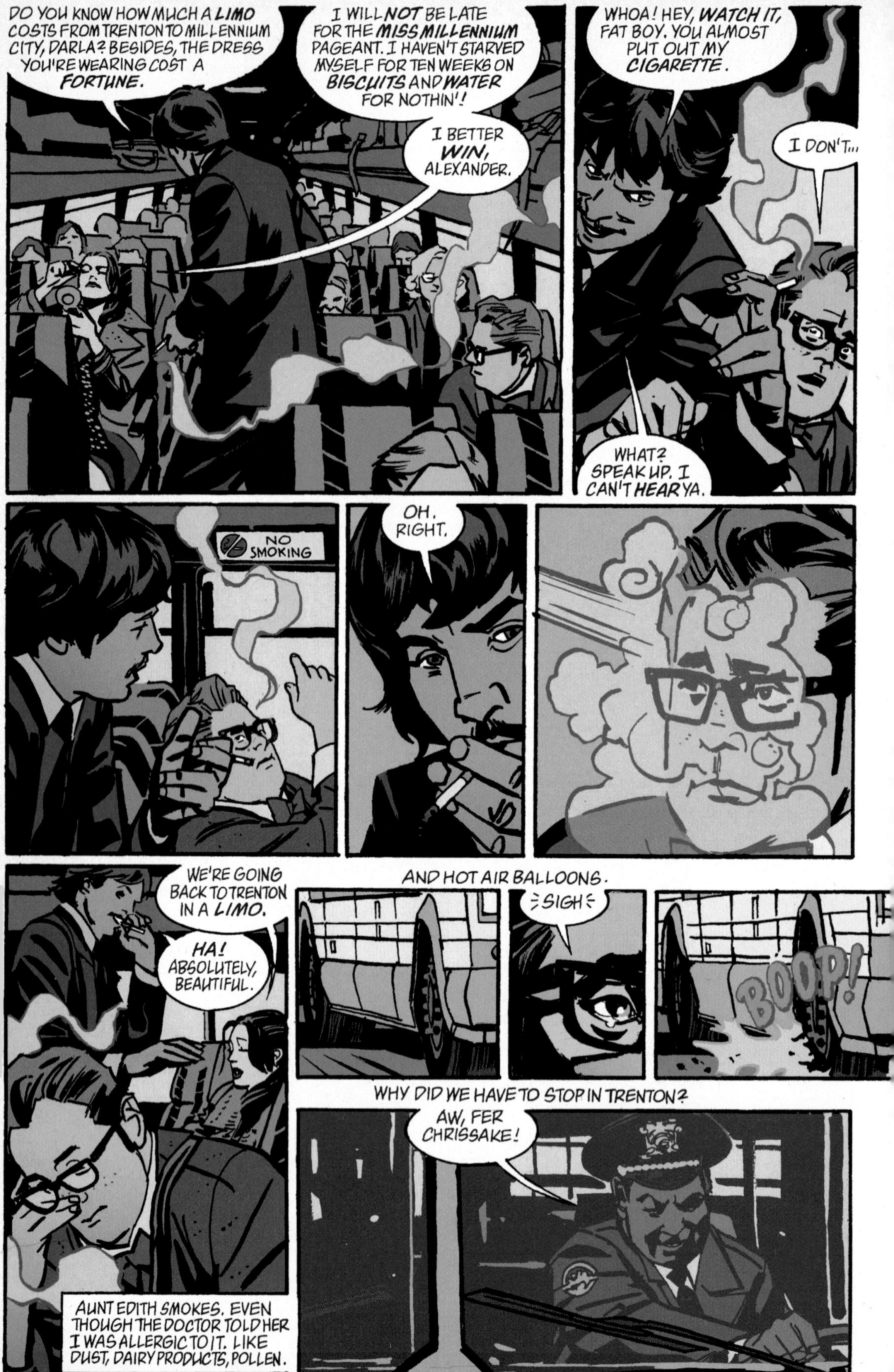

DO YOU KNOW HOW MUCH A LIMO COSTS FROM TRENTON TO MILLENNIUM CITY, DARLA? BESIDES, THE DRESS YOU'RE WEARING COST A FORTUNE.
I WILL NOT BE LATE FOR THE MISS MILLENNIUM PAGEANT. I HAVEN'T STARVED MYSELF FOR TEN WEEKS ON BISCUITS AND WATER FOR NOTHIN'!
I BETTER WIN, ALEXANDER.
WHOA! HEY, WATCH IT, FAT BOY. YOU ALMOST PUT OUT MY CIGARETTE.
I DON'T...
WHAT? SPEAK UP. I CAN'T HEAR YA.
NO SMOKING
OH. RIGHT.
WE'RE GOING BACK TO TRENTON IN A LIMO.
HA! ABSOLUTELY, BEAUTIFUL.
AUNT EDITH SMOKES. EVEN THOUGH THE DOCTOR TOLD HER I WAS ALLERGIC TO IT. LIKE DUST, DAIRY PRODUCTS, POLLEN.
AND HOT AIR BALLOONS.
SIGH
BOOP!
WHY DID WE HAVE TO STOP IN TRENTON?
AW, FER CHRISSAKE!

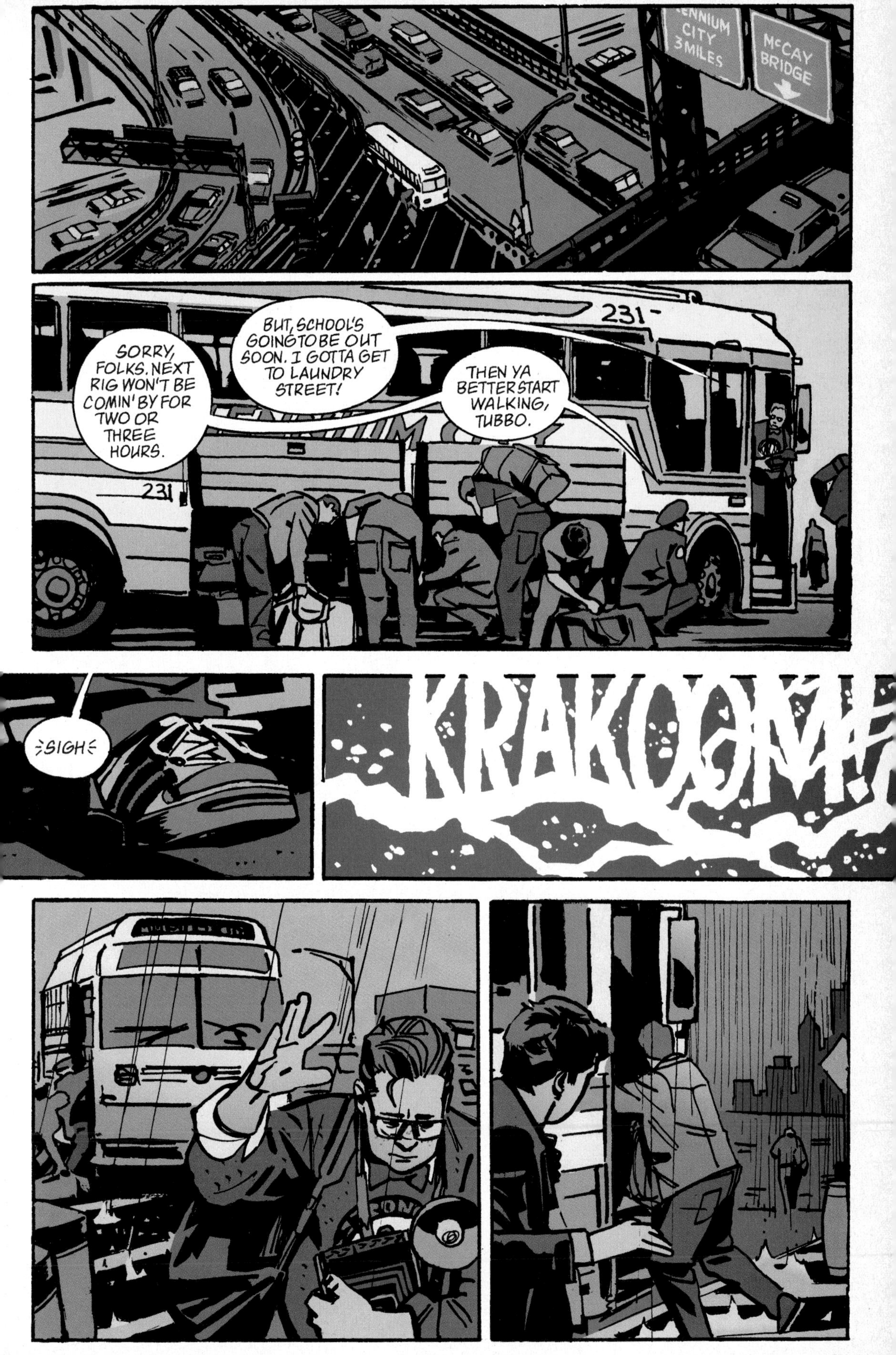

MILLENNIUM CITY 3 MILES
McCAY BRIDGE
231
SORRY, FOLKS. NEXT RIG WON'T BE COMIN' BY FOR TWO OR THREE HOURS.
BUT, SCHOOL'S GOING TO BE OUT SOON. I GOTTA GET TO LAUNDRY STREET!
THEN YA BETTER START WALKING, TUBBO.
231
SIGH
KRAKOOM!

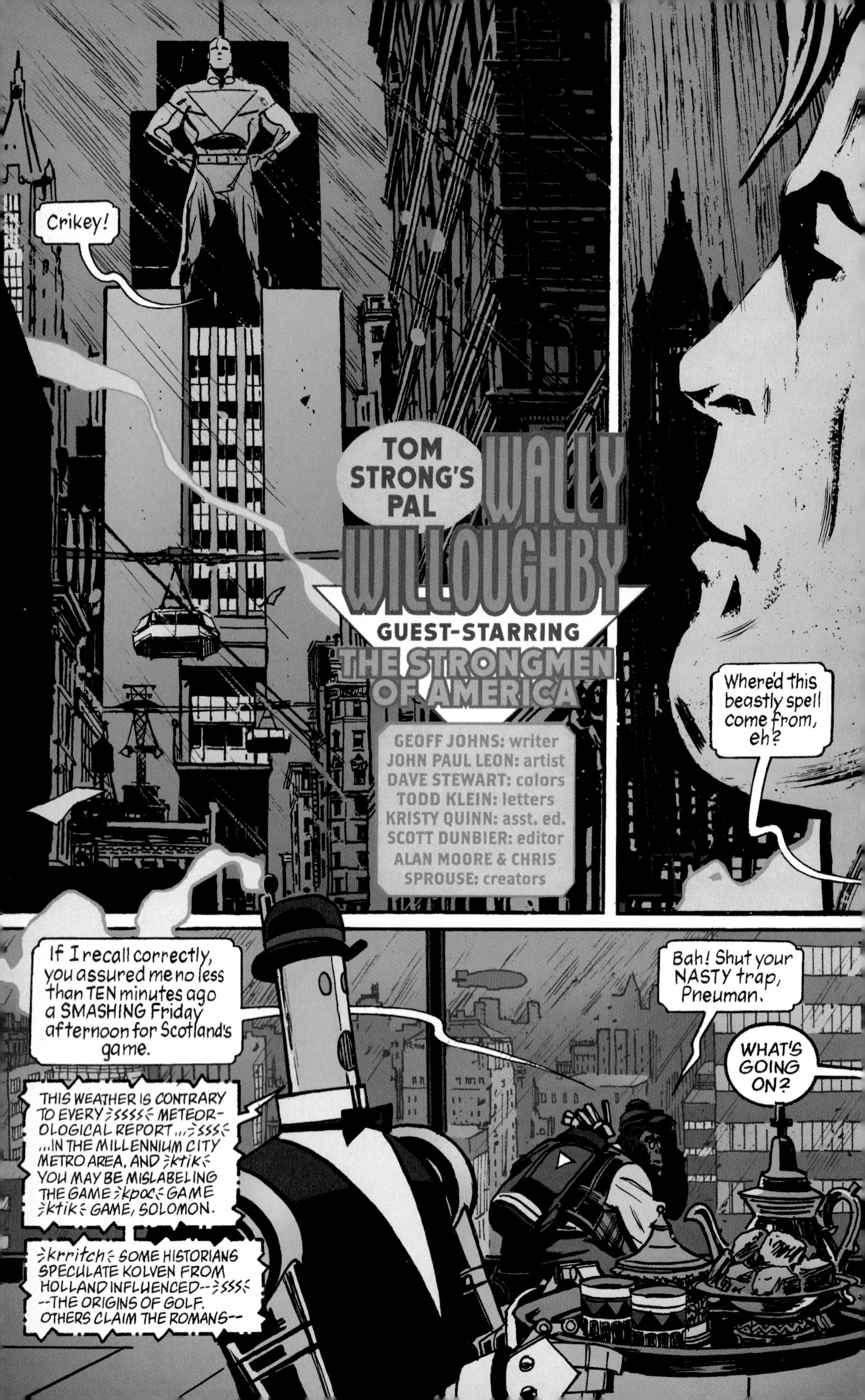
Crikey!
TOM STRONG'S PAL
WALLY WILLOUGHBY
GUEST-STARRING
THE STRONGMEN OF AMERICA
GEOFF JOHNS: writer
JOHN PAUL LEON: artist
DAVE STEWART: colors
TODD KLEIN: letters
KRISTY QUINN: asst. ed.
SCOTT DUNBIER: editor
ALAN MOORE & CHRIS SPROUSE: creators
Where'd this beastly spell come from, eh?
If I recall correctly, you assured me no less than TEN minutes ago a SMASHING Friday afternoon for Scotland's game.
THIS WEATHER IS CONTRARY TO EVERY ≷ssss≶ METEOROLOGICAL REPORT... ≷sss≶ ...IN THE MILLENNIUM CITY METRO AREA. AND ≷ktik≶ YOU MAY BE MISLABELING THE GAME ≷kpoc≶ GAME ≷ktik≶ GAME, SOLOMON.
≷krritch≶ SOME HISTORIANS SPECULATE KOLVEN FROM HOLLAND INFLUENCED-- ≷sss≶ --THE ORIGINS OF GOLF. OTHERS CLAIM THE ROMANS--
Bah! Shut your NASTY trap, Pneuman.
WHAT'S GOING ON?

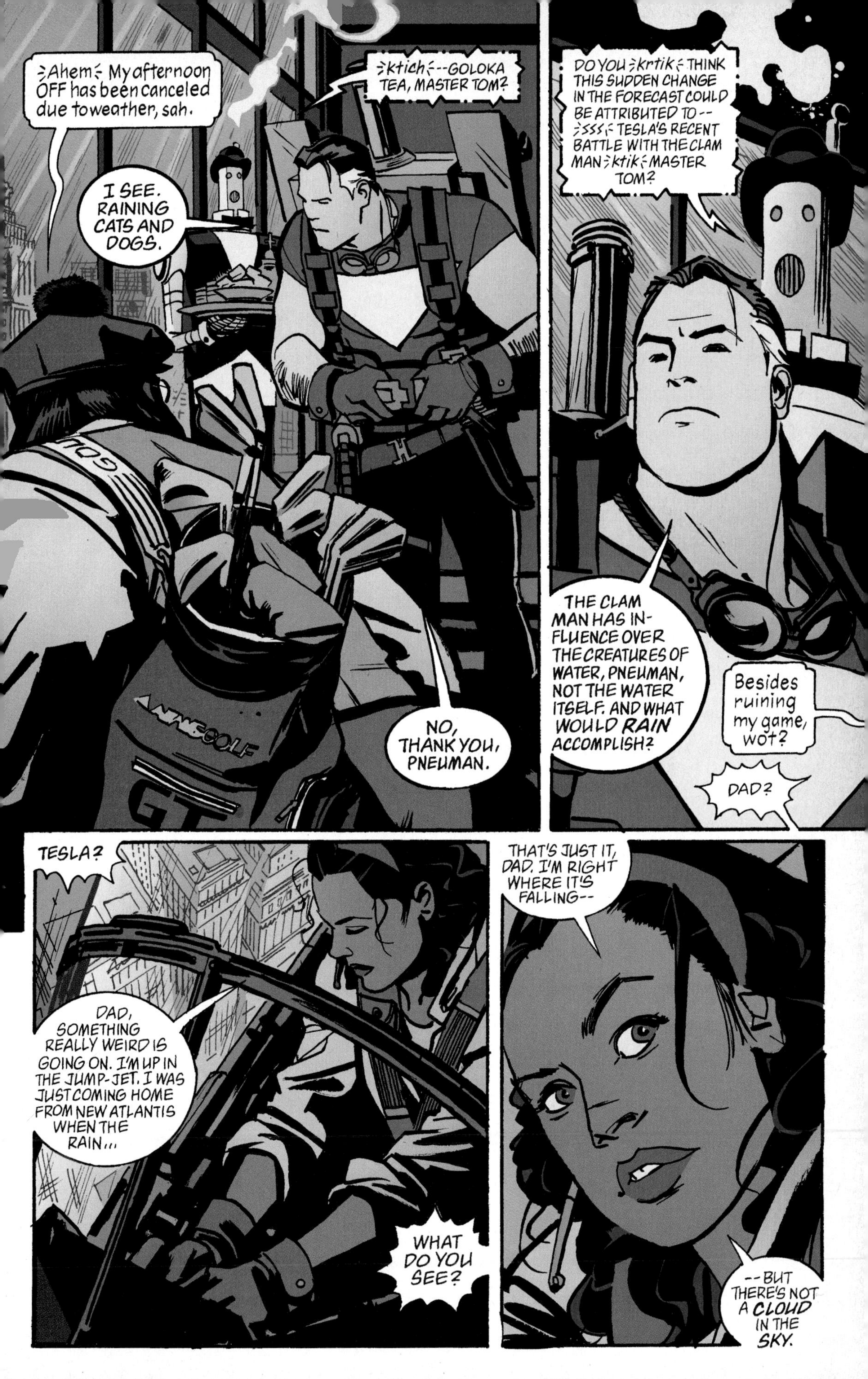

Ahem My afternoon OFF has been canceled due to weather, sah.
I SEE. RAINING CATS AND DOGS.
ktich --GOLOKA TEA, MASTER TOM?
NO, THANK YOU, PNEUMAN.
AMAGOLF
GT
DO YOU krtik THINK THIS SUDDEN CHANGE IN THE FORECAST COULD BE ATTRIBUTED TO-- sss TESLA'S RECENT BATTLE WITH THE CLAM MAN ktik MASTER TOM?
THE CLAM MAN HAS INFLUENCE OVER THE CREATURES OF WATER, PNEUMAN, NOT THE WATER ITSELF. AND WHAT WOULD RAIN ACCOMPLISH?
Besides ruining my game, wot?
DAD?
TESLA?
DAD, SOMETHING REALLY WEIRD IS GOING ON. I'M UP IN THE JUMP-JET. I WAS JUST COMING HOME FROM NEW ATLANTIS WHEN THE RAIN...
WHAT DO YOU SEE?
THAT'S JUST IT, DAD. I'M RIGHT WHERE IT'S FALLING--
--BUT THERE'S NOT A CLOUD IN THE SKY.

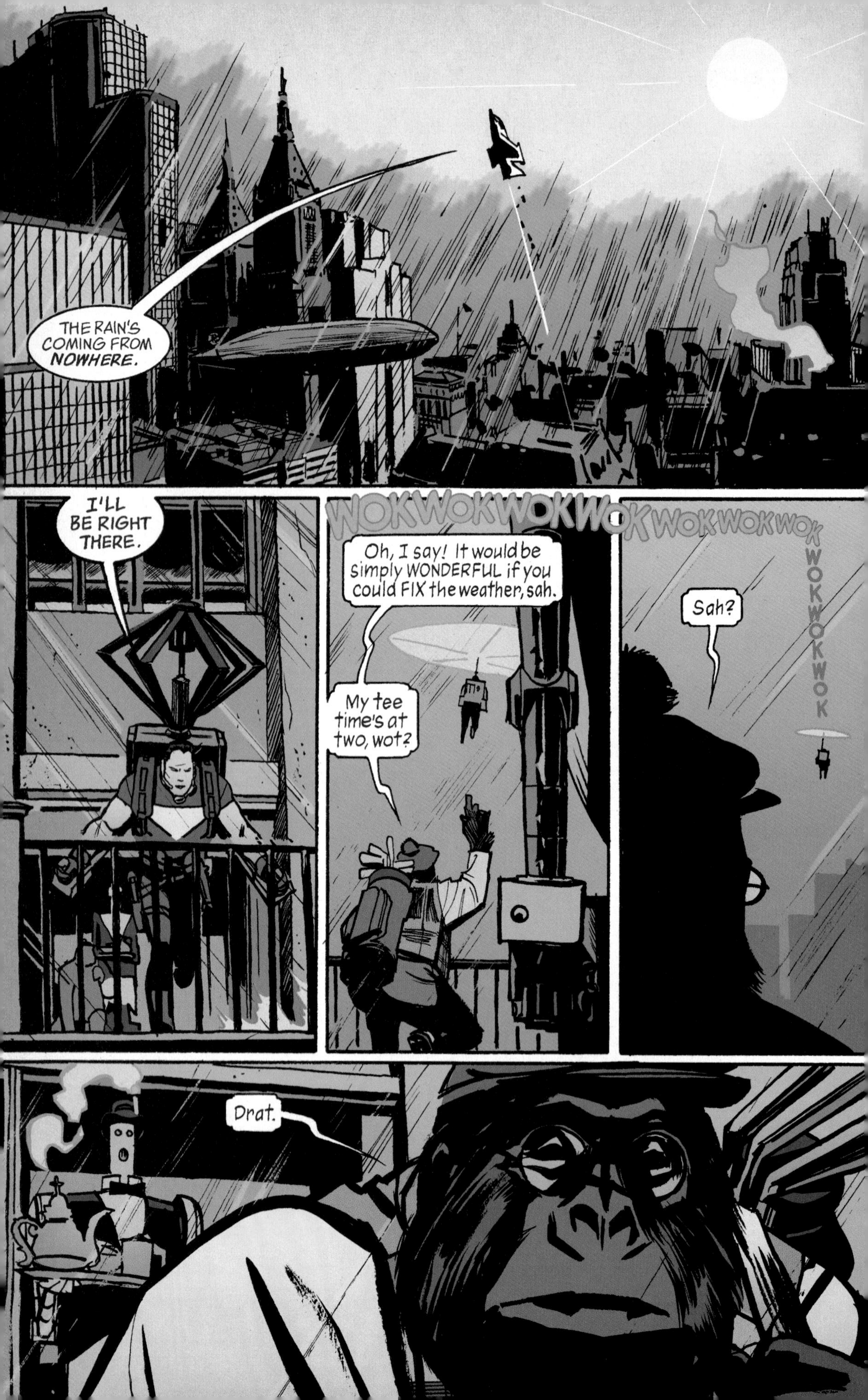
THE RAIN'S COMING FROM NOWHERE.
I'LL BE RIGHT THERE.
WOKWOKWOKWOKWOKWOKWOKWOK
Oh, I say! It would be simply WONDERFUL if you could FIX the weather, sah.
My tee time's at two, wot?
WOKWOKWOKWOK
Sah?
Drat.

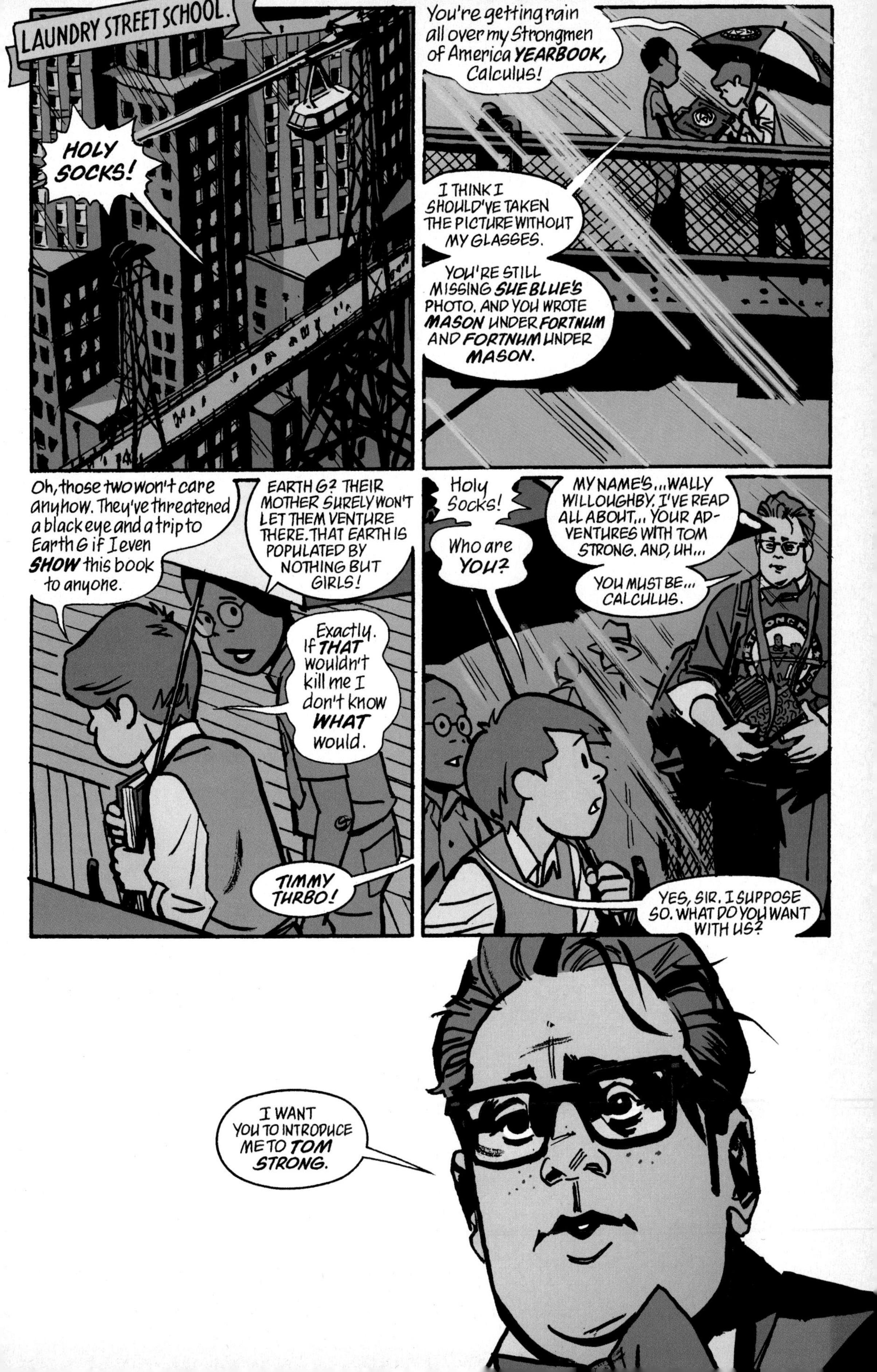
LAUNDRY STREET SCHOOL.
HOLY SOCKS!
You're getting rain all over my Strongmen of America YEARBOOK, Calculus!
I THINK I SHOULD'VE TAKEN THE PICTURE WITHOUT MY GLASSES.
YOU'RE STILL MISSING SUE BLUE'S PHOTO, AND YOU WROTE MASON UNDER FORTNUM AND FORTNUM UNDER MASON.
Oh, those two won't care anyhow. They've threatened a black eye and a trip to Earth G if I even SHOW this book to anyone.
EARTH G? THEIR MOTHER SURELY WON'T LET THEM VENTURE THERE. THAT EARTH IS POPULATED BY NOTHING BUT GIRLS!
Exactly. If THAT wouldn't kill me I don't know WHAT would.
TIMMY TURBO!
Holy Socks!
Who are YOU?
MY NAME'S... WALLY WILLOUGHBY. I'VE READ ALL ABOUT... YOUR ADVENTURES WITH TOM STRONG. AND, UH...
YOU MUST BE... CALCULUS.
YES, SIR. I SUPPOSE SO. WHAT DO YOU WANT WITH US?
I WANT YOU TO INTRODUCE ME TO TOM STRONG.

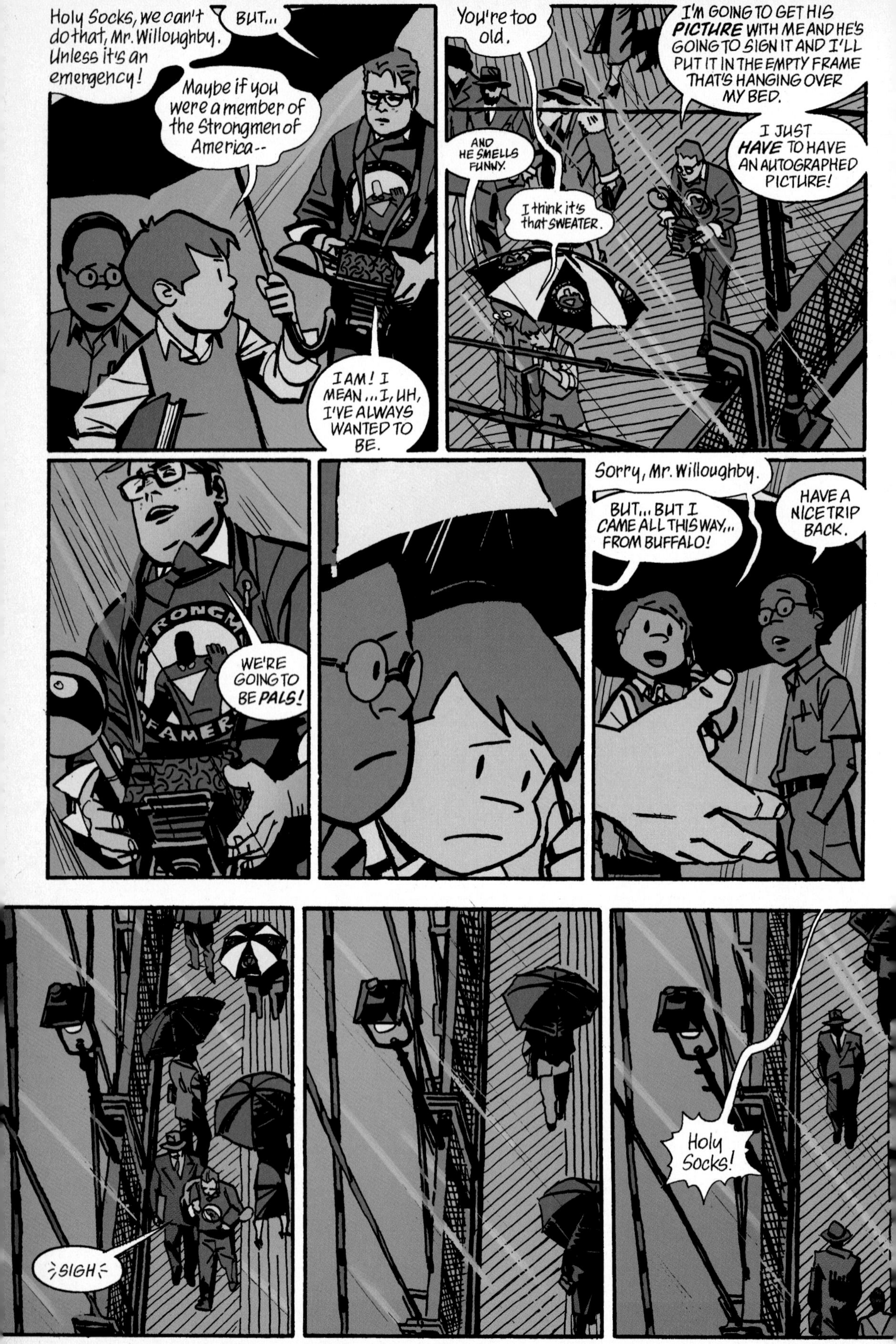

Holy Socks, we can't do that, Mr. Willoughby. Unless it's an emergency!
BUT...
Maybe if you were a member of the Strongmen of America--
I AM! I MEAN... I, UH, I'VE ALWAYS WANTED TO BE.
You're too old.
AND HE SMELLS FUNNY.
I think it's that SWEATER.
I'M GOING TO GET HIS PICTURE WITH ME AND HE'S GOING TO SIGN IT AND I'LL PUT IT IN THE EMPTY FRAME THAT'S HANGING OVER MY BED.
I JUST HAVE TO HAVE AN AUTOGRAPHED PICTURE!
WE'RE GOING TO BE PALS!
Sorry, Mr. Willoughby.
BUT... BUT I CAME ALL THIS WAY... FROM BUFFALO!
HAVE A NICE TRIP BACK.
SIGH
Holy Socks!

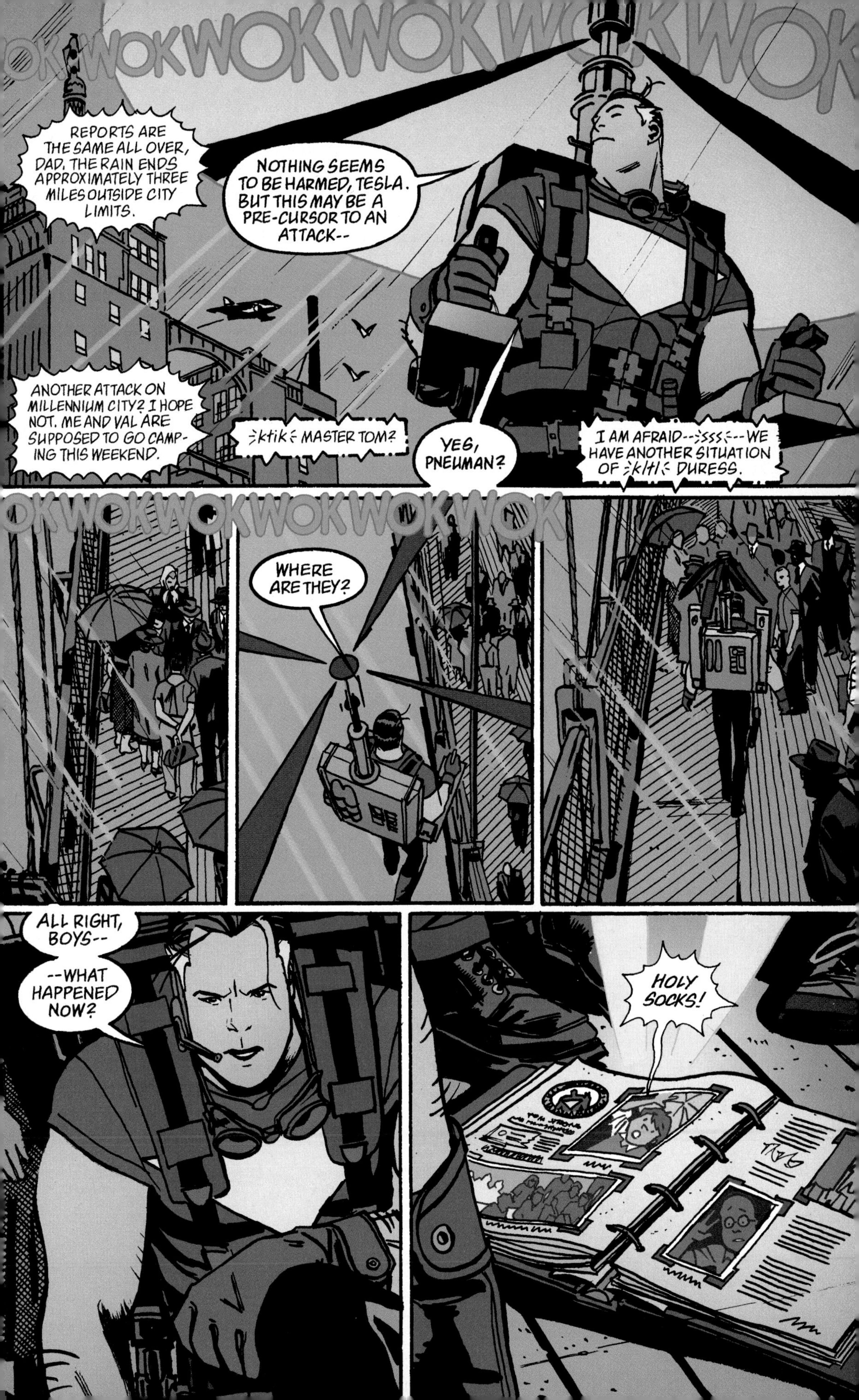
WOKWOKWOKWOKWOKWOK
REPORTS ARE THE SAME ALL OVER, DAD. THE RAIN ENDS APPROXIMATELY THREE MILES OUTSIDE CITY LIMITS.
NOTHING SEEMS TO BE HARMED, TESLA. BUT THIS MAY BE A PRE-CURSOR TO AN ATTACK--
ANOTHER ATTACK ON MILLENNIUM CITY? I HOPE NOT. ME AND VAL ARE SUPPOSED TO GO CAMPING THIS WEEKEND.
ktik MASTER TOM?
YES, PNEUMAN?
I AM AFRAID-- sss -- WE HAVE ANOTHER SITUATION OF ktl DURESS.
WOKWOKWOKWOKWOKWOK
WHERE ARE THEY?
ALL RIGHT, BOYS--
--WHAT HAPPENED NOW?
HOLY SOCKS!

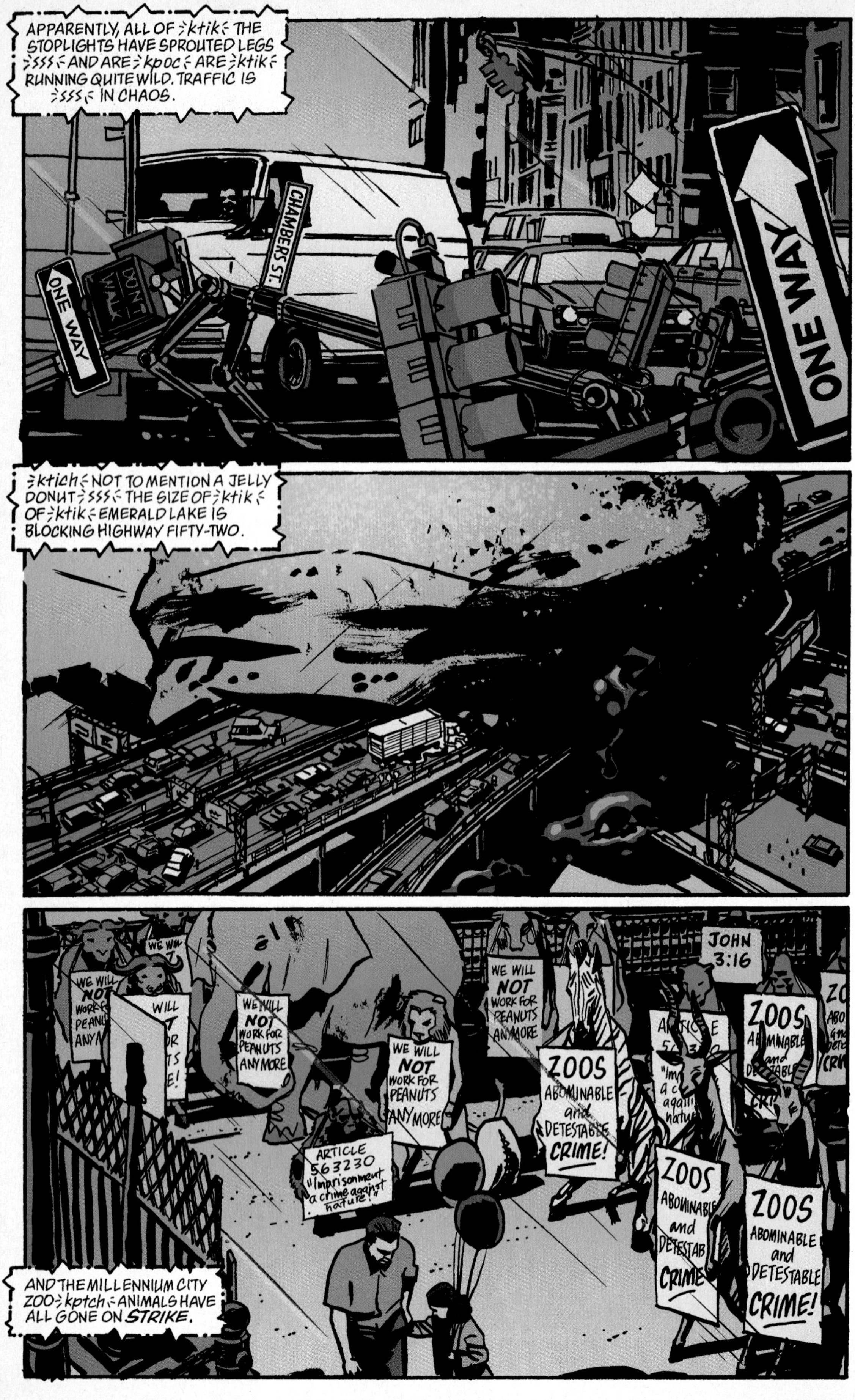
APPARENTLY, ALL OF ⸗ktik⸗ THE STOPLIGHTS HAVE SPROUTED LEGS ⸗sss⸗ AND ARE ⸗kpoc⸗ ARE ⸗ktik⸗ RUNNING QUITE WILD. TRAFFIC IS ⸗sss⸗ IN CHAOS.
ONE WAY
DON'T WALK
CHAMBERS ST.
ONE WAY
⸗ktich⸗ NOT TO MENTION A JELLY DONUT ⸗sss⸗ THE SIZE OF ⸗ktik⸗ OF ⸗ktik⸗ EMERALD LAKE IS BLOCKING HIGHWAY FIFTY-TWO.
JOHN 3:16
WE WILL NOT WORK FOR PEANUTS ANYMORE
WE WILL NOT WORK FOR PEANUTS ANYMORE
WE WILL NOT WORK FOR PEANUTS ANYMORE
ZOOS ABOMINABLE and DETESTABLE CRIME!
ARTICLE 563230 "Imprisonment a crime against nature!"
ZOOS ABOMINABLE and DETESTAB CRIME
ZOOS ABOMINABLE and DETESTABLE CRIME!
AND THE MILLENNIUM CITY ZOO ⸗kptch⸗ ANIMALS HAVE ALL GONE ON STRIKE.

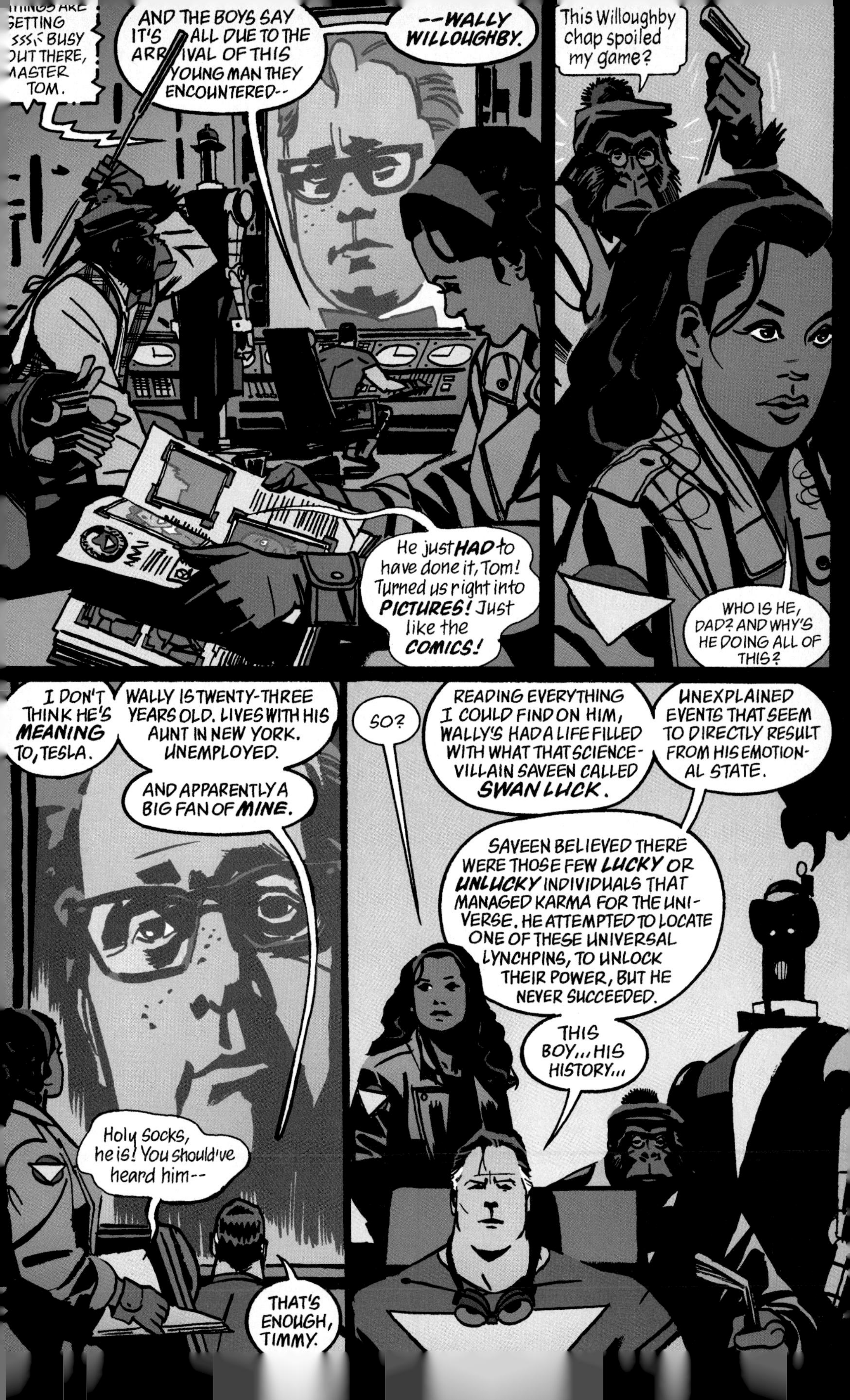
GETTING BUSY OUT THERE, MASTER TOM.
AND THE BOYS SAY IT'S ALL DUE TO THE ARRIVAL OF THIS YOUNG MAN THEY ENCOUNTERED--
--WALLY WILLOUGHBY.
This Willoughby chap spoiled my game?
He just HAD to have done it, Tom! Turned us right into PICTURES! Just like the COMICS!
WHO IS HE, DAD? AND WHY'S HE DOING ALL OF THIS?
I DON'T THINK HE'S MEANING TO, TESLA.
WALLY IS TWENTY-THREE YEARS OLD. LIVES WITH HIS AUNT IN NEW YORK. UNEMPLOYED.
AND APPARENTLY A BIG FAN OF MINE.
Holy socks, he is! You should've heard him--
THAT'S ENOUGH, TIMMY.
SO?
READING EVERYTHING I COULD FIND ON HIM, WALLY'S HAD A LIFE FILLED WITH WHAT THAT SCIENCE-VILLAIN SAVEEN CALLED SWAN LUCK.
UNEXPLAINED EVENTS THAT SEEM TO DIRECTLY RESULT FROM HIS EMOTIONAL STATE.
SAVEEN BELIEVED THERE WERE THOSE FEW LUCKY OR UNLUCKY INDIVIDUALS THAT MANAGED KARMA FOR THE UNIVERSE. HE ATTEMPTED TO LOCATE ONE OF THESE UNIVERSAL LYNCHPINS, TO UNLOCK THEIR POWER, BUT HE NEVER SUCCEEDED.
THIS BOY... HIS HISTORY...

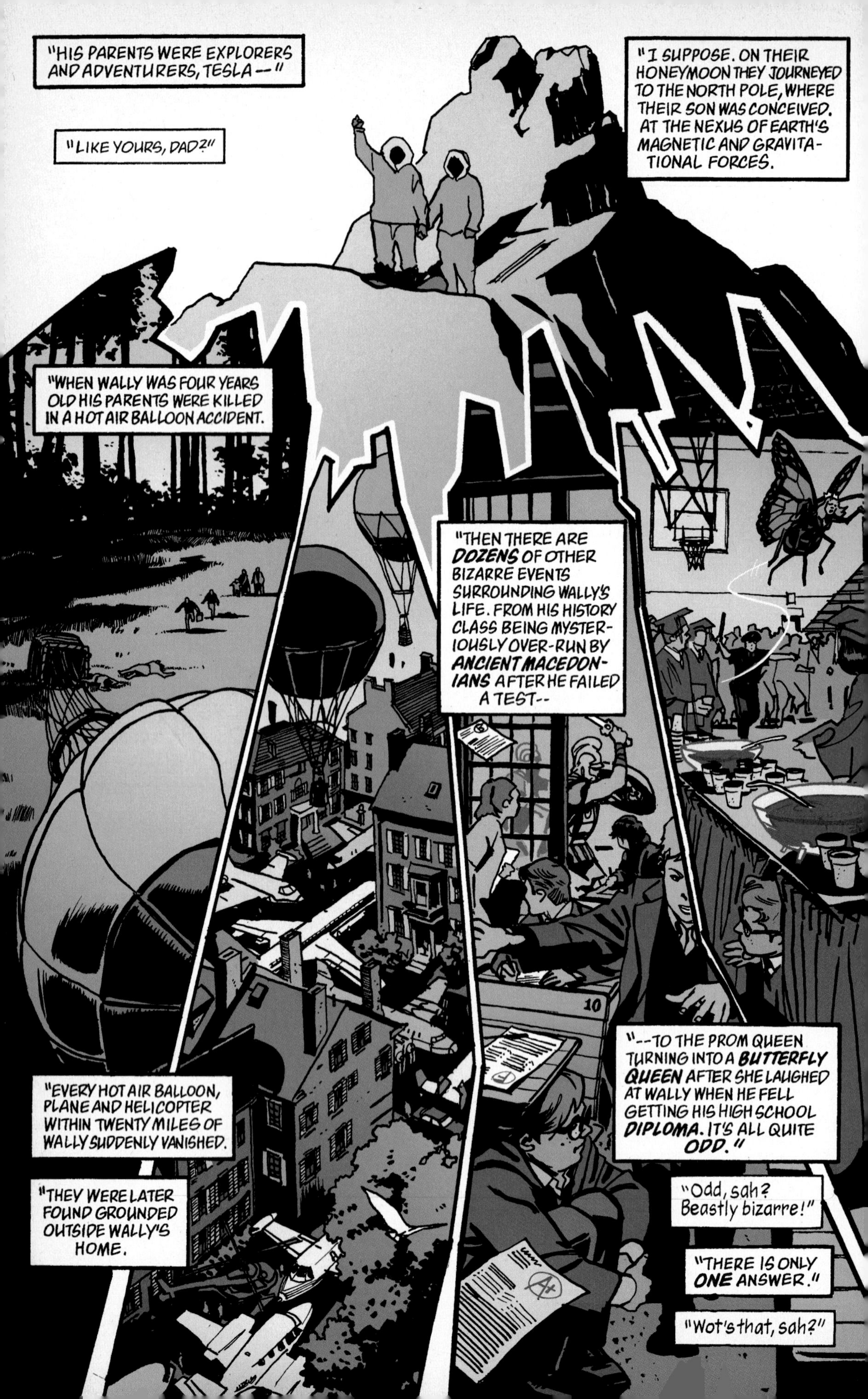
"HIS PARENTS WERE EXPLORERS AND ADVENTURERS, TESLA --"
"LIKE YOURS, DAD?"
"I SUPPOSE. ON THEIR HONEYMOON THEY JOURNEYED TO THE NORTH POLE, WHERE THEIR SON WAS CONCEIVED. AT THE NEXUS OF EARTH'S MAGNETIC AND GRAVITATIONAL FORCES.
"WHEN WALLY WAS FOUR YEARS OLD HIS PARENTS WERE KILLED IN A HOT AIR BALLOON ACCIDENT.
"THEN THERE ARE DOZENS OF OTHER BIZARRE EVENTS SURROUNDING WALLY'S LIFE. FROM HIS HISTORY CLASS BEING MYSTERIOUSLY OVER-RUN BY ANCIENT MACEDONIANS AFTER HE FAILED A TEST--
"EVERY HOT AIR BALLOON, PLANE AND HELICOPTER WITHIN TWENTY MILES OF WALLY SUDDENLY VANISHED.
"THEY WERE LATER FOUND GROUNDED OUTSIDE WALLY'S HOME.
"--TO THE PROM QUEEN TURNING INTO A BUTTERFLY QUEEN AFTER SHE LAUGHED AT WALLY WHEN HE FELL GETTING HIS HIGH SCHOOL DIPLOMA. IT'S ALL QUITE ODD."
"Odd, sah? Beastly bizarre!"
"THERE IS ONLY ONE ANSWER."
"Wot's that, sah?"

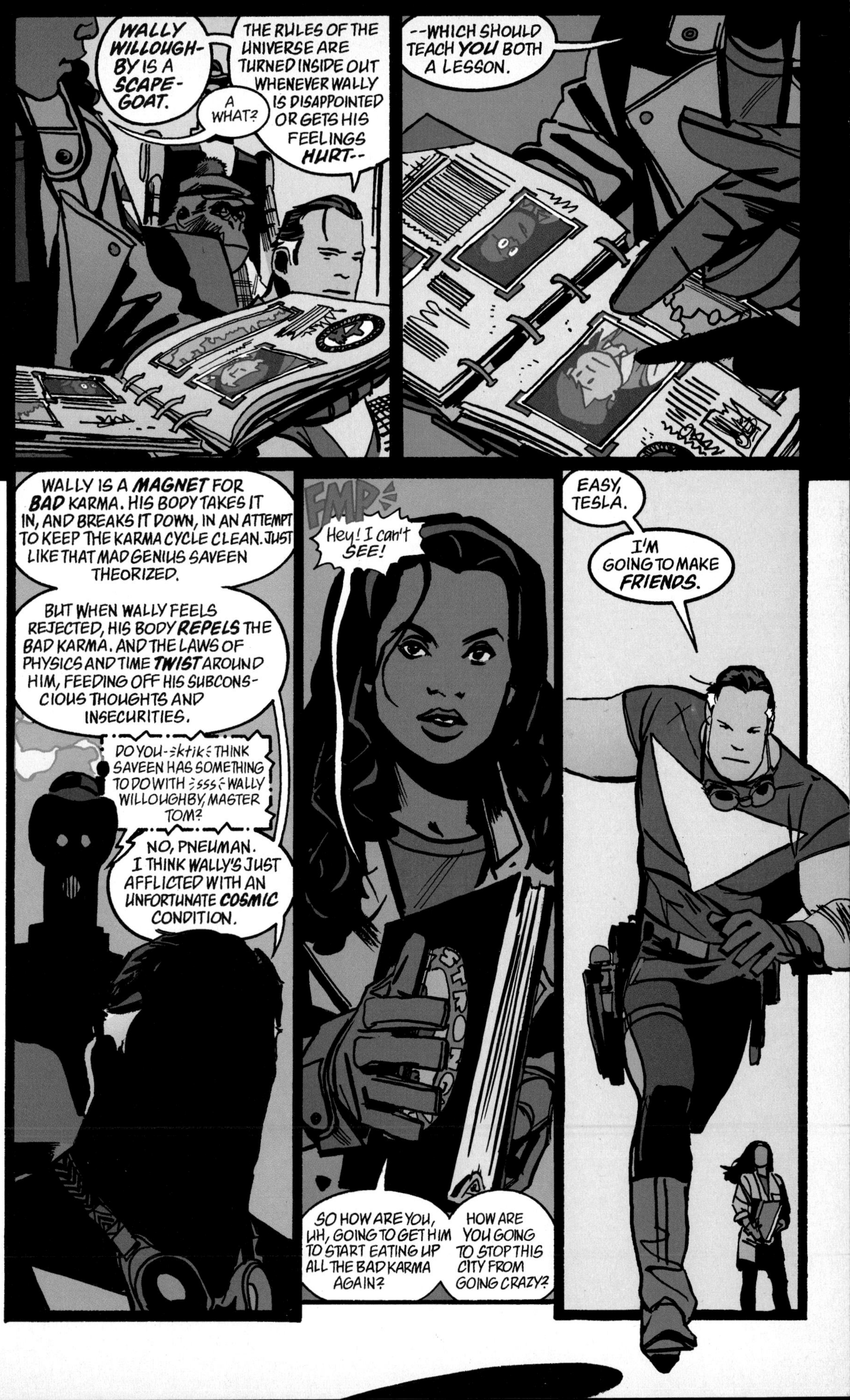
WALLY WILLOUGHBY IS A SCAPEGOAT.
A WHAT?
THE RULES OF THE UNIVERSE ARE TURNED INSIDE OUT WHENEVER WALLY IS DISAPPOINTED OR GETS HIS FEELINGS HURT--
--WHICH SHOULD TEACH YOU BOTH A LESSON.
WALLY IS A MAGNET FOR BAD KARMA. HIS BODY TAKES IT IN, AND BREAKS IT DOWN, IN AN ATTEMPT TO KEEP THE KARMA CYCLE CLEAN. JUST LIKE THAT MAD GENIUS SAVEEN THEORIZED.
BUT WHEN WALLY FEELS REJECTED, HIS BODY REPELS THE BAD KARMA. AND THE LAWS OF PHYSICS AND TIME TWIST AROUND HIM, FEEDING OFF HIS SUBCONSCIOUS THOUGHTS AND INSECURITIES.
DO YOU- ktik THINK SAVEEN HAS SOMETHING TO DO WITH sss WALLY WILLOUGHBY, MASTER TOM?
NO, PNEUMAN. I THINK WALLY'S JUST AFFLICTED WITH AN UNFORTUNATE COSMIC CONDITION.
FMP
Hey! I can't SEE!
SO HOW ARE YOU, UH, GOING TO GET HIM TO START EATING UP ALL THE BAD KARMA AGAIN?
HOW ARE YOU GOING TO STOP THIS CITY FROM GOING CRAZY?
EASY, TESLA.
I'M GOING TO MAKE FRIENDS.

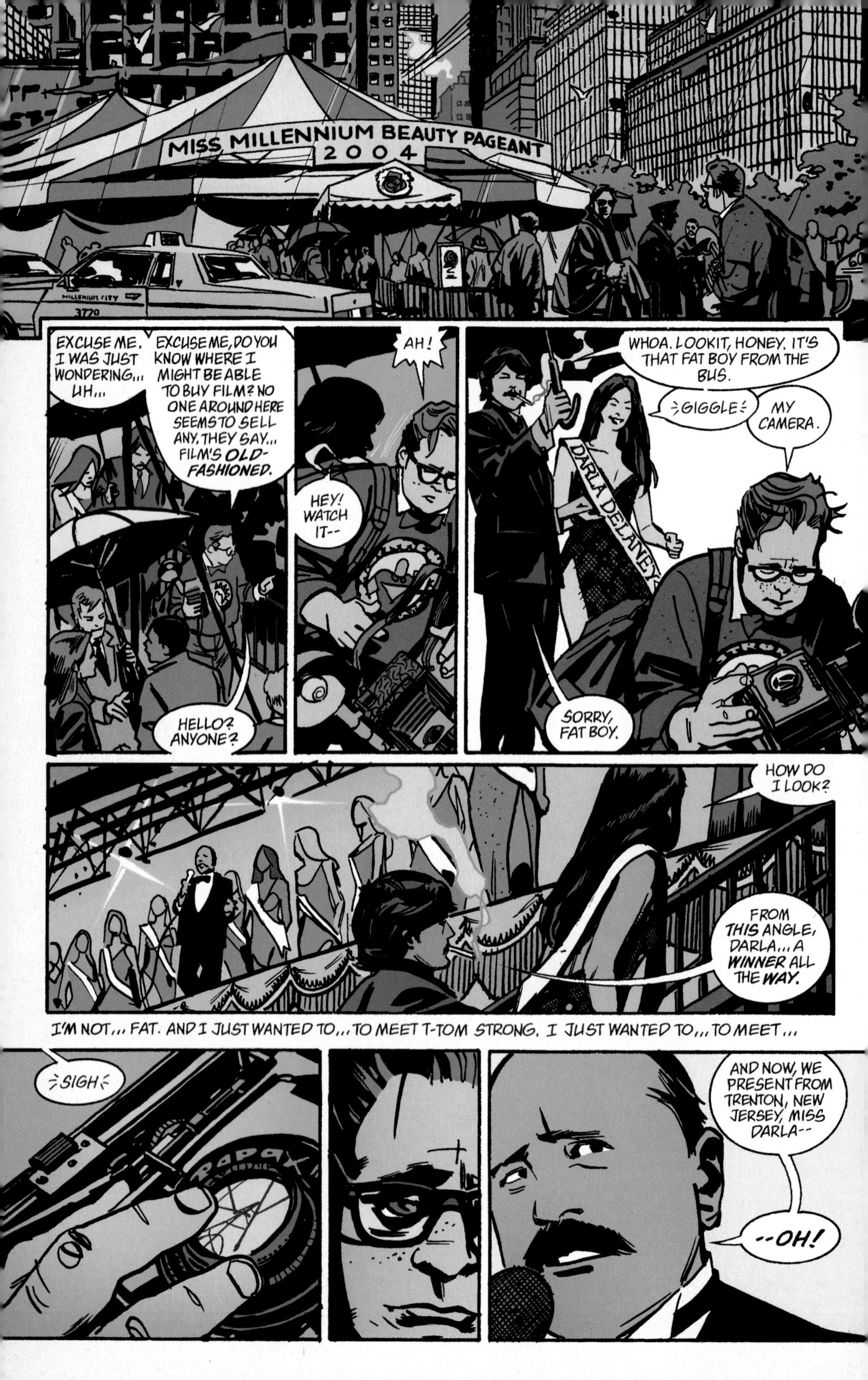
MISS MILLENNIUM BEAUTY PAGEANT
2004
MILLENNIUM CITY
EXCUSE ME. I WAS JUST WONDERING... UH...
EXCUSE ME, DO YOU KNOW WHERE I MIGHT BE ABLE TO BUY FILM? NO ONE AROUND HERE SEEMS TO SELL ANY. THEY SAY... FILM'S OLD-FASHIONED.
HELLO? ANYONE?
AH!
HEY! WATCH IT--
WHOA. LOOKIT, HONEY. IT'S THAT FAT BOY FROM THE BUS.
GIGGLE
MY CAMERA.
DARLA DELANEY
SORRY, FAT BOY.
HOW DO I LOOK?
FROM THIS ANGLE, DARLA... A WINNER ALL THE WAY.
I'M NOT... FAT. AND I JUST WANTED TO... TO MEET T-TOM STRONG. I JUST WANTED TO... TO MEET...
SIGH
AND NOW, WE PRESENT FROM TRENTON, NEW JERSEY, MISS DARLA--
--OH!

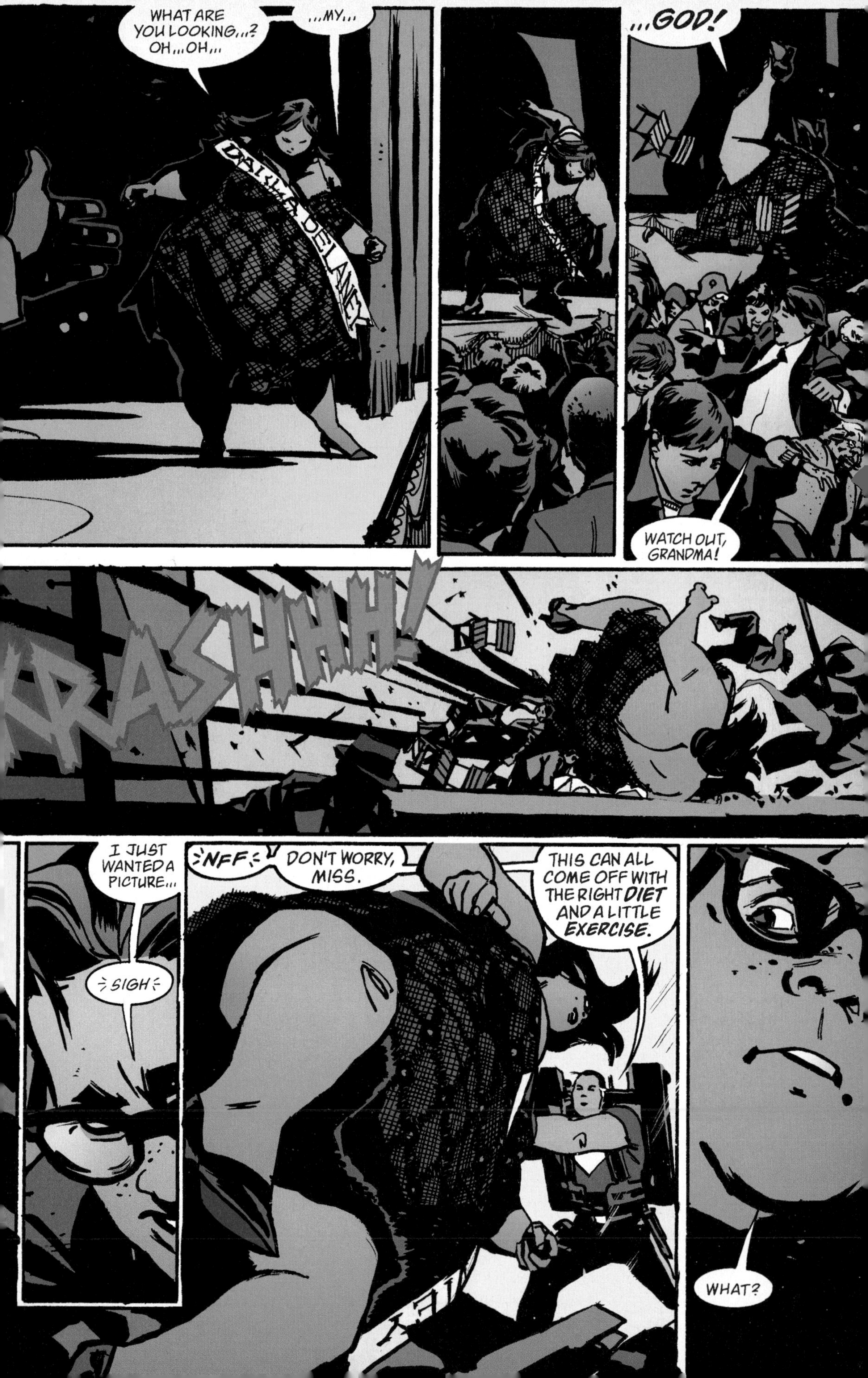
WHAT ARE YOU LOOKING...? OH...OH...
...MY...
...GOD!
WATCH OUT, GRANDMA!
DAISHA DELANEY
KRASHHH!
I JUST WANTED A PICTURE...
SIGH
NFF
DON'T WORRY, MISS.
THIS CAN ALL COME OFF WITH THE RIGHT DIET AND A LITTLE EXERCISE.
WHAT?

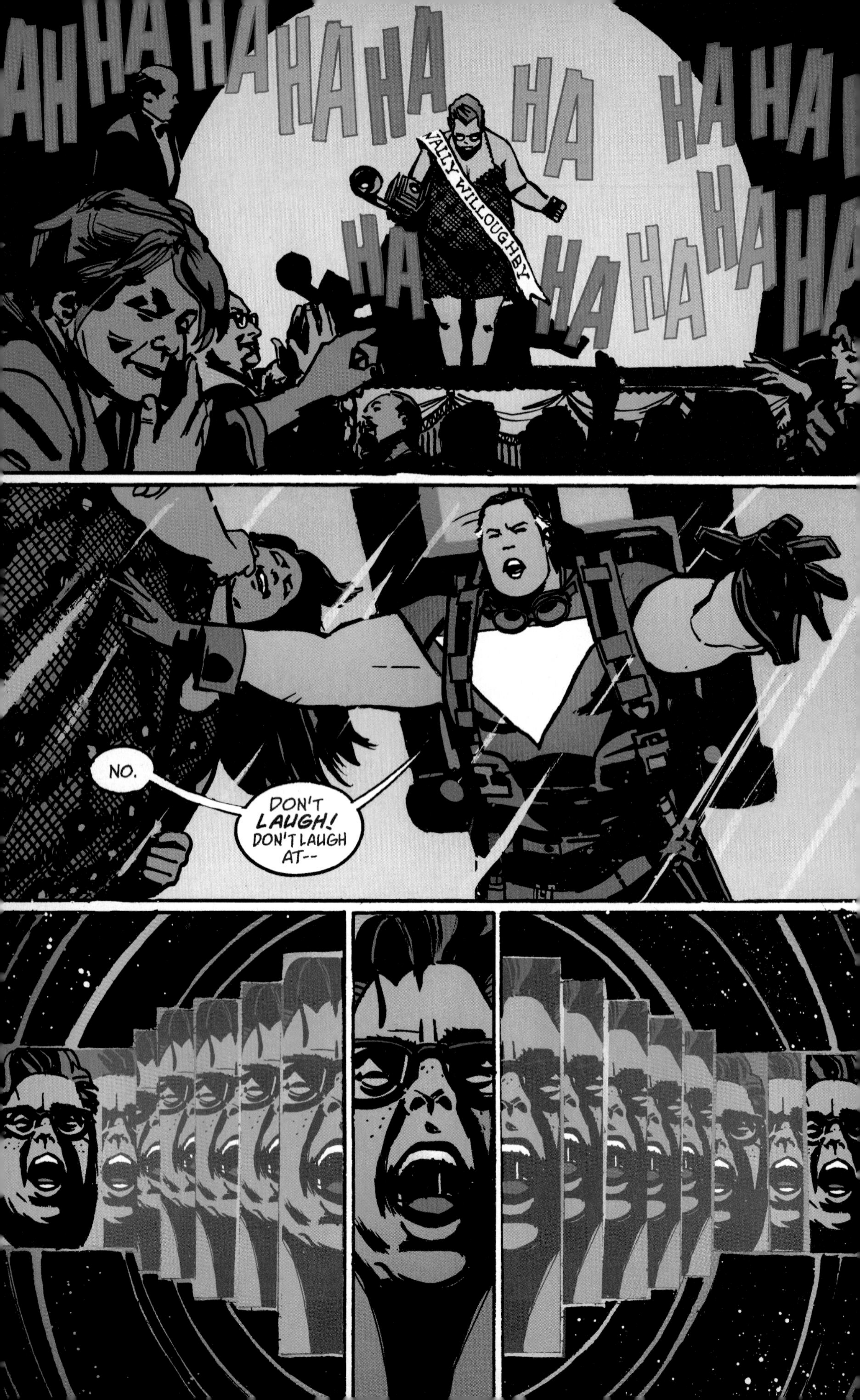
HAHAHAHAHAHA
HA
HA HA HA HA
VALLY WILLOUGHBY
HA HA HA HAHA
NO.
DON'T LAUGH! DON'T LAUGH AT--

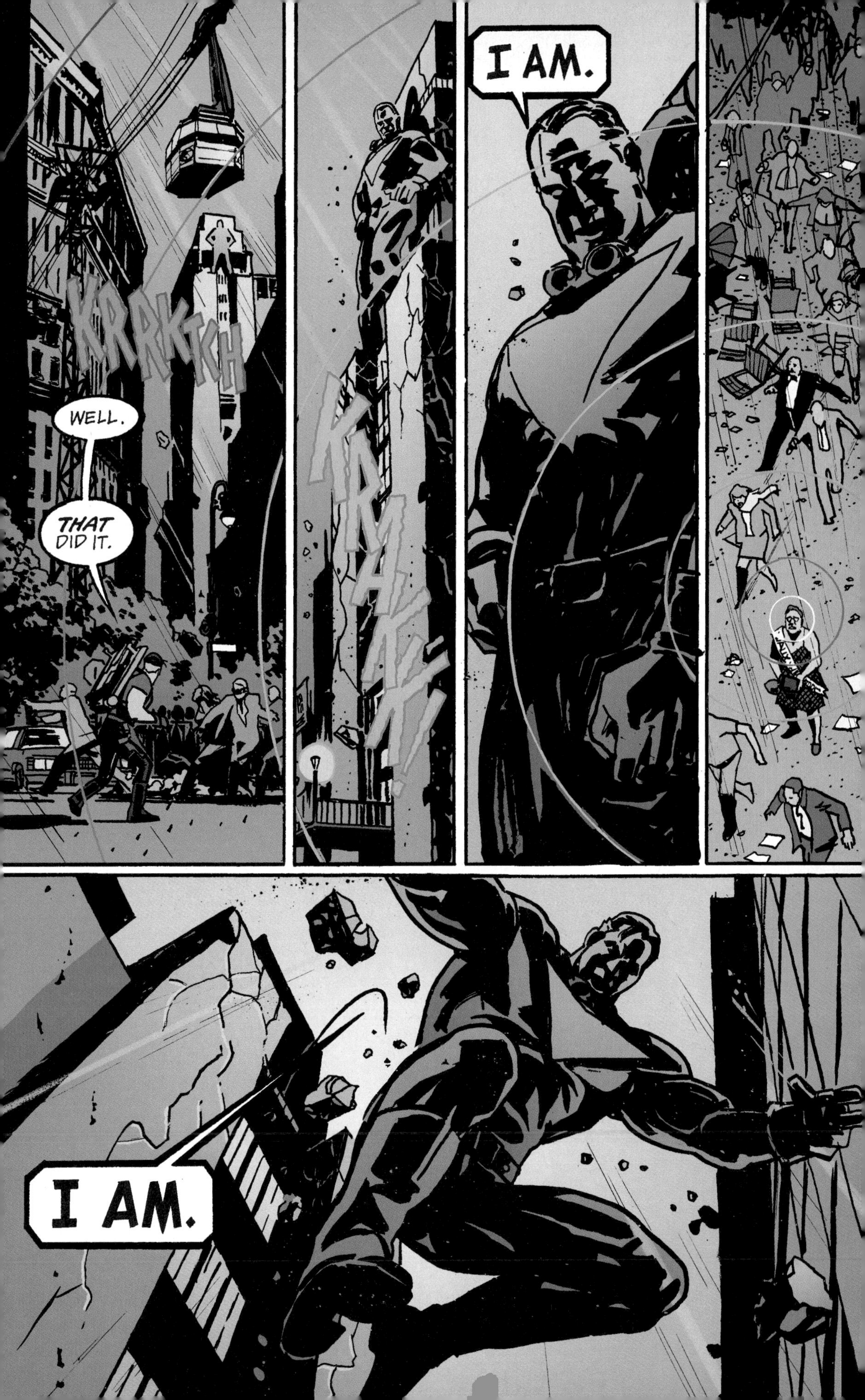
KRRKTCH
WELL.
THAT DID IT.
KRAKAKK!
I AM.
I AM.

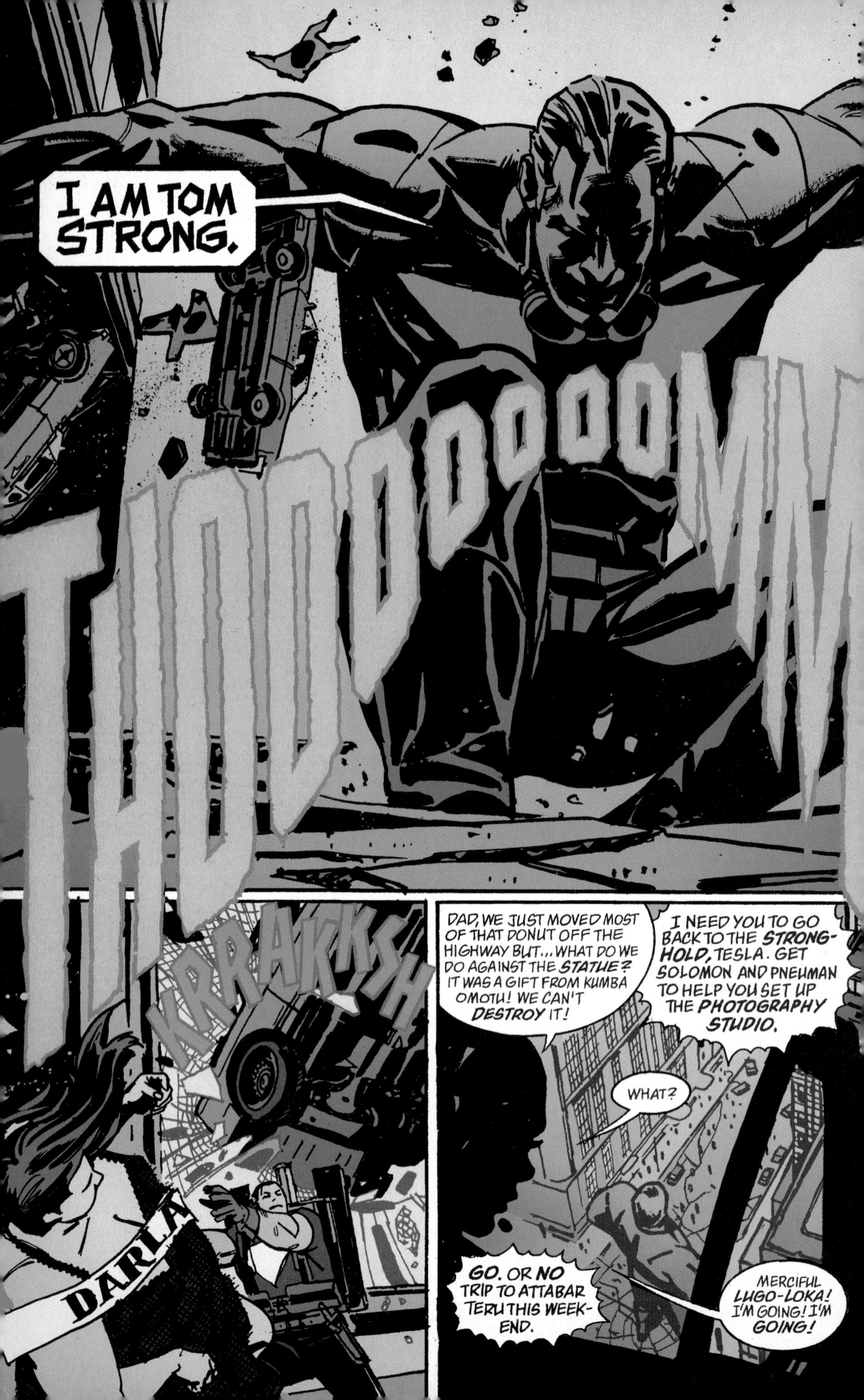
I AM TOM STRONG.
THOOOOOOMM
KRRAKKSH
DARLA
DAD, WE JUST MOVED MOST OF THAT DONUT OFF THE HIGHWAY BUT... WHAT DO WE DO AGAINST THE STATUE? IT WAS A GIFT FROM KUMBA OMOTU! WE CAN'T DESTROY IT!
I NEED YOU TO GO BACK TO THE STRONG-HOLD, TESLA. GET SOLOMON AND PNEUMAN TO HELP YOU SET UP THE PHOTOGRAPHY STUDIO.
WHAT?
GO. OR NO TRIP TO ATTABAR TERU THIS WEEK-END.
MERCIFUL LUGO-LOKA! I'M GOING! I'M GOING!

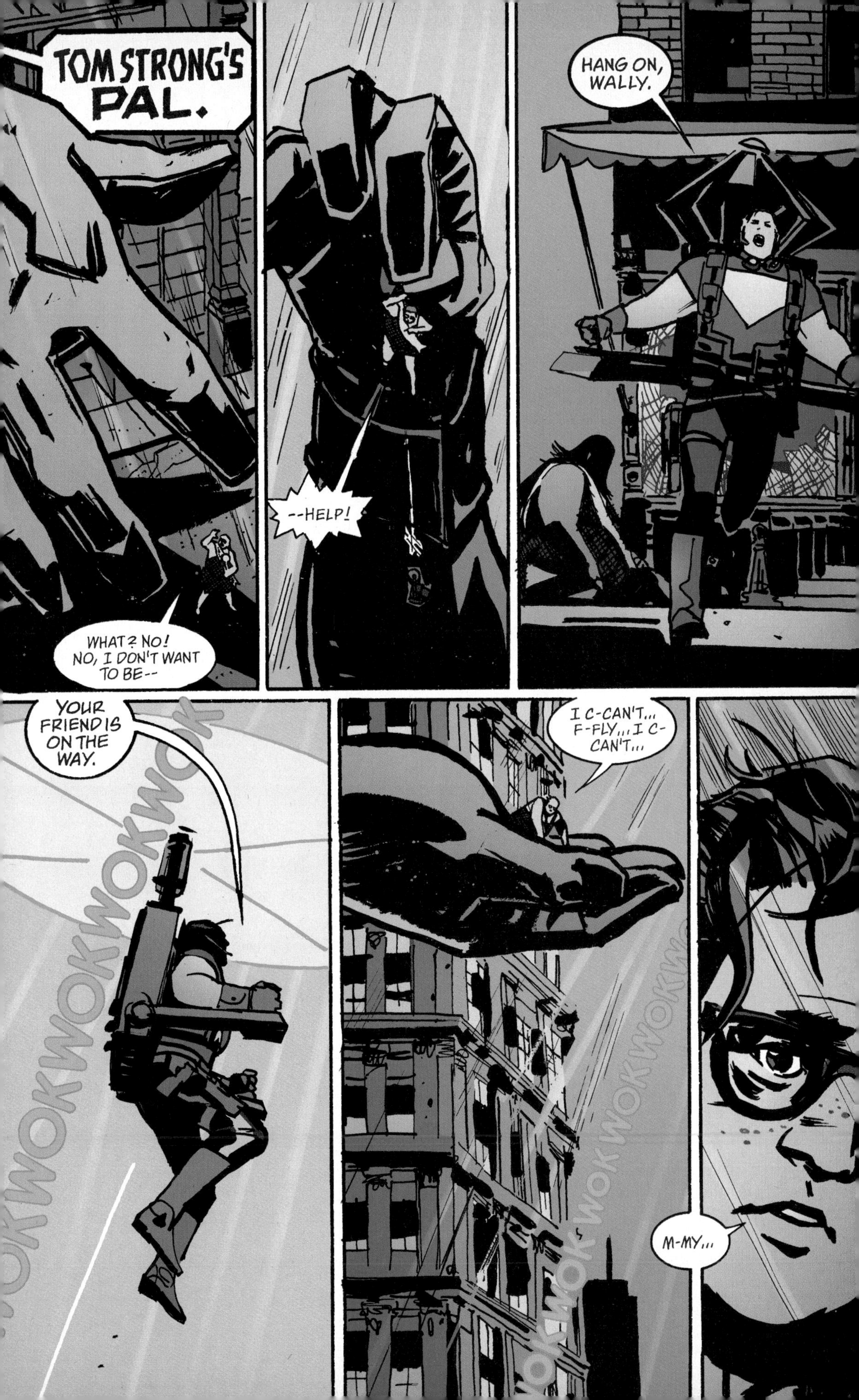
TOM STRONG'S PAL.
WHAT? NO! NO, I DON'T WANT TO BE--
--HELP!
HANG ON, WALLY.
YOUR FRIEND IS ON THE WAY.
WOKWOKWOKWOK
I C-CAN'T... F-FLY... I C-CAN'T...
M-MY...

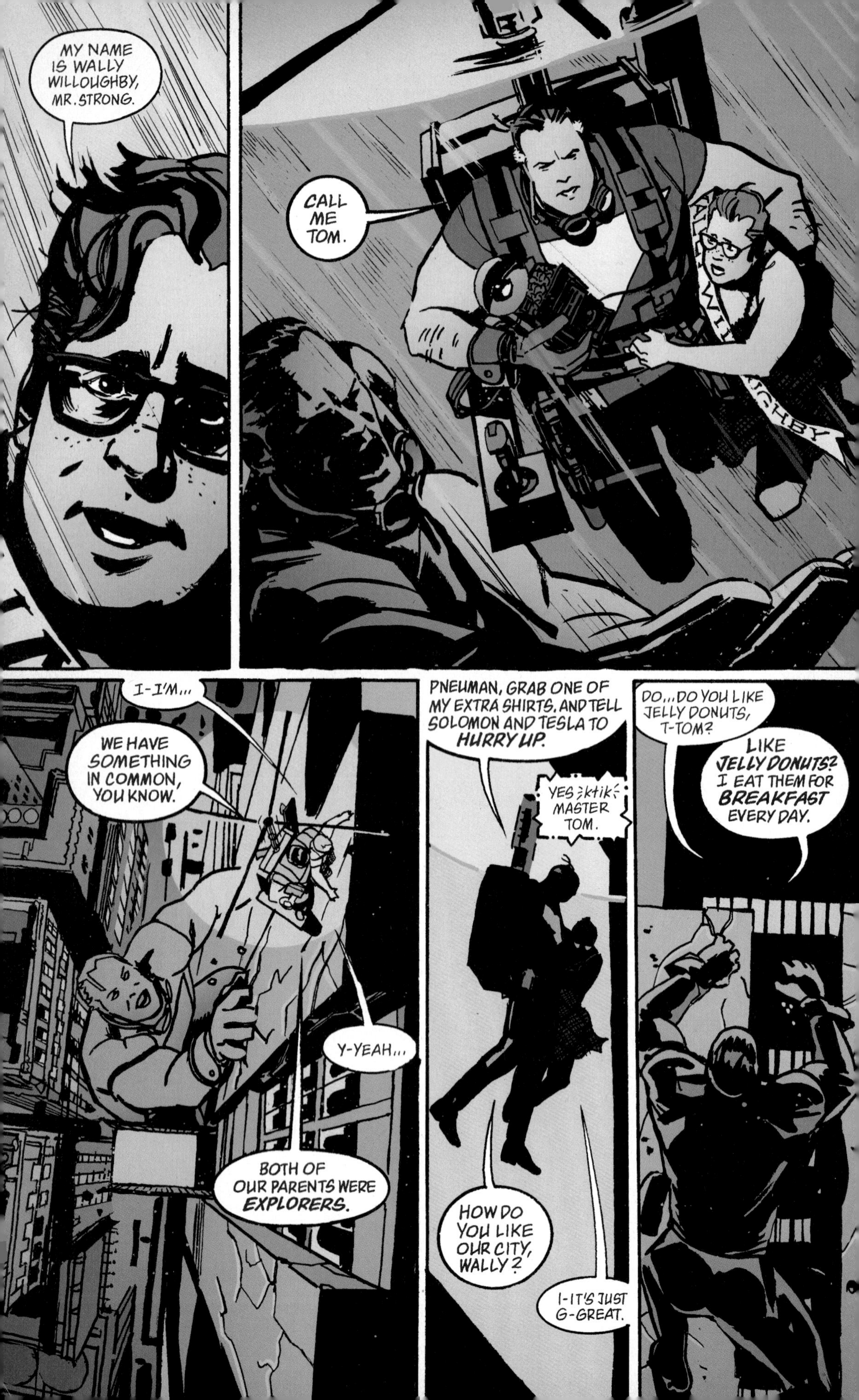
MY NAME IS WALLY WILLOUGHBY, MR. STRONG.
CALL ME TOM.
I-I'M...
WE HAVE SOMETHING IN COMMON, YOU KNOW.
Y-YEAH...
BOTH OF OUR PARENTS WERE **EXPLORERS**.
PNEUMAN, GRAB ONE OF MY EXTRA SHIRTS. AND TELL SOLOMON AND TESLA TO **HURRY UP**.
YES ktik MASTER TOM.
HOW DO YOU LIKE OUR CITY, WALLY?
I-IT'S JUST G-GREAT.
DO... DO YOU LIKE JELLY DONUTS, T-TOM?
LIKE **JELLY DONUTS?** I EAT THEM FOR **BREAKFAST** EVERY DAY.

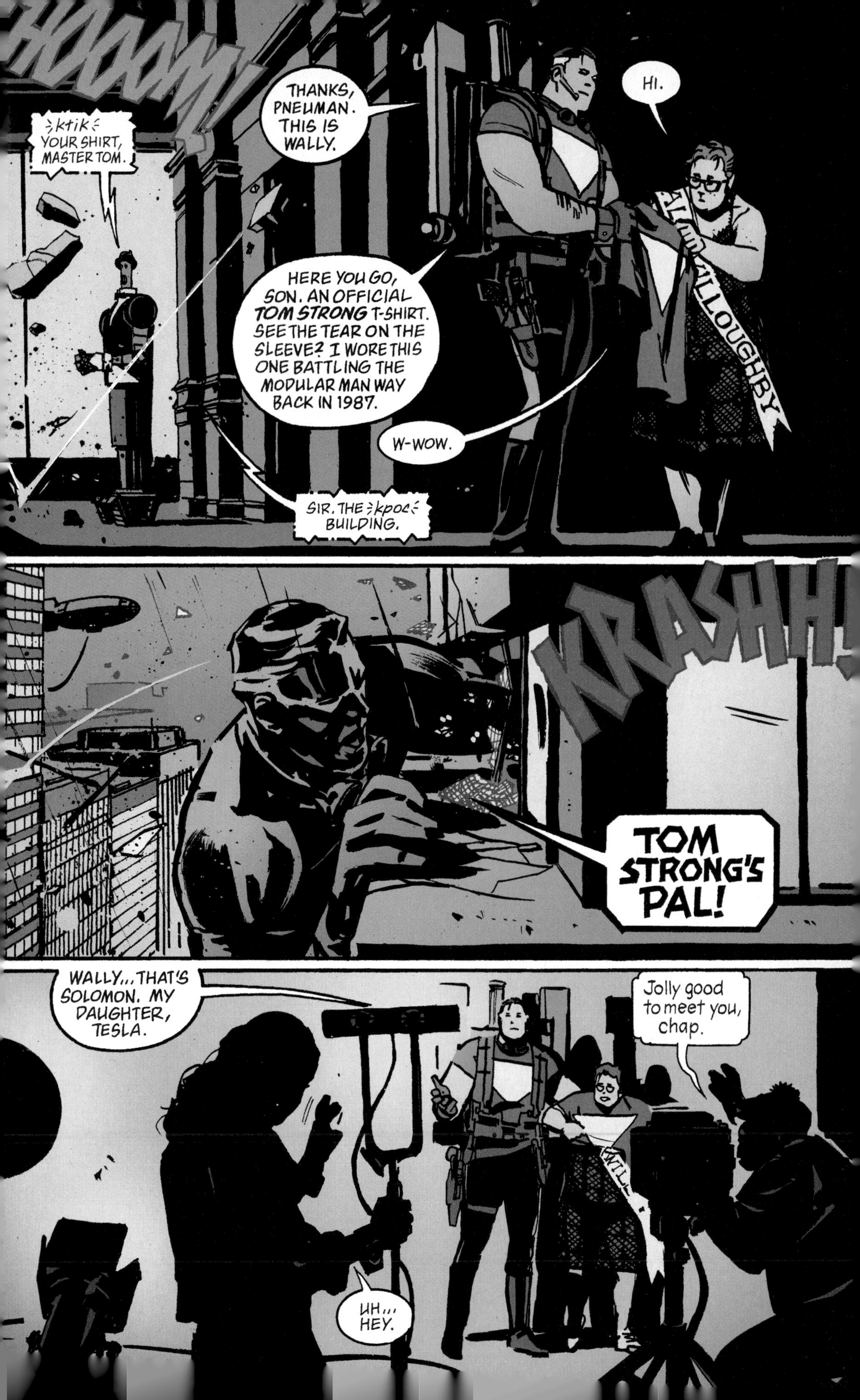

THANKS, PNEUMAN. THIS IS WALLY.
HI.
ktik YOUR SHIRT, MASTER TOM.
HERE YOU GO, SON. AN OFFICIAL TOM STRONG T-SHIRT. SEE THE TEAR ON THE SLEEVE? I WORE THIS ONE BATTLING THE MODULAR MAN WAY BACK IN 1987.
W-WOW.
SIR. THE kpoc BUILDING.
KRASHH!
TOM STRONG'S PAL!
WALLY... THAT'S SOLOMON. MY DAUGHTER, TESLA.
Jolly good to meet you, chap.
UH... HEY.

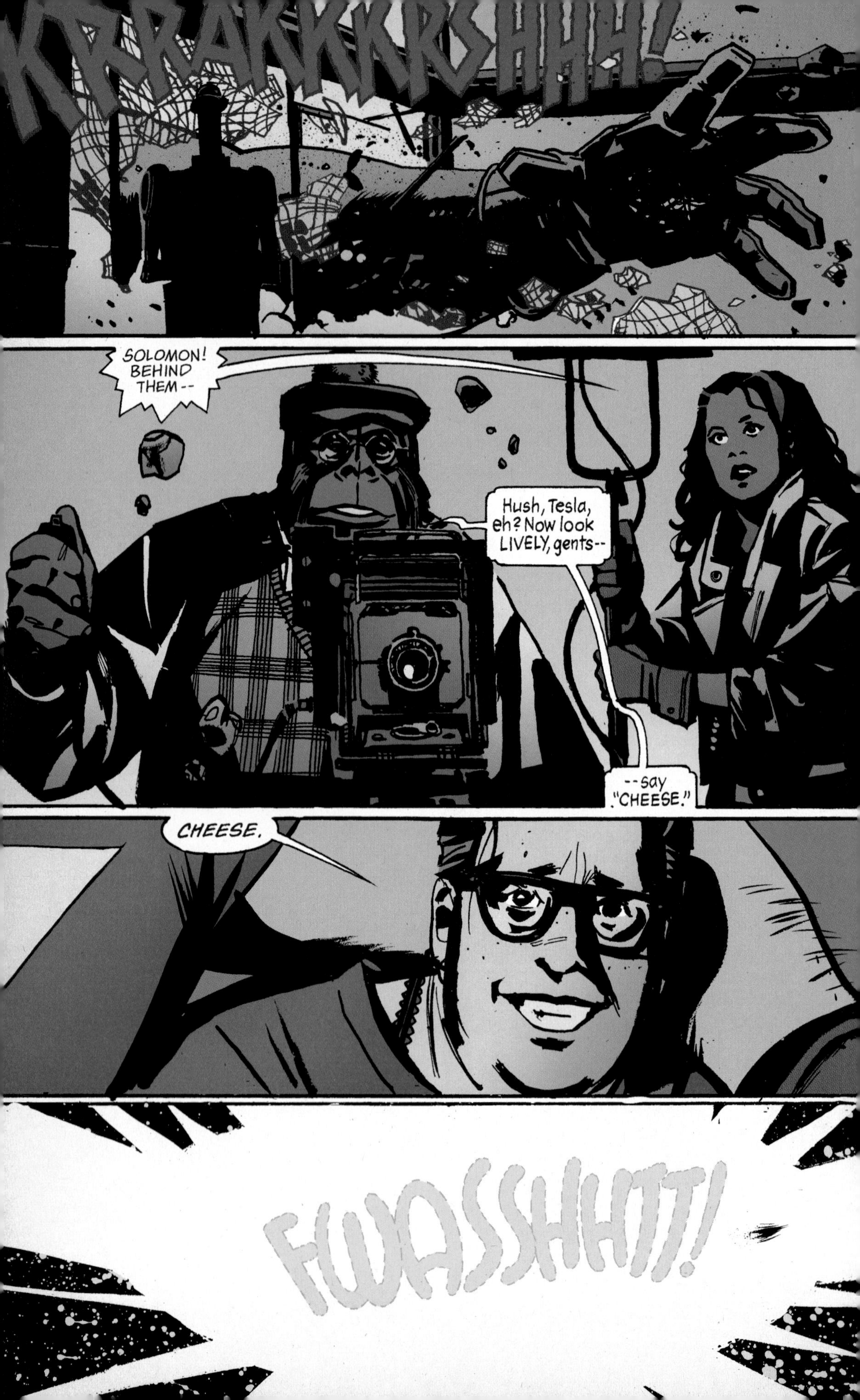
KRRAKKKRSHHH!
SOLOMON! BEHIND THEM --
Hush, Tesla, eh? Now look LIVELY, gents --
-- say "CHEESE."
CHEESE.
FWASSHHT!

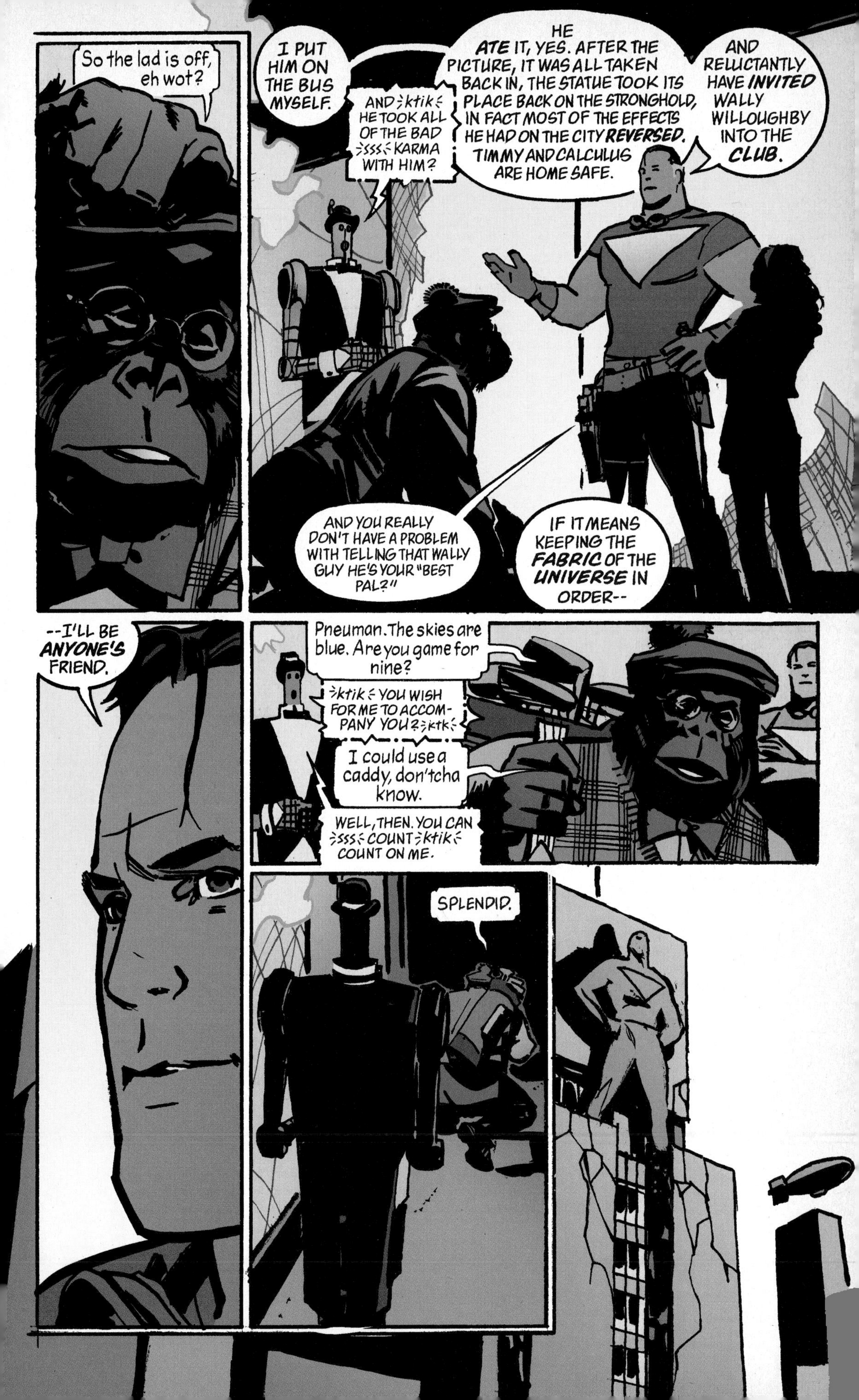
So the lad is off, eh wot?
I PUT HIM ON THE BUS MYSELF.
AND ktik HE TOOK ALL OF THE BAD sss KARMA WITH HIM?
HE ATE IT, YES. AFTER THE PICTURE, IT WAS ALL TAKEN BACK IN, THE STATUE TOOK ITS PLACE BACK ON THE STRONGHOLD, IN FACT MOST OF THE EFFECTS HE HAD ON THE CITY REVERSED. TIMMY AND CALCULUS ARE HOME SAFE.
AND RELUCTANTLY HAVE INVITED WALLY WILLOUGHBY INTO THE CLUB.
AND YOU REALLY DON'T HAVE A PROBLEM WITH TELLING THAT WALLY GUY HE'S YOUR "BEST PAL?"
IF IT MEANS KEEPING THE FABRIC OF THE UNIVERSE IN ORDER--
--I'LL BE ANYONE'S FRIEND.
Pneuman. The skies are blue. Are you game for nine?
ktik YOU WISH FOR ME TO ACCOMPANY YOU? ktk
I could use a caddy, don'tcha know.
WELL, THEN. YOU CAN sss COUNT ktik COUNT ON ME.
SPLENDID.

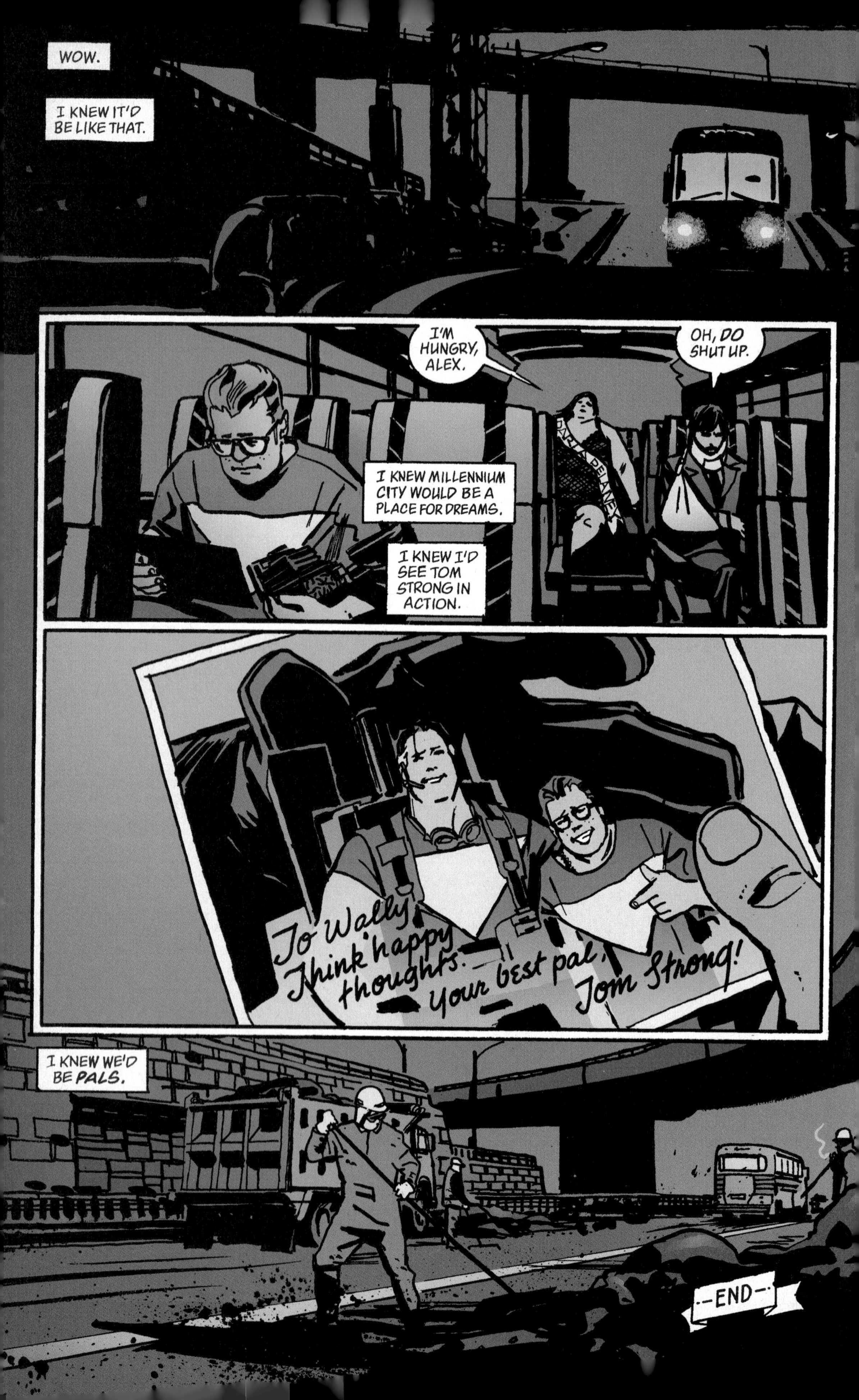
WOW.
I KNEW IT'D BE LIKE THAT.
I'M HUNGRY, ALEX.
OH, DO SHUT UP.
I KNEW MILLENNIUM CITY WOULD BE A PLACE FOR DREAMS.
I KNEW I'D SEE TOM STRONG IN ACTION.
To Wally
Think happy thoughts.
Your best pal,
Tom Strong!
I KNEW WE'D BE PALS.
END

# CONTRIBUTORS

**ALAN MOORE** is perhaps the most acclaimed writer in the graphic story medium, having garnered many awards for works such as WATCHMEN, V FOR VENDETTA, FROM HELL, MIRACLEMAN, SWAMP THING and SUPREME, among others, along with the many fine artists he has collaborated with on those works. He is currently masterminding the entire America's Best Comics line, writing PROMETHEA, TOM STRONG'S TERRIFIC TALES, and TOP 10: THE FORTY-NINERS. He resides in central England.

**PETER HOGAN** writes things down, because otherwise he forgets them. These have included issues of THE DREAMING and THE SANDMAN PRESENTS: LOVE STREET, as well as THE MANY WORLDS OF TESLA STRONG and TERRA OBSCURA (co-plotted with Alan Moore). He lives in South London, and usually stays up way past his bedtime.

**GEOFF JOHNS** began his writing career with screenplays for film and TV, but for the last few years has moved into comics with popular runs on such titles as TEEN TITANS, JSA, THE FLASH and HAWKMAN. Geoff lives in Sherman Oaks, California.

**JERRY ORDWAY** began his drawing career in the 1980s on ALL-STAR SQUADRON and INFINITY INC., and later served and artist and writer of both SUPERMAN and POWER OF SHAZAM for several years. Recently Ordway has drawn stories for WONDER WOMAN and JLA. He lives in Connecticut with wife Peggy and three children, Rachel, Thomas and James.

**CHRIS SPROUSE**, the penciller and co-creator of TOM STRONG, began working in comics in 1989, gathering approval for his work on such books as LEGIONNAIRES. He previously worked with Alan Moore on SUPREME. Chris currently lives in Ohio.

**KARL STORY** has been inking comics since 1988, and in 1991 co-founded Gaijin Studios in Atlanta. His work has been found lurking in such books as LEGIONNAIRES, NIGHTWING, BATMAN, TERRA OBSCURA and, of course, TOM STRONG. Karl lives in Georgia with his wife Cat and his very grumpy dog Strega.

**JOHN PAUL LEON**, born in 1972 in New York City, began working in comics while attending NYC's School of Visual Arts, where he studied illustration. His early work on ROBOCOP: PRIME SUSPECT and STATIC through more recent titles like CHALLENGERS OF THE UNKNOWN and EARTH X shows growth as a draftsman and storyteller. John Paul is currently working on WINTER MEN. He lives in Florida.

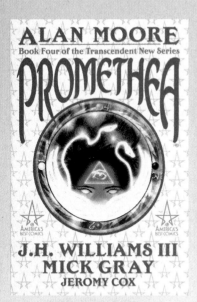

# CHAPTER ONE

**In which an intruder spins a wild tale,
Strong history takes a different turn,
and Tom Stone gets started.**

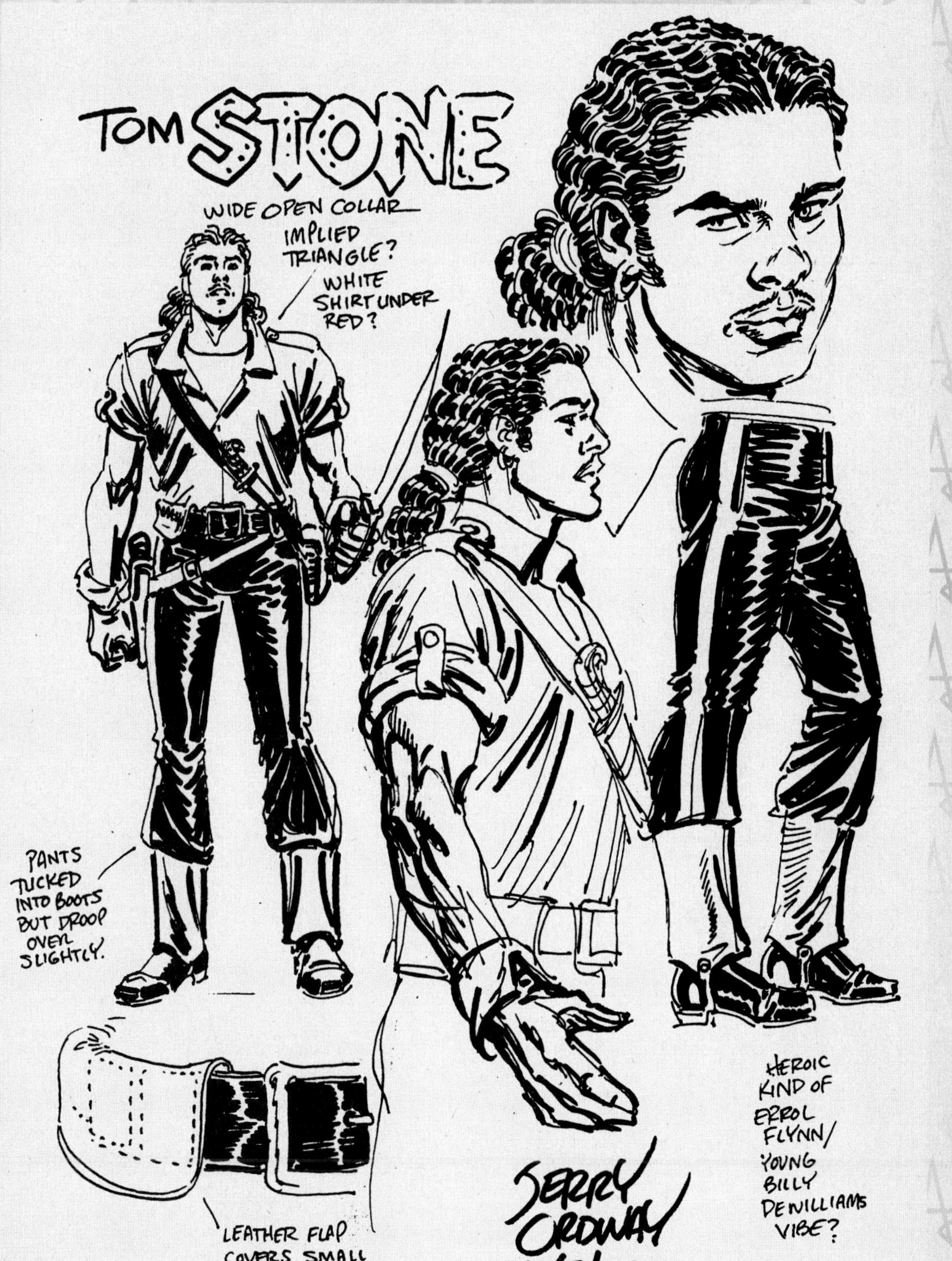
TOM STONE
WIDE OPEN COLLAR
IMPLIED TRIANGLE?
WHITE SHIRT UNDER RED?
PANTS TUCKED INTO BOOTS BUT DROOP OVER SLIGHTLY.
LEATHER FLAP COVERS SMALL COMPARTMENTS
HEROIC KIND OF ERROL FLYNN/ YOUNG BILLY DEWILLIAMS VIBE?
JERRY ORDWAY 11/5/02

**Cover art:
Chris Sprouse and Karl Story**

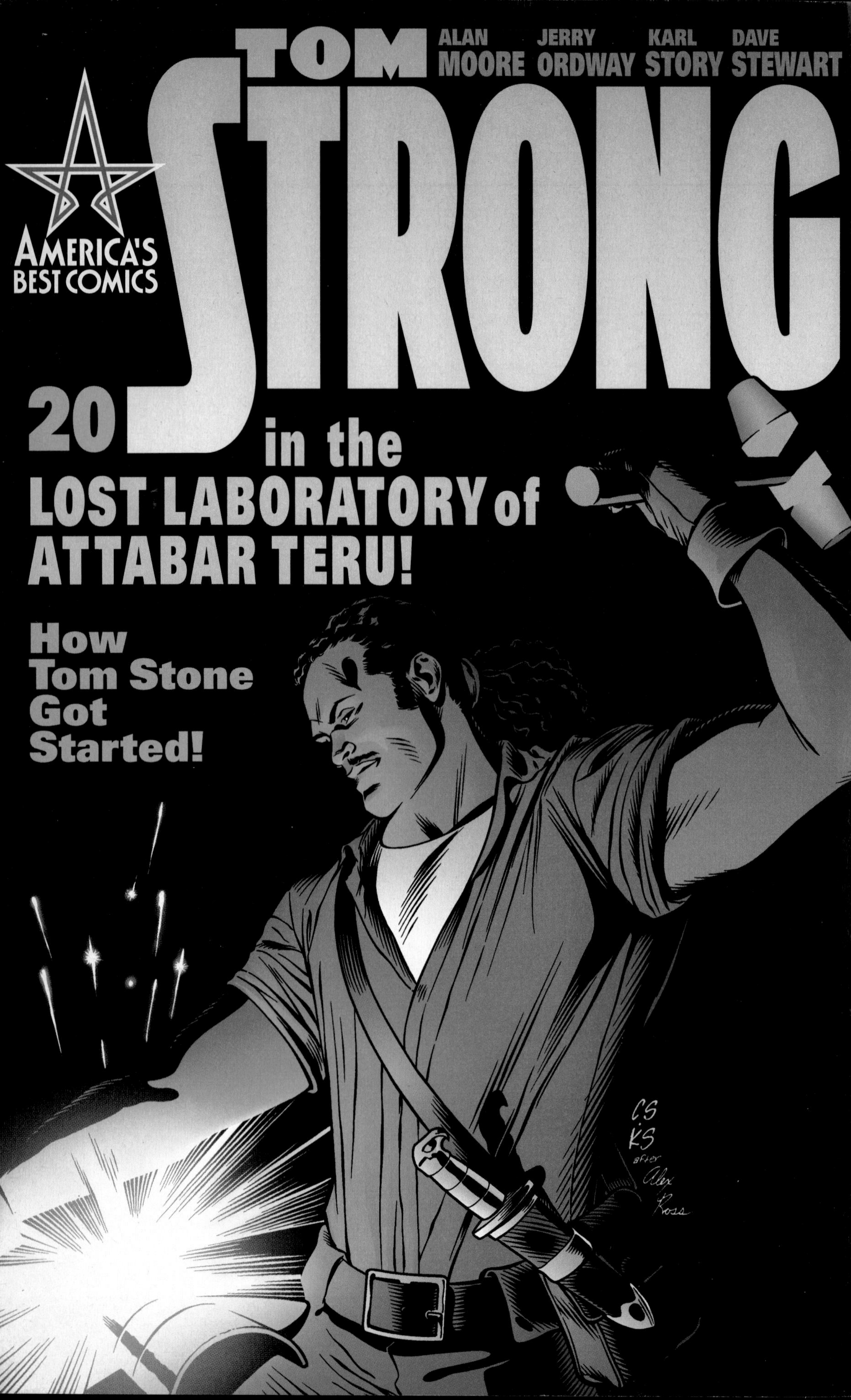
AMERICA'S
BEST COMICS
TOM
STRONG
ALAN
MOORE
JERRY
ORDWAY
KARL
STORY
DAVE
STEWART
20
in the
LOST LABORATORY of
ATTABAR TERU!
How
Tom Stone
Got
Started!
CS
KS
after
Alex
Ross